Das Brecht-Jahrbuch 40

Herausgeber:
Theodore F. Rippey

In Zusammenarbeit mit der Internationalen Brecht-Gesellschaft

The Brecht Yearbook 40

Editor:
Theodore F. Rippey

For the International Brecht Society

Edited at Bowling Green State University
Bowling Green, Ohio 43403, USA

First published 2016 by Camden House for the International Brecht Society

Camden House is an imprint of Boydell & Brewer Inc.
668 Mt. Hope Avenue, Rochester, New York 14620, USA
www.camden-house.com
and of Boydell & Brewer Limited
P.O. Box 9, Woodbridge, Suffolk, IP12 3DF, UK
www.boydellandbrewer.com

ISSN 0734-8665
ISBN 978-0-9851956-3-2

This publication is printed on acid-free paper.
Printed in the United States of America

Submissions
Manuscripts in either English or German should be submitted to The *Brecht Yearbook* via email as attachments. Hard-copy submissions are also acceptable, but they should be accompanied by an electronic file. For English language submissions, American spelling conventions should be used, e.g., "theater" instead of "theatre," "color" instead of "colour," etc. Submissions in German should use the new, not the old, spelling conventions. Endnote format should be internally consistent, preferably following The Chicago Manual of Style. Specific guidelines for the Yearbook in both English and German can be found at the website address listed on the next page. Address contributions to the editor:

Theodore F. Rippey
College of Arts & Sciences, 702 Administration Bldg.
Bowling Green State University
Bowling Green, OH 43403, USA
Email: theodor@bgsu.edu

Inquiries concerning book reviews should be addressed to:
Matthias Rothe
Department of German, Scandinavian & Dutch
University of Minnesota
320 Folwell Hall, 9 Pleasant Street NE
Minneapolis, MN 55455, USA
Email: mrothe@umn.edu

Officers of the International Brecht Society

Stephen Brockmann, President
Department of Modern Languages
Baker Hall 160, Carnegie Mellon University
Pittsburgh, PA 15213, USA
smb@andrew.cmu.edu

Günther Heeg, Vice President
Institut für Theaterwissenschaft
Universität Leipzig
Ritterstr. 16, 04109 Leipzig, Germany
guenther.heeg@gmx.de

Paula Hanssen, Co-Secretary/Treasurer
Department of International Languages and Cultures, Webster University
470 E. Lockwood
Saint Louis, MO 63119, USA
hanssen@webster.edu

Sylvia Fischer, Co-Secretary/Treasurer
University of West Florida
11000 University Pkwy. 50/125
Pensacola, FL 32514, USA
sfischer@uwf.edu

Jack Davis, Co-Editor, *Communications from the International Brecht Society*
Dept.. of Classical and Modern Languages
Truman State University
100 E. Normal Avenue
Kirksville, MO 63501, USA
jackdavis@truman.edu

Kris Imbrigotta, Co-Editor, *Communications from the International Brecht Society*
Department of German Studies
University of Puget Sound
1500 N. Warner Street #1073
Tacoma, WA 98416, USA
kimbrigotta@pugetsound.edu

IBS online: www.brechtsociety.org

The Brecht Yearbook vols. 1–34 online:
uwdc.library.wisc.edu/collections/German/BrechtYearbook

Membership:
Members receive *The Brecht Yearbook* and the annual *Communications from the International Brecht Society.* Dues should be sent in US$ to the Secretary/Treasurer or in Euro to Deutsche Bank Düsseldorf, Konto Nr. 76-74146, BLZ 300 700 24, IBAN—DE53 3007 0024 0767 4146 00, BIC bzw. Swift Code: DEUTDEDBDUE.

Student Member (up to three years)	$30.00	€30
Low Income and Emeritus Faculty	$30.00	€30
Regular Member (full-time employed)	$45.00	€45
Sustaining Member	$50.00	€50
Institutional Member	$50.00	€50
Lifetime (retirees only)	$200.00	€200

Online credit card payment is possible at the IBS website listed above; click on "membership" for instructions.

The International Brecht Society

The International Brecht Society has been formed as a corresponding society on the model of Brecht's own unrealized plan for the Diderot Society. Through its publications and regular international symposia, the society encourages the discussion of any and all views on the relationship of the arts and the contemporary world. The society is open to new members in any field and in any country and welcomes suggestions and/or contributions in German, English, Spanish, or French to future symposia and for the published volumes of its deliberations.

Die Internationale Brecht-Gesellschaft

Die Internationale Brecht-Gesellschaft ist nach dem Modell von Brechts nicht verwirklichtem Plan für die Diderot-Gesellschaft gegründet worden. Durch Veröffentlichungen und regelmäßige internationale Tagungen fördert die Gesellschaft freie und öffentliche Diskussionen über die Beziehungen aller Künste zur heutigen Welt. Die Gesellschaft steht neuen Mitgliedern in jedem Fachgebiet und Land offen und begrüßt Vorschläge für zukünftige Tagungen und Aufsätze in deutscher, englischer, spanischer oder französischer Sprache für *Das Brecht-Jahrbuch.*

La Société Internationale Brecht

La Société Internationale Brecht a été formée pour correspondre à la société rêvée par Brecht, "Diderot-Gesellschaft." Par ses publications et congrès internationaux à intervalles réguliers, la S.I.B. encourage la discussion libre des toutes les idées sur les rapports entre les arts et le monde contemporain. Bien entendu, les nouveaux membres dans toutes les disciplines et tous les pays sont accueillis avec plaisir, et la Société sera heureuse d'accepter des suggestions et des contributions en français, allemand, espagnol ou anglais pour les congrès futurs et les volumes des communications qui en résulteront.

La Sociedad Internacional Brecht

La Sociedad Internacional Brecht fué creada para servir como sociedad corresponsal. Dicha sociedad se basa en el modelo que el mismo autor nunca pudo realizar, el plan "Diderot-Gesellschaft." A través de sus publicaciones y los simposios internacionales que se llevan a cabo regularmente, la Sociedad estimula la discusión libre y abierta de cualquier punto de vista sobre la relación entre las artes y el mundo contemporáneo. La Sociedad desea, por supuesto, la participación de nuevos miembros de cualquier área, de cualquier país, y accepta sugerencias y colaboraciones en alemán, inglés, francés y español para los congresos futuros y para las publicaciones de sus discusiones.

Contents

Editorial

Theodore F. Rippey

Much of the work in the fortieth *Brecht Yearbook* has to do with forging images that grow out of then re-enter experience—either Brecht's experience of his own time, or others' experience of Brecht's work and their times. This dynamic is perhaps most concrete in the engaging and illuminating set of graphic works from Berlin artist Dieter Goltzsche, one of which also graces the cover, but it manifests itself across the range of contributions.

The opening section of the volume includes the first of the Goltzsche images, which were created in response to his experiences of Brechtian theater in Berlin, as well as a brief introductory statement by the artist. Thirteen further pieces, ranging from the 1960s to 2015, are ordered chronologically and interspersed throughout the volume. We are grateful to Dieter Goltzsche for the opportunity to share his work with our audience. Following the Goltzsche statement and first image is an open letter to Brecht from Hans-Thies Lehmann and Helene Varopoulou, offered in the context of the inaugural DURCHEINANDER theater project in August 2015. A brief statement from the project organizers accompanies the letter, and both documents wrestle with questions of how to draw on Brecht in today's efforts to renew theater as form and act, re-functionalize it as space, re-imagine and reclaim its aesthetic and political impact.

The volume's first two research articles focus on Brecht's efforts to see and show crucial components of modern life. With specific attention to the Jae Fleischhacker project and Brecht's and Hauptmann's thinking about theatrical representation of the markets and trading world of the mid-1920s, Matthias Rothe analyzes how epic manipulations of time dismantle a suspense-based mode of narration (*Erzählen mit Arglist*) and enable a narrative and performative stance that has greater capacity to expose two things: the contingency of social and economic structures like futures trading and the limits of causal reasoning as a tool for understanding such structures. Thomas Pekar elucidates the different meanings of *Apparat* in *Der Ozeanflug* in order to assess the impact of Brecht's affirmative stance toward technology on his conceptualization and artistic framing of the re-fitting of the human subject that the technological transformation of interwar society catalyzed.

The next two pieces offer critical correctives to scholarly images of two pieces of Brecht's life and work. In the first, Jürgen Hillesheim recovers the figure of Oscar Lettner, an Augsburg friend of Brecht's who had become all but lost in the extant scholarly and biographical record. In the second, Klaus-Dieter Krabiel works against the scholarly trend of interpreting the poem "Die Nachtlager" as a Marxist critique of reformism, a concept grounded in the belief that positive social transformation could be achieved without social revolution. Krabiel recaptures the poem's key intertextual link (to Theodore Dreiser's *Sister Carrie*) and illuminates the complex balance of charitable initiatives and revolutionary politics in the 1920s, providing an analysis of the poem that embraces its rich contradictions and offers an alternative to its image as a revolutionary rallying cry.

Arnold Pistiak's article focuses on a very specific type of image, the *Bild* of Hanns Eisler's *Bilder aus der Kriegsfibel.* Working musicologically, historically, and aesthetically, Pistiak characterizes the *Bild* in Eisler's composition as a Gesamtkunstwerk in miniature, a concentrated, complex form that integrates musical, verbal, and photographic elements. Pistiak argues that Eisler's project incorporates and extends the self-critical dimension of Brecht's antifascist critique, moving beyond a simple condemnation of fascism toward a reflective stance that allows artist and audience to confront questions of suffering, guilt, responsibility, and resistance. Following Pistiak's piece is a brief set of Eisler-related texts, published here as accompaniments to the English translation of the Eisler-Bunge interview volume *Fragen Sie mehr über Brecht.* The texts, a tribute to Bunge by Manfred Bierwisch and an introduction to the original German volume that was not included in the English volume, are introduced by translator and editor Sabine Berendse. The original introduction author is the pianist, conductor, and scholar Georg Knepler, who was remembered upon his death in 2003 as the last of a generation of Marxist artists and thinkers who shaped the cultural life of interwar Vienna and Berlin.

The next three pieces shift focus to adapting and disseminating Brechtian work in three globally dispersed settings. In the first of these articles, Lin Cheng focuses on a brief set of encounters between Brecht and the Chinese scholar and translator Feng Zhi. Cheng's work with sources in Germany and China sheds light on an interesting moment in Brecht's biography and provides an impression of the image of Brecht that formed in post-revolutionary China in the 1950s. Adapting Brecht's projects and propagating the results was the life's work of the Peruvian author and activist Sara Joffré. Joffré is a key figure in Carlos Vargas-Salgado's article, which examines how different artists and groups appropriated Brecht in the context of the Peruvian internal war. (Joffré also receives a tribute from Vargas-Salgado in the opening pages of this volume.) A theater-historical contribution by Laura Ginters looks at working with Brecht in the context of a very different struggle. Ginters reconstructs the creation of and response to student productions of Brecht plays, framing them as part of the broader effort to establish an independent theater in Australia in the 1960s.

The three closing articles consider possible and actual relationships between Brecht and three other major literary figures. In the first, Cora Lee Kluge investigates whether Mark Twain's concept of the magnanimous-incident hero, in particular the paradox of suffering for behavior deemed virtuous by "the books," could have served as point of reference for *Der gute Mensch von Sezuan*. The question of direct influence remains open, but Kluge's examination of the conceptual resonance is fruitful in any case. Vera Stegmann then unpacks what connects and separates Brecht and Navid Kermani, looking principally at aesthetic-conceptual issues (the relationship of empathy and *Verfremdung*, for instance) but considering as well the historical parallels between today's migrations from the Middle East to Europe and the period of exile from Europe brought on by fascism. The volume's final essay comes to us from the magisterial hand of Jost Hermand, who sets his sights on the incomparable pair of Brecht and Karl Kraus. Providing both an overview of and a new direction in scholarly work on the topic, Hermand focuses in particular on the friendly Brecht-Kraus encounters in Berlin in the late 1920s, for which Kraus's new level of political engagement in Vienna had helped prepare the ground. Those encounters inaugurated a relationship, grounded in a fundamentally anti-bourgeois stance, which resulted in artistic cross-pollination that had lasting effects on the work of both great satirists.

In closing, some brief updates and acknowledgments. With volume 40, the *Yearbook* begins publication with Camden House. The IBS is excited about this new partnership, and we look forward to many years of fruitful collaboration. I am also pleased to welcome three new members to the editorial board: Laura Bradley (Edinburgh), Meg Mumford (Sydney), and Matthias Rothe (Minneapolis). With these colleagues, our board deepens its expertise in theater and performance studies and interwar and post-war dimensions of Brecht's life and work. As new colleagues join, one valued colleague departs: Joy Calico has assumed the prestigious editorship of the *Journal of the American Musicological Society* and so is stepping down. We wish her well for the new venture, and I thank her for her excellent work on recent volumes. My thanks are also due to Marc Silberman, for collaboration in preparing this volume; to Jim Walker and his colleagues, for their advice and assistance as the *Yearbook* settles in to its new home; and finally to Friedemann Weidauer, for his work as book review editor on volumes 38 through 40 and his commitment to continue as a member of the editorial board. Looking forward, we anticipate a stimulating special interest section on teaching Brecht in volume 41 and a fascinating range of articles that will grow out of the 2016 Recycling Brecht IBS Symposium to compose volume 42. For now, I hope that readers will find use-value in the pages that follow.

Bowling Green, Ohio

Photo by Cesar De Maria.

Tribute

Sara Joffré, Soul of Peruvian Theater

Carlos Vargas-Salgado

It is still too early to make a just assessment of the voluminous legacy of Sara Joffré (1935–2014) to the theater and culture of contemporary Peru. Sara herself told me of one time when, during a discussion comparing the Peruvian theater with other Latin American theater systems, a colleague and countryman pointed out: "In Peru we don't have a National Institute of Theater or something like that; in Peru we have Sara Joffré." Sara recalled this and laughed with a touch of irony. But I think that there are many of us, Peruvian cultural producers and cultural critics, who have often thought about her exactly in this way.

Sara Joffré was an acclaimed playwright, whose works included *La Hija de Lope*, *Camille Claudel*, *Se administra justicia*, *Niña Florita*, and many others, including several plays for children. She was particularly gifted at continuously reinventing herself: an avant-garde, renowned director during the 1960s; an extraordinary critic during the '80s and '90s; and a perennially leading researcher (and promoter of research) of the Peruvian theater during her last years. But probably the most visible of her legacies are directly connected to the support and spread of playwriting in Peru. Joffré was the creator of the *Muestra de Teatro Peruano* (Peruvian Theater Festival, inaugurated in 1974 and still running). She subsequently also became the managing editor of a journal with the same name (*Muestra,* 2000–2014), exclusively devoted to publishing Peruvian dramas. These undertakings were critical contributions to Peruvian theater culture because they put Peruvian authors on the map and fostered a culture in which Peruvian stages became more interested in disseminating the work of Joffré and her fellow Peruvian playwrights.

Joffré was also significant because of her connection to Bertolt Brecht's work. Clearly, she was the most important scholar and disseminator of Brecht in Peru. In the eyes of Peruvian theater artists, Joffré's image is always tied to that of Brecht. From her very early career (mid-1960s) on, she directed Brecht's plays. Later, she was a key figure in teaching the importance of the Brechtian approaches to theater as a collective practice, particularly in the context of a country suffering a deep social crisis. As I explore in an article in this volume of the *Brecht Yearbook*, Brecht's work, either as dramatist or as thinker, has become undeniably influential in the Peruvian scene during the last forty years. With no doubt, Sara Joffré can take credit for this permanent presence of Brecht in Peru. Joffré educated several generations of theater actors and directors on the basics of Brechtian aesthetics through workshops, conferences, venues, and even performances (e.g., *Hablando de Bertolt Brecht*, 2000).

But Sara has been, above all, a devotee of living life through drama. Thus, in light of the news of her death (December 2014), between so many outstanding memories perhaps the foremost that her friends, colleagues, and even occasional adversaries have recalled is her unforgettable presence in our theatrical panorama. Sara has been, first and foremost, an activist of Peruvian theater. As a great admirer of Brecht, Sara appeared to have embodied the well-known maxim: "the theater is not a mirror that reflects reality, but a hammer that gives it shape." It is precisely in giving it shape that Sara makes her most visible bequest to Peruvian theater. Her own work has created a totally different map of Peruvian theatricality, through patient and tenacious labor, similar to the tenacity with which a hammer hits a rock to shape it.

In a wonderful final lesson, Sara herself organized the *funeral* for her journal, *Muestra*, in Lima, in October 2014. Frank, jovial, provocative as always, at that soiree she closed her own project while challenging the audience in the *Casa de la Literatura Peruana* (Peruvian Literature Center) to reflect on all the things already accomplished and think about all the things that we still need to pursue, in order to keep creating, discussing, re-working this common passion of ours called "Peruvian theater."

Fig. 1. Helene Varopoulou (left) and Hans-Thies Lehmann (center) reading the "Brechtbrief" at HAU1 in Berlin, August 2015. Image © Simone Steiner, photographer.

Brechtbrief

Verehrter Bert Brecht,

hier stocken wir schon, denn an wen richten wir dieses Schreiben? An Sie, den anarchischen, manchmal expressionistischen Dichter der frühen Gedichte und des *Baals*? An Sie, den Brecht der Neuen Sachlichkeit, der schreiben konnte "Das Abc heißt: man wird mit euch fertig werden"? An den marxistisch denkenden Brecht, der das Modell der Lehrstücke erdachte? An Sie, den Erfinder tragischer Figuren vom jungen Genossen des Lehrstücks *Die Maßnahme* bis zu Gestalten ihrer Klassiker des epischen Theaters, zum Beispiel *Mutter Courage*? Auch wenn es besonders der eine Brecht ist, nämlich der "Andere," den wir ansprechen, so meinen wir doch auch irgendwie Sie, die anderen, mit.

Sie waren eben nicht einer, sondern immer ein "Anderer," und dadurch ein Veränderer. Sie sahen sich nie als den "Besitzer" von Ideen und notierten früh in Ihren Tagebüchern 1932:

> Ich glaube nicht, dass ich jemals eine so ausgewachsene Philosophie haben kann wie Goethe oder Hebbel, die die Gedächtnisse von Trambahnschaffnern gehabt haben müssen, was ihre Ideen betrifft. Ich vergesse meine Anschauungen immer wieder, kann mich nicht entschließen, sie auswendig zu lernen.

Und wir vergessen nicht Ihre wundervolle Beschreibung, als Sie einmal ihr Gesicht betrachteten, vor dem Spiegel Kirschen essend:

> Mein Gesicht hat viele Elemente von Brutalität, Stille, Schlaffheit, Kühnheit und Feigheit in sich, aber nur als Elemente, und es ist abwechslungsvoller und charakterloser als eine Landschaft unter wehenden Wolken. Deshalb können viele Leute mein Gesicht nicht behalten ("es sind zu viele"' sagt die Hedda).

"Wer immer es ist, den ihr sucht—ich bin es nicht." Wir beide, die Ihnen diesen Brief schreiben, fanden das so wahr, dass wir—damals noch unbekannt miteinander—zur gleichen Zeit, 1991, das Motto "Der andere Brecht" für eine Brechtveranstaltung wählten. Der eine in Augsburg, die andere in Athen. Damals reichte unsere Bekanntschaft mit dem, was Sie schrieben, schon weit zurück. Bei dem einen bis in seine Bremer Jugendzeit, als er als Schüler in einem der blassgelben schmalen Einzelausgaben Ihrer Stücke am Fenster einer Bibliothek oder Buchhandlung der Innenstadt diesen Satz las und elektrisiert war: "Dass da gehören soll, was da ist, denen die für es gut sind." Elektrisiert vom Inhalt, der den jugendlichen Sinn für Gerechtigkeit ansprach; aber ebenso sehr formal, durch das wundervolle kleine Stolpern in Syntax und Klang, "die *für es* gut sind." Ein so schlagend einfacher Dreh, den der Deutschlehrer vermutlich moniert hätte.

Auch bei der anderen gab es die ersten Begegnungen mit Ihnen in der Kindheit und Jugend. Brecht: das war in Griechenland der 1950er und 1960er Jahre mehr ein Mythos als ein konkret gekannter Autor, eine Figur des antifaschistischen Deutschen, eine Größe der deutschen Exilliteratur, ein "Linker" mit dem starken Gefühl für soziale Gerechtigkeit, Leiter des Berliner Ensembles. Zunächst gab es Texte, programmatische Schriften, auch Gedichte, präsentiert in einem vor allem ideologischen Kontext. Und es gab die erste Erfahrung einer Aufführung: *Der kaukasische Kreidekreis* im Künstlertheater von Karolos Koun. Das große Erlebnis kam aber später, als sie in den 1970er Jahren die umwerfende Erfahrung des Gastspiels des Berliner Ensembles in Paris machte. Ihre Sprache, Bert Brecht, nun im Originalton; das Spiel der Helene Weigel. Das war der Brecht, der ihre intellektuelle Biographie lebenslang prägen sollte.

Wenn wir beide heute als Paar an Sie schreiben, als ein Paar, das auch zusammen arbeitet, so hoffen wir, welcher BB es auch sei, den wir antreffen, vor allem eines: dass Sie sich in Ihrem Himmel der guten Bösewichte nicht langweilen. Oder haben Sie es doch in die Hölle geschafft? Sie hatten doch deutlich geahnt, dass, wie schon Hegel wusste, im Paradies nur Gott und die Tiere es aushalten—weil es da eben so schrecklich langweilig ist. Und Sie schrieben ein Gedicht darüber, dass gerade die Sünder, die "Unreinen," denen man auf dem Weg in die Hölle zuvor noch im Überflug den Himmel zeigt, sich sehr enttäuscht von ihm zeigen—"denn gerade sie / Haben ihn sich strahlender gedacht."

Nach dieser *captatio benevolentiae* fassen wir uns nun ein Herz, denn wir müssen Sie gleich in einem wichtigen Punkt womöglich enttäuschen. Bei aller Liebe und Bewunderung für die Episierung des Theaters, denken wir nämlich, wenn wir an Sie denken, und das tun wir sehr oft, weniger an das epische Theater im engeren Sinn als an Sie, den Dichter und Denker des Modells der Lehrstücke. Natürlich, Sie waren, mit Erwin Piscator, der Erfinder und bleiben als Dichter und Theaterdenker der eigentliche Begründer des epischen Theaters. Sie könnten in dieser Hinsicht mehr als zufrieden sein: denn das epische Theater hat ja gesiegt. Ihre Forderung nach einem epischen—und das hieß ja vor allem: nach einem intelligenten—Theater ist heute bei allen, die künstlerisch zählen, zum selbstverständlichen Maßstab geworden. Ihre Ideen sind auch dort wirksam, wo nicht Ihre eigenen Stücke aufgeführt werden. Und die epische Spielweise als verfremdendes Spiel ist bei vielen der besten Schauspieler der neueren Zeit schon der gewöhnliche Habitus. Sie erlauben uns sogar im Hollywoodfilm immer wieder, Distanz zu ihren Figuren zu nehmen. Sie zeigen, historisieren und demonstrieren, ironisieren und zitieren Gesten. Kurz: Sie verfremden und episieren, was das Zeug hält.

Ihr episches Theater war eine epochale Wendung der Theater- und Schauspielkunst im zwanzigsten Jahrhundert, und es bleibt maßgebend in seiner Wendung gegen das Spektakuläre, gegen den Pleonasmus, gegen das Großtun im Theater, gegen alle neobarocken Versuchungen. Ihr materialistischer Minimalismus, das Bestehen auf Stil und Präzision des Theaters, lässt alles "Zuviel" auf der Bühne blamabel wirken. Ihre Strenge, die uns bei allen Unterschieden der Konzeption immer wieder an Beckett erinnert, stellt unausgesprochen eine Kritik am allzu Leichtfüßigen mancher Ihrer Adepten dar. Gewiss geht es darum, das Gezeigte im Theater "leicht" zu machen. Aber Sie hätten jederzeit Einstein zugestimmt, der betonte, man müsse die Dinge so einfach wie irgend möglich machen—aber nicht einfacher. Ihr Theater, verehrter Brecht, sollte Denkprozesse skandieren, einen Diskurs der Widersprüche quer zum Bewusstsein Ihrer Protagonisten artikulieren, sollte Konflikte darstellen, keine Lösungen auf Kosten der widersprüchlichen Wahrheit.

Wenn trotzdem heute die drängende Frage, der heftige Wunsch nach einem NEUEN epischen Theater auftaucht, so handelt es sich nicht um eine Sache der Mode. Sondern darum, dass für Sie die formale Erneuerung des Theaters—im Unterschied zu bloß formalistischen Neuerungen—stets nur eine Seite der Medaille war, deren andere hieß: das Politische im Theater. Und wenn wir nicht orthodox "brechtgläubig" die Augen davor verschließen, dann müssen wir heute erkennen, dass in der gegenwärtigen Bilderflut die Techniken des epischen Theaters einen großen Teil ihrer den Betrieb und das Bewusstsein einst verstörenden Kraft verloren haben. Vermutlich weit über Ihre eigenen schlimmsten Befürchtungen hinaus verwandelt der kapitalistische Kulturbetrieb, wie der Kapitalismus insgesamt, das gegen ihn gespritzte Gift in Rauschgift und genießt dieses.

Trotzdem geben sich viele unverdrossen mit dem schulischen Gedanken zufrieden, der Brecht hätte revolutionärerweise das Denken ins Theater eingelassen. Wir beide können uns, ehrlich gesagt, überhaupt nicht vorstellen, Sie hätten je bezweifelt, dass man auch im dramatischen Theater "des Shakespeare," wie Sie ihn gern nannten, viel und sehr viel gedacht hat. Das allein kann also nicht das Wesentliche an Ihrer Theaterrevolution gewesen sein. Es war jedoch wohl bequemer zu meinen, es genüge, etwas Intelligenz, Denken, Theorie, Wissen auf der Bühne, um das Theater einer Grunderneuerung zu unterziehen. Geht man über diesen Gesichtspunkt nicht hinaus, so bleibt aber davon ganz unberührt und unangefochten das Institut, der Apparat des Theaters. Ihre Idee des Theaters hatte aber immer eine politische, zumal eine institutionskritische Pointe.

Darum wollen wir das, was in unseren Augen das eigentlich Revolutionäre Ihres Denkens, Ihrer Praxis ausmacht, anders definieren. Sie haben als ein "Kippernikus" des Theaters tatsächlich die ganze Grundidee von dem, was Theater sei, gekippt und einen radikal anderen Begriff davon begründet. Indem Sie das Theater nicht mehr als *Aufführung vor*, sondern als *szenische Praxis von und mit* allen, auch den Besuchern = Teilnehmern, imaginiert haben. Theater in aller Konsequenz als gemeinsame Veranstaltung aller Beteiligten zu denken—das, so scheint uns, ist die veränderte Sehweise, die uns bei der Suche nach einem NEUEN epischen Theater Orientierung gibt. Und daher werden Sie verstehen, warum wir gerade Sie, den Inspirator der Idee des *learning play*, des Lehrstücks, als unseren Paten und Schutzpatron auf diesem Weg zu gewinnen hoffen.

Vermutlich ist die Kunde schon bis zu Ihrem Himmels-Saloon oder zu Ihrer Höllenkneipe gedrungen (wo Sie gestern noch mit Marx und Lessing, heute mit Nietzsche, Sophokles und Lukrez ewige Gespräche führen), dass sich viele der Jüngeren zur Zeit vor allem für Sie als den Erfinder der Idee des *learning play*, d.h. für ein Theater der Recherche und Selbstverständigung der Spielenden interessieren.

Es ist nicht lange her, dass uns jüngere Theatermacher auf die Tonaufzeichnung eines Gesprächs aufmerksam gemacht haben, in dem Sie 1953 erklärten, was man "jetzt" brauche, seien "kleine bewegliche Formen, Theaterchen." Sie erinnern da an die Tradition des Agitprop und meinen, kleine Theaterkollektive könnten auch an den großen Theatern selber entstehen, durch—hier hört man auf dem Band förmlich Ihr kleines erfreutes Schmunzeln über die eigene Formulierung—"durch Selbstzündung." Sie haben in diesen späten Jahren Ihres viel zu kurzen Lebens die *Buckower Elegien* geschrieben, Gedichte voller Skepsis. Und diese Skepsis hat Sie, so will uns scheinen, schon damals ahnen lassen, von welch lähmender Erstarrung die großen Theaterapparate bedroht waren und sind.

Welche Art von "Theaterchen," welche beweglichen Formen und Strukturen benötigen wir für ein neues episches Theater? Wir können Ihnen nicht versprechen, wie das neue epische Theater aussehen wird. Manche werden vielleicht statt eines Stücks eine Installation oder einen getanzten Prozess machen, zumal ja große Dichter, die mit der Kunst der komplexen Einfachheit ihrer Lehrstücktexte heute rivalisieren könnten, nicht in Trauben zur Welt kommen. Andere interessiert vielleicht eine Adaptation Ihres Modells auf andere Texte der dramatischen Literatur. Wieder andere schicken das Publikum vielleicht auf eine Erkundungsreise in ihre Umwelt oder arbeiten mit dokumentarischem Material. Das alles und viel mehr, was wir uns nicht im Voraus ausdenken können und wollen, ist möglich. Angeknüpft wird jedenfalls, wie sagten Sie so treffend: beim schlechten Neuen, nicht beim guten Alten.

Nennen wir trotzdem etwas wie unsere "Wunschliste": von den Räumen die kleineren, von den Spielern die klügeren, von den Gedanken die geräumigeren, von den Zeiten die längeren, von den Künstlern überhaupt die mehr am gesellschaftlichen Leben als an ihrem Selbst interessierten.

Warum nur selten ein Theater der großen Dimension? Weil Theater die Kunst *par excellence* ist, in der wir mit Blicken und Gesten, mit Schwingung und Färbung der Stimme, mit Haltung und sinnlicher Ausstrahlung, kurzum: mit dem Körper kommunizieren. Darum plädieren wir für die physische Nähe zwischen den Akteuren, Spielern, Zuschauern. So können sie sich mental voneinander entfernen, wie Sie es immer verlangt haben, aber diese Ferne nicht nur theoretisch, sondern körperlich erfahren—als "entferntes Verstehen."

Warum die klügeren Spieler? Manchen mag, was wir eben sagten, zu wenig intellektuell klingen für ein Theater in Ihrem Geist. Das neue epische Theater braucht aber gerade die klugen Spieler, die nicht einfältig genug sind, im Theater Ideen zu propagieren, eine Botschaft an den Mann bringen zu wollen, mit der Absicht einer direkten Beeinflussung der Leute. Wir wissen doch längst, dass sich diese Vorstellung bei der ersten Besinnung, spätestens beim Verlassen des Theaters widerlegt. Vielmehr wird ein NEUES episches Theater von Ihrem gelegentlich geäußerten Gedanken ausgehen, dass die Schauspieler als "Delegierte" des Publikums zu verstehen sind. Sie sind dazu bestellt, gemeinsam interessierenden Themen, besonders den schwer lösbaren Grundkonflikten des gesellschaftlichen Zusammenlebens, sinnliche Gestalt zu verleihen. Sie sollen sich nicht wie Zauberer aufführen, die den Zuschauern magische Wundertaten der Verkörperungskunst anbieten, sondern als besonders aktive Teilnehmer Theater als einen auf Zeit gemeinsam bewohnten Denkraum realisieren. Siegreiche Parolen waren nicht Ihre Sache. Ihr "Theater des konstruktiven Defaitismus" fängt ja schon damit an, dass Sie nie die erfolgreiche Revolution ins Bild setzten, sondern immer nur ihre Probleme. Nie den siegreichen, heroischen Kampf, immer die Niederlage, den Deserteur, den, der nicht mitspielt.

Warum von den Gedanken die geräumigeren? Die geräumigen Gedanken sind die, die das Undenkbare mit einschließen. Ihr ganzes Theaterdenken zielte nicht auf die schlichte Vorstellung ab, die viele noch immer bei Ihnen zu finden glauben, dass Theater solle mit seiner Sinnlichkeit etwas illustrieren, was man auch theoretisch denken und als Gelerntes schwarz auf weiß nach Hause tragen kann. Vielmehr haben Sie immer wieder implizit und manchmal auch explizit auf etwas bestanden, was den Liebhabern des belehrenden Theaters in die Parade fährt: Theaterspiel ist eine Praxis, durch die und mit deren Hilfe man "begreift," was man rein *theoretisch* eben *nicht* begreifen kann—sondern nur gestisch, sinnlich, stimmlich, körperlich. Der Prozess des Spielens, des Darstellens eröffnet ein "Lernen," das nicht in fixierbarem Gelerntem mündet. Viel näher als dem Bild, das viele von Ihnen malen, scheinen Sie uns darum Hölderlin, der den Menschen als "unter Undenkbarem wandelnd" zeigen wollte.

Warum von den Zeiten die längeren? Es wird ein Theater sein, dessen Aufführungen der Idee nach als fortgesetzte Probenarbeit unter Zulassung der Öffentlichkeit verstanden werden sollen. Ein Theater der Erforschung, das viele Mitautoren hat und sucht. Ein Theater, das sich dafür die nötige Zeit nimmt und entsprechenden Zeitaufwand auch seinen Besuchern zumutet. Wir denken, das neue epische Theater soll sich jene Haltung zum Vorbild nehmen, mit der Sie den Funktionären der Partei, die die Länge einer geplanten Aufführung monierten, weil die Leute morgens zur Arbeit müssten, zur Antwort gaben: Da gebe es wirklich ein Problem. Man müsse ganz offenbar die Arbeitszeiten ändern.

Grüße in Ihr Exil jenseits von Zeit und Arbeit senden

Hans-Thies Lehmann und Helene Varopoulou

Fig. 2. The audience for the new epic theater at HAU1 in Berlin, August 2015. Image © Simone Steiner, photographer.

Letter to Brecht

Dear Bert Brecht,

Here we already start to falter, because to whom do we address this letter? To you, the anarchic, sometimes expressionist writer of the early poems and of *Baal*? Or to the Brecht of New Objectivity, the one who wrote "The ABC says: they will get you down"? To the Brecht who thought as a Marxist and invented the model of the *Lehrstücke*? To the inventor of "tragic" figures, from the young comrade in the learning play *The Measures Taken* to the characters of your classics of epic theater, such as *Mother Courage*? Even when it is particularly that one Brecht, the "other," whom we address, we somehow also include all the others.

You were never just one, but always another, and because of that, also someone who brought about change. You never conceived of yourself as the "owner" of ideas, and wrote early on in your diaries:

> I don't think that I can ever have such a matured philosophy as Goethe or Hebbel, who must have had, in regards to their own ideas, the memories of tram conductors. I always forget my own convictions and cannot make myself learn them by heart.

And we cannot forget your wonderful description when you once observed your face as you ate cherries in front of a mirror:

> My face contains many elements of brutality, quiet, slackness, cunning, and cowardice, but only as elements, and it is more varied and less principled than a landscape under passing clouds. This is why many people can't remember my face ("There are too many," says Hedda).

"Whoever you are looking for—it's not me." The two of us who are writing this letter to you found this to be so true that in 1991 we separately—at the time still unacquainted with one another—chose the motto "The Other Brecht" for Brecht events: one in Augsburg, the other in Athens. At the time, our acquaintance with your writings already went back quite far: for one of us, back to his youth in Bremen. As a schoolboy, in the window of a library or bookshop in the city, he read the following sentence in one of the thin, pale-yellow single editions of your work. He was electrified: "That that of what is there should belong to those who are good to it." Electrified by the content that spoke to a youthful sense of justice, but also by the very formality of that wonderful stumble of syntax and sound: "those *who are good* for *it*," such a simple twist, which the grammar teacher probably would have rejected.

The other one of us also had her first experiences with you during her youth and early years. In 1950s and 1960s Greece, "Brecht" was more of a legend than a real, known author: a representative of the antifascist Germans, a giant of German literature in exile, a "leftist" with a strong sense of social justice, the director of the Berliner Ensemble. She first knew you through texts: programmatic writings and poems usually presented in an ideological context. Then came the first live performance, *The Caucasian Chalk Circle*, at the artist theater of Karolos Koun. The truly transformative experience came later, when she saw the stunning performance of the Berliner Ensemble in Paris during the 1970s. Here was your language, Bert Brecht, as it was written; here was the acting of Helene Weigel. This was the Brecht that would so affect the rest of her intellectual life.

We write to you today as a couple working together. We both hope for one thing, regardless of which BB we reach: that you aren't bored in your heaven of good villains. Or did you make it to hell? In life you certainly suspected (as Hegel already knew) that only God and animals could survive paradise—it is so terribly boring. Once you wrote a poem about the sinners, the "unclean" who were flown over heaven on their way to hell: they were disappointed, "because precisely they were the ones / who thought it would be more splendid."

After this *captatio benevolentiae* we must be brave, because now we may perhaps have to disappoint you on an important point. With all our love and admiration for epic theater, when we think of you (and we do this frequently), we think less of epic theater in its narrower sense and more of you as the poet and the inventor of the *Lehrstück* model. Of course you invented the epic theater, together with Erwin Piscator, and as a poet and theater theorist you remain its founder. From this perspective you can be more than satisfied: epic theater has triumphed. Your call for an epic theater—an intelligent theater—has become the self-evident measure for anyone who matters artistically. Your ideas are effective even in places where your works are not performed. The epic style with its estranged acting has become habitual for many of the best contemporary actors. They allow us, even in Hollywood films, to distance ourselves from their characters: they show, historicize, demonstrate, ironize, and cite gestures; in short they estrange for all they are worth.

Your epic theater was a hallmark shift in the art of theater-making and acting in the twentieth century, and it remains a standard against spectacle, against redundancy, against the swagger of theater, against all neo-baroque temptations. This materialist minimalism, this insistence on simple elegance and precision, makes any excess on stage feel embarrassing. Your rigor (which despite all its differences reminds us time and again of Beckett) is a form of silent criticism of the whimsy of some of your acolytes. (Certainly what is shown in the theater can be made "light," but you would have agreed with Einstein when he emphasized that it is about making things as easy as possible—but not easier.) Your theater, dear Brecht, was to scan our thinking process and articulate a discourse of contradictions at odds with the awareness of its protagonists. It should present conflicts, not solutions at the expense of contradictory truths.

If today the urgent question, the undeniable desire for a NEW epic theater arises, then this is not a question of passing fashions. For you, the formal renewal of the theater (in contrast to mere formalist innovations) was only one side of the coin; the other side was the political in the theater. We must not close our eyes (as does the Brecht orthodoxy) to the fact that, in the contemporary flood of images, the techniques of epic theater have lost a large part of their power to unsettle the establishment and our own consciousness. Probably far beyond your own worst fears, the capitalist cultural establishment (like the rest of capitalism) is able to transform the poison used against it, and to enjoy it as a narcotic.

Perhaps many take a childish comfort in the idea that, in some revolutionary way, the Great Brecht brought thinking into the theater. To be honest, neither of us can imagine that you ever doubted people were thinking, and thinking a lot, also in the dramatic theater of "the Shakespeare," as you liked to call him. So this aspect *cannot* be the essence of your revolution of the theater. It would be so nice to believe that bringing a bit of intelligence, thinking, theory, or knowledge onto the stage would suffice to fundamentally renew the theater. If one does not go beyond this perspective, however, then everything—the institution, the apparatus of the theater—remains unchanged and uncontested. Your notion of theater always meant a political and institutional criticism of its very apparatus.

And this is why we would like to define differently what, in our eyes, is the truly "revolutionary" part of your thought and practice. Like a Copernicus of the theater, you subverted the foundational idea of what theater is and established a radically different idea for it. You no longer imagined theater as a performance *in front of* and *for* the visitors, but as a scenic practice *by* and *with* everyone participating, audience and performers alike. To think of theater as a communal event of all participants—to think through this concept, in all its consequences—this is what appears to us as the changed way of seeing that offers us direction in the search for a NEW epic theater. And this is why we hope to win you, who inspired the idea of the learning play, as our godfather and patron.

Perhaps the message has already reached your heavenly saloon or your dive bar in hell (where yesterday it was perhaps Marx and Lessing, today Nietzsche, Sophocles, and Lucretius with whom you share eternal conversations). These days, many young people are more interested in you as the inventor of the learning play, in the theater of research and of self-understanding (*Selbstverständigung* was your term for this) among its players, than in you as the inventor of epic theater.

It was not so long ago that young theater-makers brought a sound recording to our attention on which, in 1953, you explained that what we needed "now" were "small, mobile forms, little theaters." You recalled the tradition of agitprop and mused that small theater collectives might even originate in the larger theaters through—here one seems to hear clearly on the tape your own delighted smirk at this formulation—*Selbstzündung*, spontaneous combustion. In these later years of your far-too-short life you wrote the *Buckower Elegies*, poems full of skepticism. And as it appears to us, it was this skepticism that allowed you to foresee even then the paralyzing immobility that threatened (and continues to threaten) the big theaters.

What type of little theaters, what flexible forms and structures, do we need for a new epic theater? We cannot paint you a picture of how the new epic theater will look. Some artists will make an installation or a danced process instead of a theater piece, perhaps because great poets who could match the high art of complex simplicity in your *Lehrstück* texts are not exactly being born *en masse*. Others are perhaps interested in the adaptation of your model to other texts of dramatic literature. Still others may send the audience on a journey of discovery through their environments, or work with documentary material. All of this and much more is possible; we cannot and do not wish to predict it. In any case (as you once said so well), it will be built not on the "good old," but on the "bad new."

Let us nevertheless state something like our "wish list" for the new epic theater: of the spaces, the smaller ones; of the performers, the smarter ones; of the thoughts, the more expansive ones; of the durations, the longer ones. And of the artists: rather those who are more interested in the life of society than in themselves.

Why do we rarely want to see a theater of large dimensions? Because theater is the art *par excellence* in which we communicate with the body: with gazes and gestures, with the modulation and timbre of the voice, with posture and sensual presence. This is why we plead for a physical closeness between actors, players, and audience: so that they can distance themselves mentally from one another, as you demanded, but at the same time experience this distance not only theoretically but physically too, as *entferntes Verstehen*, which means both an incomplete understanding and a removed understanding.

Why the smarter performers? What we just spoke of may not appear to be intellectual enough for some. However, the new epic theater needs specifically clever actors: those who are not so simple as to want to propagate ideas in the theater, to sell a message to the people, to desire a direct influence on them. After all, we have known for a long time that this influence will fade away upon closer examination, at the latest upon leaving the theater. Rather, the new epic theater will depart from your occasionally expressed thought that the actors should be understood as delegates of the audience; commissioned to lend sensual form to shared themes of interest, especially those difficult-to-solve, fundamental conflicts about our ways of living together as a society. They should not present themselves as magicians who offer the audience magical acts of the art of embodiment. Instead, they should offer themselves as especially active participants in a theater that is conceived as a shared space for thinking, inhabited for a certain amount of time. Victory slogans were never your thing. Your "theater of constructive defeatism" never showed the successful revolution, but always only its problems. You never portrayed the victorious, heroic battle, but always the defeat, the deserter, the one who didn't play along.

Why do we need the more expansive thoughts? Expansive thoughts are those that contain the unthinkable within them. Your entire concept of theater never aimed at the simplistic idea that many still adhere to: that theater should illustrate with its sensuality something that one can also grasp theoretically, something you can take home, black-on-white, as something learned. Instead, you always implicitly (and sometimes explicitly) insisted on the opposite of what aficionados of the theater of instruction uphold. Theater is a practice, through which and with the help of which one is able to grasp what one *cannot* grasp theoretically, but *only* through practice: through gestures and movements, sensually, vocally, physically. The process of performing, of acting, opens a space for learning that does not end in something fixed, something learned. Much closer than the image that many have of you, you appear to us close to Hölderlin, who wished to show the human being as "wandering among the unthinkable."

And why the longer duration? A theater of discovery with many authors, a theater that takes the necessary time, expects the necessary expenditure of time from its visitors. The new epic theater will be a theater whose performances can be considered conceptually as a continuation of rehearsals—with an invitation to the audience. We think that the new epic theater should adopt one of your own stances. Once you were scolded by party functionaries about the length of a performance, because after all, people needed to go to work the next morning. You responded that this was indeed a problem: obviously one would have to change the work schedules.

Many greetings to your exile beyond time and work from

Hans-Thies Lehmann und Helene Varopoulou

Fig. 3. The theater space for 24h Durcheinander during the discussion of the "Brechtbrief" at HAU1 in Berlin, August 2015. Image © Simone Steiner, photographer.

24h DURCHEINANDER

Kattrin Deufert und Thomas Plischke

Der Brechtbrief von Hans-Thies Lehmann und Helene Varopoulou wurde für unser erstes DURCHEINANDER verfasst, das im August 2015 im Berliner Theater HAU1 im Rahmen des Festivals "Tanz im August" Premiere hatte. *DURCHEINANDER* ist der Titel einer Projektreihe und auch Motto für unsere künstlerischen Arbeitsweisen. Das Projekt DURCHEINANDER untersucht und produziert eine gewisse gesellschaftliche Unordnung, fordert aber auch gegenseitige Bezugnahme und soziale Interaktion und sucht die Kommunikation im Chaos des künstlerischen Handelns. Unsere Arbeitsprozesse fordern es geradezu heraus, Entscheidungen und Erfahrungen verstärkt durch-die-anderen zu machen und zu verstehen und im eigenen Handeln öfter mal einen Schritt zur Seite zu treten.

Seit mehreren Jahren denken wir Theater als eine soziale Situation, die bestimmte Merkmale wie die Publikumsbehandlung oder Raum- und Zeitbezüge des Brecht'schen epischen Theaterdiskurses weiterführt und umsetzt. Was wir mit Anderen ein neues episches Theater nennen, ist ein choreografisches Theater, das Aktionen, Akteure, Besucher, Räume und Objekte in komplexen Partituren im Auf- und Abbau seiner selbst verknüpft. Das neue epische Theater re-funktionalisiert Theater als Raum: es kann getrennt Parlament, Akademie und Lebensraum oder alles in einem sein. Als Parlament verhandelt es Meinungen, die noch nicht geäußert wurden, als Akademie verhandelt es das Nichtwissen und das Nochnichtwissen, als Lebensraum gibt es uns Zeit und Raum zum Leben in der Gemeinschaft der Fremden. Zuallererst ist Theater immer ein lebendiger und sozialer Ort, der sich auf unterschiedliches Wissen, unterschiedliche Kulturen, Sprechweisen und Meinungen öffnet. Das neue epische Theater ist ein Theater der sozialen Realität in seiner temporär geteilten Ausweglosigkeit. Mehr noch als die Notausgangsschilder braucht das Publikum im Theater eine Aufgabe in neuen gemeinsamen Lebensformen, um den Alltag in der Umgebung aufzuheben. Das neue epische Theater nimmt seine Zuschauer ernst, es macht kein Theater für sie, sondern mit und von ihnen. Wie im Lehrstück von Brecht aktivieren wir den Zuschauer und beziehen ihn ein. Das Publikum ist das Theater. Das Publikum macht unser Theater. Es gibt keine Vorführung und keinen Vorführeffekt, sondern Aufführung und Teilhabe. Auch in der Welt der Theaterumgebung ist jeder verantwortlich für sein Tun. Im

THE BRECHT YEARBOOK | DAS BRECHT-JAHRBUCH 40
(ROCHESTER, NY: CAMDEN HOUSE, 2016)

neuen epischen Theater gilt das Gesetz der polyphonen Antistatik und des temporären Durcheinanders. Seien Sie auf der Hut!

Das DURCHEINANDER im August 2015 brachte etwa fünfundzwanzig Künstlerinnen und Künstler sowie ein vielfaches an Publikum im Berliner HAU1 zusammen, um in vierundzwanzig Stunden ein ganzes Theater um-, auf-, und wieder abzubauen. Es wurde gemeinsam getanzt, gegessen, geschlafen und dazwischen vieles umgestellt, verschoben, durcheinander gebracht und wieder aufgeräumt.

Überall im Haus verstreute das Publikum auf losen Zetteln Erinnerungen an vergangene persönliche Theatererlebnisse. Im oberen Foyer wuchsen schon seit mehreren Wochen Pilze heran, die einem mykologischen Gemeinschaftsexperiment dienten und dann als Risotto verzehrt wurden. Zur Mitternacht wurde ein Vorhang vor die große Bühne gehängt, der in vielen bunten Stoffresten eine Karte von Berlin zeigte, die das Publikum in vierstündiger Arbeit zusammengeflickt hatte, während gleichzeitig auf der Bühne ein Vortrag zum Thema des Exodus in der Musik des zwanzigsten Jahrhunderts gehalten wurde. Für alle Besucherinnen und Besucher war nonstop eine Bücherei geöffnet, die Schreib- und Lesehilfen für eigene und fremde Texte des neuen epischen Theaters bereitstellte. In der Nachtruhe wurde ein Parlament geöffnet und nach der Kundgebung am Morgen gab es Schauspielunterricht für Anfänger. Ganz am Anfang spazierten in der ersten Stunde alle mit einem Kopfhörer durch das Theater und sahen sich gegenseitig von Raum zu Raum hören:

Unsere Zeit gehört uns nicht.
Nicht mir und nicht dir
und nicht ihnen,
auch wenn wir alle bezahlen,
oft mehr als wir können.

Aber vielleicht wollen wir sie gar nicht haben,
sondern sie vertreiben und
durcheinander bringen.
Nicht nichts tun,
sondern gemeinsam etwas tun:
zuhören zum Beispiel
und später noch mehr,
denn es bleibt immer wieder
alles zu tun
in unserer Zeit.

Hier gibt es manches zu verschwenden,
zu verplempern,
zu verprassen,

so vieles auf den Kopf zu hauen.
Lassen sie sich Zeit.
Unser Theater hat 24 Stunden.

Zum Schluss erinnern wir gerne an den Moment, als wir am Sonntag früh am Morgen vor Sonnenaufgang ins Theater zurückkehrten und beim Eintritt ins leere Foyer ein leises ganz unspektakulär regelmässiges Schnarchen der Zuschauer hören konnten, die spät nachts im DURCHEINANDER auf der Bühne geschlafen haben. Es schien für einen kurzen Augenblick fast so, als würde das hundert Jahre alte Foyer selbständig atmen. Wir dachten für einen Moment an unsere beiden kleinen Kinder, die wir gerade zuhause verabschiedet hatten und wie beruhigend es sein kann in unserer Welt der Menschen, noch Schlafende zu hören.

deufert&plischke (Künstlerzwilling), Berlin, Januar 2016

Endredaktion: Kareth Schaffer und Marc Silberman
24h DURCHEINANDER ist eine Produktion von deufert&plischke GbR und Tanzfabrik Berlin e.V., gefördert aus Mitteln des Hauptstadtkulturfonds Berlin und im Rahmen von "apap—advancing performing arts project—Performing Europe 2011–2016," unterstützt durch EU Kultur.
24h DURCHEINANDER ist eine Produktion von und mit: Kattrin Deufert, Thorsten Eibeler, Alain Franco, Roni Katz, Hans-Thies Lehmann, Sandra Noeth, Thomas Plischke, Kareth Schaffer, Cecilie Ullerup Schmidt, Marcus Steinweg, Yair Vardi, Helene Varopoulou, Stefanie Wenner, Arkadi Zaides.
www.deufertandplischke.net

24h MUDDLE

Kattrin Deufert and Thomas Plischke

Hans-Thies Lehmann and Helene Varopoulou wrote the letter to Brecht for our first MUDDLE, which premiered at the Berlin Theater HAU1 in August 2015 as part of the festival "Dance in August." *MUDDLE* is the title of a project series as well as the motto for our artistic working method. The MUDDLE project examines and produces a certain social disorder, but also requires a mutual relationship and social interaction, and seeks communication within the chaos of artistic activity. Our working methods literally provoke participants to make decisions and have experiences more intensely through the others and to understand and, when taking an action, to step aside now and again.

For several years we have been thinking about theater as a social situation that extends and transforms certain aspects of the Brechtian epic theater discourse, such as the treatment of the audience or spatial and temporal references. What we—along with others—call a new epic theater is a choreographic theater that connects actions, actors, visitors, spaces, and objects in complex performance scores for its own setup and dismantling. The new epic theater re-functionalizes theater as space: it can be divided into parliament, academy, and living space or it can be all in one. As parliament it debates opinions that were not yet expressed, as academy it debates the unknown and the not-yet-known, as living space it offers us time and space to live in a community of strangers. In the first instance theater is always a lively and social place that opens into different kinds of knowledge, different cultures, ways of speaking, and opinions. The new epic theater is a theater of social reality in its temporarily shared dead end. More than emergency exit signs the theater public needs a task in the new, mutual forms of living in order to preserve the everyday in our surroundings. The new epic theater takes seriously its audience; it makes theater with and by them, not for them. As in Brecht's learning play, we activate the audience and draw it in. The public is our theater. The public makes our theater. There are no presentations and no show effects, but instead performance and participation. Even in the world of the theater environment all are responsible for their actions. In the new epic theater the law of polyphonic anti-stasis and temporary muddle pertains. Be on your guard!

The MUDDLE in August 2015 brought together about twenty-five artists and a much larger public at the Berlin HAU1 to convert, set up, and then dismantle an entire theater. There was dancing, eating, sleeping, and in between much was converted, shifted, messed up, and cleaned up.

Throughout the building the public scattered notes with its memories of past personal theater experiences. In the upper lobby mushrooms had been cultivated for several weeks, which served as a shared mycological experiment and were then eaten as a risotto. Around midnight a curtain made of many colorful cloth remnants that the public had sewn together over a period of four hours was hung in front of the large stage, showing a map of Berlin. Simultaneously a lecture was delivered from the stage on the topic of exodus in twentieth-century music. All visitors had nonstop access to a library that provided writing and reading advice for their own and others' texts for the new epic theater. During the night's rest time a parliament was called into session, and after the morning announcements there was acting instruction for beginners. At the very beginning everyone walked through the theater building with headphones and, passing through space after space, saw each other listening:

> Our time does not belong to us
> Not to me and not to you
> and not to them,
> even though all of us pay,
> often more than we are able to.
>
> But maybe we don't really want to have it,
> we want instead to kill it and
> muddle it up.
> Don't do nothing,
> but rather do something together:
> for example listen
> and later even more,
> because there is always
> everything to do
> in our time.
>
> Here there is much to waste,
> to fritter away,
> to squander,
> so much to blow.
> Take your time.
> Our theater has 24 hours.

Finally, we like to think back on that moment on Sunday morning before the sun came up when we returned to the theater and—stepping into the lobby—we could hear a soft, very unspectacular, rhythmical snoring of the audience, which, after the late night, was sleeping in a MUDDLE on the stage. For one brief moment it seemed almost as if the one-hundred-year-old lobby was itself breathing. We thought for a minute about our two small children to whom we had just said goodbye and about how reassuring it can be in our human world to still hear those who are sleeping.

deufert&plischke (artistwins), Berlin, January 2016

Translation and proofreading: Kareth Schaffer and Marc Silberman
24h MUDDLE is a production by deufert&plischke GbR and Tanzfabrik Berlin e.V., with support from Hauptstadtkulturfonds Berlin and the European network "apap—advancing performing arts project—Performing Europe 2011–2016," which receives funding from the EU Culture Program.
24h MUDDLE was created by and with: Kattrin Deufert, Thorsten Eibeler, Alain Franco, Roni Katz, Hans-Thies Lehmann, Sandra Noeth, Thomas Plischke, Kareth Schaffer, Cecilie Ullerup Schmidt, Marcus Steinweg, Yair Vardi, Helene Varopoulou, Stefanie Wenner, Arkadi Zaides.
www.deufertandplischke.net

Erinnerungen an das Brecht-Theater

Dieter Goltzsche

Seit 1953 besuchten wir Kunststudenten aus Dresden häufig Berlin: Ziel waren immer die Kunstmuseen und abends das Brecht-Theater BE. Die durchgefeilten, so lange geprobten Aufführungen gaben uns einen ganz neuen Eindruck von Theater—keine Illusionen, Denken und Empfinden gehörten zusammen. Die großen Eindrücke, außer der *Mutter Courage*, waren *Pauken und Trompeten* von George Farquhar in der Bearbeitung von Brecht, Regie Besson; das Stück *Die Mutter*; *Der Hofmeister* (Lenz); *Der gute Mensch von Sezuan*; *Die Dreigroschenoper* (der Bandit wird zum Bürger, eine scharfe Anklage, die bis heute an Bedeutung nichts verloren hat!); *Dickicht der Städte*; *Herr Puntila und sein Knecht Matti*; *Galileo Galilei*.

Später dann *Arturo Ui*—ein Gangsterspektakel. Aus der frühen Zeit sind die großen Schauspieler zu nennen: die Weigel, Regine Lutz, Therese Giehse, Ernst Busch, Wolf Kaiser und andere. Zu nennen ist auch die begabte Regieschülerschaft, Manfred Wekwerth, Peter Palitzsch, Egon Monk—Benno Besson, ein Schweizer von größter Eigenart.

Berlin war ja trotz der vier Sektoren und der immensen Zerstörungen noch eine offene Stadt, in der man sich kulturell vollsaugen konnte. Museen, später die Ausstellungen in der neuerbauten Akademie der Künste am Hanseatenweg, in der Maison de France. Die Galerie Gerd Rosen war eine Legende, das Kino am Steinplatz, die Städtische Oper und die Komische Oper unter Felsenstein, und eben das BE.

Da wir von Dresden aus die Spielpläne nicht kannten, sah ich die *Courage* sechsmal, andere Aufführungen auch mehr als einmal. Wir Studenten hatten immer die billigsten Plätze für fünfzig Pfennige, nahe den Scheinwerfern, oft fehlte die Sicht auf ein Viertel der Bühne. Interessant war im BE das vielfach internationale Publikum. Das doch kleine Theater am Schiffbauerdamm mit seinen Vergoldungen, dem Stuck, und dem vielen Plüsch stand im absoluten Gegensatz zur Brecht-Gardine und zur Nüchternheit der Szenen. Allein dieser Kontrast war eine geniale Idee. Der von Brecht intendierte V-Effekt wandte sich gegen Naturalismus und Einfühlung. Der Schauspieler soll zeigen, dass er zeigt. Es gab aber hier, von der Seite der Einheitspartei, immer wieder Sentimentaleinwände.

THE BRECHT YEARBOOK | DAS BRECHT-JAHRBUCH 40
(ROCHESTER, NY: CAMDEN HOUSE, 2016)

Indem ich diese Zeilen schreibe, merke ich, dass die tatsächlichen Eindrücke jener Zeit kaum zu übermitteln sind. Aber die Erinnerungen sind fest im Kopf.

Januar 2016

Dieter Goltzsche, geboren 1934 in Dresden, ist Graphiker und Maler. Er ist Mitglied der Akademie der Künste und lebt in Berlin.

Editor's note: The set of images selected for publication encompasses fourteen works that range from the 1960s to 2015. The pieces are ordered chronologically and interspersed throughout the volume, starting on the following page. The Brecht Yearbook *thanks Dieter Goltzsche for the opportunity to share his work with our audience.*

Dieter Goltzsche, *Tagebuch b. b.*, 1967, Graphit.

Die Temporalität der Kritik: Bertolt Brechts Fragment *Jae Fleischhacker in Chikago* (1924–1929)

Das Dramafragment *Jae Fleischhacker in Chikago* ist von der Brechtforschung bisher kaum beachtet worden. Das ist besonders überraschend angesichts der Tatsache, dass Brechts und Hauptmanns Arbeit an diesem Stück, das auf dem Frank Norris Roman *Die Getreidebörse* von 1903 beruht, weithin als wichtiges Moment in der Genealogie des epischen Theater gilt. Der hier vorliegende Artikel nimmt die Idee einer "Krise der dramatischen Form" zu seinem Ausgangspunkt und versucht, sich auf Archivmaterialen stützend, zu bestimmen, worin genau diese Krise besteht. Die zentrale These des Artikels lautet, dass es sich um eine Krise des Erzählens handelt. Das Erzählen, das den Leser bannt und interessiert, macht zugleich die Kritik an den ökonomischen Praktiken, die es zum Gegenstand hat, unmöglich. Aber *Jae Fleischhacker* ist nicht lediglich ein gescheitertes Projekt; das Fragment steht bereits für einen Ausweg aus der Krise. Es schlägt eine neue Temporalität des Erzählen vor. Brecht illustriert diese Temporalität in Form eines Gedichtes von 1926: "Diese Babilonische Verwirrung der Wörter." Das Gedicht wird daher den interpretativen Rahmen für diesen Artikel abgeben.

The drama fragment *Jae Fleischhacker in Chikago* based on Frank Norris's 1903 novel *The Pit* has gotten little scholarly attention. This is all the more surprising in view of the fact that it is widely accepted that Brecht and Hauptmann's work on *Fleischhacker* contributed largely to the emergence of a new form of theater. By drawing on archive material this paper proposes a way of understanding the crisis of dramatic form for which the Fleischhacker fragment purportedly stands. This crisis is best captured, the paper maintains, as a crisis of storytelling: stories that captivate their readers also render impossible any critique of the economic practices they depict. However, *Jae Fleischhacker* is not simply a failed project; it already provides an escape by reconfiguring the temporality of storytelling. Brecht programmatically illustrates such a procedure in a poem from 1926, "Diese Babilonische Verwirrung der Wörter," which thus functions here as an interpretative frame.

The Temporality of Critique: Bertolt Brecht's Fragment *Jae Fleischhacker in Chikago* (1924–1929)

Matthias Rothe

Stories from the Perspective of Redemption

Neulich wollte ich euch
Erzählen mit Arglist
Die Geschichte eines Weizenhändlers in der Stadt
Chikago, mitten im Vortrag
Verließ mich die Stimme in Eile
Denn ich hatte
Plötzlich erkannt: welche Mühe
Es mich kosten würde, diese Geschichte
Jenen zu erzählen, die noch nicht geboren sind
Die aber geboren werden und in
Ganz anderen Zeitläufen leben werden
Und, die Glücklichen! Gar nicht mehr
Verstehen können, was ein Weizenhändler ist
Von der Art, wie sie bei uns sind
Da fing ich an, es ihnen zu erklären, und im Geist
Hörte ich mich sprechen sieben Jahre
Aber ich begegnete
Nur stummem Kopfschütteln bei allen
Meinen ungeborenen Zuhörern
Da erkannte ich, dass ich
Etwas erzählte, was
Ein Mensch nicht verstehen kann[1]

Brecht wrote the poem "Diese Babilonische Verwirrung der Wörter" in 1926, at a time when he and Elisabeth Hauptmann were working intensively on *Jae Fleischhacker in Chikago*, originally titled *Mortimer Fleischhacker*. Material (*Stoff*) for the play was Frank Norris's 1903 novel *The Pit*, the story of the speculator Curtis Jadwin, a wheat trader (*ein Weizenhändler*) who succeeds in cornering the wheat market.[2] Norris tells the story of Jadwin's ever-growing obsession with the game of speculating, a fixation that eventually causes his bankruptcy and threatens to destroy his marriage, conceived of as a refuge from the world of the Pit, the Chicago futures exchange. Norris also describes in detail the various financial maneuvers that lead to Jadwin's corner. When Brecht first turned his attention to Norris in 1924, this type of story was topical: strong fluctuation in prices of staple foods, especially bread, was the order of the day in Germany, widely attributed to the trading of commodity futures. The events at the stock exchange and the Chicago Pit were reported in the newspapers as if they were boxing matches.[3] Many of these articles, which Brecht collected for his play project, are preserved in the Brecht Archive. This poem can thus be understood in the context of such narratives (and Norris employs them too): it does not announce the failure of the *Fleischhacker* project, as Patrick Primavesi claims in the *Brecht Handbuch*[4]—the project was in full swing in 1926—but offers a reflection on the failure of a certain form of storytelling, namely "Erzählen mit Arglist." More important, as I will attempt to show, the poem suggests an alternative to "Erzählen mit Arglist" through its poetic procedure.[5]

"Erzählen mit Arglist," to narrate cunningly, means to not yet reveal the end of the story, but instead to continuously feed the readers' expectations, confirm and disappoint them by twists and turns, and make them eager to know what comes next, until this tension is released in a solution provided by the ending (which is at the same time *Lösung* and *Auflösung* of the story). This is also how the lyric I seeks to proceed, yet halfway through, the lyric I is unable to continue. It suddenly imagines its audience to be the yet unborn listeners and thus becomes aware that the twists and turns will only work if they still know what a wheat trader is. As the lyric I begins to explain this profession, it realizes that it will have to explain much more: most likely it will have to define "stock exchange" and its function, spell out "commodity"—that is, the difference between wheat as food and wheat as trade object—and surely the meaning of gain and loss and prices and their fluctuation, and so on ("hörte ich mich sprechen sieben Jahre"). And still these explanations of objects, functions, and causal connections would fail to yield comprehension ("nur stummes Kopfschütteln"). It becomes clear to the lyric I that it is not the solutions that need explanation, as it were, but the existence of the problem. The lyric I comes to look at these economic proceedings—in alliance with the unborn listeners—as if such practices had already ceased to exist. And it understands that for a human being, for someone who lives in a just society, the pertinent question is: why did people once live in such a way that was obviously—as the last verse of the poem states—"zu durchschauen als falsch und unmenschlich"? This question implies that economic practices such as speculations on food are not without alternative; they ultimately reveal themselves as contingent, as belonging to a specific form of society.[6]

Through the failure of "arglistiges Erzählen" all this emerges—"all this" being an image of society as a whole. In other words, if it succeeds, "arglistiges Erzählen" necessarily hides all these so-called structural aspects (and their temporal index) by simply making them functional prerequisites.[7] Worse, in doing so, it renders its objects comprehensible in both senses: intelligible and acceptable.[8] Paradoxically, that "arglistiges Erzählen" fails is told here quite cunningly. The lyric I employs all the tricks of fiction: an innocuous beginning ("neulich wollte ich"), an unexpected incident ("mitten im Vortrag"), various twists and turns ("plötzlich," "da fing ich an," "da erkannte ich"), and a solution in the twofold sense of the word (the lyric I catches up with the point of view from which the story fails, that is, with the point of view of those who deserve the name of a human being). Thus the problem at hand is not one of storytelling *tout court*, but rather it is a problem of perspective or temporality. The second story, the story of the failure of storytelling, is successful because it is told, to quote T. W. Adorno, "vom Standpunkt der Erlösung."[9] And instead of speaking of two stories—one story that fails and one that succeeds—it is perhaps more precise to say that there is only one story, namely the story of the wheat trader retold from the point of view of redemption, an endeavor that backhandedly replaces the target of storytelling: the end of *the* story, the solution of the plot, is gradually substituted by the end of THE story, of all such stories. And only when the greater story comes to its end, it turns out that its end was already the starting point of *the* story, the story of the wheat trader.[10]

Adapting Narration for the Stage

The problem with storytelling is strictly speaking a problem of story-showing. Storytelling, writing, was already more advanced and it did not have to proceed cunningly, even though, in Norris's novel, it does so. Brecht and his collaborators were aware of this difference in media. Not only had Brecht closely followed and commented on the narrative inventions of writers such as Alfred Döblin, Franz Kafka, or Sherwood Anderson at the time, but it can also be assumed that the poem itself had its origin in an attempt to adapt a story for the stage: Bouck White's *The Book of Daniel Drew*. This novel proceeds cunningly yet in quotation marks, and the stage, as Brecht famously claimed on the occasion of his first plagiarism scandal, still lacked inverted commas.[11] Thus the actual question was how to reproduce the effects of writing on the stage.

Bouck White's quotation marks apply to the form of autobiographical storytelling. Faithfully basing his work on the life of the real Dan Drew, he writes a fake autobiography. Brecht read the book in early 1925, and perhaps it became a model case for his request, formulated in a memo in 1926, to fabricate documents, to produce "Monographien bedeutender Männer, Aufrisse gesellschaftlicher Strukturen . . . durch die Form nicht . . . neutralisiert."[12] White had risen to this challenge. His novel was celebrated as a real autobiography, for example, in a review from 1920 known to Brecht and as an autobiography that allowed its readers more insights into the workings of capitalism than the author could have intended.[13] The book's hidden impersonal narrator had evidently managed to walk the thin line between caricature and heroic story, and accomplished something like a cross-section (*Aufriss*) of Dan Drew's individual story. He had brought to the fore the societal structures on which it was inscribed. This was reason enough for Brecht, Hauptmann, and Emil Hesse-Burri to turn the novel into a play between December 1925 and March 1926—just before the work on *Jae Fleischhacker* entered its most intensive and, according to the Berlin-Frankfurt edition, decisive phase. *Dan Drew,* very much like *Jae Fleischhacker*, depicts a speculator (in railways) and the mechanisms and effects of commodity futures trading. Thus, it is safe to assume that Brecht and his collaborators were able to draw conclusions for *Fleischhacker* from the difficulty they encountered with the adaptation of White's book.[14]

Adaptation is indeed the right name for the Dan Drew project. The play, which was eventually abandoned with only a few scenes missing, follows the original story's linear order, borrows a great number of descriptions and dialogues word for word from the original, and often marks the places of missing scenes with the page numbers of White's book. Changes mostly concern the adjustment to a conventional drama format: side stories, and along with them continuous changes of times and places, are cut in favor of the main conflict over the Erie railways. The differences in character between the adversaries, Dan Drew and Cornelius Vanderbilt, are more strongly emphasized: pessimism versus optimism, features that also determine their speculation strategies. The conflict itself often evolves in the form of direct confrontations, and events that successively unfold in White's novel are presented as happening simultaneously. For example, Dan Drew's semi-illegal printing of new Erie stocks and their release at the stock exchange, which happen on different days in White's book, are combined in a single scene. The Erie stocks are carried over to the stock exchange as they come out of the printer; the turmoil they cause is immediately reported back:

> *Boten haben während der ganzen Szene schon Pakete abgeholt*
> **Drew**: Wieviel habt ihr schon verkauft?
> **Der Mann**: Smith hat die ersten 2000 angeboten, aber jetzt wird Gardener seine 5000 anbieten und ich zehn . . .
> **Drew**: Hier nehmen Sie die Pakete, ihr müsst schneller arbeiten . . .
> **Ein Agent**: Vanderbilt gibt Auftrag den Markt zu stützen.
> **Ein Anderer**: Herr Drew, die Aktien sind noch nass. Man hat es gemerkt und sucht Sie.[15]

Questions arise. How long can Drew pursue this without being caught—and earn money through falling prices? Will he be able to print another set and still escape? "Aufrisse der gesellschaftlichen Strukturen"[16] are neutralized here through the form: the reader is captivated and absorbed, eager to know what comes next. In other words, "arglistiges Erzählen" presupposes what demands to be questioned in the first place, namely the financial apparatus of stocks and futures trading.

There are a few scenes (most of them included in the Berlin-Frankfurt edition) that exemplify a different approach to the original story. Yet these seem to fall on the other side of the spectrum: if the adaptation discussed above tends to erase the quotation marks in favor of the captivating story of a clever speculator, the protagonists are now turned into caricatures:

> Dan Drew, scene 1
> [variation 1, featuring "arglistiges Erzählen" –MR]
>
> *Prärie. Wellblechschuppen, dürres Gras, Hudsonspiegel grau, dünner Wind. Dan, Drew, Jimmy Fisk, Jay Gould*
> **Fisk:** Sag einmal, Onkel, was denkst du, wenn du dieses Land ansiehst
> **Drew:** Es ist der übelste Strich der Welt. Wenn einer nicht mit Klappenschlangen handelt und die platten Steine aus dem Hudson verkaufen kann, wird er hier nie ein Geschäft machen
> **Fisk:** Und dabei wird New York eine dicke Stadt und du hast keinen Gedanken, um Geld zu machen.
> **Drew:** Ich will euch was sagen. Solang die verrückten New Yorker noch Krieg führen, kann man noch etwas verdienen. Wenn der Krieg aus ist, dann ist alles aus . . .
> **Fisk:** Ich meine, man müsste eine Ader anstechen, bei der wir alle drei in einigen Jahren volle Taschen haben. Verstehst du mich
> **Gould:** Er hat Recht, Drew. Sie haben doch mit Dampfschiffen ihre schönen Geschäfte gemacht. Und Vanderbilt hat ein Riesenhaus sich jetzt bauen können . . .
> **Jimmy**: Willst du wieder Ochsen verkaufen?
> **Drew**: Jimmy spotte nicht . . . Ich denke nämlich, dass die Zeit reif ist . . . ich möchte meine Hände ganz gern in Eisenbahngeschäfte stecken . . .
> **Fisk:** Meiner Ansicht nach, Onkel, kannst du allein mit deiner Bahn fahren, keine Sau setzt sich drauf.
> **Drew:** Jimmy du bist ungläubig . . .
> **Gould:** Sagen Sie, lieber Onkel, wollen Sie mit allem ihrem Geld einfach Schienen kaufen und losbauen? Ich denke, dass ihr nicht bis ans Ufer von New Jersey kommt . . .
> **Drew:** Ich bin heut schon ein alter Mann, aber ich habe immer gewusst, wie man es macht . . .
> **Fisk:** Dan, ich finde es nicht so schlecht, was du sagst.
> **Drew:** . . . Der Krieg wird ja doch verloren . . . und wir müssen auf der Lauer liegen, um aus dem Untergang uns noch etwas zu holen . . .[17]

Dan Drew, scene 1 *Steppe. Drei Männer*
[variation 2, moving away from "arglistiges Erzählen" –MR]

Dan Drew *sagt*:
Dies ist ein Land, das nur für Menschen taugte
Die satt von Klappenschlangen werden und
Sich nähren können von den platten Steinen
Aus des Hudsons Tief. Für Wölfe, lebend
Vom Schneewind, denen der reine Himmel
Unterschlupf genug ist.
Fisk
Doch da wir gerade hier
Leben und nicht anderswo, lasst uns
Umschauen nach Fleisch von Fleische dieses Lands
Und auch nach Tischen von dieses Landes Holz
Gould
Und nach des Menschen besten Zugtier, welches
Der Mensch ist. Also schaut nicht aus nach dem, was da ist, sondern
Nach dem, was noch fehlt. Und wär's so Kleines
Wie die Eisenbahn von diesem Land, das nichts ist
Zu einem anderen Land, das auch nichts ist.
Die drei Männer lachen.

White's impersonal narrator makes an appearance in variation 2 through the seemingly innocuous insertion of "Dan Drew *sagt*." The scene reveals itself as a narration. With it, the back-and-forth of opinions that leads to a (contested) decision, namely to invest in railways, is reduced in favor of the posture that is inherent or underlies such an exchange of opinions. Accordingly Fisk, Dan, and Gould no longer figure as distinguishable individuals. They are "three men" who complete jointly one sentence in a unified language (blank verse) and produce the same physical expression: laughter. As the protagonists assess what they see ("umschauen," "ausschauen," "dies," "hier"), they turn into the wolves they talk about ("dies ist ein Land für Wölfe"). They become visible as predators.

In pushing White's narrator to the fore and thus making the scene a presentation (three men exhibited on a plain: "Steppe"), Brecht and his collaborators create types from the flow of events. The concept of type (*Typus*) had already undergone various modifications in Brecht's work. Brecht had understood the type—a legacy of naturalism—as the result of an "imprint" of a specific milieu, and the milieu that interested him most at the time was "the big city."[18] Yet in *Im Dickicht der Städte* in particular, contrary to a naturalist aesthetic and Brecht's earlier "city play" *Trommeln in der Nacht*, it is not the relation between individuals and their specific milieus that actually drives the plot. This play shows "typing" on a more abstract level. The protagonist is the city itself, represented through personalizing descriptions such as "kaltes Chikago," "erwachendes Chikago," "Stadt aus Eisen und Dreck," "Chikago wirft das Handtuch," "das immerwährende Geräusch Chikagos," and so on. And the object of the city's impression throughout the play is not an individual but a face: "Wir sind in die Stadt verschlagen mit den Gesichtern des Landes," "das Gesicht ist . . . wie vor einem Plan," "milchglasiges Gesicht," "der Mensch bleibt was er ist auch wenn sein Gesicht zerfällt," "das Gesicht ist in guter Ordnung."[19] The city makes faces unreadable; what is readable in its place is the destruction that this process causes. In *Dan Drew,* the milieu making the impression finally becomes society; society turns individuals into functions and erases them as much as the city erases their individual faces. Although Brecht and his collaborators ascend to yet another level of abstraction, the causal model remains the same. In a new preface to the 1926 edition of *Trommeln in der Nacht,* Brecht identified the bourgeois as type with a view to George Grosz's drawings and conceived type in a still naturalist manner as the truth behind appearance: "jeder Bourgeoistyp machte Geschäfte, indem er besser erschien als er war." Grosz's physiognomies would force the truth to emerge (much like Brecht with the new initial scene from *Dan Drew*).[20] Brecht elaborated on this perspective and in 1927 declared the depiction of types as the cornerstone of a theater to come in various publicized discussions with the Marxist sociologist Fritz Sternberg.[21] Yet the initial scene of *Dan Drew* already exemplifies both the political and the aesthetic limits of "typing." What Brecht and his collaborator offer (the image of the speculator as predator) is no more capable of providing an insight into societal structures than the captivating stories. Such an image does not expose, but re-personalizes these structures. It blends seamlessly with popular, largely anti-Semitic attacks against financial capitalism. The type constitutes an aesthetic problem as well, because a reconfiguration of the story in terms of types would arrest every development and turn fulfilled time (that is, the developmental time of White's characters) into empty time, and an inflexible constellation would emerge (variances being the only changes conceivable).[22] Thus an adaption seemed to have failed. The subtle balance in distance—White's quotation marks—proved irreproducible on stage. Perhaps "adaptation" was the wrong project in the first place.

The Time of the Gestus[23]

Beyond Adaptation: "Aus dem Gedächtnis spielen"

The sources of *Jae Fleischhacker in Chikago* are Frank Norris's novels *The Pit (1903)* and *The Octopus (1901),* and his posthumously published story "A Deal in Wheat" (1903); all these texts are part of Norris's project to trace the path of wheat from its production to its consumption. In contrast to *Dan Drew,* not many *Fleischhacker* scenes were completed. The three *Fleischhacker* folders in the Brecht Archive contain numerous scene sketches, variations of scenes, two songs, a number of outlines, reflections on style and economy, extracts from Norris's novel prepared for Brecht by Elisabeth Hauptmann, and a variety of paratextual materials such as a floor plan of the Chicago Pit, photos of Chicago, and articles on commodity futures trading from various German and Austrian papers. The completed scenes as well as the many sketches show that Brecht and Hauptmann have moved away from depicting persons or types. The focus is on actions, on social relations, and on the protagonist's emotional states,[24] which are revealed through self-reflection in the form of short monologues.[25] More important, an obvious connection between these scenes and sketches is missing. The events at the Chicago Pit, the futures exchange, which make up the most captivating passages in Norris's novel and guarantee its cohesion, are relegated to the background. They are presented in a first version—the BFA identifies three work phases—through newspaper articles,[26] and in a later version by means of simple prose passages.[27] Although it is undoubtedly true that every claim about the play's ultimate form has to remain speculative, it might nevertheless be possible to account for the heterogeneity of the material and its seeming incoherence. Evidently Brecht and Hauptmann attempted something other than an adaptation. I would like to argue that Brecht instead employed the procedure depicted in "Diese Babilonische Verwirrung der Wörter," namely to retell a story from the perspective of the ending of all such stories.

Such a claim is supported by Elisabeth Hauptmann's work diary. In March 1926—while working on *Fleischhacker*—she writes: "Brecht findet die Formel für das 'epische Theater': aus dem Gedächtnis spielen." Presumably some years later she reworked her diary entry (without making the modifications noticeable) and added: "und arbeitet beim Schreiben ganz in diese Richtung." She now defines "aus dem Gedächtnis spielen" as "Gesten, Haltungen zitieren." Brecht "spielt sich Vorgänge vor. So entstehen die Zeigeszenen, wie er sie nennt."[28] Her revisions call for some caution. Brecht only began to use the term "episches Theater" in late 1926 and early 1927, for example, in his discussions with Fritz Sternberg. And he did so in a way that was still unsystematic. Gestus or stances ("Haltungen") were not theorized before 1929.[29] Hauptmann, however, suggests an already systematic understanding of these terms. Retroactively, she seems to apply the concepts that determine Brecht's acting theory of the late 1920s to his writing process. Yet in 1926 writing still carried the main burden of innovation; and Hauptmann's entry, far from being a mere projection, perhaps reveals instead a moment of the genealogy of Brecht's acting philosophy.[30] Writers, like later actors, should not simply write a story down—in stage terms act it out as if it unfolds in the here and now—but rather, they should assume knowledge of the entire story beforehand and *re*-present the story ("aus dem Gedächtnis spielen") with a view to

"Gesten, Haltungen." Moving against the "natural" flow of the story, they have to make"bestimmte Vorgänge unter Menschen auffällig"—as it is called in the annotations to *Mann ist Mann* (1929)—produce "Brechungen und Sprünge," and will be (wrongly) considered "Episodisten."[31] In short, the *Fleischhacker* fragment could be understood as what remained of Norris's stories after they had been subjected to the disruptive process of a re-presentation that cites their constitutive moments. And the act of *re*-presentation—a delay assumed and made noticeable when going over the original story again—defines "die Zeigeszene,"[32] and distinguishes it from adapted scenes.

To be more precise, Brecht and Hauptmann seem to have gone even further with Norris's stories, because the scenes and sketches from *Fleischhacker* are, strictly speaking, not quotations of "Gesten, Haltungen." Rather, they are the result of a deromanticizing and a belated reinsertion of what had been "omitted" in the original story's natural flow, "im arglistigen Erzählen." Only a revisiting of the original story makes the gaps noticeable. In a notebook entry from 1929, Brecht characterizes such a "radicalized" procedure as "herausstellen des gestischen gehalts eines bekannten stoffes . . . die haltungen auf die es ankommen soll . . . (werden) richtig gesetzt, gegen den stoff."[33] "Richtig setzen" should be read then as a corrective intervention, a reworking. Accordingly, the original story turns into mere material (*Stoff*).

De-narratization, Historicization

The *Fleischhacker* scene, presumably envisioned by Brecht and Hauptmann as the play's opening scene, can perhaps exemplify what it means "to correctly place, against the material, those stances ['Haltungen'] that count." From the perspective of chronology, the scene constitutes the beginning of Jae's story, his entry into the speculation business. It focuses on Jae Fleischhacker's social advancement and its prerequisites: betrayal and the disavowal of his previous life. This moment of transition is merely a side remark in Norris's novel. We are told in passing that Jadwin Curtis, who grew up in a farmer's family, went into the livery stable business before moving into real estate and speculation. Jae, likewise a farmer's son, then moves from the slaughterhouse business to commodity futures trading.

> **Weizenbörse**
> *Jae Fleischhacker und vier Bullen: Table, Brown, Shaw and Becket.*
> *Abseits Matthew Milk*
> **Jae**:
> Weil jetzt das milchglasige Gesicht dieses Chikago
> Auf mich, Jae Fleischhacker, gerichtet ist
> Gehorch ich dem Wunsch des ungeheuren Chikago
> Anders zu werden auf solcher Höh

An Tugend zuzunehmen und
Mich zu prüfen, eh ich weiter steige, wie
gesund ich bin, und drum
Geht auf Milk zu
Hacke ich jetzt dich, meine rechte Hand
Heute noch nützlich, einst ganz unentbehrlich
Schmutzige Hand aus trüber Zeit, heut ab
Shaw
s'ist mehr als wir erwarten, Jae
Brown
s'ist gut
Table
s'ist gefährlich gut
Jae
s'ist gefährlich zu steigen, geh Milk, deine Hand
Wenngleich für mich seit sieben Jahren roh
Stinkt doch nach Schmutz der Tief, mit dir
Tue ich ab des Schlachthof rohen Nackenschlag und kämpf
WEITER MIT DEM KOPF
Milk:
Kämpf gut, kämpf verzweifelt gut und schlaf
Nicht ein nachts, iss nicht, trink nicht, schrei nicht
Denn von dem Tag an, den du jetzt gezeichnet
Wird nicht mehr wegsehen von dir dieses milchglasige
Gesicht Chikagos. Sondern zählen
Schlag deines Herzens, Röt und Leere der Wang und wird
Nicht abgewendet sein, vor's deinen Schrei vernimmt
In deiner ganz eigentlichen Sprache, Sprache deiner Milz
In der du nach deiner Mutter schreien wirst.
Jae *lacht und stößt ihn weg*
Doch jetzt geht weg und lass dich
Nicht auffischen, wenn wir Netze werfen
Milk ab
Denn
Es hebt höchst gute Zeit jetzt an. Der Weizen[34]

The scene went through four revisions, and the BFA identifies this version as the last. The changes made are small but significant. Their overall tendency is a "de-narratization." Comparable to the initial scene from *Dan Drew,* a disagreement has turned into a unanimous position, a constellation has replaced a discursive development. Each of the new allies now supports Fleischhacker's decision to dissociate from Milk, his collaborator from the slaughterhouse business. Furthermore, older versions of this scene are either set in unspecific locations or at the slaughterhouse. Thus, the narrative moment implied in the setting—*first* Jae has to rid himself of his old companion to *then* move onto the next stage—has been erased. Jae is at the Pit. The transition has already happened, and his speech—performative in the first place—now becomes entirely declarative. Milk's removal is no longer one step in an unfolding story, but emphasized as a prerequisite for the story to unfold. It is emphasized as one of its constituting moments. Taken together with the actions defined in the stage directions, which are in none of the previous versions ("Geht auf Milk zu" and "stößt ihn weg"), the individual decision and the actions accompanying it can be recognized as a ritual, a social gestus. The scene is structured around a central image: "the cutting off of the right hand." The harmless proverb "he is my right hand" suddenly has a literal meaning, not least in the context of Jae's origin, the slaughterhouse. The (social) violence of the gestus is revealed as well as the fact that the "slaughtering" will continue:[35] far from becoming a distant memory, it is also the first step on his new career path.

This de-narratization traceable through the revisions of the scene reflects Brecht and Hauptmann's production method. Norris's stories are revisited, knowledge of them is fully acknowledged, and they are retold. Jadwin's advancement, nothing but a fleeting moment in Norris's story, is thereby brought to the fore and disrupts the original story's flow. In "Diese Babilonische Verwirrung der Wörter," the story of the wheat trader is disrupted ("mitten im Vortrag") in the same manner when the lyric I revisits it. More important, the episodic retelling of Norris's stories gives them an entirely new temporal order. The retelling, on the one hand, presupposes the completed story and, on the other, anticipates this completed story and all such stories, because the social gestus[36] that emerges as an effect of revisiting the original story transcends individual motives and constitutes their "horizon of possibility," as Hermann Kappelhoff calls it.[37] "Diese Babilonische Verwirrung der Wörter" programmatically depicts or stages the process of such a "retroactive anticipation." Step by step, losing the thread of "arglistiges Erzählen," the lyric I catches up with the perspective from which this and all such stories are told—the perspective of the yet unborn listeners. The point of view of the gestus—from which Brecht and Hauptmann lose the thread of Norris's story—almost corresponds to this perspective. But only almost: although the gestus can provide a cross section of societal structure, it does not yet historicize them. Brecht and Hauptmann then furnish Norris's stories with a temporal index by way of presentation. This scene of social advancement, Fleischhacker's entry into the wheat business, recalls or inscribes itself onto another one: a scene from Shakespeare's *Henry IV, Part Two*. This inscription can be understood as a functional equivalent to the perspective of the not yet born.

Hal, newly crowned, bans John Falstaff, his old drinking buddy and fellow highwayman, from the royal premises immediately after his crowning ceremony. The new King Henry V, like Jae Fleischhacker, the new King of Wheat, walks past Falstaff in company of his retinues and dismisses him. Comparing his ascension to the rising sun,[38] he publicly declares: "[werfe] ich ab dies lose Wesen . . . merken soll's die Welt, Dass ich mein vor'ges Selbst hinweggetan."[39] According to Bernhard Reich, a friend and collaborator, Brecht had planned to place the Norris stories entirely within a Shakespearean setting.[40] It is also conceivable that Brecht had thought of Christopher Marlowe's *The Life of King Edward II* as a frame for *Fleischhacker*. He had reworked this play with Lion Feuchtwanger in 1923–24 and directed it in 1924. Earl Roger Mortimer is one of its protagonists, and Mortimer Fleischhacker was the play project's first title.[41] Yet the existing *Fleischhacker* sketches and scenes do not cohere stylistically. Brecht and Hauptmann, it seems, experimented with various historical forms of presentation.[42] Besides these Shakespearean forms, there are scenes, sketches, and constellations reminiscent of the Bible,[43] Schiller's *Räuber*,[44] and Goethe's *Faust*.[45] In this particular scene, however, the historicity of the gestus of disavowal is established through an anachronism: financial speculations are rephrased as feudal power politics.

Walter Benjamin associates Brecht's theater with the *Trauerspiel* of the Baroque era; Brecht's protagonists would be entirely un-tragic.[46] This is the case, it could now be added, because like the *Trauerspiel*, the form of theater represented by *Jae Fleischhacker* commences with its end, the end of all such stories about commodity speculation. Fleischhacker's downfall is a confirmation of this beginning. Through the Shakespearean setting, we come to see the events as if they had already passed.[47] The scenes are written from the perspective of redemption.[48]

Composition

Can the poem "Diese Babilonische Verwirrung der Wörter" also indicate the play's envisioned composition? The difficulty that Brecht and Hauptmann might have encountered with the composition seems again comparable to the core challenge of the epic actor: "Da alles auf die Entwicklung, den Fluss ankommt . . . muss der epische Schauspieler vielleicht ein noch längeren Atem haben als der alte Protagonist," Brecht writes in 1929. The development or the flow of events has to be accomplished "trotz oder besser vermittels der Brüche und Sprünge."[49] In other words, the production process itself or Norris's linear story needed to find some kind of representation. Its collapse into the temporality of the gestus must become visible, comparable to the poem, which stages the story of the wheat trader *and* its disruption.

Accordingly, the two outlines that Brecht and Hauptmann propose preserve the linearity of the original plot, namely Fleischhacker/Jadwin's rise and fall. The plot unfolds in a classic five-act schema[50] and is reconceived at a later phase as a succession of eleven pictures.[51] More important, the

Fleischhacker plot is flanked by another plot, which also unfolds in linear time: the story of the downfall of the Mitchels, a farmer's family, who come to Chicago to look for work (likewise employing Norris's stories as its material).[52] Elisabeth Hauptmann notes in her diary on 29 March 1926:

> B. will jetzt doch den *Fleischhacker* machen, + zwar nach neuerlichem Plan, ihn mit der Geschichte von der Familie zusammenzulegen. Glücklicher Einfall: Joe ist der Bruder in der Stadt den die Familie sucht . . . Durch Calvin + Joe geht die Familie kaputt.[53]

In the first outline, the fate of the Mitchels' and Fleischhacker's speculations are still causally linked: Calvin's death in the electric chair, following a strike—the exact nature of the strike remains unclear—is "beschlossen von J."[54] And a scene sketch directly connects the rising price of flour with the Mitchel family's eviction from their home: "Mehl kaufen oder Miete zahlen?"[55] Such close causal connections disappear in the second outline. Scenes with Fleischhacker and the Mitchels strictly alternate. Whereas the first outline talks about the Mitchels' ruin, the second calls the same events a robbery ("Beraubung"), and as such it is unrelated to Fleischhacker's speculation. Fleischhacker's "grosser Corner" now follows Calvin Mitchel's strike. Thus Calvin cannot have gone on strike against Fleischhacker. His death is no longer explicitly linked to Jae's business. Moreover, the causal connections seem to have disappeared within each story as well. The stages of the plot do not directly correspond to the existing scenes or scene sketches; a clear assignment remains difficult. They seem to merely mark temporal spots, representing, on the one hand, the linearity of each story and, on the other, their parallelism.[56] There is nevertheless causality at work, but an entirely different and indirect one: all relations are mediated by money.[57]

After the combination had been decided, Brecht and Hauptmann most likely wrote a preface to *Jae Fleischhacker* titled "Geld," a complex text that illustrates by means of its argumentative procedure and simultaneously explains how money mediates every aspect of life without emerging as a mediating force. The text concludes: "von vielen Dingen ist das, was über sie unbekannt ist, weil es mit Geld zusammenhängt, viel bezeichnender als das, was über sie bekannt ist. Dadurch entsteht ein falscher Eindruck."[58] By severing direct causal links, the new structure of the play—the juxtaposition of Fleischhacker and the Mitchels' story—undoes the "wrong impression" (money's false appearance) that the problem at hand is a conflict between a good family and a greedy speculator. Calvin/Billy, the Mitchels' son (Brecht and Hauptmann repeatedly interchange names) is as restless and as dissatisfied as Jae. At every moment of calm and safety, Calvin/Billy responds: "hier ist es schlecht."[59] Furthermore, the Mitchels justify their move to Chicago not with their poverty but the opportunities ahead: "(um) einen Penny zu setzen / unser Stück Fleisch herauszuschneiden / Und ihnen zu zeigen wie man Geld macht."[60] The real problem then, as it appears, is not personal but systemic. Jae and Calvin "richten die Familie zugrunde," because they are both defined by money. Money is at work as a mediating force. Their restlessness can be compared without their differences being leveled.[61] In Norris's story, money is nothing but one topic among others and the "spirit of money" is in conflict with "the spirit of love," which prevails in the end.[62] In Brecht and Hauptmann's play, money subjectivizes the protagonists and money determines the composition as well: differences within parallels reflect money's overall mediation.[63] In other words, the focus on money allows for the identification of the stories' constitutive elements (the gestus) and at the same time relieves the order of events from the burden of causality; a chronology can unfold within the gestus without becoming meaningful on its own.

Trading Futures

Yet *Jae Fleischhacker in Chikago* remained a fragment. In conclusion I would like to offer some tentative considerations on the interrelation between aesthetic form and economic subject by suggesting that the fragmentary character might have something to do with a moment in the genealogy of the gestus, in particular with its close connection to matters of money.[64] *Jae Fleischhacker* depicts the cornering of a market through futures commodity trading; this topic is central to *Dan Drew* and *Die heilige Johanna der Schlachthöfe* (1929–1932) as well. In the *Fleischhacker* folders of the Brecht Archive, a great variety of drawings, tables, and notes bears testimony to Brecht and Hauptmann's attempts to analyze in detail the functioning and effects of futures trading.[65] The trading in futures relies on a complex temporality: processes are computed as running against a future that has already been anticipated. A speculator who in May buys September wheat anticipates the amount and quality of the cereal that will be available in September. The price paid reflects this anticipation. As current production moves forward, with all the factors that influence it—weather, international relations, domestic politics, and so on—it will be continuously judged from the perspective of an envisioned September stock; the anticipation based on these various factors constitutes its horizon of possibility. Accordingly, the price for September wheat will fluctuate. In short, the present becomes criticizable—the price reflects this critique—because the future emerges as a current probability. A trading of futures happens here quite literally. A blind future is exchanged against an already determined one, very much as in Brecht's poem "Diese Babilonische Verwirrung der Wörter" where the future (a just society) precedes a blindly unfolding present that thereby becomes recognizable in its contingency and changeability. Perhaps futures trading is relegated to the background in the *Fleischhacker* fragment because the play itself takes over its temporality. *Fleischhacker* would aim at reproducing—though not in the form of a deliberate pursuit—the technicalities of speculation on the level of its subjective prerequisites.

The emergence of money as the fragment's structuring force would then be far from the result of a genius intuition, but first and foremost reflects the function of money within futures trading. In futures trading money is a goal, the commodity that needs to be accumulated. Yet more important, it also is the condition of possibility of any such speculation. Money applied as a common quantifying measurement ensures that there is a future to anticipate, because money provides unique objects—plants in different places, of different shapes, quality and stages of development, and so on—with a common denominator. It makes them calculable by ensuring identity in time; it constitutes the commodity form. In *Fleischhacker*, accordingly, money functions as both: as a mere drive and as a constituting force because it subjectivizes the protagonists. This artistic reproduction of the speculation scheme is far from being its mere repetition. Whereas the many speculators translate scattered and random external events—weather conditions, politics, and policies—into speculation strategies, which blindly generate a price as effect of their non-coherence, Brecht and Hauptmann work on the events of Norris's stories, which are already depictions of futures trading. Thus, it is within the frame of self-reflection that they become the subject of strategies that ideally cohere in the play's composition, differences within parallels. However, money itself still escapes representation. It becomes palpable only through its effects: Dickensian misery, as Fredric Jameson puts it (the figure of the peasant)[66] or splendid disaster (the grand capitalist). Such expressions are not without risk. It is at times a thin line between a social gestus and a stereotype. *Mahagonny* then it is! With it, money takes center stage, and the new temporality of critique can emancipate itself from its (economic) origin.[67]

Notes

[1] Bertolt Brecht, *Werke: Große kommentierte Berliner und Frankfurter Ausgabe*, Werner Hecht et al., eds., vol. 13 (Berlin and Frankfurt am Main: Aufbau and Suhrkamp, 1988–2000), 356–357. Hereafter BFA volume, page. The poem consists of three strophes; the one quoted here is the second.

[2] Finance, in particular the figure of the speculator, was already a popular topic in American literature around 1900. See Urs Stäheli, *Spektakuläre Spekulationen: Das Populäre der Ökonomie* (Frankfurt am Main: Suhrkamp, 2007), p. 3 for a list of plays, short stories, and novels on this theme. Norris's novel itself was adapted for the stage in 1904 and in 1909 for film by D. W. Griffith. Brecht, it seems, had not known of these adaptions when he worked on *Jae Fleischhacker*.

[3] For example: "Eine Milliarde Dollars verspekuliert! Wahnsinnsszenen an der New Yorker Börse," announced the *National Zeitung* on 4 March 1926: "Die Baisse ist auf der ganzen Linie siegreich. Vor Schluss glich die Börse einem Tollhause. Vor den

Wasserständen wurden Besucher in manchen Fällen handgemein, Kleider wurden zerrissen, Hüte unter die Füße getrampelt . . ." (Bertolt Brecht Archive, BBA 524/62.)

[4] Primavesi writes: "Schon 1926 hatte er [Brecht] es [das Projekt *Fleischhacker*] in dem Gedicht 'Diese Babilonische Verwirrung der Wörter' als auswegloses Unterfangen kommentiert." Patrick Primavesi, "Jae Fleischhacker in Chikago," in Jan Knopf, ed., *Brecht Handbuch*, Bd. 1 (Stuttgart/Weimar: Metzler, 2001), pp. 147–152, here p. 151.

[5] Brecht regularly employs poems for poetological reflections. The form of a poem, through the contractions and reductions it enforces, provides considerations assumed as necessarily transient with a provisional consistency.

[6] Brecht's recurring characterizations of wheat trading as "schlechthin unerklärlich," "von der Vernunft nicht erfassbar" (BFA 21, 703), or as something that "ein Mensch nicht verstehen kann" do not so much reflect, as Dommann maintains, that Brecht searched painstakingly for causal explanations. See Monika Dommann, "Bühnen des Kapitalismus: Der Getreidehandel als Wissensobjekt zwischen den Weltkriegen," *Berichte zur Wissenschaftsgeschichte* 37.2 (2014): pp. 112–31, here pp. 117–118. Rather, with the depiction of economic practices, Brecht experienced the shortcomings of causal explanations. The narrative challenge—with *Jae Fleischhacker* and still with *Mahagonny*—was not to unfold causality, but to shift the focus of critique by showing the insufficiency of a reasoning that relies on causality. Primavesi (*Brecht Handbuch*, p. 151) and Parmalee, author of one of the few studies that discusses *Fleischhacker* at some length, also read these statements as illustrating Brecht's attempt to find an exhaustive causal explanation and consequently as an admittance of the play's failure. Parmalee claims: "The reason Joe *Fleischhacker* was never finished is precisely because Brecht did not understand the functioning of the market well enough." Patty Lee Parmalee, *Brecht's America* (Columbus: Ohio State University Press, 1981), p 120.

[7] "Strukturen als solche lassen sich entweder gar nicht oder nur in blasser Weise erzählen. Sie werden vor allem indirekt kenntlich, im unausgeführt mitlaufenden Hintergrund von Situationen. Insofern ist das Erzählen mit der Verflüssigung des Sozialen solidarisch; es liebt Helden und ihre Aktionen und formt noch die abstraktesten Zusammenhänge in Handlungsabläufe um," Koschorke maintains. See Albrecht Koschorke, *Wahrheit und Erfindung: Grundzüge einer allgemeinen Erzähltheorie* (Frankfurt am Main: Fischer, 2012), pp. 73–74. In letting "Erzählen mit Arglist" fail, Brecht's poem forces "den unausgeführt mit laufenden Hintergrund" to emerge.

[8] Brecht raises the same points in his "campaign" against Thomas Mann's realism in 1926 and concludes: "Unsere einzige Chance besteht darin . . . nicht mehr zu verstehen . . . Man kann von mir nicht verlangen, den *Zauberberg* zu begreifen . . . Von Anfang an verstehe ich nichts mehr: keine Regung dieses Mannes, desgleichen ich nie gesehen habe oder nie hätte sehen mögen" (BFA 21, 168). The short circuit of understanding and accepting also becomes the target of his critique of naturalist plays in 1928: "Warum finde ich diese Stücke langweilig? . . . Weil ich hier etwas tragisch finden soll, dass man ohne Weiteres . . . aus der Welt schaffen kann" (BFA 21, 229).

[9] "Erkenntnis," Adorno writes "hat kein Licht, als das von der Erlösung her auf die Welt scheint: alles andere erschöpft sich in Nachkonstruktion und bleibt ein

Stück Technik." See Theodor W. Adorno, *Minima Moralia* (Frankfurt am Main: Suhrkamp, 2003), p. 283.

[10] Another famous example of the use of such interlacing temporal perspectives is Brecht's poem from 1934 "An die Nachgeborenen."

[11] Brecht used various passages from Rimbaud and Verlaine's poems for *Im Dickicht* and objected to the accusation of plagiarism: "Im Buch sind diese Stellen durch Anführungszeichen kenntlich gemacht. Die Bühne besitzt anscheinend keine Technik, Anführungszeichen auszudrücken" (BFA 21, 103).

[12] BFA 21, 163–165. Documentary techniques and the use of documents were highly popular in the 1920s; they marked the style of *Neue Sachlichkeit* as well as of the Piscator theater. Yet as Wilke points out, Brecht's focus was on the *fabrication* of documents. He was not interested in documents as evidence and guarantors of authenticity. See Judith Wilke, *Brechts "Fatzer"-Fragment: Lektüren zum Verhältnis von Dokument und Kommentar* (Bielefeld: Aisthesis, 1996), p. 74.

[13] See the introduction to the German edition of Bouck White, *Das Buch des Daniel Drew* (München: Georg Müller, 1922), p. 7. Hanns Heinz Ewers discusses in it the American reception of the novel and quotes from a review.

[14] The fact that the *Dan Drew* project is based on a novel or fake autobiography is rarely mentioned in the discussion of the project. Mittenzwei mentions Brecht's use of "biographisches Material." See Werner Mittenzwei, *Das Leben des Bertolt Brecht oder der Umgang mit den Welträtseln* (Berlin: Aufbau, 1986), p. 253. Parker calls White's book "a biography." See Stephen Parker, *Bertolt Brecht: A Literary Life* (London: Bloomsbury, 2014), p. 227. The exception is Seliger, who provides detailed information on Bouck White and his novel. See Helfried W. Seliger, *Das Amerikabild Bertolt Brechts* (Bonn: Bouvier, 1974), pp. 74–77.

[15] BFA 10.1, 361.

[16] BFA 21, 165.

[17] BFA 10.1, 377 and 340–341, abridged by the author.

[18] He had planned a drama series with the title "Der Einzug der Menschheit in die großen Städte" (a line from Rimbaud), and his *Lesebuch für Städtebewohner* was part of the same project.

[19] All quotations are from *Im Dickicht der Städte* in BFA 1, 438–497.

[20] BFA 25, 16.

[21] See BFA 21, 202–204, and Fritz Sternberg, *Der Dichter und die Ratio* (Frankfurt am Main: Suhrkamp, 2014), pp. 69–80. Hecht comments: "Die Beschäftigung mit der Soziologie brachte eine Überbewertung der Materialität mit sich, eine Tendenz, die sich auch in Sternbergs Briefen fand (Liquidierung des Individuums)." See Werner Hecht, "Der Weg zum epischen Theater," in Werner Hecht, ed., *Brechts Theorie des Theaters* (Frankfurt am Main: Suhrkamp, 1986), pp. 54–90, here pp. 51–52.

[22] The terms empty time and fulfilled time are borrowed from Louis Althusser. In *Mutter Courage* and *Leben des Galilei* Althusser sees two timelines simultaneously at work and understands the dramaturgy of these plays through their interrelation. A developmental time, the time of the protagonist, unfolds within and against a time that does not stand for any development, for example, the time of war, the time

of society; it is through this juxtaposition and the interplay of timelines that the audience comes to know more than the protagonists and recognizes their limits. The empty time that comes into existence through "typing" would, by contrast, be reduced to a mere background from which the characters would always stand out as the same types. See Louis Althusser, "Brecht and Bertolazzi: Bemerkungen über materialistisches Theater," *alternative* 97.17 (August 1974), pp. 130–145.

[23] This subtitle is taken from Hermann Kappelhoff, *Nach '68—Politik der Form* (2011), accessed 18 January 2016, http://www.empirische-medienaesthetik.fu-berlin.de/multimediale_publikationen/nach_68_politik_der_form/index.html.

[24] The scenes depict the moment of Fleischhacker's entrance into the futures trading business, his management of alliances, his fear of social relegation, a self-reflection on his declining capacity to adapt to ever-changing circumstances, his employment of physical violence to silence an adversary, reflections on the burden of rootlessness, the separation from his wife in the context of his downfall, and so on.

[25] Primavesi comments on this as follows: "So wollte Brecht weniger den Kampf des großen Mannes zeigen . . . als vielmehr die Verhältnisse, die solche Einstellungen nicht zulassen," Primavesi, *Brecht Handbuch*, p. 149.

[26] Brecht quotes newspaper articles verbatim, for example, an article from the *Wiener Journal* (10 March 1926) "Das Getreide wird billiger. Der Preissturz in Amerika und der österreichische Markt" (BBA 678/37): "Seit einigen Tagen wird von den amerikanischen Getreidebörsen ein panikartiges Fallen der Weizenpreise gemeldet . . ." (BFA 10.1, 300).

[27] It could be argued that these passages only provide the material for scenes to be written, yet they are clearly artistically designed in contrast to texts that merely serve as summaries or offer information. See BFA 10.1, 311–312.

[28] Elisabeth Hauptmann, *Julia ohne Romeo: Geschichten, Stücke, Aufsätze, Erinnerungen* (Berlin: Aufbau, 1977), p. 172. Parts of the diary were included in an essay by Hauptmann in 1930. The diary itself was first published in *Sinn und Form* (1957).

[29] See for example Jan Knopf, "Verfremdung," in Werner Hecht, ed., *Brechts Theorie des Theaters* (Frankfurt am Main: Suhrkamp, 1986), pp. 93–114, here p. 119.

[30] Brecht developed a theory of epic theater—*the* epic theater never existed, rather it was in continuous development—between late 1928 and 1932 in a series of essays such as "Ödipus letzte Etappe" (1929) or "Über Stoffe und Formen" (1929) and in the booklet series *Versuche* (1929–1932). In profiling his own theory, he also claimed distance to forms of contemporary theater with which he had allied himself. Piscator and Jessner, for example, become subject to biting criticism.

[31] BFA 4, 49.

[32] When tracing the origin of epic theater, Parker also emphasizes the importance of the diary entry discussed here. He claims though that Hauptmann refers to Brecht's own plays, which Brecht would quote from memory after having written them. See Parker, *Bertolt Brecht*, p. 230. However, in the context of Brecht's notebook entry quoted in the following passage, and given the fact that at the time the diary entry was written, Brecht and Hauptmann were working on *Fleischhacker,* it is more likely that the entry discusses the usage of foreign material. Ultimately, both readings can coexist without contradiction.

[33] BBA 10331/157; © Bertolt-Brecht-Erben/Suhrkamp Verlag.

[34] The scene breaks off. BFA 10.1, 303–304.

[35] Accordingly, Jae announces in another scene with a view to his financial speculations: "Die Stadt wartet auf ihren Genickschlag," BFA 10.1, 302.

[36] These (temporal) operations perform the rupture that, according to Silberman, constitutes the gestural or the social gestus: they break the "equation between expression and form, dramatic content and performative gesture." See Marc Silberman, "Brecht's Gestus or Staging Contradictions," *Brecht Yearbook* 31 (2006), pp. 319–335, here p. 321. This is not to say that the gestural receives its ultimate form here; rather, something like a social gestus becomes a possibility. It can take various forms, and Silberman carefully traces them from the 1920s to the 1950s.

[37] Kappelhoff writes: "der Gestus (bezeichnet) eine zeitliche Korrelation welche die Linearität des erzählten Geschehens durchbricht und die Figuren in jedem Moment der Handlung auf ihren Möglichkeitshorizont bezieht." See Kappelhoff, *Nach '68*, 2.5.

[38] The personal (and spatial) constellation is not the only parallel between the scenes. When Fleischhacker dismisses his old companion Milk, he evokes Chicago as "die Welt" and employs words that complement Hal's comparison with the rising sun. "Gehorch ich dem Wunsch des ungeheuren Chikago / anders zu werden auf solcher Höh / An Tugend zuzunehmen" (BFA 10.1, 303). Moreover, both scenes talk about debauchery and health. Hal comments on Falstaff's decaying body: "so aufgeschwellt vom Schlemmen" (Shakespeare, *Heinrich der Vierte*, p. 199, see note 39). Whereas Fleischhacker, once a participant in Milk's debauchery, intends "zu prüfen eh ich weiter steig, wie gesund ich bin" (BFA 10.1, 304), in the last act of *Henry IV, Part One*, Falstaff asks "Kann Ehre ein Bein ansetzen? Nein. Oder einen Arm? . . . Ehre versteht sich also nicht auf die Chirurgie?" (Ibid., p. 84). Fleischhacker, metaphorically cutting of his right hand in the name of virtue, seems to respond to these questions. Response or continuation ("Weiterschreiben") of the Shakespearean scene seems to be Brecht's method of inscription throughout. Schulz calls Brecht's use of Schiller in *Die heilige Johanna der Schlachthöfe* a "Weiterdichten." See Gudrun Schulz, *Die Schillerbearbeitungen Bertolt Brechts* (Tübingen: Niemeyer, 1972), p. 103. Brecht knew the Falstaff story (although it remains difficult to prove that he had already known it in 1926). He compared Falstaff to Galileo in 1948 (BFA 14, 247), and Volker Klotz identifies a scene from *Der Kaukasische Kreidekreis* as a replay of Falstaff's dismissal in *Henry IV, Part One*. See Volker Klotz, *Bertolt Brecht: Versuch über das Werk* (Darmstadt: Gentner, 1957), p. 47.

[39] William Shakespeare, *König Heinrich der Vierte: Erster und Zweiter Teil*. Schlegel-Tieck Übersetzungen in Einzelbänden (Berlin: Contumax, 2015), p. 199. Brecht most likely used this translation.

[40] Reich recalls a conversation in which Brecht told him "Dieser Joe Fleischhacker . . . bringt die Mitkönige zu Fall . . . Der Stoff ist episch. Die Helden sind Geschäftsleute. Wegen höchst prosaischer Dinge—wegen des Profits—bekriegen sie sich und führen dabei höchst prosaische Aktionen—wie hausse and baisse—durch. Diese 'Helden' will ich in shakespeareschen Versen sprechen lassen. Dieses Verse-sprechen steht ihnen von Rechts wegen zu; denn die Unternehmungen der Händler und Wechsler sind nicht weniger folgenschwer—Leben oder Tod Zehntausender bestimmend—als die Schlachten der Heerführer." See Bernhard Reich, *Im Wettlauf mit*

der Zeit: Erinnerungen aus fünf Jahrzehnten deutscher Theatergeschichte (Berlin: Henschel, 1970), p. 287.

41 There is a variety of correspondences between Mortimer and Jae Fleischhacker. Both ascend to their position—King of England, King of Wheat—through a betrayal, both are characterized through their adaptability; constant change and Fortuna's wheel are recurrent themes.

42 Brecht's note seems to indicate this: "Zum Fleischhacker und anderen Historien 1) Zuerst ganzer Stoff wie in der Bibel darstellen . . . 2) Dann als Zeitungsbericht" (BFA 10.1, 281).

43 See for example: "Ich habe gehabt / Den Weizen Amerikas und ich wollte / Haben den Weizen der Erde . . ." (BFA 10.1, 299).

44 Brecht planned to restructure the play around the opposition of two brothers after he had decided to combine *Jae Fleischhacker* with another play project, *Eine Familie aus der Savannah*: Jae Fleischhacker and Calvin, see BFA 10.1, 1071–1072. Calvin, rebellious and finally sentenced to death, could be read as a Karl Moor character, not least because Brecht had employed this motif before. "Mit *Dickicht* wollte ich *Die Räuber* verbessern," he writes in 1926 in his work journal. Furthermore, in September 1926 Piscator's *Räuber* premiered and became immediately famous. Brecht followed Piscator's work closely at the time.

45 The character of Kate Mitchel, originally from *Eine Familie aus der Savannah* (see note 53), a farmer's daughter, can be read as a modern version of Gretchen, one who fully acknowledges her desires and renounces religion. Whereas Gretchen in *Faust I* still accepts her brother's blame—"Du fingst mit einem heimlich an / Bald kommen ihrer mehre dran, / Und wenn dich erst ein Dutzend hat, / So hat dich auch die ganze Stadt"—(Goethe, *Faust I*, in *Sämtliche Werke in 5 Bänden* [Paris: Baudry, 1840], vol. 2, p. 189), Kate Mitchel declares with self-confidence: "seit wir in diesen Städten, Verführung uns so ausgedörrt hat dass / unser durst nach mehr an Männern äugt / vor einer uns anrührt schon ist's uns wenig." (BBA 524/13); © Bertolt-Brecht-Erben/Suhrkamp Verlag.

46 Walter Benjamin, *Versuche über Brecht* (Frankfurt am Main: Suhrkamp, 1971), p. 20.

47 This procedure of historicization achieves what Brecht had attempted with *Dan Drew*, namely to "fabricate documents" (BFA 21, 163–165). Wilke, tracing the meaning of the documentary in her book on the *Fatzer* fragment (on which Brecht worked simultaneously), defines the function of the document in Brecht's work as follows: "Gegenwart als etwas von vornherein Vergangenes [behandelt], es dokumentiert für den fremden, zukünftigen Betrachter." See Wilke, *Brechts "Fatzer"-Fragment*, p. 67.

48 In a 1932 review of the radio play *Die heilige Johanna der Schlachthöfe* that employs similar presentational forms, Fritz Walter captures the effect of historicization: "die klassischen Formen wieder sind es, die ihre . . . sinnvolle Funktion bekommen, weil sie . . . die Vorgänge des Dramas in jene Distanz, in jenen überschaubaren Abstand rücken, in dem sich die Probleme nicht verkleinern . . . sondern in dem die Zusammenhänge des Dargestellten ersichtlich und erkennbar werden . . ." See Bertolt Brecht, *Die heilige Johanna der Schlachthöfe: Bühnenfassung, Fragmente, Varianten*, ed. by Gisela Bahr (Frankfurt am Main: Suhrkamp, 1974), pp. 219–220.

[49] BFA 14, 49.

[50] BFA 10.1, 276–277.

[51] BFA 10.1, 278–279.

[52] Hauptmann, published in Sabine Kebir, *Ich fragte nicht nach meinem Anteil: Elisabeth Hauptmanns Arbeit mit Bertolt Brecht* (Berlin: Aufbau, 2006), p. 50. The decline of a farmer's family who moves to a big city, San Francisco, is a side story in Norris's *The Octopus*. The family becomes homeless, the mother dies of hunger, and the daughter falls into prostitution. Norris's "A Deal in Wheat" juxtaposes financial speculations with the fate of a farmer who has to give up his farm and searches for work in Chicago.

[53] The BFA published *Jae Fleischhacker* and *Eine Familie aus der Savannah*—the original title of the family story—as one play fragment under the title of *Jae Fleischhacker in Chikago*. Two outlines support this decision. Yet it should be noted that there are hardly scenes that work out such a combination. Most of the Savannah material probably predates Brecht's combination plan and has not been reworked and integrated into the *Fleischhacker* project. Its style is noticeably different. With the exception of three very brief sketches, which *suggest* scenes in which the Mitchel father looks for Jae, and a short scene that shows an effect of Jae's speculation on the Mitchel family (rising bread prices), nothing indicates that Brecht and Hauptmann followed through with their plans.

[54] BFA 10.1, 277.

[55] BFA 10.1, 278.

[56] Brecht and Hauptmann come close to a parallel montage. D. W. Griffith's film version of Frank Norris's novel employs it throughout. Griffith struggled with the same problem, the insufficiency of storytelling. In his detailed analysis of the film, Helmut Färber describes it as follows: "Alles Erzählen ist ein Schildern von Lebensverhältnissen zwischen Menschen; es bestehen aber durchaus keine zwischen Bauern, Spekulanten und Hungernden . . . [M]it jeglichem Erzählen [ist] der Anschein eines menschlichen Verhältnisses angefälscht." See Helmut Färber, *A Corner in Wheat von D. W. Griffith: Eine Kritik* (München: Färber, 1992), p. 62.

[57] Hauptmann's diary confirms this new focus of the play: "am Schluss fing Brecht an Nationalökonomie zu lesen. Er behauptete die Praktiken mit Geld seien sehr undurchsichtig und er müsse jetzt sehen, wie es mit den Theorien über Geld stehe . . . 'Diese Dinge,' sagte B., 'sind nicht dramatisch . . . und wenn man sieht, dass unsere heutige Welt nicht mehr ins Drama passt, dann passt das Drama eben nicht mehr in die Welt.'" See Kebir, *Ich fragte nicht nach meinem Anteil*, p. 61. Again, some caution is necessary. According to Kebir this entry was belatedly inserted for a 1930 publication of the work diary in the theater journal *Der Scheinwerfer* (Ibid., p. 252).

[58] BFA 10.1, 278. Brecht seems to rephrase Hegel's famous words from the perspective of money: "Das Bekannte überhaupt ist darum, weil es bekannt ist, nicht erkannt." See G. W. F. Hegel, *Phänomenologie des Geistes* (Berlin: Duncker und Humblot, 1832), p. 25.

[59]Ibid., p. 292.

[60] Ibid., p. 283.

[61] In Brecht and Hauptmann's decision to combine *Fleischhacker* with the *Savannah* play, Seliger sees a problematic relativism at work "denn dadurch würde bewiesen, dass weder Arme noch Reiche im kapitalistischen System sicher sind . . . Wäre 'der gerechte und verdiente' Untergang des Spekulanten wirklich noch 'lehrreich'?" Seliger, *Das Amerikabild*, p. 124. Such relativism would indeed be unavoidable if Brecht and his collaborators had still pursued their original plan to emphasize the influence of the big city on human beings. The city of Fleischhacker and the city of the Mitchels are clearly not the same city, and the differences would have been leveled. Yet I maintain that the merging of the plays had only become possible because the city had already ceased to be the driving agent.

[62] In Brecht and Hauptmann's version of Norris's love story, Fleischhacker's relationship ends when his wife, Annabel, contractually stipulates that her property will not be involved in her husband's possible ruin (BFA 10.1, 317–318), whereas Laura, Jadwin's wife, sacrifices her belongings for her husband.

[63] The Mitchel story, for example, includes reflections of Kate Mitchel, the daughter, on her marriage and the status of the wife as a commodity, followed by the husband's disillusioned considerations (BFA 10.1, 287–288). The same constellation is repeated in the Fleischhacker story. Annabel's fear of her husband's appetite (BFA, 10.1, 315–316) is juxtaposed with her husband's reflection: "die trockenen frauen das wässrige / fleisch und die kalte betrachtung des / rauchs—alles das missfällt mir. / vom grund auf" (BBA 818/35); © Bertolt-Brecht-Erben/Suhrkamp Verlag. This sketch from Brecht's notebook is not part of the Fleischhacker folders and hence has not been identified by the BFA as belonging to the play project, yet its theme strongly suggests that it does: "Heut fürcht ich eines Mannes Appetit, wünschend nur / Einen, der sitzt täglich / In einer Ecke hinter Rauch," says Annabel in her monologue.

[64] Hauptmann's claims that Brecht's work on *Fleischhacker* induced him to study money and "(i)m Laufe dieser Studien stellte Brecht seine Theorie des epischen Dramas auf" (Kebir, *Ich fragte nicht nach meinem Anteil*, p. 61) are widely accepted as unproblematic. See for example Mittenzwei, *Das Leben des Bertolt Brecht*, pp. 255–256); Jan Knopf, *Bertolt Brecht: Lebenskunst in finsteren Zeiten* (München: Hanser, 2012), p. 167; or Primavesi, *Brecht Handbuch*, p. 147. But how exactly should this interrelation between economy and dramatic form be conceptualized? It would be reductive to depict the attempt to capture in dramatic form such "undramatic matters like money" (Kebir, *Ich fragte nicht nach meinem Anteil*, p. 61) as mere adjustment of the representational tools. Within the frame of an aesthetic project the development of artistic forms and of economic knowledge takes place "in one go," and there is struggle going on. Matters of money also attempt to capture the drama, and aesthetic forms become necessarily contaminated in the process.

[65] See BBA 524/23, 524/25–26, 514/50–51, 524/85, 524/117, 678/7–8, 678/11, 678/15–16, 378/17–18, and the various articles collected on the subject of speculations (BBA 524/62–63, 524/91, 524/99–101).

[66] Fredric Jameson, *Brecht and Method* (London: Verso, 1998), p. 191.

[67] "Die Stadt Mahagonny ist eine Darstellung der sozialen Welt in der wir leben, entworfen aus der Vogelperspektive einer real befreiten Gesellschaft," Adorno writes in a 1930 review. See Theodor W. Adorno, "Mahagonny," in David Drew, ed., *Über Kurt Weill* (Frankfurt am Main: Suhrkamp, 1975), pp. 58–66, here, p 58.

Dieter Goltzsche, *Bettleroper*, 1961, Radierung.

Devices and Bodies: Reflections on Bertolt Brecht's Radio Play *Der Ozeanflug*

Brecht's engagement with technology, a topic that has received little discussion to date, can be analyzed through the central concept of the device (*Apparat*), a concept that, in his didactic radio play (*Radiolehrstück*) *Der Ozeanflug* (1929), encompasses: (a) the airplane itself, (b) the radio as a new communication system, and (c) the theater. Through this concept of the device Brecht is responding to the new relationship between man and machine in the working environment, which had been produced specifically through the introduction of Taylorism. These altered conditions were understood as consistent with a "new type of human" (BFA 24, 40) that was approaching a kind of symbiotic relationship with technical devices, as exemplified by the airplane, yet was also being placed, through the didactic role of the radio, into the service of the collective. The practice (*Einübung*) of these new relationships was intended to occur within the theater. The various aspects of the device were to be conclusively related to the death of an individual and understood as opportunities for the overcoming of the fear of dying.

Brechts bislang nur wenig thematisiertes Verhältnis zur Technik lässt sich unter dem zentralen Begriff des "Apparates" diskutieren, der in Hinsicht auf sein "Radiolehrstück" *Der Ozeanflug* (1929) (a) das Flugzeug selbst, (b) das Radio bzw. ein neues Kommunikationssystem und (c) das Theater umfasst. Brecht reagierte mit diesem "Apparat" auf das neue Verhältnis von Mensch und Maschine, welches sich besonders durch die Einführung des Taylorismus in der Arbeitswelt ergeben hatte. Diesen veränderten Bedingungen sollte "ein neuer Typus von Mensch" (BFA 24, 40) entsprechen, der zum einen in Bezug auf den technischen Apparat, beispielhaft das Flugzeug, in ein fast symbiotisches Verhältnis rückte und der zum anderen durch die "Radio-Erziehung" in den Dienst des Kollektivs gestellt werden sollte. Die Einübung in diese neuen Verhältnisse sollte im Theater geschehen. Die unterschiedlichen Aspekte des Apparates werden abschließend auf den individuellen Tod bezogen und hier als Möglichkeiten der Überwindung der Todesangst verstanden.

Apparate und Körper: Überlegungen zu Bertolt Brechts Radiolehrstück *Der Ozeanflug*

Thomas Pekar

> Es ist Gesang in der Luft, Gesang der Winde, Motorengesang, fröhliche Menschenstimmen und strömende Musik. (BFA 19, 717)[1]

Einleitung

Ästhetische und technische Moderne sieht man nach wie vor oft in einem Spannungsverhältnis zueinander stehen. Diesem Standpunkt entspricht die Kernaussage der 1985 von Odo Marquard formulierten "Kompensationshypothese," die besagt, dass die "Geisteswissenschaften" den beschleunigten wissenschaftlich-technisch-industriellen Fortschritt verlangsamen, sozusagen "entschleunigen" sollen, indem sie vertraute Geschichten erzählen und so den Menschen in einer sich durch technische Innovationen zu schnell verändernden Welt Orientierungshilfen anbieten können.[2] Diese *entschleunigende* Funktion wird dann überhaupt oft der Kunst, dem Theater, der Literatur usw. zugesprochen. Vor dem Hintergrund dieser Vorstellungen erscheint Kunst, die Technik, den sogenannten "technischen Fortschritt," unterstützt, ja antreiben und *beschleunigen* will, wie beispielsweise die avantgardistische Kunstbewegung des Futurismus, suspekt. Dieser Argwohn gegenüber einer Kunst, die sich mit dem "technischen Fortschritt" verbindet, muss allerdings auch gegenüber Bertolt Brecht gehegt werden, der, zumindest in einer bestimmten Phase seines Lebens, technische Entwicklungen positiv aufnahm und diese auch in seinem persönlichen Leben zu schätzen wusste, z. B. als Vorliebe für schnelle Autos, denen er das Gedicht "Singende Steyrwagen" widmete (vgl. BFA 13, 392–393). Brecht selbst besaß einen solchen Wagen.[3] Aus dieser Haltung einer grundsätzlichen Bejahung der Technik heraus, die sich mit seinen gesellschaftlich-marxistischen Ansichten durchaus vertrug, versuchte Brecht, so meine Ausgangsthese, das Verhältnis der Menschen zur Technik überhaupt zu bestimmen; und dies bedeutete auch, das Selbstverständnis des Menschen und seine Beziehung zu anderen Menschen neu zu definieren, da diese Grundlagen des Menschseins und seiner Beziehungen durch Technik fundamental verändert wurden. Die grundsätzliche Frage nach dem Verhältnis von Brecht zur Technik kann im Rahmen dieses Aufsatzes nicht geklärt werden; ich werde mich hier auf Brechts Radiolehrstück *Der Ozeanflug* beschränken (der ursprüngliche Titel war *Lindbergh*, dann *Lindberghflug* dann *Der Flug der Lindberghs*).[4] Ein Grund für die Titeländerung war die Tatsache, dass der historische Ozeanflieger, Charles Lindbergh (1902–1974), sich in den 1930er Jahren immer mehr den Nationalsozialisten angenähert hatte, so dass Brecht seinen Namen vermeiden wollte. Es wird hier also darum gehen, diese bejahende Einstellung Brechts zur Technik, auf die u. a. auch Helmut Lethen hingewiesen hat,[5] am Beispiel seines Lehrstücks *Der Ozeanflug* zu untersuchen.

Dieses Verhältnis zur Technik wird bei Brecht unter einem zentralen Begriff verhandelt, nämlich dem des "Apparates," der, in Hinsicht auf den *Ozeanflug*, aber auch über ihn hinausweisend, zumindest drei Bedeutungsdimensionen hat:

> a) Apparat benennt das Flugzeug, den Flugapparat selbst, betrifft also das Verhältnis des Menschen zu seiner Maschine bzw. zu Maschinen überhaupt.
> b) Apparat benennt weiter das Radio, den Radioapperat, d. h. ein damals neues Kommunikationsmedium, betrifft also das Verhältnis der Menschen zu diesem Medium bzw. das neue Verhältnis der Menschen zueinander, die nun, vermittelt durch dieses Medium, miteinander kommunizieren.
> c) Schließlich benennt Apparat auch noch das Theater, den Theaterapparat, also die Gesamtheit von Bühne, Kulisse, Kostüme, Zuschauerraum, Regisseur, Schauspieler, Bühnenarbeiter, Zuschauer etc. Dieser Apparat sollte—und das war wohl Brechts dringlichstes Anliegen—auf die Veränderungen, die sich durch die anderen Apparate, die Apparate der Beschleunigung, des rasanten Ortswechsels und der, wenn man so sagen will, "entfesselten" Kommunikation ergeben haben (oder sich in einer anderen Gesellschaftsform hätten ergeben können) reagieren.

"Apparat" ist damit ein vieldeutiger, sowohl inhaltliche wie auch formale Aspekte betreffender Begriff, der im Folgenden näher beleuchtet werden soll.

Mit der experimentellen Serie seiner *Lehrstücke*, zu denen der *Ozeanflug* gehört, reagierte Brecht wesentlich auf die technischen Veränderungen, die sich im und nach dem Ersten Weltkrieg (und da besonders in der zweiten Hälfte der 1920er Jahre) im Verhältnis von Mensch und Maschine ergeben hatten. Diese—sicherlich krisenhaften—Veränderungen betrafen und destruierten insbesondere die traditionelle Vorrangstellung des Subjekts,[6] welches sich nun, enger als je zuvor, an die Maschine angeschlossen vorfand, weshalb die Position und überhaupt das Selbstverständnis dieses Subjekts neu justiert werden musste.[7] Diese Neu-Justierung des

Individuums geschah bei Brecht experimentell, mit dem Schwerpunkt in zwei Bereichen: Der erste umfasste das Verhältnis des Individuums zu seiner Körperlichkeit vor allem in Hinsicht auf die Hinfälligkeit dieser Körperlichkeit, d.h. letztlich in Hinsicht auf den Tod; der zweite Schwerpunkt betraf sein Verhältnis zu den anderen, d.h. zum Kollektiv.

Der historische Kontext des *Ozeanflugs*

Historisch gesehen ist Brecht in den Kontext der technikfreundlichen Diskurse seiner Zeit einzurücken; Stichwörter dafür sind "Neue Sachlichkeit" oder "Amerikanisierung." Entstehungs- und Aufführungszeit des *Ozeanfluges* sind die Jahre 1928/1929, die als die Endphase einer Zeit relativer wirtschaftlicher Stabilität und politischer Festigung in Deutschland angesehen werden, die Ende 1923 begann und bis zum 23. Oktober 1929, dem schwarzen Freitag, dem Zusammenbruch der New Yorker Börse, reichte. Die USA waren in dieser Zeit ein wichtiger Wirtschaftspartner Deutschlands. Es ist daher kein Wunder, dass sich Deutschland in dieser Zeit in seinen wirtschaftlichen und technischen Zielen stark an Amerika orientierte, insbesondere in Hinsicht auf die Produktionsmethoden. Dort hatte sich "die wissenschaftliche Betriebsführung (*scientific management*), wie sie vor allem von Taylor, Gilbreth und Ford vertreten wurde, als allgemein anerkannte Grundlage unternehmerischen Handelns durchgesetzt."[8]

Der amerikanische Ingenieur Frederick Winslow Taylor (1856–1915) hatte die Tätigkeit eines Arbeiters in kleinste Einheiten systematisch zerlegt, diese gemessen, um eine Optimierung der Arbeitsleistung zu erreichen; der oberste Lehrsatz seines *Scientific Management* lautete: "Die größte Prosperität ist das Resultat einer möglichst ökonomischen Ausnutzung des Arbeiters und der Maschinen, d.h. Arbeiter und Maschinen müssen ihre höchste Ergiebigkeit, ihren höchsten Nutzeffekt erreicht haben."[9] Taylors Schüler, Frank Bunker Gilbreth (1868–1924), entwickelte photografische Bewegungsstudien in Hinsicht auf die Arbeitsbewegungen, um den täglichen Arbeitsablauf optimal zu normieren; der Automobilhersteller Henry Ford (1863–1947), dessen 1923 auf Deutsch erschienene Autobiografie gleich ein Bestseller wurde, schließlich setzte das *Scientific Management* konsequent in Massenproduktionsverfahren um, zu dessen Grundlagen das Fließband und die Austauschbarkeit der Einzelteile gehörten. Diese sogenannte "Rationalisierungsbewegung," die allerdings die Arbeitsbedingungen für die Arbeiter wesentlich verschlechterte, ergriff auch die Betriebe in Deutschland.[10] Man träumte davon, gesellschaftliche Probleme technisch-rational lösen zu können, wodurch dann eben diese technisch-ökonomischen Fragen gesellschaftlich-kulturelle wurden: Mit Begriffen wie "Amerikanisierung," "Neue Sachlichkeit," "Rationalisierung," "Chauffeurmenschentum" usw. wurde hier von Philosophen, Künstlern und nicht zuletzt auch Ingenieuren eine intensive Technik-Debatte geführt. Wenn man diese Diskussionen in den Kontext der von Foucault so genannten "Mikrophysik der Macht" stellt,[11] die auf den Körpern direkt ansetzt und dort "Schnittstellen" zu den Maschinen implantiert, so hat man damit m.E. auch die Ebene erreicht, auf der sich Brecht mit seinen Überlegungen bewegte. Er hatte—und darauf hat die Forschung schon hingewiesen[12]—an dieser "Rationalisierungsbewegung," an "Fordismus" und "Taylorismus" großes Interesse, ja sein Lustspiel *Mann ist Mann* (1926), das den "Umbau" des irischen Packers Galy Gay zum Soldaten der britischen Indienarmee zeigt, setzt diese Spezialisierung und Mechanisierung der Fabrikarbeit dramaturgisch um. So heißt es im Stück: "Hier wird heute abend ein Mensch wie ein Auto ummontiert . . ." (BFA 2, 123). Auch der *Ozeanflug* fügt sich in diese Disziplinierungs- und Mechanisierungsgeschichte des Körpers ein, ist sein in den späteren Fassungen namenlos gewordener (Anti-)Held, ganz ähnlich wie Galy Gay, doch kein Individuum, sondern vielmehr ein Typus—und zwar "ein neuer Typus von Mensch" (BFA 24, 40).

Der Flugapparat

Ich möchte nun diesen Typus der "technischen Intelligenz," für den der Ingenieur-Flieger repräsentativ ist, in seinem Verhältnis zum "Apparat" genauer bestimmen—und zwar zunächst zum Flug-Apparat. Um Brechts Einstellung dazu zu verdeutlichen, sei auf eine Notiz und ein ihr gegenübergestelltes Bild aus Brechts *Arbeitsjournal* hingewiesen.[13] Es handelt sich hier um eine Text-Bild-Kombination, was aus Brechts *Kriegsfibel* bekannt ist, im *Arbeitsjournal* allerdings nur selten zu finden ist. Es gibt keine Erklärung zu dem Bild selbst; wir haben es mit einem Flugzeugcockpit zu tun, welches eine gewisse kühle Eleganz ausstrahlt. Dieses Cockpit ist demjenigen von Lindberghs Flugzeug, der legendären *Spirit of St. Louis*, mit dem er am 27. Mai 1927 den Atlantik überquerte, sehr ähnlich.[14]

Was schreibt der Exilant Brecht, der sich an diesem Augusttag des Jahres 1940 auf seiner Flucht vor den Nazis gerade in Finnland befand, über den technischen Apparat "Flugzeug," der sich bei verschiedenen Einsätzen, z. B. bei der Bombardierung der spanischen Stadt Guernica 1937 durch deutsche Flugzeuge, durch die Bombardierung Warschaus 1939 und durch die sogenannte "Luftschlacht um England," die Mitte 1940 begann, bereits als eine Tod und Verderben bringende Waffe erwiesen hatte? Erstaunlich Positives! Brecht verteidigt "die Schönheit eines Flugzeuges" (BFA 26, 420) im Verweis auf altgriechische Epigramme, die Waffen preisen, und appelliert an "den einfachen Traum der Menschheit vom Fliegen" (ebd.). Allerdings fügt er hinzu, dass diese Schönheit "etwas Obzönes" (ebd.) habe. Brecht spricht hier einen Film an; genauer gesagt, geht es um ein Filmexposé, welches er zusammen mit dem schwedischen Schriftsteller Henry Peter Matthis (1892–1988) geschrieben hatte mit dem Titel "Wir wollen fliegen / Vi vill Flyga." Es gibt nur ein schwedisches Typoskript;

der deutsche Text ist eine Übersetzung aus dem Schwedischen.[15] Es geht in diesem Drehbuch um einen armen, proletarischen Jungen, Erik, der sich für Flugzeuge begeistert und Flieger werden möchte. Er kann sein Ziel aber nicht erreichen, sondern wird nur Flugzeugmechaniker. Fliegen bleibt für ihn ein Traum. Hier kämpft Brecht, um es kurz zu resümieren, gegen die Tatsache, dass, wie es im Text heißt, "Arbeiter . . . nicht Flieger werden" können und hat am Ende die Vision eines global-proletarischen Luftverkehrs: Man sieht dann in der allerdings nie zustande gekommenen filmischen Realisierung dieses Drehbuchs "seinen Traum—große Flugzeuge in der Luft, über dem Flugplatz und über dem Atlantik—Postflugzeuge, Passagierflugzeuge—ihre eleganten Landungen" (BFA 19, 717). An diesem Beispiel kann man deutlich erkennen, dass Brecht selbst noch in diesem Kriegsjahr 1940 eine von ästhetischer Faszination geprägte Einstellung zu Flugzeugen—eben auch zu Flugzeugen als Waffen—hatte, unter der einzigen Einschränkung, dass sie im "proletarischen Besitz" bzw., wie es im Text hier heißt, "in festen Händen" (BFA 26, 420), sein sollten.

Walter Benjamin (1892–1940) hat diese Bemerkung zu Brechts *Ozeanflieger* gemacht:

> T. E. Lawrence, der Verfasser der *Sieben Säulen der Weisheit*, schrieb, als er zur Fliegertruppe ging, . . . dieser Schritt sei für den Menschen von heute [d. h. also der 1920er Jahre], was für den mittelalterlichen der Eintritt in ein Kloster gewesen sei. In dieser Äußerung findet man die Bogenspannung wieder, die dem *Flug der Lindberghs*, aber auch den späteren Lehrstücken eigen ist. Eine klerikale Strenge wird der Unterweisung in einer neuzeitlichen Technik zugewandt—hier der im Flugwesen, später der im Klassenkampf.[16]

In diesem Zitat sind wesentliche Punkte angesprochen: Zum einen wird erneut auf die unglaubliche Faszination des Fliegens hingewiesen, die auch in Lindberghs Büchern über seinen Transatlantikflug immer wieder zu finden ist, die durchaus auch religiös-mythologische Tiefenschichten ansprach; so heißt es bei ihm beispielsweise: "Welche Freiheit liegt im Fliegen! Gottähnlich ist die Macht, die es dem Menschen gibt."[17] Davon kann man sich natürlich heute als Economy-Klasse-Passagier (also als lebendige Luftfracht) keinen Begriff mehr machen. Zum zweiten wird hier erneut auf diesen "disziplinierenden" Aspekt hingewiesen, insbesondere den körperdisziplinierenden Aspekt, der mit dem Mönchs-/Fliegerleben verbunden wird. Diese Körperdisziplinierung wird bei Lindbergh selbst bis hin zu einem völligen Vergessen des Körpers getrieben.[18] Und zum dritten wird hier auf diesen strengen didaktischen Zug bei Brecht hingewiesen, der eben diese "Unterweisung" in neuzeitlicher Technik—und, damit verbunden, "Klassenkampf" betrifft. Dieser Punkt scheint allerdings heute historisch (vorerst?) erledigt zu sein, nachdem in den 1970er Jahren Brechts

Lehrstücke als Beispiele für ein modellhaftes und zukunftsweisendes "sozialistisches Theater" gefeiert worden waren.[19] Nicht erledigt ist allerdings die von Benjamin angesprochene Frage nach der "Unterweisung" bzw., weniger "klerikal" formuliert, nach dem Umgang mit der neuzeitlichen Technik.

Gedanken, dass der Mensch in ein neues, gleichsam "symbiotisches" Verhältnis zur Maschine rücke, waren in diesen 1920er–1930er Jahren *en vogue*; man denke hier nur an Ernst Jüngers (1895–1998) Begriff der "organischen Konstruktion" für die neue Mensch-Maschine-Verbindung, den er im Übrigen in seinem 1934 erschienen Essay "Über den Schmerz" am Beispiel eines japanischen Selbstmord-Torpedos entwickelte.[20] Der Typus, der für Brecht diese Mensch-Maschine-Verbindung verkörperte, war der des "Ingenieurs" bzw. "Fliegers"; und eine solche Verkörperung war eben der amerikanische Pilot Charles Lindbergh, der mit seinem Flugzeug *Spirit of St. Louis* 1927 als erster im Alleinflug den Atlantischen Ozean überquerte, indem er von New York nach Paris flog. Er wurde in der Öffentlichkeit als der moderne Held schlechthin betrachtet, der, anders als die Piloten des Ersten Weltkrieges, den neuen Typus des "zivilen" Piloten vertrat. So feierte ihn auch die deutsche Presse, wie z.B. die *Vossische Zeitung* vom 24. Mai 1927 mit einem begeisterten Kommentar, aus dem Brechts Hörspieltext dann wörtlich zitierte.[21]

Zwei Momente sind es nun, die Brecht bei Lindbergh hervorhob: (a) sein Verhältnis zur Maschine, d.h. hier zum Flugzeugmotor, und (b) sein Verhältnis zu den Produzenten des Flugapparates, d.h. zum "Kollektiv" der Mechaniker. Das Verhältnis zu diesem Kollektiv wird im *Ozeanflug* durch den Hinweis auf die Arbeiter in den Ryanwerken, die, wie es im Stück heißt, "Kameraden in San Diego" (BFA 3, 15), die auch der historische Lindbergh erwähnt, hergestellt.[22] Auf diesen Aspekt, der dann vor allem in dem späteren Lehrstück *Die Maßnahme* (1930) im Mittelpunkt steht, gehe ich hier nicht weiter ein, sondern konzentriere mich auf das Verhältnis des Menschen zur Maschine, genauer gesagt: auf das Verhältnis von Lindberghs Körper zum Motor. Sowohl bei Brecht als auch in Lindberghs Büchern über seinen Flug wird eine Disproportionalität zwischen Körper und Maschine konstatiert: Während der Körper sich als hinderlich und hinfällig erweist, zeigt der Motor hingegen mechanische Präzision und Unermüdlichkeit. Brecht antizipiert gewissermaßen in seinem Stück den späteren Volkswagen-Werbeslogan "Er läuft und läuft und läuft": Viermal taucht diese Zeile "Der Motor läuft" bei Brecht in "Lindberghs Gespräch mit seinem Motor" auf (BFA 3, 20–21). Und *dass* Lindbergh überhaupt mit seinem (eben dadurch personifizierten) Motor *spricht*—er fragt ihn direkt: "Geht es dir gut?" (BFA 3, 20)—und mit ihm so ein dialogisches, ja fast symbiotisches Verhältnis eingeht, wenn er in Hinsicht von sich und dem Motor von "wir" spricht: "Wir zwei" (BFA 3, 20), zeigt, wie eng hier Mensch und Maschine aneinander gekoppelt sind. Dies entspricht Lindberghs tatsächlichem

Verhalten: Er nannte sein erstes Buch über seinen Transatlantikflug einfach *We* (womit er sich und sein Flugzeug meinte)[23] und gab seinem zweiten Buch dann gleich den Namen seine Flugzeuges, *The Spirit of St. Louis*.[24]

Während einige Jahre nach Brecht Ernst Jünger die eben erwähnte Konzeption der "organischen Konstruktion" fasste, um einen "gerüsteten," d.h. für Schmerzen unempfindlich gewordenen und von Todesangst befreiten Körper auf die Standards eines von—oft auch tödlichen—Maschinen geprägten Raumes zu bringen (die Ausgangserfahrung dafür sind die Materialschlachten des Ersten Weltkriegs), geht Brecht nicht so weit: Bei ihm behält der Körper sein Eigenleben, was sich gerade in seinen Defiziten, wie Schwäche und Schmerz, zeigt. Lindbergh bleibt ein "schwacher" Held—und auch noch mit einer "schwachen" Technik, mit einem "schwachen" Apparat ausgestattet:

> Freilich mein Apparat
> Ist schwach, und schwach ist
> Mein Kopf . . . (BFA 3, 19)

Dieser "Schwäche" entspricht im Übrigen die "Vorläufigkeit," in Form einer (noch) primitiven Technik in einer (noch) primitiven Gesellschaftsform. Allerdings muss dieser schwache Körper—gerade wegen seiner Schwäche—bei Brecht diszipliniert werden; und dafür ist Lindbergh sicherlich ein Vorbild, der seinem Körper sogar das "Recht" absprach, ihn durch das Schlafbedürfnis von seinem Flug abzulenken.[25] Der Körper hat sich somit zu mechanisieren; er wird, z.B. in Hinsicht auf das Flugzeug, zu einem untergeordnetem Bestandteil. Damit nimmt Brecht Teil an dem umfassenden Diskurs der Mechanisierung, der versucht, "menschliche Körper auf die Standards von Maschinen" zu bringen.[26] Um es mit Lindberghs Worten zu sagen: "Dem Fleische nach bin ich ein Automat, den man an eine im voraus geschaltete Leitung gekuppelt hat."[27]

Der Radioapparat

Ich komme nun zu dem zweiten Apparat, dem Radio. Es soll hier nicht der Ort sein, Brechts Radiotheorie erneut zu rekapitulieren.[28] Für den von mir hier vorgestellten Disziplinierungs-Zusammenhang sei lediglich erwähnt, dass Brecht seine Radio-Erziehung ganz in den Dienst dieses Kollektivismus stellte—und in einer "bürgerlichen" Staatsform dafür nur einen ganz unzureichenden Rahmen sah (vgl. BFA 21, 219). Natürlich erscheint uns heute die Art und Weise, *wie* Brecht den Hörer aktivieren und dieses Schauspieler- bzw. Sprecher-Hörer-Kollektiv erzwingen wollte, recht merkwürdig: "[D]er Hörer soll . . . den *Flug der Lindberghs* mit dem Text in der Hand rezipieren und mitsprechen; vor der Ursendung wurde der Text tatsächlich zu diesem Zweck in Rundfunkzeitschriften verbreitet,"[29] aber was Brecht damit forderte, war damals durchaus nicht ungewöhnlich, wie zeitgenössischen Bilder zeigen: So stellt das Bild *Der Radionist* (1927) des Malers Kurt Günther (1893–1955) einen kleinbürgerlichen Radiohörer dar, der während des Radiohörens eine Zigarre raucht und eine Flasche Wein neben sich stehen hat.[30] Bei dem Bild *Radiohörer* (1930) des neusachlichen Malers Max Radler (1904–1971) handelt es sich hingegen offensichtlich, wie die Fabrik im Hintergrund und die karge Wohnung zeigen, um einen proletarischen Radiohörer.[31] Beide, Kleinbürger wie Arbeiter, tragen Kopfhörer, da die damals üblichen Radios Detektorenempfänger waren, bei denen man aus technischen Gründen diese tragen musste—und beide sind vorbildliche Radiohörer, ganz im Sinne Brechts, indem sie nämlich den Text der Radiosendung mitlesen, wobei der Arbeiter noch einen Stift vor sich liegen hat, wohl um sich gegebenenfalls Notizen machen zu können.

Brechts Forderungen des Mitsprechens und Mitlesens schließen sich somit an den damaligen Hörgewohnheiten, dass man eben per Kopfhörer hörte und die Texte von Radiosendungen mitlesen konnte, nur an; was er daran anknüpfend anstrebte, war aber eine Disziplinierung des Hörers bzw. der Versuch, ihn aus seiner Rezipientenrolle herauszuholen, was, besonders dann von Walter Benjamin mit dem Begriff der "Umfunktionierung" bezeichnet wird.[32] Brechts Interesse galt also nicht der Radiotechnik selbst, nicht den durch diese Technik erzeugten "neuen Klängen," von denen Kurt Weill 1926 sprach,[33] sondern sein Interesse galt den mit diesen "Apparaten" gekoppelten Körpern, deren Verbindung "mechanistisch" hergestellt werden sollte (vgl. BFA 14, 101)—und die somit "diszipliniert" werden mussten; noch einmal Brecht: "Diese Übung dient der Disziplinierung, welche die Grundlage der Freiheit ist" (BFA 24, 88).

Der Theaterapparat

Was nun den Theater-Apparat betrifft—und Brecht selbst nennt das Theater immer wieder einen "Apparat," z.B. einen "schwerfälligen" (vgl. BFA 21, 126)—so kann man Brechts Anliegen kurz und bündig mit Walter Benjamins Worten so bezeichnen: "Es geht um die Verschüttung der Orchestra";[34] d.h. um die Verschüttung jenes "Abgrundes," "der die Spieler vom Publikum, wie die Toten von den Lebendigen scheidet. . . ."[35]

Bekanntlich wollte Brecht das Theater-Publikum in "Fachleute" verwandeln, so wie man dies heute vielleicht von Fans in einigen Fußball-Stadien kennt; Brechts Vorbild waren die "sachkundig und kritisch urteilenden Zuschauer von Boxkämpfen."[36] Hier verknüpft sich dann auch die Idee des *Lehrstücks* mit der des *epischen Theaters*. Der herkömmliche Theater-Apparat, der als Kultur-Apparat, als Apparat bestimmter Produktionsverhältnisse immer mit der Gesellschaft und den jeweiligen Staatsformen verkoppelt ist, sollte, und dies ist eine Grundthese Brechts, nicht mehr einfach "beliefert," sondern, genau eben wie das Radio auch, "umfunktioniert" werden. Doch was bedeutete diese "Umfunktionierung" eigentlich konkret? Meist wird dies in der Forschungsliteratur recht beschönigend, wenn auch dann unverbindlich so gesagt, dass Brecht das Publikum "einbeziehen" wollte; die "verbreitete Passivität sollte durchbrochen, das Publikum selbst an der Aufführung beteiligt werden."[37] Dies mag beim epischen Theater, etwa durch die Handlungsunterbrechung, den Montagecharakter, den Anti-Illusionismus, eine komplexe und wirkungsvolle Form gefunden haben, beim Lehrstück hingegen war an eine direkte Disziplinierung und Schulung gedacht, so Brecht in einer Erläuterung zum Stück: "Der *Flug der Lindberghs* hat keinen Wert, wenn man sich nicht daran schult. Er besitzt keinen Kunstwert, der eine Aufführung rechtfertigt, die diese Schulung nicht bezweckt" (BFA 24, 87).

Diese "Schulung" kann man sich eigentlich gar nicht mechanisch genug vorstellen, weshalb Brecht hier den "Staat," den "sozialistischen Staat" (der Zukunft), anruft, der—ja, was soll der eigentlich tun?—wenn nicht die Zuschauer und Zuhörer dazu *zwingen* sollte, sich dieser disziplinierenden Schulung zu unterwerfen. Deshalb halte ich sowohl den Vorschlag Steinwegs, die "Lehrstücke" in "Lernstücke" umzubenennen für falsch,[38] wie auch die m.E. zu postmodernistische Sicht Müller-Schölls, der die Lehrstücke "Leerstücke" nennt, da es in ihnen seiner Meinung nach darum gehe, die "Grund- und Haltlosigkeit jeder Autorität, eben auch der "marxistischen," zu demonstrieren.[39] Ich denke, man sollte hier Brecht nicht zu (post-)modern machen, sondern seine historisch bedingten Grenzen anerkennen und sehen, dass diese Stücke ganz klar Lehr-, Schulungs-, Disziplinierungsstücke waren[40]—und, wie ich dies versucht habe auszuführen, als Teil dieses damaligen umfassenden, auf Technik bezogenen gesellschaftlichen Disziplinierungs- und Rationalisierungs-Diskurses zu verstehen sind. Wenn es Brecht um eine "Umfunktionierung der Kunst in eine pädagogische Disziplin" (BFA 21, 466) ging, so kann man sich dies eigentlich nicht konkret genug vorstellen, d.h. es ging um "Training," um direktes Körpertraining, um Sprech- und Bewegungsvorschriften, die zu befolgen waren.[41] Dieses Verständnis der Lehrstücke als "Trainingseinheiten" teilt im Übrigen die postmarxistische Sichtweise, dass aus diesen Lehrstücken "keine einfache Botschaft oder Lehre herausgelöst werden kann."[42] Vielmehr ist es so, dass die Teilnahme an ihnen, als "Schauspieler," als "Zuschauer" oder als "Hörer," d.h. sich also ihren körperdisziplinierenden und kollektivbildenden "Exerzitien" zu unterwerfen, die Botschaft, die "Lehre" selbst ist. Dies wäre dann allerdings medienhistorisch avanciert, variierte es doch McLuhans bekannten Satz "The medium is the message."

Schluss

Versucht man alle drei genannten Aspekte des "Apparates" schließlich zusammenzubringen, dann lässt sich sagen, dass sie alle auf das Kollektiv verweisen, welches sich bei Brecht damit als neue, das bürgerliche Individuum überwindende oder, wenn man dies dialektisch formulieren will, "aufhebende" menschliche Lebensform ankündigt. Es unterstreicht diesen Zusammenhang nur, wenn Brecht einmal schreibt: "Der Kollektivist sieht die Menschheit als einen Apparat, der erst teilweise organisiert ist" (BFA 21, 518). Dies wäre dann noch eine weitere Bedeutung von "Apparat"—die kollektiv organisierte Menschheit, was uns heute doch eher als eine Dystopie erscheinen mag. So verweist der Flugapparat auf das Kollektiv der Mechaniker, das ihn produziert hat; so verweist der Radioapparat in seiner ganzen medialen Innovationskraft auf das Kollektiv der Zuhörer bzw. der Radiohörer, für die vollkommen neue Rezeptionsbedingungen gelten als z.B. für den individuellen Leser eines Buches. Und so verweist schließlich der neu zu konzipierende Theaterapparat, in Verbindung mit dem Staatsapparat, auf ein neues Schauspieler-Zuschauer-Kollektiv, für welches diese alten Begriffe, "Schauspieler," "Zuschauer," nicht mehr gültig sind.

Nun scheint es mir aber so zu sein, dass dies noch nicht alles ist, dass nämlich dieser aufgeblähte Gedanke des Kollektivs bei Brecht—Ernst Schumacher spricht einmal davon, dass "beim Materialisten Brecht . . . an die Stelle Gottes das abstrakte Kollektiv getreten" sei[43]—doch vielleicht einen ganz individuellen Hintergrund haben mag, vielleicht sogar *den* individuellen Grund schlechthin, den Tod nämlich. Trotz der (von Brecht formulierten) Einsicht des chinesischen Weisen Me Ti von der Überschätzung der Todesfurcht (vgl. BFA 18, 80), ist er doch die *conditio sine qua non* von menschlicher Individualität und mag wohl auch in der besten aller möglichen Welten unaufhebbar einen dunklen Schatten aufs Leben werfen.[44] Dieser Gedanke des Todes liegt nicht fern, hat Brecht doch selbst einmal in Notizen die *Lehrstücke* als "Sterbelehre" bezeichnet.[45] Alle drei Kollektive nämlich wollen den individuellen Tod—und damit eben den Tod als solchen—überwinden, denn der Gedanke eines möglichen kollektiven Todes, d.h. den Tod des Gattungswesen Mensch (z.B. durch Umweltzerstörungen oder Klimaveränderungen), ist bei Brecht, wenn ich es recht sehe, noch nicht bedacht. Man könnte auch sagen, dass alle drei "Apparate" als Transformatoren arbeiten, die Individuelles in Kollektives und damit Sterbliches in (nahezu) Unsterbliches verwandeln wollen: Der technische Apparat—als Produkt oder "Vergegenständlichung" des Kollektivs der Mechaniker—verhindert den individuellen Tod dieses einen Piloten wie sich dieser eine Pilot überhaupt als Teil dieses Mechaniker-Kollektivs versteht. Kennzeichen dieses so als defizitär begriffenen individuellen Lebens werden deshalb auch schamhaft verborgen wie z.B. die Schwäche; Brecht lässt Lindbergh nach seinem Flug sagen:

> . . . Bitte tragt mich
> In einen dunklen Schuppen, daß
> Keiner sehe meine

Natürliche Schwäche. (BFA 3, 23)

Gleich darauf kommt—als eben Gegenvorstellung zu dieser individuellen Schwäche—das Kollektiv (und die Maschine) ins Spiel, fährt der Text doch fort:

Aber meldet meinen Kameraden in den Ryanwerken San Diego
Daß ihre Arbeit gut war.
Unser Motor hat ausgehalten
Ihre Arbeit war ohne Fehler. (BFA 3, 23)

Schwäche, Schmerzen, letztlich der Tod erscheinen hier als defizitäre Marker von Individualität; die Überwindung dieser Individualität, das Kollektiv also, wäre von all diesen Negativitätsmerkmalen befreit. Und so wie der Pilot durch seinen Eintritt ins Kollektiv nahezu unsterblich wird, so werden auch die toten Bühnenfiguren durch die "Verschüttung der Orchestra" (als "Abgrund"), d.h. durch den Eintritt in ein noch namenloses Figuren-, Akteure- und Zuschauer-Kollektiv, gleichsam zum Leben erweckt.

Brechts "Lösung" des Todesproblems kann aber heute, nachdem der Verlauf der Geschichte selbst diesen Gedanken des Kollektivs vollkommen desavouiert hat und indem wir gegenwärtig sehen, dass uns der "technische Fortschritt" an den Abgrund globaler Katastrophen geführt hat (vor denen er uns allerdings auch allein nur retten zu können scheint), nicht mehr überzeugen; ja, wenn wir ein wenig böswillig sein wollen, so drängt sich geradezu die Vermutung auf, dass es letztlich vielleicht doch Brechts individuelle und einsame, menschlich-allzumenschliche Todesangst war, die diese merkwürdigen Apparate als imaginär-kollektive Todesüberwindungs-Szenarien gebar.[46]

Anmerkungen

[1] Ich zitiere Brecht nach: Bertolt Brecht, *Werke: Große kommentierte Berliner und Frankfurter Ausgabe*, Werner Hecht u. a., Hrsg. (Berlin und Frankfurt am Main: Aufbau und Suhrkamp, 1988–2000). Im Folgenden BFA Band, Seite.

[2] Vgl. vor allem Odo Marquard, "Über die Unvermeidlichkeit der Geisteswissenschaften," in ders., *Apologie des Zufälligen* (Stuttgart: Reclam, 1986), S. 98–116.

[3] Vgl. Hans-Christian von Herrmann, *Sang der Maschinen: Brechts Medienästhetik* (München: Fink, 1996), S. 170–171.

[4] Text von Brecht, Musik von Paul Hindemith und Kurt Weill. Das Stück wurde, unter der Regie von Ernst Hardt, im Rahmen des Musikfestes "Deutsche Kammermusik Baden-Baden" am 27. Juli 1929 zum ersten Mal öffentlich vorgeführt und dann, wenig später, auch vom Südwestfunk in Frankfurt gesendet. Es wurde dann 1930 in *Der Flug der Lindberghs* umbenannt und erhielt nun, in Heft 1 der *Versuche*, auch den Untertitel: *Ein Radiolehrstück für Knaben und Mädchen*. 1949-1950 erhielt das Stück seinen letzten Titel *Der Ozeanflug* und einen Prolog, vgl.

dazu BFA 3, 401 und u.a. auch Klaus Völker, *Brecht-Kommentar zum dramatischen Werk* (München: Winkler, 1983), S. 114ff. und Klaus-Dieter Krabiel, "Der Lindberghflug/Der Flug der Lindberghs/Der Ozeanflug," in Jan Knopf, Hrsg., *Brecht Handbuch* (Stuttgart und Weimar: Metzler, 2001), Bd. 1, S. 216–226.

[5] Vgl. Helmut Lethen, "Ernst Jünger, Bertolt Brecht und der Habitus des Einverständnisses mit der Modernisierung," *Studi Germanici* 21/22 (1983-1984): S. 273–289.

[6] Vgl. Nikolaus Müller-Schöll, *Das Theater des "konstruktiven Defaitismus": Lektüren zur Theorie eines Theaters der A-Identität bei Walter Benjamin, Bertolt Brecht und Heiner Müller* (Frankfurt am Main: Stroemfeld/Nexus, 2002), S. 187ff.

[7] Vgl. Helmut Lethen, "Brechts Hand-Orakel," *The Brecht Yearbook* 17 (1992): S. 77–99; hier, S. 79.

[8] Ingeborg Güssow, "Kunst und Technik in den 20er Jahren," in Helmut Friedel, Hrsg., *Kunst und Technik in den 20er Jahren: Neue Sachlichkeit und gegenständlicher Konstruktivismus* (München: Städtische Galerie im Lenbachhaus, 1980), S. 30–45; hier, S. 30.

[9] Frederick Winslow Taylor, *Die Grundsätze wissenschaftlicher Betriebsführung* (München und Berlin: Oldenbourg, 3. Aufl., 1922 [1912]), S. 10; zit. nach Herrmann, *Sang der Maschinen*, S. 148.

[10] Vgl. Güssow, *Kunst und Technik*, S. 33.

[11] Vgl. Michel Foucault, *Überwachen und Strafen: Die Geburt des Gefängnisses* (Frankfurt am Main: Suhrkamp, 1995).

[12] Vgl. z.B. Helfried W. Seliger, *Das Amerikabild Bertolt Brechts* (Bonn: Bouvier, 1974), S. 269 und Herrmann, *Sang der Maschinen*, S. 143ff.

[13] Bertolt Brecht, "Vi vill Flyga / Wir wollen fliegen," in ders., *Texte für Filme: Drehbücher, Protokoll "Kuhle Wampe," Exposés, Szenarien* (Frankfurt am Main: Suhrkamp, 1973), S. 356–365; hier, S. 160–161. Vgl. auch BFA 26, 419, wo, wohl aus Platzgründen, diese Gegenüberstellung von Text und Bild leider aufgelöst ist.

[14] Lindberghs Cockpit kann unter dieser Adresse angesehen werden: http://ww1.prweb.com/prfiles/2007/01/03/495081/SpiritofStLouis.jpg (accessed 30 November 2014). Das Flugzeug selbst ist im National Air and Space Museum, Washington, DC ausgestellt.

[15] Vgl. Brecht, "Vi vill Flyga," S. 356–365 und S. 664, und BFA 19, 433–437 und 714–717.

[16] Walter Benjamin, *Versuche über Brecht*, in Rolf Tiedemann, Hrsg. (Frankfurt am Main: Suhrkamp, 1966), S. 28. Thomas Edward Lawrence (1888–1935) war bekannt als Lawrence von Arabien.

[17] Charles A. Lindbergh, *Mein Flug über den Ozean* (Berlin und Frankfurt am Main: Fischer, 1954), S. 110.

[18] Vgl. z. B. Lindbergh, *Mein Flug*, S. 401.

[19] Vgl. Reiner Steinweg, "Das Lehrstück—ein Modell des sozialistischen Theaters. Brechts Lehrstücktheorie," *Alternative* 14 (1971), S. 102–116; hier, S. 103. Zur Kritik an ihm vgl. u.a. schon Heinrich Berenberg-Gossler, Hans-Harald Müller und Joachim Stosch, "Das Lehrstück—Rekonstruktion einer Theorie oder Fortsetzung eines Lernprozesses," in Joachim Dyck u. a., Hrsg., *Brechtdiskussion* (Kronberg/

Taunus: Scriptor, 1974), S. 121–171 und Heiner Müller, "Absage," in Reiner Steinweg, Hrsg., *Auf Anregung Bertolt Brechts: Lehrstücke mit Schülern, Arbeitern, Theaterleuten* (Frankfurt am Main: Suhrkamp, 1978), S. 232.

[20] Vgl. Ernst Jünger, "Der Schmerz," in ders., *Blätter und Steine* (Hamburg: Hanseatische Verlagsanstalt, 1934), S. 154–213; hier, S. 173–174.

[21] Vgl. Herrmann, *Sang der Maschinen*, S. 157–158.

[22] Vgl. Lindbergh, *Mein Flug*, S. 122.

[23] Vgl. Charles A. Lindbergh, *We: The Famous Flier's Own Story of His Life and Transatlantic Flight* (New York and London: Putnam, 1927).

[24] Vgl. Charles A. Lindbergh, *The Spirit of St. Louis* (New York: Scribner, 1953).

[25] Vgl. Lindbergh, *Mein Flug*, S. 267.

[26] Herrmann, *Sang der Maschinen*, S. 193.

[27] Lindbergh, *Mein Flug*, S. 402.

[28] Vgl. dazu z.B. Norbert Schachtsiek-Freitag, "Bertolt Brechts Beitrag zur Geschichte des deutschen Hörspiels," *Brecht heute—Brecht today: Jahrbuch der internationalen Brecht-Gesellschaft* 2 (1972): S. 174–186; Peter Groth und Manfred Voigts, "Die Entwicklung der Brechtschen Radiotheorie 1927–1932. Dargestellt unter Benutzung zweier unbekannter Aufsätze Brechts," *Brecht-Jahrbuch* (1976): S. 9–42 und Heinrich Vormweg, "Zur Überprüfung der Radiotheorie und -praxis Bertolt Brechts," in Klaus Schöning, Hrsg., *Hörspielmacher: Autorenporträts und Essays* (Königstein/Taunus: Athenäum, 1983), S. 13–26.

[29] Vormweg, "Zur Überprüfung der Radiotheorie," S. 23.

[30] Im Internet kann man das Bild z.B. unter dieser Adresse sehen: http://www.ausstellung-weimarer-republik.de/Bilder/00011188.gif (accessed 15 April 2015).

[31] Dieses Bild ist z.B. hier zu sehen: http://dokufunk.org/jpeto_cache/radler_1.jpg (accessed 15 April 2015).

[32] Vgl. Benjamin, *Versuche über Brecht*, S. 104.

[33] Vgl. Herrmann, *Sang der Maschinen*, S. 103–104.

[34] Benjamin, *Versuche über Brecht*, S. 7.

[35] Ebd.

[36] Wolf-Dietrich Junghanns, "Öffentlichkeiten: Boxen, Theater und Politik," *The Brecht Yearbook* 23 (1998): S. 56–59; hier, S. 56.

[37] Albrecht Dümling, *Laßt euch nicht verführen: Brecht und die Musik* (München: Kindler, 1985), S. 249.

[38] Vgl. Steinweg, "Das Lehrstück—ein Modell," S. 106.

[39] Müller-Schöll, *Das Theater des "konstruktiven Defaitismus,"* S. 310.

[40] Vgl. dazu auch Ernst Schumacher, *Die dramatischen Versuche Bertolt Brechts 1918–1933* (Berlin: Rütten & Loening, 1955), S. 322.

[41] Vgl. auch Rainer Nägele, "Augenblicke: Eingriffe. Brechts Ästhetik der Wahrnehmung," *The Brecht Yearbook* 17 (1992): S. 29–51; hier, S. 30.

[42] Müller-Schöll, *Das Theater des "konstruktiven Defaitismus,"* S. 315.

[43] Schumacher, *Die dramatischen Versuche*, S. 323.

[44] Vgl. dazu auch Gerlinde Wellmann-Bretzigheimer, “Brechts Gedicht ‘Als ich in weißem Krankenzimmer der Charité’: Die Hilfe des Sozialismus zur Überwindung der Todesfurcht,” *Brecht-Jahrbuch* (1977): S. 30–51; hier, S. 47.

[45] Vgl. Müller-Schöll, *Das Theater des “konstruktiven Defaitismus,”* S. 326 und Nikolaus Müller-Schöll, “Brechts ‘Sterbelehre,’” in Stephen Brockman, Mathias Mayer und Jürgen Hillesheim, Hrsg., *Ende, Grenze, Schluss? Brecht und der Tod* (Würzburg: Königshausen & Neumann, 2008), S. 23–35.

[46] Vgl. zur Todesproblematik bei Brecht auch Brockman, Mayer und Hillesheim, *Ende, Grenze, Schluss?*

Dieter Goltzsche, *Die Ausnahme ist die Regel*, 1967, Kugelschreiber.

Who Is Oscar? An Unpublished Letter to Brecht from a POW in Scotland, 12 June 1918

Very little is known about Brecht's Augsburg circle of friends, and the image of those relationships is further compromised by misreading or misattribution of the few pertinent documents we have. One example of this is a letter to Brecht, written by a German prisoner of war in Scotland on 12 June 1918. The letter is published here in its entirety for the first time. Who is Oscar Lettner, the author of the letter? He was born 10 February 1893 and lived in Brecht's neighborhood. Excerpts from Lettner's diary, which is in the collections of the Bertolt Brecht Archive in Berlin, show how close and durable the Brecht-Lettner friendship was. It dates back at least to 1912, and Lettner was a frequent guest in the Brecht home. The two took bicycle tours together, went on city walks, attended festivals and fairs, and the like. The letter reflects these experiences in concentrated form.

Über den Augsburger Freundeskreis Brechts ist immer noch wenig bekannt. Umso schlimmer ist es, wenn dann die wenigen vorliegenden Dokumente falsch gelesen bzw. falschen Autoren zugeordnet werden. Ein Beispiel, das den Blick auf eine wichtige Jugendfreundschaft Brechts verstellt, ist ein Brief, der am 12. Juni 1918 aus der Kriegsgefangenschaft an Brecht nach Augsburg geschrieben wurde. Er wird hier erstmals komplett veröffentlicht. Wer ist Oscar Lettner, der Autor des Briefes? Er wurde am 10. Februar 1893 geboren und wohnte in Brechts Nachbarschaft. Auszüge aus Lettners Tagebuch, die sich im Bertolt-Brecht-Archiv in Berlin befinden, zeigen, wie eng und dauerhaft die Freundschaft mit Brecht war. Sie reicht bis mindestens 1912 zurück; Lettner ging in Brechts Wohnung ein und aus. Man unternahm gemeinsam Radtouren, spazierte durch die Stadt, besuchte das Volksfest. Lettners Brief aus der Gefangenschaft reflektiert gebündelt diese Freundschaft.

Wer ist Oscar? Ein unveröffentlichter Brief an Brecht vom 12. Juni 1918 aus schottischer Kriegsgefangenschaft

Jürgen Hillesheim

Neue Forschungsergebnisse resultieren in der Regel aus neuen Funden, neu erworbenen Manuskripten, Dokumenten oder aus philologischer Arbeit, aus Textanalysen oder dem Nachweis unbekannter Quellen und Anregungen, die Eingang in ein dichterisches Werk fanden. Dass die Wissenschaft—zugegebenermaßen wohl eher unfreiwillig—aufgrund von Nachlässigkeit und Ungenauigkeit auch imstande sein kann, relevante Zusammenhänge, die Leben und Werk eines Autoren betreffen, zu verschleiern, sogar auf falsche Fährten zu führen, sollte die Ausnahme sein. Es kommt aber vor, wie im Folgenden zu zeigen sein wird, und im Falle Brechts gar nicht einmal so selten. Mit anderen Worten: Es handelt sich dann um neue Erkenntnisse, die gerade durch Infragestellung, durch die Widerlegung und Aufhebung wissenschaftlicher Befunde zustande kommen, durch Falsifizierung eines vermeintlich bereits gewonnenen Erkenntnisstands. Wie gesagt: Das ist wohl eher ungewöhnlich; doch recht spannend und im Resultat ergiebig ist es allemal.

Eine der wichtigsten Erwerbungen der Staats- und Stadtbibliothek Augsburg für deren Brechtsammlung ist zweifellos der Teilnachlass von Brechts Bruder Walter. Möbelstücke gehörten zu ihm, das Tauf- und Konfirmationsbesteck Brechts, ein Fotoalbum seiner Familie, aber auch ein auffallend umfangreiches Konvolut von zum Zeitpunkt der Erwerbung nicht veröffentlichen Briefen: Es waren insgesamt dreißig Briefe Brechts an seine Augsburger Jugendliebe Paula Banholzer, aber auch sieben Briefe des Augsburger Freundes Fritz Gehweyer an Brecht, vier Briefe von Augsburger Mädchen und Frauen an den jungen Dichter[1] und ein singulärer Brief, der ihn in Augsburg am 12. Juni 1918 aus der Kriegsgefangenschaft erreicht hatte.

Oscar Lettner, Brief an Bertolt Brecht, Stobs (Schottland), 12. Juni 1918.

Stobs, 12. Juni 1918.
Mein lieber Eugen.

> Da bin ich nun seit über einem Jahre "geschnappt," wie der Stobser Fachausdruck für gefangen lautet. Als sogen. Oberprisoner steige ich nunmehr im Lager herum und beteilige mich als künftiger Holland-Anwärter auch schon an den beliebten Austauschgesprächen. Freilich heißt es noch mindestens ein halbes Jahr absitzen. Nun ja, vielleicht ist der große Austausch direkt nach der Heimat näher als wir glauben.—Hier herrscht das schönste Wetter seit einigen Tagen. Ich sitze täglich im Freien und lasse mich von der Sonne braun brennen. Dann schließen sich meist die Augen & Bilder aus der Heimat ziehen vorüber: unsere Jugendjahre, mit den tollen Streichen, die Tage auf dem Jakoberwall, der Plärrer, mein Urlaub . . . All diese lieben Bilder folgen rasch aufeinander & die Sehnsucht nach der Heimat wird immer brennender. Dein lieber Brief vom 6. April führte mir so recht die schöne alte Zeit vor Augen.—Dein Entschluß, Dich der Naturwissenschaft zu widmen, hat mich freudig überrascht. Es ist doch das idealste aller wissenschaftlichen Fächer. Walter wird wohl bereits ein rauhes Handwerk ergriffen haben; wünsche ihm viel Glück. Schreibe mir bitte bald wieder, kannst mir damit die größte Freude bereiten.
>
> Auf bald. Wiedersehen. Dein tr. Freund Oscar.
>
> Herzliche Grüße an Deine Eltern und innigen Dank für gesandte Rauchwaren![2]

Werner Hecht zitiert erstmals eine kurze Phrase aus dem Dokument. Er schreibt in seiner großen *Brecht-Chronik*, die 1997 erschien, Folgendes: "12. Juni, Mittwoch. Fritz Gehweyer schreibt B aus der Gefangenschaft, ihm zögen, wenn er die Augen schließt, die 'Bilder aus der Heimat' vorbei. 'Unsere Jugendjahre mit den tollen Streichen, die Tage auf dem Jakoberwall, der Plärrer, mein Urlaub . . .'"[3] Fritz Gehweyer, dem Hecht damit die Autorschaft des Briefes eindeutig zuschreibt, war einer der Freunde Brechts, die ihm in seinem ersten Freundeskreis, der um die Entstehungszeit der Schülerzeitschrift *Die Ernte* entstanden war, und zu dem beispielsweise Caspar Neher und Otto Müllereisert noch nicht gehört hatten, am nahesten stand. Mit ihm edierte Brecht die Zeitschrift; er selbst war Autor, Redakteur, der Beiträge anderer zu akquirieren hatte. Gehweyer oblag die graphische Gestaltung des Blattes und dessen Illustrierung in Jugendstil-Manier. Gemeinsam mit Brecht stellte er nach Beginn des Ersten Weltkriegs eine Reihe von Postkarten für die Augsburger Kriegsfürsorge her, bei gleicher Arbeitsteilung: Brecht trug die Texte bei, Gehweyer illustrierte. Auf ihn ist ein genauerer Blick nötig. Er wurde 1897 geboren und war der Sohn eines Kaufmanns. Die Familie betrieb in der Steingasse, mitten in Augsburg, ein Textilgeschäft. Brechts und Gehweyers Väter waren befreundet und beide Mitglied der "Augsburger Liedertafel," einem renommierten

Gesangverein. Am Realgymnasium gingen Brecht und Gehweyer auch in eine Klasse, bis letzterer im Schuljahr 1912-1913 nicht versetzt wurde. Er musste dann 1914 die Schule verlassen und zog nach München, wo er die Kunstakademie besuchte. Nicht nur die Tatsache, dass während dieser Zeit jene Postkarten für die Kriegsfürsorge entstanden, zeugt davon, dass die Bindung zwischen Brecht und Gehweyer nach wie vor eng war, sondern auch deren Briefkorrespondenz, in erster Linie die sieben schon erwähnten Briefe Gehweyers an Brecht aus den Jahren 1914 und 1915. Im August 1915 unternahmen beide eine mindestens dreiwöchige Reise ins Bregenzer Land; Brecht, offenbar völlig unbeeindruckt vom Krieg, der nun schon ein Jahr gewütet hatte, schrieb von dort zwei Postkarten an den Freund Max Hohenester nach Augsburg.[4] Die Tradition gemeinsamer Reisen oder Ausflüge sollten beide beibehalten. Auch Fritz Gehweyer wurde eingezogen, am 29. Dezember 1917 befand er sich, wie Brecht schreibt, im Range eines Unteroffiziers.[5] Im Sommer 1918 sollte es mit Brecht in den Bayerischen Wald gehen; zwei Briefe, die Brecht an seine Freundin Paula Banholzer nach Augsburg schrieb, entstanden zwischen 10. und 12. August 1918. Auch diese Texte sind vom Kriegsgeschehen völlig ungetrübt. Gehweyer allerdings kann davon, über die eigene Involvierung hinaus, nicht unberührt gewesen sein, denn seine beiden älteren Brüder blieben, wie es damals und fatalerweise auch später noch lange hieß, "auf dem Feld der Ehre": Schon am 24. April 1915 war sein 1890 geborener Bruder Georg gefallen, und nun, gerade einmal einen Monat zuvor, am 17. Juni 1918, der 1894 geborene Bruder Franz. Damit wäre Fritz Gehweyer von weiteren Fronteinsätzen freigestellt gewesen. Dies war eine offizielle Gepflogenheit, um den Familien die Gefahr zu ersparen, dass alle Söhne im Krieg umkommen. Dennoch meldete sich Fritz freiwillig, seinen Waffendienst fortzuführen, zum Unverständnis Brechts, wie die Vielzahl seiner Briefe dieser Zeit belegt, die er Caspar Neher an die Front schickte und in denen er ihn dringend aufforderte, diese existenziell bedrohliche Situation zu fliehen. Dass seine Befürchtungen im Falle seines einstmaligen *Ernte*-Mitherausgebers in besonders tragischer Weise wahr werden sollten, ist hinlänglich bekannt: Gehweyer wurde kurz nach der Reise, die er mit Brecht unternommen hatte, eingezogen und fiel am 14. Oktober 1918, kurz vor Kriegsende. Auf dem Augsburger Westfriedhof erinnert noch heute ein Gedenkstein an dieses schreckliche Schicksal der Familie.[6]

Fritz Gehweyer also war zu der Zeit, als der hier nun erstmals veröffentlichte Brief entstand, nicht in Kriegsgefangenschaft, sondern kurz danach noch mit Freund Brecht in der "Sommerfrische." Der Schreiber hingegen war, wie er selbst betont, schon über ein Jahr in Gewahrsam, in einer Zeit, in der Gehweyer noch als Unteroffizier aktiv war. Der Brief kann also nicht von ihm stammen; nichts deutet auf seine Autorschaft, rein gar nichts. Dies legen nicht nur diese leicht zu recherchierenden Fakten zwingend nahe, sondern auch die Unterschrift im Original, die vielleicht nicht auf

Anhieb zu entziffern ist, die aber gewiss nicht “Fritz” lauten kann. Hinzu kommt: Hecht hat während der Arbeit an der *Brecht-Chronik* den gesamten Nachlass von Walter Brecht gesichtet, auch aus anderen Dokumenten dieser Provenienz zitiert. Ein Blick auf die sieben originalen Briefe Gehweyers an Brecht aus den Jahren 1914 und 1915, sämtliche mit “Fritz” unterzeichnet, hätte genügen müssen, um sofort zu erkennen, dass es sich um zwei völlig verschiedene Handschriften handelt. So auch in einem anderen Fall, gleichfalls innerhalb seiner Augsburger Recherchen für die *Brecht Chronik* und mit Bezug auf den Nachlass Walter Brechts: Ebenfalls schon Erwähnung fanden Briefe von Augsburger jungen Frauen an Brecht. Auch sie lagen Werner Hecht vor, er zitiert aus allen,[7] datiert einen falsch, ihm entgeht, dass einer, unterzeichnet mit “E. Krause,” von Lilly Prem stammt (Krause war ihr Mädchenname, was bereits länger bekannt war), und die beiden Briefe, datiert auf den 30. Januar und den 27. November 1917 und mit “Rosmarie” und “Rosl” unterschrieben, weist er kurzerhand Rosa Maria Amann zu, ohne über diese Vornamen hinaus weitere Anhaltspunkte zu haben und völlig ungeachtet der Tatsache, dass die Schriftbilder auch dieser beiden Briefe völlig unterschiedlich sind.[8]

Von wem aber stammt nun jener Brief an Brecht vom 12. Juni 1918? Nicht leicht zu erkennen, weil der letzte Buchstabe eine kleine kalligraphische Verzierung aufweist, aber nach längerer Betrachtung eindeutig ist er mit “Oscar” unterzeichnet. Doch damit ist man zunächst keinen Schritt weiter, gleich die nächste Frage schließt sich nämlich an: Wer ist denn “Oscar”? Schließlich, so doch der Eindruck, gibt es keinen engeren Freund Brechts mit diesem Vornamen, weder in diesem frühen Freundeskreis zu Zeiten der *Ernte* noch in jenem berühmten späteren noch kennt man, jenseits dieser Cliquen, eine Einzelperson dieses Namens.[9] Auch Walter Brecht spricht in seinem Erinnerungsbuch in Zusammenhang mit engeren und entfernteren Freunden und Bekannten nicht von einem Oscar, obwohl er dessen Brief ja über Jahrzehnte aufbewahrt hat. Und doch muss jener Oscar Brecht nahe gestanden haben, dies erweist der Inhalt des Briefes doch recht eindeutig. Machen wir uns also auf die Suche nach Intimus “Oscar” und wenden uns zunächst der *Ernte*, aber auch Brechts frühen Tagebüchern und Briefen zu, also den BFA-Bänden 26 und 28. Damit landen wir abermals bei Werner Hecht und dessen permanentem Changieren zwischen Oberflächlichkeit und wissenschaftlichem Unvermögen.

Wir finden—in verschiedener, uneindeutiger Schreibweise—gleich zwei “Oscars” bzw. “Oskars”: Einer war Mitarbeiter der *Ernte*. Er heißt mit Familiennamen Lettner und wurde am 10. Februar 1893 geboren, er war also auf den Tag genau fünf Jahre älter als Brecht. Auch er war der Sohn eines Kaufmanns bzw. “Handlungsbevollmächtigen,” wie es im Adressbuch heißt, und genau so alt wie Georg Pfanzelt, über den Brecht ihn kennengelernt haben dürfte. Lettner wohnte in der ehemaligen Sonnenstraße Nr. 6.[10] Sie war eine Querstraße zwischen Kanalstraße und der Bleichstraße, in der Brecht wohnte; Lettner lebte also in dessen engster Nachbarschaft.[11] Wie auch Fritz Gehweyer war Lettner einige Jahre Schüler des Augsburger Realgymnasiums, ab dem Schuljahr 1904-1905, das er jedoch 1910 mit dem "Einjährigen" verließ, um städtischer Angestellter zu werden.[12] Zur Zeit der *Ernte*, 1913-1914, war Lettner bei der Augsburger Marktinspektion tätig. Bei der Schülerzeitschrift tat er sich weniger mit eigenen Texten als mit guten Französischkenntnissen hervor: Er übersetzte eine Kurzgeschichte, die offenbar als Sprachübung gedacht war.[13] Eine engere Freundschaft zwischen Brecht und Lettner ist daraus noch nicht abzuleiten; allerdings verweist Gerhard Seidel bereits 1988 in seinem Beitrag über die Schülerzeitschrift *Die Ernte* darauf, dass im Brecht-Archiv in Berlin Auszüge aus Tagebuchaufzeichnungen Lettners vorhanden seien, die "zahlreiche Begegnungen mit Brecht" dokumentieren.[14] Oscar Lettner starb 1973 in Augsburg.

Zeit, einen Blick in Brechts eigene frühe autobiografische Notate dieser Zeit zu werfen, um "gegenzulesen," in den von Werner Hecht besorgten BFA-Band 26. Wieder wird man rasch fündig, doch findet man zwar einen Oskar, aber keinen Lettner. Der Oskar des berühmten *Tagebuchs No. 10* heiße vielmehr Sternbacher. Er war der Sohn eines Fotografen und 1896 geboren. Oskar Sternbacher also war ein Mitschüler Brechts und kommt in dessen "Satirischer Biographie" *Der Geyer*, in der er nicht nur jenen Freund Georg Geyer, sondern auch eine Reihe ihm ferner stehende Schulkameraden keineswegs wohlwollend karikiert, gar nicht gut davon: "Sternbacher, der herrliche Pathetiker, dem eine schöne Schmachtlocke ins Gesicht fällt. Er gefällt mir nicht, sein Lächeln ist schmierig und nicht gut!"[15] Das hinderte Brecht aber nicht, folgt man Hechts Zuweisung, mit Sternbacher häufiger zu verkehren, gar Schach zu spielen.[16] So schreibt Brecht am 23. Mai 1913: "Nachmittags bei Oskar, der Urlaub hat, Schach gespielt. Ist ein guter Freund."[17] Einen Tag später heißt es: "Nachmittags bei Oskar."[18] Gut drei Wochen später, am 15. Juni, notiert Brecht: "Abends heim und mit Oskar Schach (Remi) gespielt."[19] Und, es waren wieder knapp zwei Wochen vergangen, am 29. Juni: "Abends zu Oskar."[20] Bleiben wir immer noch bei Hechts Zuweisung, existiert Oscar Lettner, der Mitarbeiter der *Ernte*, in Brechts frühen Tagebuchaufzeichnungen also nicht, Sternbacher allerdings findet vermeintlich noch 1918 in einem Brief Brechts Erwähnung, und zwar ausgerechnet in einem jener, die er im Sommer 1918, als er mit Gehweyer im Bayerischen Wald unterwegs war, Paula Banholzer schreibt: "Grüße meinen Freund Oskar, wenn Du ihn siehst."[21] Diesen Band 28 der BFA, vier Jahre später erschienen als Band 26 mit den frühen Tagebüchern, bearbeitete allerdings Günter Glaeser unter der Mitarbeit Wolfgang Jeskes und Paul-Gerhard Wenzlaffs, und man schränkt im Zeilenkommentar bezüglich Oskar ein: "vermutlich Oskar Sternbacher."[22]

Doch kann jener von Brecht zweimal im Abstand von mehreren Jahren so genannte "Freund" und Schachpartner tatsächlich jener Sternbacher mit der “Schmachtlocke,” und dem “schmierigen, unguten Lächeln” sein? In diesem Zusammenhang gleich eine zweite Frage: Wieso schreibt Brecht, Oskar habe zur Zeit ihres Schachspiels Urlaub gehabt, wenn Sternbacher doch ein Mitschüler war, der keinen Urlaub, keine Arbeitsbefreiung, bestenfalls Ferien haben konnte, allerdings, wie sich leicht feststellen lässt, definitiv nicht am 23. Mai 1913, als noch Schulzeit war? Diese Widersprüche sind sehr einfach zu lösen. Werner Hecht ging im Kommentar der BFA ebenso vor, wie bei der Zuweisung unseres Briefes an Fritz Gehweyer. Er ermittelte—durchaus korrekt—den Vornamen jenes nur einmal erwähnten und dabei geschmähten Sternbacher und übertrug dessen Nachnamen dann einfach auf den anderen, in sehr positiver Stimmung noch dreimal genannten “Oskar,” auf niemand anderen als Brechts guten Schachfreund und *Ernte*-Mitarbeiter Oscar Lettner, der also fälschlicherweise von Lettner zu Sternbacher wurde und damit gleichzeitig eine ganze Reihe seiner Erwähnungen seitens Brecht einbüßt. Er kommt, folgt man der BFA, einfach seltener vor, man verliert ihn leicht aus dem Blick. Erkennt man aber, dass Lettner gemeint ist, ergibt sich ein schlüssiges und einheitliches Bild zwischen all jenen Erwähnungen Oskars, den Brecht mit “k” schreibt, in Zusammenfassung mit der *Ernte*, in den frühen Tagebüchern und in jenem Brief aus dem Jahr 1918. Es ist eine Stimmung, die genau derjenigen des Briefes entspricht, der von Oscar Lettner—er selbst schreibt seinen Vornamen mit “c”—stammt. Auch wird so klar, warum Brecht in Zusammenhang mit dem Schachspiel bei einer Gelegenheit erwähnt, dass Oskar Urlaub habe: Im Gegensatz zu Mitschüler Sternbacher war er zu dieser Zeit bereits bei der Stadt beschäftigt und hatte sich eben einige Tage frei genommen. Oskar Sternbacher wiederum gibt es nicht in Brechts näherem Umfeld. Mit ihm hatte der junge Autor nichts zu schaffen. Ein einziges Mal nur erwähnt er ihn; und dies auch noch abfällig, benannt lediglich mit seinem Nachnamen.

Das Dokument, das diese Theorien gänzlich außer Zweifel stellt, liegt in Berlin, es handelt sich um jene bis heute gleichfalls nicht veröffentlichten Auszüge aus den Tagebuchaufzeichnungen des jungen Oscar Lettner.[23] Sie umfassen ca. fünfzig Manuskriptseiten und einen Berichtszeittraum vom 1. Januar 1912 und 31. Dezember 1919. Während, trotz größerer Fehlstellen, die Jahre 1912 und 1913 und das erste Halbjahr 1914 im Wesentlichen kontinuierlich dokumentiert sind, reißt die Überlieferung am 30. August 1914 ab. Sie beginnt erst wieder mit dem 15. November 1919, es sind also nur Aufzeichnungen über die letzten sechs Wochen dieses Jahres überliefert. Die Notate sind nicht spektakulär; sie zeugen gar von einer gewissen Pedanterie, wenn zum Beispiel stereotyp an mehreren Tagen hintereinander Formeln wie “Den ganzen Tag in der Sparkasse” zu lesen sind. Dennoch gewähren sie nicht uninteressante Einblicke in das Leben eines jungen Mannes, der das Gymnasium verlassen hatte, nun in der Verwaltung beschäftigt ist, sich aber dennoch mit Goethes *Faust* befasst[24] und tatsächlich recht gut Französisch gekonnt haben muss,[25] eine Kompetenz, von der, wie erwähnt, Brecht für seine Schülerzeitschrift *Die Ernte* profitierte. Dennoch passierte auch Einiges, durchaus auch Spektakuläres, von dem Brecht mit Sicherheit Kenntnis genommen haben dürfte. Am 13. März 1913 notiert Oscar Lettner sehr aufgeregt:

> Abends erfuhr ich von Georg Zeitler, daß Marie im englischen Institut dimittiert worden sei. Kurz darauf traf ich Walter Brecht, der diese Äußerung bestätigte. Letzterer gab mir auch zu, dass Marie einen Selbstmordversuch machen wollte, in dem sie sich ins Wasser zu stürzen beabsichtigte.[26]

Es handelte sich dabei nicht etwa um Rosa Maria Amann, Brechts spätere Freundin, die gleichfalls das Englische Institut in der Frauentorstraße besuchen sollte, sondern um, wie Lettner in einer Randnotiz angibt, eine Marie Lehner.[27] Diese war Lettners Schwarm, minuziös hält er in seinen Aufzeichnungen jede Begegnung mit ihr fest; ganz verschämt kürzt er häufig ihren Namen mit den Anfangsbuchstaben ab. Dies sind interessante Einblicke in den Dunstkreis des noch sehr jungen Brecht, in eine Zeit, über die man sehr wenig weiß; Einblicke, die sogar als amüsant bezeichnet werden dürfen, da Fräulein Lehner ihre Pläne in jener Phase exogener Depression ja glücklicherweise nicht in die Tat umsetzen sollte. Sie wird später noch öfters erwähnt; Brecht muss sie definitiv gekannt haben. Doch warum wohl ist sie der Schule verwiesen worden? Was hatte sie angestellt, hatte es möglicherweise einen moralischen Fehltritt gegeben? Einen solchen wie den, der Brechts Jugendliebe Paula Banholzer, die von ihm schwanger war, später ins allgäuer Exil treiben sollte? Marie Lehners in Betracht gezogene pathetische Reaktion deutet darauf hin. Doch Marie, in Brechts Frühwerk dann Synonym für die Austauschbarkeit der Frauen, überlebte ja und scheidet somit als zweite Vorlage neben Shakespeares Ophelia für Brechts Gedicht "Vom ertrunkenen Mädchen" aus,[28] es sei denn, der junge Autor dachte in der Fiktion das Schicksal des jungen Mädchens in unerfreulicher Konsequenz fort.

Eines stellen die Tagebuchaufzeichnungen außer Zweifel: Brechts guter Freund Georg Pfanzelt ist auch eine enge Bezugsperson Oscar Lettners; niemand anderes wird namentlich so oft erwähnt wie er. Und Brecht selbst? Auch er ist erstaunlich oft präsent, insgesamt kommt er, über den Berichtszeitraum gleichmäßig verteilt, fünfundzwanzig Mal vor, wobei fast alle Erwähnungen ein Treffen zwischen ihm und Lettner dokumentieren.[29] Erstmals tritt er im Notat vom 2. März 1912 in Erscheinung, die wohl früheste gesicherte Erwähnung Brechts in einem Dokument dieser Art.[30] Auch hier wirkt vieles banal, stereotyp; die Eintragungen sind in vielen Fällen tatsächlich nichts als das Festhalten eines Treffens in Form von drei, vier Worten. Man erfährt aber auch sehr Wissenswertes, Dinge, die, neben dem kontinuierlichen Schachspiel beider, auf die enge dieser Freundschaft deuten, so etwa, das Lettner Brecht morgens häufig auf seinem Schulweg begleitete.[31] Oder am 7. April 1912: "Nachmittags . . . mit Eugen und Pfanzelt kleinen Spaziergang gemacht."[32] Noch ergiebiger werden die Informationen mit dem Frühjahr des Jahres 1913. So notiert Lettner am 21. April: "Eugen kam dann zu mir in die Wohnung und wir unterhielten uns bis abends."[33] Die nächsten beiden Tage spielten sie dann, worauf auch Hecht verweist, ausgiebig Schach, Lettner am 24. April sehr stolz: "Um 5 h heim und mit Eugen 3 Partien Schach gespielt, von denen ich 2 gewann." Dann schließt sich unmittelbar an: "Marie ging heute abend absichtlich zweimal an meinem Haus vorbei und lächelte herüber."[34] Wie schön also, dass sie Wochen zuvor nicht ernst gemacht hatte. Genau einen Monat später begleitete Lettner Brecht zu einem Einkauf: "Nachmittgas zuerst mit Eugen in die Stadt, da er sich eine Mundharmonika kaufte."[35] Dies ist ein sehr frühes Zeugnis für Brechts Affinität zur Musik, die auch immer wieder in dessen eigenen Notaten dieser Zeit, dem *Tagebuch No. 10*, zum Ausdruck kommt. Die Mundharmonika zählte im Übrigen zu den Instrumenten, die gelegentlich bei den Ausflügen des Kreises um Brecht mitgeführt wurden.[36] Am 11. September 1913 machte Lettner mit Brecht eine "kleine Radtour,"[37] und eine knappe Woche später ist nun wirklich Wichtiges zu vermelden, Brechts Busenfreund dieser Zeit, Georg Pfanzelt betreffend, ohne den das Frühwerk in weiten Bereichen anders aussehen würde. Es muss ein schlimmes Zerwürfnis zwischen den beiden gegeben haben, in diesem Alter nicht unbedingt selten, aber dennoch erwähnenswert. Lettner konstatiert jedenfalls in einer Randnotiz erleichtert: "Eugen und Pfanzelt haben sich in den letzten Tagen wieder gefunden."[38] Diese sollte offenbar von Dauer sein. Denn am 19. Oktober gehen, wie auch Hecht dokumentiert, alle drei gemeinsam auf die Lechhauser Kirchweih.[39] Doch keineswegs schlug man dort über die Stränge, denn: "Dann zu Eugen in die Wohnung mit Pfanzelt und uns dort unterhalten; Pfanzelt spielte Klavier."[40] Dies fand nicht etwa in Brechts Mansarde, die er seit 1910 bewohnte, sondern im Wohnzimmer der Familie, in dem ein Klavier stand, statt.[41] Diese Harmonie sollte anhalten. Zehn Monate später, im August 1914, berichtet Lettner: "Abends mit Pfanzelt und Brecht kleine Runde um die Bleich und an den Königsplatz."[42] Der Weg scheint sie also an diesem Tag aus der beschaulichen Jakober-Vorstadt bis über das Zentrum Augsburgs hinaus und wieder zurück geführt zu haben.

Diese Fülle an Begegnungen zwischen Brecht und Oscar Lettner, zu denen auch sämtliche gehören, die Brecht in seinem *Tagebuch No. 10* mit einem Freund namens "Oscar" oder "Oskar" erwähnt, zeigen, dass es sich hier tatsächlich um eine recht enge, durchaus als innig zu bezeichnende und langwährende Jugendfreundschaft Brechts handelt, die durch Hechts Fehlleistungen über Jahrzehnte aus dem Fokus der Aufmerksamkeit gedrängt wurde. Lettner war kein begabter Künstler, kein angehender Intellektueller, gewiss auch kein "Bürgerschreck," sondern ein braver Mitarbeiter des, wie es heute heißt, "öffentlichen Dienstes." Doch der doch um fünf Jahre Ältere hielt den Kontakt zu Brecht und dessen Kreis; ebenso wie Fritz Gehweyer, dem der Brief ursprünglich zugeschrieben wurde. Scheinbar fungierte im Falle Lettners Georg Pfanzelt, ebenfalls in Brechts enger Nachbarschaft wohnend, immer wieder als Bindeglied, er, der ja als einziger des engeren Kreises keine weiterführende akademische Ausbildung absolviert hatte, dem Brecht allerdings, nicht zuletzt wegen seiner musikalischen Qualitäten, seines "Verquälten,"[43] aber auch Obszön-Diabolischen besonders zugetan war. Im *Baal* wie auch in Gedichten der *Hauspostille* wird er zu einer besonderen Art der Figur eines Weisen stilisiert.

Ein anderer Gesichtspunkt kommt hinzu. Die vorliegenden Dokumente der Tagebücher Lettners und Brechts und Aussagen seiner Freunde und Kameraden in Werner Frischs und Kurt Walter Obermeiers Dokumentation *Brecht in Augsburg* belegen, dass Brecht in seiner späten Kindheit und frühen Jugend ein begeisterter Schachspieler war, eine Passion die, obwohl auch im Exil dokumentiert, sich dann ein wenig legen sollte. Mit seinem Vater spielte Brecht Schach, auch mit Franz Xaver Schiller, Adolf Seitz, Stephan Bürzle und anderen; zu diesem Kreis gehörte aber auch Oscar Lettner. Es ist die Rede davon, dass im Umfeld der Schule ein regelrechter kleiner Schachverein gegründet wurde, dessen "Heimstätte" allerdings das Brechtsche Wohnzimmer war.[44] Er hatte zunächst den Namen *Amicitia*, dann hieß er *Die lustigen Steinschwinger*. Er gab eine kleine Zeitschrift heraus, die recht genau beschrieben, jedoch verschollen ist.[45] Sie wäre dann, wenn man so will, eine Art themengebundener Vorstufe von Brechts und Gehweyers Schülerzeitschrift *Die Ernte* gewesen. Wie dem auch gewesen sein mag; fest steht, dass in dieses Umfeld wohl auch Oscar Lettner gehört, der in den Erinnerungen des Zeitzeugen vielleicht deshalb ein wenig aus den Augen geraten ist, weil er die Schule frühzeitig verlassen hatte.

Oscar Lettners Brief an Brecht vom 12. Juni 1918 hält sehr konkrete Informationen bereit. Lettner leistete seit längerem Kriegsdienst. Keineswegs ausgeschlossen ist, dass auch er, wie viele andere, sich freiwillig gemeldet hatte. Doch, im Gegensatz zu vielen anderen und auch Neher, der fast vier Jahre im Einsatz war, wie Julius Bingen und Fritz Gehweyer, hatte er Glück. Zwar kam auch er nicht ganz unbeschadet davon; er wurde als Mitglied des vierundzwanzigsten Infanterieregiments, zwölfter Kompagnie der Bayerischen Armee, am 17. Juli 1916 als leicht verwundet gemeldet.[46] Doch nun jedenfalls, am 12. Juni 1918, kann Lettner in seinem Brief berichten, dass er schon über ein Jahr in Gefangenschaft ist, in diese also spätestens Mitte 1917 geraten war. Mit anderen Worten: er war nun in Sicherheit, und es ging ihm während dieser Zeit, der Brief verrät es trotz Zensur, trotz allen Heimwehs gewiss nicht sonderlich schlecht. Geradezu entspannt wirkt der Schreiber, sogar ein wenig von fatalistischem Humor bestimmt, trotz seines Wunsches, gerne wieder nach Hause zurückzukehren.

Untergebracht war er in Schottland, im Kriegsgefangenenlager Stobs. Dies war das zentrale schottische Internierungslager, gelegen bei Hawick in Südschottland. Zuvor als Übungs-Camp benutzt, war es im November 1914, also nicht allzu lange nach Beginn des Ersten Weltkriegs, als Kriegsgefangenenlager eingerichtet worden. Mit einer geplanten Kapazität von zwölftausend Internierten sollte es eines der größten Lager in Großbritannien werden; mehr als 4500 Kriegsgefangene waren aber nie in Stobs untergebracht. Das gesamte Lager war von einem Stacheldrahtzaun umgeben und nachts beleuchtet. Es bestand aus vier Camps mit jeweils vierzig Wohnhütten der Ausmaße sechs mal sechsunddreißig Meter, die im Durchschnitt mit dreiunddreißig Insassen belegt waren. In den Abteilungsküchen und Backstuben arbeiteten nur inhaftierte deutsche Köche und Bäcker, auch verrichteten deutsche Ärzte und Pfleger ihren Dienst. Am südlichen Ende des Lagers befand sich ein Feldlazarett. Auf dem kleinen Friedhof, der angelegt worden war, befanden sich am Ende des Krieges sechsunddreißig Gräber.[47]

Brecht selbst hatte einmal ein Kriegsgefangenenlager kurz nach Beginn des Krieges und buchstäblich “von außen” kennengelernt. Als nämlich in Augsburgs Umfeld schon nach wenigen Tagen mehrere tausend französische Kriegsgefangene untergebracht werden mussten, reaktivierte man das Militärlager “Lager Lechfeld,” ca. zwanzig Kilometer von Augsburg entfernt. Brecht machte mit seinem Bruder Walter dorthin einen Ausflug mit dem Fahrrad, um sich das Lager anzuschauen und konnte gar durch den Zaun mit Gefangenen sprechen.[48] Er schrieb darüber einen Zeitungsbeitrag, der am 27. August 1914 in den *Augsburger Neuesten Nachrichten* erschien.[49]

“Oberprisoner” nennt Lettner sich in seinem Brief. Der Kontext deutet darauf hin, dass bei Gefangenen über längere Zeit, zu denen er nach über einem Jahr wohl gehörte, Austauschmaßnahmen vorgesehen waren, die offenbar in Holland vollzogen wurden, und Lettner darauf hofft. Er geht zwar davon aus, dass das noch dauere; Brechts bereits zitierter Brief vom 10. August 1918, in dem er Paula Banholzer auffordert, seinem Freund Oscar Grüße auszurichten, verrät allerdings, dass Lettner zu dieser offenbar schon wieder länger in Augsburg verweilte, seine Entlassung also nicht allzu lange nach Verfassen seines Briefes an Brecht stattgefunden haben muss. Dieser ist ein Antwortbrief; Brecht seinerseits hatte an Lettner, so die genaue Angabe, am 6. April 1918 geschrieben, mitten in einer Zeit, in der Briefe an seinen Freund Neher an der Front seine Korrespondenz dominieren. Was wird er wohl Lettner in jenem Brief, der nicht erhalten ist, geschrieben haben? Er wird ihn kaum wie Neher unter Druck gesetzt haben.[50] Dem nüchternen Brecht war ja sehr wohl bewusst, dass Lettner in Stobs erst einmal in Sicherheit ist, seine Entlassung jedoch einen neuerlichen Fronteinsatz ermöglicht hätte. So also hat er offenbar von anderem, zum Beispiel von seinem begonnenen Medizinstudium berichtet. Dass Lettner die Vermutung äußert, Brechts Bruder Walter sei wohl inzwischen Handwerker, mag auf den ersten Blick hin überraschen;

schließlich weiß man doch, dass er Ingenieur wurde, bei den Haindlschen Papierfabriken begann und später in Darmstadt als erster deutscher Professor für Papiertechnologie Karriere machte. Doch wie Lettner selbst hatte Walter, ganz im Gegensatz zu seinem Bruder, zeitweise schulische Probleme, er berichtet davon in seinen Memoiren.[51] Lettner konnte also nach der recht langen Zeit der Trennung durchaus vermuten, dass auch Walter Brecht die weiterführende Schule, in seinem Falle die Oberrealschule, verlassen haben könnte.

Auch hatte Brecht in seinem Brief an Lettner scheinbar über gemeinsame "alte Augsburger Zeiten" geschrieben, was den Empfänger offenkundig in Wehmut versetzte. Mit dem Jakoberwall und dem Plärrer nennt er in seiner Reminiszenz gleich zwei Orte, die in Brechts "Augsburger Topografie" von Bedeutung sind. Dass Lettner in diesem Zusammenhang besonders einen seiner Urlaube hervorhebt, deutet darauf hin, dass er in diesem viel Zeit mit Brecht verbracht haben muss, wann auch immer das gewesen sein mag. War er vielleicht einmal mit auf einer mehrtägigen Tour, die Brecht mit Freunden ja des Öfteren machte? Der Schluss seines Briefes belegt, wie nahe Lettner Brecht und seiner Familie stand. Gar Zigaretten oder Tabak hat man ihm in die Gefangenschaft geschickt, um ihm die Zeit zu erleichtern; so wie man es bei einem guten Freund macht, der Oscar Lettner ohne Zweifel war.

GEBR. MARTIN
INH. K. RESSLER

Anmerkungen

[1] Bertolt Brecht, *Liebste Bi. Briefe an Paula Banholzer*, Helmut Gier und Jürgen Hillesheim, Hrsg. (Frankfurt am Main: Suhrkamp, 1992); Jürgen Hillesheim und Stephen Parker, "'Ebenso hieß das Mädchen nicht andauernd Marie': Vier (fast) unbekannte Frauenbriefe an Bertolt Brecht aus den Jahren 1916 bis 1918," *German Life and Letters* 64.4 (2011): S. 536–551.

[2] Abdruck mit freundlicher Genehmigung der Staats- und Stadtbibliothek Augsburg.

[3] Werner Hecht, *Brecht Chronik: 1898–1956* (Frankfurt am Main: Suhrkamp, 1997), S. 57.

[4] Hierzu Jürgen Hillesheim und Erdmut Wizisla, "'Was macht Deine Dichteritis?' Bertolt Brecht im Bregenzer Land," *The Brecht Yearbook* 26 (2001), S. 3–13; Brecht, "*Wie ich mir aus einem Roman gemerkt habe . . .*" *Früheste Dichtungen,* Jürgen Hillesheim, Hrsg. (Frankfurt am Main: Suhrkamp, 2006), S. 199, 202–203.

[5] BFA 28, 40.

[6] Zu Fritz Gehweyer ausführlich vgl. Bertolt Brecht, *Die Ernte: Die Augsburger Schülerzeitschrift und ihr wichtigster Autor*, Jürgen Hillesheim und Uta Wolf, Hrsg. (Augsburg: Maro, 1997), S. 32–36.

[7] Hecht, *Brecht Chronik*, S. 42–55.

[8] Hierzu ausführlich Hillesheim und Parker, "'Ebenso hieß das Mädchen nicht andauernd Marie,'" S. 540–541.

[9] Für Hinweise und Recherchen in diesem Zusammenhang, den engeren und erweiterten Freundeskreis des jungen Brecht und Lettners Militärzeit betreffend, sei Dr. Michael Friedrichs und Wolfgang Mayer, Staats- und Stadtbibliothek Augsburg, herzlich gedankt.

[10] Sie gibt es unter diesem Namen nicht mehr; eine heutige Sonnenstraße in Augsburg befindet sich in einem anderen, recht weit entfernten Stadtteil.

[11] *Adreßbuch der Stadt Augsburg für das Jahr 1913* (Augsburg: Stadtmagistrat, 1912), S. 171, 285–286.

[12] Bertolt Brecht, *Die Ernte*, S. 37.

[13] Ebd., S. 62.

[14] Gerhard Seidel, "Die Augsburger Schülerzeitschrift *Die Ernte*. Zu den ersten Veröffentlichungen Bertolt Brechts. Mit einer Bibliographie," *Zeitschrift für deutsche Philologie* 107.2 (1988): 233–253; hier, S. 237.

[15] BFA 26, 24.

[16] BFA 26, 498.

[17] BFA 26, 15.

[18] Ebd.

[19] BFA 26, 35.

[20] BFA 26, 48.

[21] BFA 28, 64.

[22] BFA 28, 589.

[23] Ich danke Prof. Dr. Erdmut Wizisla für die entgegenkommende und unkomplizierte Bereitstellung dieser Materialien.

[24] Tagebuch Oscar Lettner, 24. November 1912, BBA Z 30/33; 19. Dezember 1912, BBA Z 30/35.

[25] Tagebuch Oscar Lettner, 7. September 1913, BBA Z 4/84.

[26] Tagebuch Oscar Lettner, 13. März 1913, BBA Z 4/80.

[27] Ebd.

[28] BFA 11, 109.

[29] Hecht, der Lettners Tagebuchauszüge auswertete, beschränkt sich darauf, in seiner *Chronik* ganze sieben Begegnungen festzuhalten, darunter nicht unbedingt die interessantesten. Er beginnt erst mit dem 24. April 1913, um zu betonen, dass Lettner mehrere Tage hintereinander mit Brecht Schach gespielt habe; vgl. Hecht, *Brecht Chronik*, S. 15, 25–26, 30, 32, 79–80.

[30] Tagebuch Oscar Lettner, 2. März 1912, BBA Z 30/25.

[31] Tagebuch Oscar Lettner, 8., 18., und 22. März 1912, BBA Z 30/25, 26.

[32] Tagebuch Oscar Lettner, 7. April 1912; BBA 30/28.

[33] Tagebuch Oscar Lettner, 21. April 1913, BBA Z 4/81; am 23. April dieselbe Formulierung.

[34] Ebd.

[35] Tagebuch Oscar Lettner, 24. April 1913, BBA Z 4/82.

[36] Walter Brecht, *Unser Leben in Augsburg, damals: Erinnerungen* (Frankfurt am Main: Suhrkamp, 1984), S. 235.

[37] Tagebuch Oscar Lettner, 11. September 1913, BBA Z 4/84; vgl. auch Hecht, *Brecht Chronik*, S. 25.

[38] Tagebuch Oscar Lettner, 16. September 1913, BBA Z 4/85.

[39] Hecht, *Brecht Chronik*, S. 26.

[40] Tagebuch Oscar Lettner, 19. Oktober 1913, BBA Z 4/86.

[41] Walter Brecht, *Unser Leben in Augsburg*, S. 51.

[42] Tagebuch Oscar Lettner, 27. August 1914, BBA Z 4/89.

[43] Walter Brecht, *Unser Leben in Augsburg*, S. 238.

[44] Walter Brecht, *Unser Leben in Augsburg*, S. 233.

[45] Werner Frisch und Kurt Walter Obermeier, *Brecht in Augsburg: Erinnerungen, Dokumente, Texte, Fotos* (Berlin: Aufbau, 1975), S. 44–45.

[46] Preußen, Armee, *Armeeverordnungsblatt/Verlustliste* Nr. 1054, S. 13458.

[47] Stefan Manz, *Migranten und Internierte: Deutsche in Glasgow, 1864–1918* (Stuttgart: Steiner, 2003), S. 78–82.

[48] Walter Brecht, *Unser Leben in Augsburg*, S. 219.

[49] Jürgen Hillesheim, "'Spottlust und viel ehrliches Mitleid.' Bertolt Brechts 'Ah . . . nous pauvres,'" *German Life and Letters* 61.3 (2008): S. 311–323, hier 315–319.

50 Z. B. BFA 28, 45, 54–55, und 57.

[51] Walter Brecht, *Unser Leben in Augsburg*, S. 222–224.

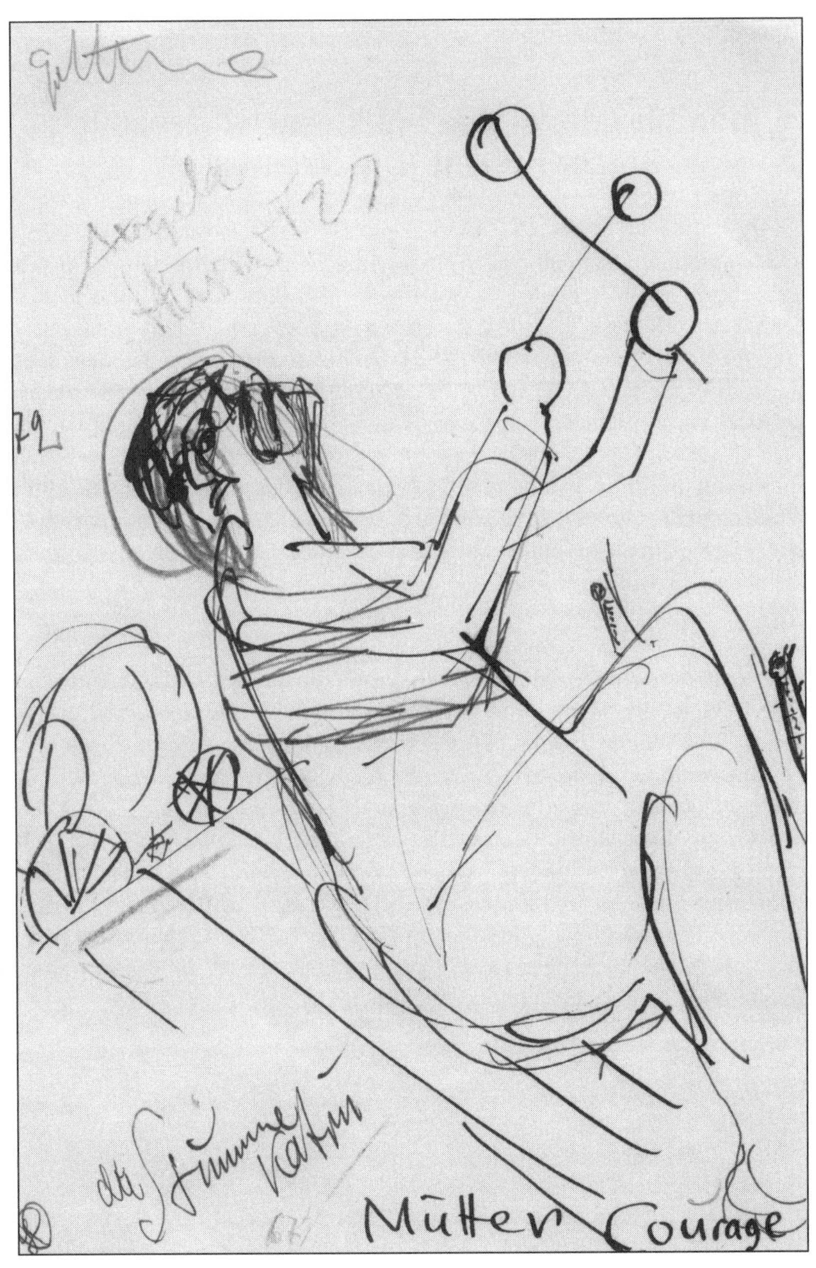

Dieter Goltzsche, *Mutter Courage (Die stumme Kattrin)*, 1967, Tusche.

“don’t lay down that book, you who read it”: Brecht’s Poem “Die Nachtlager”

The common denominator of virtually all scholarly interpretations of this 1931 poem is its treatment as a critique of “reformism,” a concept that served as a rallying cry of the German Communist Party (KPD) in its battles with the Social Democratic Party (SPD) in the interwar era. The poem does not convey the one-dimensional message attributed to it, nor are its social-political themes identical to those of other Brecht works from this time. From a historical perspective, there are grounds for differentiating between reformism as political strategy and reformism as charitable work. The latter was a component of the KPD’s social agenda, which is easily demonstrable. It is more difficult to answer the question of why Brecht never published the poem.

Gemeinsamer Nenner nahezu aller Interpretationen des Gedichts aus dem Jahr 1931 ist die Formel von der Kritik am “Reformismus,” ein Begriff, der als Kampfbegriff der KPD gegen die konkurrierende Sozialdemokratie von zentraler Bedeutung war. Das Gedicht vermittelt weder die eindeutige Botschaft, die allgemein unterstellt wird, noch ist sein Thema mit den sozialpolitischen Motiven anderer Dichtungen Brechts aus dieser Zeit identisch. Historisch besteht Anlass, zwischen dem “Reformismus” als politischer Strategie und karitativer Hilfeleistung zu differenzieren. Letztere war Bestandteil auch der Sozialpolitik der KPD, wie sich leicht belegen lässt. Nicht überzeugend beantwortet ist bislang auch die Frage, warum Brecht sein Gedicht selbst nie veröffentlicht hat.

"leg das buch nicht nieder, der du das liesest, mensch": Brechts Gedicht "Die Nachtlager"

Klaus-Dieter Krabiel

die nachtlager

ich höre, dass in newyork
an der ecke der 26. strasse und des broadway
während der wintermonate jeden abend ein mann steht
und den obdachlosen, die sich ansammeln
durch bitten an vorübergehende ein nachtlager verschafft.

die welt wird dadurch nicht anders
die beziehungen zwischen den menschen bessern sich nicht
das zeitalter der ausbeutung wird dadurch nicht verkürzt
aber einige männer haben ein nachtlager
der wind wird von ihnen eine nacht lang abgehalten
der ihnen zugedachte schnee fällt auf die strasse.

leg das buch nicht nieder, der du das liesest, mensch.

einige menschen haben ein nachtlager
der wind wird von ihnen eine nacht lang abgehalten
der ihnen zugedachte schnee fällt auf die strasse
aber die welt wird dadurch nicht anders
die beziehungen zwischen den menschen bessern sich dadurch nicht
das zeitalter der ausbeutung wird dadurch nicht verkürzt.[1]

Das Gedicht "Die Nachtlager," dessen Entstehung allgemein um 1931 angesetzt wird, gehört zu den bekannten, häufig analysierten Gedichten Brechts. Die Episode, von der eingangs berichtet wird ("ich höre, dass . . ."), stammt aus einer literarischen Quelle, aus Theodore Dreisers Roman *Sister Carrie* (1900), der 1929 unter dem Titel *Schwester Carrie* im Paul Zsolnay Verlag (Wien) in deutscher Übersetzung erschienen war.[2] Diese Übertragung lag Brecht vor, auf sie bezog er sich.[3] Dreiser (1871–1945), einer der bedeutendsten amerikanischen Erzähler in der ersten Hälfte des 20. Jahrhunderts und Hauptvertreter des Naturalismus in den USA, war vor allem an den Konflikten interessiert, in die der Mensch—vor allem in den Großstädten—im harten Daseinskampf gerät. Die Themen seiner Romane kreisen um Sexualität, Geld, Macht und um daraus resultierende Verbrechen. Im Dezember 1928 hatte Brecht in seiner Antwort auf die Rundfrage der Zeitschrift *Das Tage-Buch* nach den besten Büchern des Jahres Dreisers Roman *Der Titan: Trilogie der Begierde*, der gerade in deutscher Übersetzung erschienen war, etwas abschätzig als "Unterhaltungsliteratur" bezeichnet.[4] Aber die schonungslos kritisch geschilderten Fakten der amerikanischen Realität, in der nur der Stärkste sich behaupten kann, und die hohe Authentizität in der Darstellung der Lebensverhältnisse in den USA fanden durchaus Brechts Interesse. Dies offensichtlich noch in den 1950er Jahren.[5]

Der frühe Roman *Sister Carrie*, dessen Handlung im späten 19. Jahrhundert angesiedelt ist, trug dem Verfasser Probleme mit der Zensur ein. Das Leben der Titelfigur verstieß gegen die moralischen Normen der Zeit; es untergrub den allgemeinen Konsens, wonach nur harte Arbeit und moralisches Verhalten zum Erfolg im Leben führen könne. Die Toleranz von Immoralität in Dreisers Roman war eine Novität in der amerikanischen Literatur. Die Titelfigur Caroline Meeber, auch "Carrie" genannt, die achtzehnjährig aus dem ländlichen Wisconsin nach Chicago geht, dort zunächst—nach gescheiterten Versuchen, Arbeit zu finden—als Liebhaberin von Männern lebt, wird am Ende eine sehr erfolgreiche, gefeierte Schauspielerin. Ganz anders der anfangs gutsituierte George W. Hurstwood, ihr letzter Liebhaber. Dass er am Schluss auf die Hilfe des "Bettenvermittlers" angewiesen ist, wird als Folge seines persönlichen Versagens dargestellt, Folge auch einer kriminellen Verfehlung. Die Konsequenz ist sein völliger sozialer Absturz. Er erkrankt schließlich an Lungenentzündung und nimmt sich am Ende das Leben.

Auf Hurstwood bezieht sich die Überschrift des fünfundvierzigsten Kapitels des Romans "Seltsam-wechselnde Schicksale des Armen" ("Curious Shifts of the Poor"), aus dem die von Brecht aufgegriffene Episode stammt. Gegen Abend, "wenn der Broadway gewöhnlich am interessantesten aussieht," heißt es in dem Kapitel,

> nahm an der Ecke der Sechsundzwanzigsten Straße und des Broadway . . . unveränderlich ein Mann seinen Standplatz ein. Dies war die Stunde, zu der die Theater ihre Gäste empfangen . . .
>
> Dieser eigentümliche Mann an der Ecke war ein früherer Soldat, der Pietist geworden. Nachdem er selbst unter den Peitschenhieben der Entbehrung, Folge unserer Gesellschaftsordnung, gelitten, war er zum Schlusse gelangt, daß es seine Pflicht gegen Gott, wie er ihn auffasste, war, seinen Brüdern zu helfen. Er wählte eine ganz seltsame Art der Hilfe. Allen heimatlosen Wanderern, die sich hier an ihn wandten, besorgte er ein Lager für die Nacht. Obgleich er kaum das Nötige besaß, sich selbst ein ordentliches Heim zu schaffen.
>
> Nachdem er, umbrandet von Lust, seinen Platz bezogen, pflegte er dazustehen, seine hagere Gestalt in einen großen Mantelkragen

> gehüllt, den Kopf von einem breitkrempigen Schlapphut geschützt. So erwartete er die Bittsteller, die irgendwie von seiner Wohltätigkeit vernommen.[6]

An dem Abend, von dem im Roman die Rede ist, strömen immer mehr Bedürftige herbei. Der Mann, den sie den "Kapitän" nennen, spricht die Vorübergehenden an und bittet um ein paar Cents für jeden Einzelnen. Schlechten Gewissens, der Not gehorchend, gesellt sich auch Hurstwood zu ihnen. Er hält sich in der Nähe der Theater am Broadway auf, weil er hofft, dort Caroline zu treffen, von der er Hilfe erwartet—vergeblich, wie sich bald zeigt. Für nicht weniger als 137 Schicksalsgenossen hat der Kapitän schließlich das Geld gesammelt und führt die Menschen dann "zu einem Hotel garni in der Achten Straße,"[7] wo sie ein kärgliches Unterkommen für die Nacht finden.

Die ersten fünf Zeilen des Gedichts, ein einziger, weit ausschwingender Satz, wie das gesamte Gedicht in prosanaher Sprechweise verfasst, knüpfen unmittelbar, teilweise wörtlich, an diese Episode an. Offenbar erkannte Brecht eine Parallele zwischen der von Dreiser geschilderten Situation in den USA des späten neunzehnten Jahrhunderts und den von der Wirtschaftskrise, von Arbeitslosigkeit und Massenelend geprägten Verhältnissen in Deutschland um 1930. Die folgenden Strophen sind ein zweigeteilter, doppelter Kommentar zur referierten Romanepisode. Er besteht aus zwei Sechszeilern (Zeilen 6–11 und 13–18), jede der beiden Strophen aus zweimal drei parataktisch aneinandergereihten Versen, die in einander widersprechender Weise Stellung beziehen zur Episode des Romans. Die technisch-inhaltliche Besonderheit des Gedichts besteht darin, dass die beiden Dreizeiler der ersten Strophe (a–c / d–f) in der zweiten Strophe wiederholt werden, allerdings in umgekehrter Reihenfolge (d–f / a–c), wobei die bedeutungsschwere adversative Konjunktion "aber" vom Beginn der Zeile d ("a b e r einige männer haben ein nachtlager") nun an den Anfang der Zeile a rückt: "a b e r die welt wird dadurch nicht anders." Diese im lyrischen Werk Brechts eher seltene Formstruktur[8] ist mehrfach und hinreichend präzise beschrieben worden. Deshalb können sich die folgenden Bemerkungen auf die Sinnstruktur des Gedichts konzentrieren.

Brecht stellt zwei gegenläufige Sichtweisen auf die Bettenvermittlung gegenüber in Form zweier—für sich genommen unwiderlegbarer—Tatsachen: der einen, dass durch die Bemühungen des Bettenvermittlers "die welt . . . nicht anders / . . . / das zeitalter der ausbeutung . . . nicht verkürzt" werde (Zeilen 6–8), und der anderen, dass "einige männer . . . ein nachtlager" haben und "der ihnen zugedachte schnee . . . auf die strasse" fällt (Zeilen 9–11). Durch die Umkehr der beiden Dreizeiler in der letzten Strophe rücken die Zeilen "die welt wird dadurch nicht anders / . . . / das zeitalter der ausbeutung wird dadurch nicht verkürzt" ans Ende des Gedichts und erhalten auf diese Weise den größeren Nachdruck. Die

Gewichtung beider gegenläufiger Tatsachen ergibt sich somit unmittelbar und ausschließlich aus der Umkehr der ursprünglichen Versfolge im zweiten Sechszeiler. Was das Gedicht mitteilt, hängt in besonderem Maße von dessen poetisch raffinierter Gestalt ab. Es läuft auf die Feststellung hinaus, dass karitative Hilfeleistung, so wohltätig sie sich für den Einzelnen auch erweisen mag, das grundlegende gesellschaftliche Problem nicht zu lösen vermag. Was im Grunde eine recht banale Feststellung ist.

Es ist auffallend, wie einhellig das Gedicht, das Brecht selbst nie veröffentlicht hat, in der Forschungsliteratur beschrieben und bewertet worden ist. Den gemeinsamen Nenner der meisten Interpretationen bildet die Formel von der Kritik am "Reformismus," ein Begriff, der aus den Debatten innerhalb der Sozialdemokratie gegen Ende des neunzehnten Jahrhunderts stammt. Reformismus (oder der in ähnlichem Sinn verwendete Begriff Revisionismus) beinhaltet die Überzeugung, dass sich soziale Verbesserungen auf dem Wege von Reformen erreichen lassen, dass es dazu keiner grundlegenden Umwälzung der Gesellschaftsstruktur bedarf—eine Überzeugung, die in den Jahren der Weimarer Republik mit der Sozialdemokratie identifiziert wurde. In der Agitation der KPD, deren strategisches Konzept auf der Notwendigkeit eines revolutionären Umsturzes der kapitalistischen Gesellschaft beruhte, spielte der Begriff Reformismus als Kampfbegriff gegen die konkurrierende SPD deshalb eine wichtige Rolle.

Vor diesem Hintergrund analysiert Klaus Schuhmann Brechts Gedicht "Die Nachtlager." In einem eigenen Kapitel, überschrieben "Episteln und Balladen. Auseinandersetzung mit dem Reformismus," subsumiert er Brechts Stücke *Die heilige Johanna der Schlachthöfe* und *Die Mutter* zusammen mit dem Gedicht "Die Nachtlager" und der für den Film *Kuhle Wampe* vorgesehenen "Ballade vom Tropfen auf den heißen Stein" unter dem Stichwort "Polemik gegen den Reformismus."[9] Die Bemühungen des Bettenvermittlers könnten "mit dem Verelendungsprozeß im Kapitalismus" nicht Schritt halten, stellt er fest; der "Menschenfreund" werde "eines Tages erkennen, daß alles umsonst war."[10] Schuhmann weiß also genau Bescheid über die (fiktive) Gestalt des amerikanischen Bettenvermittlers und dessen künftige Entwicklung (die literarische Quelle des Gedichts kannte er noch nicht). Auch über das zukünftige Verhalten der Obdachlosen gibt er präzise Auskunft: Sie "werden die Wahrheit finden und schließlich bereit sein, ihre Forderung nach Arbeit und Obdach mit dem sozialen Kampf der Arbeiterklasse zu identifizieren."[11] Nichts dergleichen findet sich in Brechts Gedicht. Schuhmann interpretiert nicht dessen Wortlaut, sondern benutzt den Text als Beleg dafür, dass Brecht Marxist war, und was die marxistische Gesellschaftslehre vorsieht, glaubt der Interpret dem Gedicht ohne weiteres hinzufügen zu können.[12]

Nicht weniger grobes Geschütz fahren Alfred Erck und Karl Gräf auf. Sie sind mit Schuhmann der Auffassung, das "Hauptobjekt der Kritik"

Brechts sei "der von den Imperialisten . . . unterstützten und gelenkten reformistischen Ideologie in ihrer organisierten Form in der modernen Arbeiterbewegung."[13] Brecht führe hier "eine grundsätzliche Auseinandersetzung mit dem Reformismus aller Schattierungen . . . nach dem Grundsatz des Marxismus, dass die chaotischen gesellschaftlichen Verhältnisse durch die revolutionäre, einheitliche Aktion der Arbeiterklasse verändert werden müssen."[14] Man sieht: Die DDR-Forschung der 1960er Jahre kämpfte noch die Kämpfe der KPD gegen die Sozialdemokratie aus der Weimarer Zeit, die allerdings nach dem Zweiten Weltkrieg im östlichen Teil Deutschlands (Stichwort Zwangsvereinigung der beiden Arbeiterparteien im Jahre 1946) ihre Neuauflage erlebten.

Was Brechts Gedicht anbelangt, so könnte man die Thesen von K. Schuhmann und A. Erck/K. Gräf getrost zu den literarhistorischen Akten legen, wären sie nicht mehrfach wieder aufgegriffen worden[15] und hätten sie nicht Eingang auch in die Werkausgabe (BFA) gefunden. Für Brecht werde "die Bettenvermittlung an Obdachlose . . . Ausdruck eines reformistischen Verhaltens," heißt es dort im Kommentar zum Gedicht "Die Nachtlager."[16] An anderer Stelle wird die Kritik am Reformismus als gemeinsamer Kontext des Gedichts vom Bettenvermittler, der *Heiligen Johanna der Schlachthöfe*, des *Brotladen*-Fragments, der "Ballade vom Tropfen auf den heißen Stein" und des "Lieds vom Flicken und vom Rock" aus der *Mutter* benannt.[17]

Mit dem *Brotladen*-Fragment und der *Heiligen Johanna der Schlachthöfe* wird der Reformismus-Begriff ganz zu Unrecht in Zusammenhang gebracht. Das gemeinsame Motiv beider Werke ist die Heilsarmee, deren Aktivitäten und profitorientierte Geschäftspraktiken Brecht und Elisabeth Hauptmann damals—im Zusammenhang zunächst mit der Komödie *Happy End*—mit großem Interesse verfolgten.[18] In der *Heiligen Johanna* tritt die Titelheldin, Mitglied der "Schwarzen Strohhüte," einer religiösideologischen Organisation der Armenhilfe, als Agitatorin auf, die "an die moralische Veränderbarkeit der verderbten Welt durch Gewaltlosigkeit und durch das Vorbild des guten Menschen" glaubt.[19]

> JOHANNA Wir sind die Soldaten des lieben Gottes. . . . Wir marschieren mit Trommeln und Fahnen überall hin, wo Unruhe herrscht und Gewalttaten drohen, um an den lieben Gott zu erinnern, den sie alle vergessen haben, und ihre Seelen zu ihm zurückzubringen.[20]

Dies hat mit Reformismus so wenig zu tun wie die Handlungsweise des Bettenvermittlers in Brechts Gedicht.[21] In einem Notat aus dem *Brotladen*-Komplex finden sich aufschlussreiche Bemerkungen über die "Geschichte der Heilsarmee." Sie zeige "vielleicht am krassesten das Schicksal aller 'idealistischen,' religiösen Korporationen und Aktionen im Hochkapitalismus," schreibt Brecht; "es ist die Geschichte einer entsetzlichen Veränderung aus einer auf persönlicher Entsagung aufgebauten Korporation in eine solche, die lediglich Ansprüche erhebt, aus einer den Profit bekämpfenden in eine profitmachende, aus einer grundsätzlich armen in eine grundsätzlich reiche, kurz, aus einer antikapitalistischen," als die Friedrich Engels sie in der Einleitung zur englischen Ausgabe seiner Schrift *Die Entwicklung des Sozialismus von der Utopie zur Wissenschaft* noch dargestellt hatte, "in eine kapitalistische."[22] Brecht kommentiert die Textstelle von Engels: "Das Element urchristlichen[23] Klassenkampfes ist längst im Keime erstickt worden. Heute bleibt das Bild einer grotesken Abnormität, eben das Bild des Urchristentums im Hochkapitalismus, ein Bild," so fügt Brecht hinzu, als wolle er sein literarisches Interesse an diesem Thema rechtfertigen, "das in einer Sammlung der Sitten und Gebräuche der Bourgeoisie nicht fehlen darf."[24]

In einem weiteren Notat aus dem *Brotladen*-Fragment stellt Brecht in zwei Kolumnen "die k[ommunistische] p[artei]" und "die heilsarmee" gegenüber (wohlgemerkt: die Heilsarmee, nicht die reformistische Sozialdemokratie):

die k[ommunistische] p[artei]		die heilsarmee
hilft zunächst niemand		hilft dem einzelnen
führt den einzelnen zur masse		trennt ihn von der masse
hat als hilfsmittel die gewalt		bekämpft die gewalt
materiell denkend		ideell denkend
	hat erfolg	
durch die schlechte lage		trotz der schlechten l[age]
ist interessiert		ist aus id[eellen] gründen
	an der änderung der l[age]	
		uninteressiert[25]

Der Bettenvermittler in Brechts Gedicht hat weder etwas mit der Heilsarmee, den "Schwarzen Strohhüten" aus der *Heiligen Johanna* zu tun, noch kennt er eine (reformistische) Perspektive im Sinne sozialdemokratischer oder gewerkschaftlicher Strategie. Das gilt sowohl für Brechts Quelle (Theodore Dreiser) als auch für seine Behandlung der Romanepisode im Gedicht.

Selbstverständlich gehörte auch der Reformismus zu den Themen, die Brecht damals beschäftigten, insbesondere im Zusammenhang mit der Arbeit an dem Stück *Die Mutter* nach Gorkis Roman. Hier ist die Konfrontation von gewerkschaftlichem Handeln und revolutionärer Strategie zentrales Thema des Stücks. Es existiert ein Lied aus dem Jahr 1931, dessen Titel ursprünglich lautete *Verurteilung des Reformismus*—eine frühe Fassung des bekannten "Lieds vom Flicken und vom Rock," das Brecht 1935 in *Die Mutter* aufnahm und das Hanns Eisler für die New Yorker Aufführung des Stücks im November des Jahres vertonte.[26] Es gibt weitere Gedichte aus der Zeit um 1931, die eine ähnlich kritische Haltung gegenüber gewerkschaftlichem, sich mit minimalen Verbesserungen begnügenden Handeln zum Ausdruck bringen und—direkt oder indirekt—auf die Notwendigkeit eines grundlegenden sozialen Umbruchs verweisen.[27] Sie waren in der Regel für bestimmte Werke verfasst und wurden zumeist von Eisler vertont, der damals der linksorientierten Arbeitermusikbewegung eng verbunden war und für seine Lieder und Chöre eine eindeutige propagandistische Aussage erwartete. Das Gedicht "Die Nachtlager" dagegen stand weder im Zusammenhang mit anderen Werken noch war es für die Vertonung gedacht oder geeignet.

Wie skeptisch Brecht im übrigen einen Erfolg der Strategie der KPD tatsächlich einschätzte, belegt ein kleines Notat, das um 1930–1931 entstanden sein dürfte. "Zur Bekämpfung des Reformismus in den Reihen der Arbeiter," heißt es da, brauche man

> eine quantitative Analyse der klassenmäßigen Zusammensetzung der Volksmassen in Deutschland. Es würde sich dann ergeben, daß die Arbeiterklasse Bündnisse braucht, um die Mehrheit zu gewinnen. Diese Bündnisse würde sie aber niemals zustande bringen, da nur eine vollständige Arbeiterpolitik, d.h. der Sozialismus, Lösungen böte. Je mehr aber diese vollsozialistische Tendenz sichtbar würde, desto weniger würde sie die Bündnisse bekommen, je nötiger diese Tendenz erschiene (und erschien), desto mehr drängte sie die Kleinbürger-(Bauern-)schichten in Bündnisse mit der herrschenden Klasse.[28]

Hierin steckt im Ansatz auch eine Kritik an der KPD, an ihrer "ultralinken" Position und Kompromissunfähigkeit.[29]

Zurück zum Gedicht "Die Nachtlager." In den Interpretationen werden Sachverhalte auf einen Nenner gebracht, die s o offenbar nicht zusammengehören. Das Gedicht kann weder mit der Formel "Kampf gegen den Reformismus" beschrieben noch mit der profitorientierten, reichen, kapitalistischen Korporation in Zusammenhang gebracht werden, als die Brecht die Heilsarmee im *Brotladen*-Fragment und in der *Heiligen Johanna der Schlachthöfe* darstellt. Der abfällig konnotierte Begriff "karitative bürgerliche Bestrebungen"[30] beinhaltet im Zusammenhang mit dem Kampfbegriff Reformismus die Unterstellung, hier werde ein mögliches soziales Unruhepotential im Interesse des Fortbestands der "Ausbeutergesellschaft" ruhiggestellt. Davon kann in der Episode, die Brecht in seinem Gedicht aufgreift, keine Rede sein. Die Handlungsweise des Bettenvermittlers, dessen sozialer Status mit dem seiner Klientel nahezu identisch ist, ist eine für den Augenblick gedachte und so wirkende solidarische Hilfeleistung, ohne Hintersinn, ohne einen Anflug von Korrumpierbarkeit.

Wichtig scheint in diesem Zusammenhang der Hinweis, dass das Gedicht keineswegs die e i n d e u t i g e Botschaft vermittelt, welche die meisten Interpreten unterstellen. Es wird übersehen, dass die drei Verse "einige menschen haben ein nachtlager / . . . / der ihnen zugedachte schnee fällt auf die strasse" auch im zweiten Sechszeiler in ihrer menschlich-sozialen Bedeutung durchaus unangetastet bleiben, nicht etwa als sinnlos, überflüssig oder kontraproduktiv verworfen werden. Brechts Gedicht relativiert die karitative Zuwendung zwar, nimmt ihr jedoch nicht ihre Berechtigung. Darauf aber laufen die Analysen des Gedichts in der Regel hinaus: auf die Auffassung, das Handeln des Bettenvermittlers fördere die Veränderung der Gesellschaft nicht nur nicht, sondern verhindere sie eher, zögere sie jedenfalls hinaus.[31] Diese Auffassung teilt Brechts Gedicht keineswegs. Notleidenden karitative Hilfe mit dem Argument zu verweigern, diese verzögere den revolutionären Umbau der Gesellschaft, wäre blanker Zynismus. Es ist dies ein Missverständnis, auf das Interpreten—seit der ersten Analyse des Gedichts durch Walter Jens[32]—immer wieder hereingefallen sind.[33]

Im übrigen besteht historisch Anlass genug, zwischen "Reformismus" als politischer, auf die Zukunft gerichteter Strategie auf der einen und karitativer Hilfe für Notleidende im Hier und Jetzt auf der anderen Seite zu differenzieren. Karitative Einrichtungen gab es in den 1920er Jahren in organisierter Form selbstverständlich vielfach. Sie erlangten in der Zeit der Massenarbeitslosigkeit zwangsläufig eine zunehmende Bedeutung und nahmen unbestrittene, kaum ersetzbare Aufgaben wahr. Dies keineswegs nur im "bürgerlichen" Lager. Anders als im zitierten Notat aus dem *Brotladen*-Fragment behauptet,[34] waren karitative Maßnahmen selbstverständlicher Bestandteil auch der Sozialpolitik der KPD. Erinnert sei nur an die im August 1921 (nach einem Aufruf Lenins anlässlich der Dürre- und Hungerkatastrophe im Wolgagebiet) gegründete "Internationale Arbeiterhilfe" (IAH). Im August-Heft 1929 der Zeitschrift *Der rote Aufbau*, der von Willi Münzenberg herausgegebenen *Zeitschrift der Internationalen Arbeiterhilfe*, findet sich unter der Rubrik *Aus der Organisation* der Artikel "Unterstützt das proletarische Kinderhilfswerk der IAH."[35] In einer redaktionellen Vorbemerkung heißt es:

> In den letzten großen Wirtschaftskämpfen in Amerika, Deutschland, Frankreich, England, der Tschechoslowakei und anderen Ländern haben die streikenden und ausgesperrten Arbeiter eine besonders große Unterstützung durch das Kinderhilfswerk der IAH. erhalten. Die Möglichkeiten, Kinder der Wirtschaftsopfer in Pflege zu nehmen, sind in fast allen Sektionen der IAH. im letzten halben Jahre ganz bedeutend gestiegen. Die amerikanische Sektion allein verfügt heute schon über 15 große Kinderlager. In Frankreich haben die Heime auf der Insel de Ré und 'Avenir Social' einen Ausbau erfahren, in Deutschland wurde kürzlich erst wieder ein neues Kinderheim in Ruhle fertiggestellt und der Benutzung übergeben. Überall befinden sich neue Heime im Bau und werden neue Lager errichtet. Dieses große Solidaritätswerk . . .

> ist nur möglich, wenn es die moralische und materielle Unterstützung der breitesten Kreise findet. Daher ist es zu begrüßen, dass die deutsche Sektion der IAH. einen Aufruf herausgebracht hat, der sich an alle Werktätigen, an alle Frauen und Männer, an alle Hand- und Kopfarbeiter mit einem Appell, die Kinderhilfe der IAH. zu unterstützen, wendet.[36]

Der Aufruf sei "von etwa 600 Persönlichkeiten" unterschrieben worden. Unter den rund dreihundert Namen, die auf zweieinhalb Druckseiten genannt werden, findet sich nahezu alles, was in den Jahren der Weimarer Republik Rang und Namen hatte: Schriftsteller, Künstler, Komponisten, Regisseure und Schauspieler, auch Ärzte, Hochschullehrer, Architekten, Anwälte, Politiker und Lehrer. Beiläufig auch der Name Brechts.[37]

Die These, karitative Maßnahmen verzögerten oder verhinderten die Lösung des grundlegenden gesellschaftlichen Problems, erweist sich nicht nur als zynisch, sie ist auch wirklichkeitsfremd. Nähme man sie beim Wort, müsste man über das Kinderhilfswerk der IAH ebenfalls urteilen: "das zeitalter der ausbeutung wird dadurch nicht verkürzt." Die Identifikation karitativer Hilfe mit politischem Reformismus geht in der geschichtlichen Realität nicht auf.

Brechts Gedicht "Die Nachtlager" erhält mit dem alleinstehenden Vers 12, zwischen die beiden Sechszeiler plaziert, einen ausgesprochen appellativen Charakter: "leg das buch nicht nieder, der du das liesest, mensch."[38] Von welchem "buch" ist in dieser Apostrophe die Rede? Da der Lesende, der Leser des Gedichts, unmittelbar angesprochen wird, kann logischerweise nur das "buch" gemeint sein, das dem Leser vorliegt.[39]

Umso bemerkenswerter ist es, dass Brecht das Gedicht selbst nie veröffentlicht hat, weder Anfang der 1930er Jahre, als es entstand, noch später. Und dies, obwohl es sich ohne Zweifel um ein abgeschlossenes, druckreifes Gedicht handelt. Es existiert als sauber typierte Abschrift (BBA 108/12), die nur eine einzige handschriftliche Korrektur aufweist: Im Vers 12 hat Brecht das ursprüngliche "liest"—offensichtlich aus rhythmischen Gründen—in "liesest" korrigiert. Auch Möglichkeiten, den Text zu veröffentlichen, gab es zur Zeit der Entstehung durchaus. Warum also blieb es unpubliziert? Auf diese Frage ist bis heute keine überzeugende Antwort gefunden worden.

Merkwürdige Begründungen liefern hierzu A. Erck/K. Gräf, ausgehend von K. Schuhmanns Behauptung: "Es ist nicht einfach, den Gedankenweg Brechts zu verfolgen. Brecht setzte bereits theoretisches Wissen voraus und adressierte die Epistel an einen Kreis von Sachkundigen."[40] Die Form des Gedichts sei nicht "volkstümlich (etwa im Sinne von 'leicht eingängig' oder 'folkloristisch-traditionell')," meinen Erck/Gräf; es sei wahrscheinlich ein Nebenprodukt der Theaterarbeit gewesen, "das Brecht für sich und vielleicht noch für einen kleinen Kreis Initiierter schrieb und nicht veröffentlichte."[41] Ist das Gedicht tatsächlich so schwer verständlich, dass es nur "Sachkundigen" und "Initiierten" zugänglich wäre? "Die Praxis hat jedoch in der Zwischenzeit"—also wohl seit Existenz der DDR—"diese Begrenzung aufgehoben," heißt es dann vielsagend.[42] Das Gedicht könnte demnach erst begriffen werden, wenn—nach dem Selbstverständnis der DDR—das gesellschaftliche Problem gelöst, "das zeitalter der ausbeutung" beendet wäre. Aber wäre eine Belehrung über den "Gedankenweg Brechts" dann noch von praktischem Interesse?

Es lohnt sich durchaus, der Frage noch einmal nachzugehen, warum Brecht sein Gedicht nie veröffentlicht hat. Die Antwort hat zweifellos etwas mit dem Inhalt des Gedichts zu tun, jedoch in anderer Weise, als bisher vermutet. Trifft es wirklich zu, dass Brechts Gedicht "mitten in aktuelle Auseinandersetzungen der Weimarer Republik, mitten in tragische Ereignisse der deutschen Geschichte" hineinführt, dass "das Problem, das in diesem Gedicht dialektisch behandelt" werde (das "Problem der Kompromißunfähigkeit zwischen den Parteien"), "eben auch ein ganz aktuelles Problem der Entstehungszeit des Gedichts" war, wie behauptet worden ist?[43] Träfe dies zu, hätte es für Brecht keinen Grund gegeben, das Gedicht n i c h t zu publizieren.

Ist es nicht wahrscheinlicher, dass Brecht das Gedicht zurückhielt, weil es ihm—im Unterschied zu anderen Texten aus dem zeitlichen Umfeld—nicht hinreichend e i n d e u t i g erschien—im Sinne der revolutionären Linken, der er sich damals, insbesondere in seiner Zusammenarbeit mit Hanns Eisler, zugehörig fühlte? Weil es—wie es nun einmal lautet—den Anforderungen der linken Theorie und Propaganda nicht gerecht wurde? Die Handlungsweise des Bettenvermittlers war weder verwertbar im Sinne der Kritik am Reformismus noch an der Heilsarmee. Es steckte auch mit seiner Thematik—der relativ positiven Wertung dieser wohltätigen Handlungsweise—zu tief in den real existierenden Widersprüchen zwischen der rigiden Theorie der revolutionären Linken und ihrer ganz anders gearteten Praxis. Das Gedicht "Die Nachtlager" führte nicht mitten hinein in die Auseinandersetzungen der Weimarer Republik, sondern bewegte sich eher am Rande dieser kleinen unausgesprochenen Unstimmigkeiten und Widersprüche.

Im übrigen wurde die Thematik des Gedichts vom Bettenvermittler spätestens mit der Etablierung der NS-Herrschaft in Deutschland bis auf weiteres obsolet. Nun traten nicht nur ganz andere Themen in den Vordergrund. Angesichts der politischen Realitäten—der Unterdrückung der KPD wie der SPD gleichermaßen—ging es nicht mehr um die Abwägung von revolutionärer Theorie und karitativer Praxis. Letztere gewann ganz im Gegenteil zunehmend an Bedeutung. Hunderttausende mussten Nazi-Deutschland verlassen; die Mehrzahl der Exilanten waren in den Gastländern bekanntermaßen auf Hilfen in der einen oder anderen Form dringend angewiesen. Diese waren, wie sich zeigte, vielfach überlebensnotwendig.

Dass man Brechts Gedicht “Die Nachtlager” in den Lyrik-Publikationen der Exil-Zeit, in den Sammlungen *Lieder Gedichte Chöre* (1934) und *Svendborger Gedichte* (1939), nicht erwarten darf, leuchtet deshalb unmittelbar ein. Das gilt mutatis mutandis auch für die ersten Nachkriegsjahre, die zwar erneut eine völlig veränderte historische Situation brachten, jedoch Hilfeleistungen für viele keineswegs überflüssig machten.

Erst 1956, im Todesjahr des Dichters, erschien das Gedicht “Die Nachtlager” in der von Peter Suhrkamp herausgegebenen Auswahl *Bertolt Brechts Gedichte und Lieder*.[44] Es existiert eine Titelliste Suhrkamps,[45] auf der das Gedicht “Die Nachtlager” verzeichnet ist; es scheint die erste Erwähnung des Gedichts seit seiner Entstehung zu sein. Brecht hat es Suhrkamp zur Verfügung gestellt, seine Veröffentlichung also gebilligt. Die Auswahl erschien Ende Mai 1956 als Band 33 der *Bibliothek Suhrkamp*.

Anmerkungen

[1] Zitiert nach dem Typoskript im Bertolt-Brecht-Archiv (BBA 108/12).

[2] Aus dem Englischen übersetzt von Anna Nußbaum.—Die Quelle wurde von A(lfred) Erck und K(arl) Gräf zuerst nachgewiesen: “Bertolt Brechts Gedicht *Die Nachtlager*. Versuch einer Interpretation,” *Weimarer Beiträge* 13.2 (1967): S. 228–245; hier, S. 237. Die Verfasser nennen in Anm. 15 allerdings nicht die Ausgabe, die Brecht vorlag, sondern eine 1958 in Moskau erschienene englische und eine 1963 im Aufbau-Verlag (Berlin/DDR) publizierte deutsche Ausgabe.

[3] Danach die folgenden Zitate.—Der Band ist in Brechts nachgelassener Bibliothek nicht überliefert; vgl. jedoch Anm. 5.

[4] Bertolt Brecht, *Werke: Große kommentierte Berliner und Frankfurter Ausgabe*, Werner Hecht, Jan Knopf, Werner Mittenzwei und Klaus-Detlef Müller, Hrsg., Bd. 21 (Berlin/Weimar und Frankfurt am Main: Aufbau und Suhrkamp, 1988–2000), 256. Im folgenden zitiert: BFA Band, Seite.

[5] In Brechts Nachlass-Bibliothek sind vier Bände von Theodore Dreiser aus den Jahren 1952 und 1954, erschienen im Aufbau-Verlag (Berlin/DDR), überliefert. Vgl. *Die Bibliothek Bertolt Brechts: Ein kommentiertes Verzeichnis*, Bertolt-Brecht-Archiv, Hrsg., bearbeitet von Erdmut Wizisla, Helgrid Streidt und Heidrun Loeper (Frankfurt am Main: Suhrkamp, 2007), S. 152, Nr. 1013–1016.

[6] Theodore Dreiser, *Schwester Carrie* (Wien: Zsolnay, 1929), S. 562–564.

[7] Ebd., S. 571.

[8] Eine ähnliche Struktur weisen, soweit ich sehe, nur die Gedichte “Der Bauer kümmert sich um seinen Acker” (BFA 14, 172) und “Alles wandelt sich” (BFA 15, 117) auf.

[9] Klaus Schuhmann, *Der Lyriker Bertolt Brecht: 1913–1933* (Berlin: Rütten & Loening 1964), S. 260–266 (danach die folgenden Zitate); hier, S. 260. S. 266 spricht K. Schuhmann von den beiden Reformismusgedichten. Die spätere Ausgabe seiner Darstellung im Deutschen Taschenbuch Verlag (München 1971) ist nur geringfügig überarbeitet.

[10] Ebd., S. 262.

[11] Ebd., S. 263.

[12] "Probleme der marxistisch-leninistischen Theorie und des praktischen Klassenkampfes," behauptet K. Schuhmann, "bilden das philosophische Sujet beider Dichtungen" (Ebd., S. 266).

[13] A. Erck/K. Gräf, "Bertolt Brechts Gedicht *Die Nachtlager,*" S. 234.

[14] Ebd., S. 235. Es sei sicher möglich, heißt es weiter, "den Nachweis zu führen, dass in den *Nachtlagern* sämtliche Grundgesetze der materialistischen Dialektik zur Anwendung gekommen sind" (Ebd., S. 236). Es bleibt bei der Behauptung; tatsächlich geführt wird der Nachweis nicht.

[15] Beispielsweise von Sigurd Paul Scheichl, "Vom Text zum historischen Kontext. Eine didaktische Möglichkeit des Landeskundeunterrichts. Am Beispiel der *Nachtlager* von Bertolt Brecht," *Informationen zur Deutschdidaktik. Zeitschrift für den Deutschunterricht in Wissenschaft und Schule* 11.1/2 (Wien 1987): S. 121–135 (zum Gedicht "Die Nachtlager" S. 125–132). Scheichl bezieht sich mehrfach auf K. Schuhmann und A. Erck/K. Gräf (vgl. besonders S. 128–130 und 134, Anm. 11–16).

[16] BFA 14, 531.

[17] BFA 3, 498.

[18] Vgl. BFA 10.2, 1170–1171.

[19] Burkhardt Lindner, "Die heilige Johanna der Schlachthöfe," in Jan Knopf, Hrsg., *Brecht Handbuch in fünf Bänden*, Bd. 1 (Stuttgart/Weimar: Metzler 2001–2003), S. 269. Im folgenden zitiert: BHB. Über die Absichten Johannas und der "Schwarzen Strohhüte" vgl. auch BFA 3, 133–139.

[20] BFA 3, 134.

[21] In seinen Artikeln über das *Brotladen*-Fragment und *Die heilige Johanna der Schlachthöfe* (BHB 1, S. 238–242 und 266–288) verzichtet Lindner auch konsequent auf den Begriff "Reformismus."

[22] BFA 10.1, 593–594 (A 31).

[23] In der BFA steht an dieser Stelle fälschlich "unchristlichen" (BFA 10.1, 594; vgl. BBA 1355/09).

[24] Ebd.

[25] BBA 1353/87. Das als Typoskript überlieferte, in der Zuordnung der Satzteile nicht ganz sinnentsprechend angelegte Notat ist in der BFA 10.1, 593 (Zeilen 21–23) aus Gründen besserer Verständlichkeit leicht bearbeitet wiedergegeben. Der Abdruck hier folgt dem Typoskript, erlaubt sich jedoch in den letzten fünf Zeilen ebenfalls geringfügige technische Eingriffe.

[26] Vgl. BFA 14, 125 und 525–526.

[27] Zu nennen sind hier neben der für den Film *Kuhle Wampe* verfassten "Ballade vom Tropfen auf den heißen Stein" (BFA 14, 120–121) und dem Lied "Wir wollten ein Obdach haben" (ebd., 126) das "Streiklied" (ebd., 121–122) für *Die Maßnahme* und das "Lied vom Flicken und vom Rock" (ebd., 125) für *Die Mutter*, allesamt 1931 entstanden und von Hanns Eisler vertont.

[28] BFA 21, 408.

[29] Vgl. hierzu S. P. Scheichl, "Vom Text zum historischen Kontext," S. 130.

[30] BFA 3, 498.

[31] So K. Schuhmann, *Der Lyriker Bertolt Brecht*, ausdrücklich: "Der Mann mit den Nachtlagern weiß um die Tragweite seiner Handlungen," er verzögere "den Erkenntnisprozess, der die Weltveränderung einleiten könnte" (S. 265).

[32] Walter Jens, *Statt einer Literaturgeschichte* (Pfullingen: Neske, 1962), S. 251: "gerade der 'Revisionismus' verschleiert die tatsächlichen Verhältnisse und verharmlost die Heilsbedürftigkeit der Welt." ". . . nicht, dass einige Menschen ein Nachtlager haben, sondern dass die Welt sich dadurch nicht ändert, ist wichtig." Walter Jens, *Deutsche Literatur der Gegenwart: Themen, Stile, Tendenzen* (München: Piper, 1961), S. 127–128: "der Wohltäter als ein gefährlicher Mann"; "nicht das Wohl des Einzelnen, das Wohl der Gesamtheit ist wichtig."

[33] K. Schuhmann, *Der Lyriker Bertolt Brecht*, S. 263: "Das soziale Elend der Krisenjahre kann nicht durch karitative und philanthropische Bemühungen gemildert werden." Albert Spieler/Norbert Thamm, *Literaturunterricht im 5.-11: Schuljahr* (Esslingen: Schneider, 1968), S. 297: "Es kommt nicht auf das Wohl des einzelnen an, sondern auf das Wohl der Gesamtheit." Manfred Herrmann, *Gedichte interpretieren: Modelle, Anregungen, Aufgaben* (Paderborn: Schöningh, 1978), S. 26: "In dieser marxistischen Auffassung erscheint das almosengebende Verhalten . . . als in keiner Weise hilfreich für eine Veränderung der Welt," meint "offenbar sogar eine Hinderlichkeit," da es "nichts zu den vom Autor aufgestellten Zielen beitrage." Soweit ich sehe, schätzen nur zwei Interpreten die Bettenvermittlung dem Text entsprechend ein. Peter Whitaker, *Brecht's Poetry: A Critical Study* (Oxford: Clarendon Press 1985), urteilt: "Brecht's opposition to reformism does not prevent his recognition of humane action—the age of exploitation is not shortened if the homeless are ignored" (S. 79). Scheichl, "Vom Text zum historischen Kontext," meint, "der Lösung der individuellen Wohltätigkeit" werde "durchaus relative Gültigkeit zugebilligt," fügt jedoch hinzu: "diese Lösung einzelner Fälle" werde "durch die generelle, revolutionäre Lösung der Spannungen des Zeitalters der Ausbeutung überflüssig gemacht" (S. 128).

[34] Vgl. Anm. 25; dort heißt es: Die kommunistische Partei "hilft zunächst niemand."

[35] *Der rote Aufbau* 2.4 (August 1929): S. 189–192.

[36] Ebd., S. 189.

[37] Ebd., S. 192.

[38] Der Vers ist mehrfach unrichtig, nämlich als erster Vers der abschließenden Strophe wiedergegeben worden: So im Erstdruck des Gedichts durch Peter Suhrkamp (vgl. die Anm. 44), bei W. Jens und A. Spieler/N. Thamm (vgl. Anm. 32 und 33), dann überraschenderweise noch einmal in BFA (14, 137).

[39] Eine grotesk zu nennende Interpretation dieser Zeile liefert K. Schuhmann, *Der Lyriker Bertolt Brecht*, S. 262: "Das Buch darf n i c h t zur Seite gelegt werden. Es ist nötig, mehr zu wissen und genauer zu studieren. Dann wird man im Buch der Klassiker finden, dass der Weg des amerikanischen Nachtlagervermittlers, der leidenden Menschheit zu helfen, falsch ist." Brecht meine hier "das Abc der Politik und der dialektischen Ökonomie. Mit einem Wort: die revolutionäre Theorie, die den Menschen leitet und bei seinen Taten beflügelt." Der Verfasser bezieht das Gedicht "Lob des Lernens" in die Interpretation des Gedichts vom Bettenvermittler

ein und folgert: "Nun erst erschließt sich der Sinn der Aufforderung ['Leg das Buch nicht nieder . . .']. Indem der Mensch liest, kämpft er." Der Mensch "wird zum Weltveränderer, indem er den objektiven Entwicklungsgesetzen der Gesellschaft zum Durchbruch verhilft" (S. 262–263).

[40] Ebd., S. 263. Die Tatsache, dass Brecht das Gedicht nicht veröffentlicht hat, bleibt häufig unbemerkt, was besonders problematisch erscheint, wenn Brechts lyrische Arbeit mit Nachdruck als Kommunikationsform aufgefasst wird. Bei Ray Ockenden, "Empedocles in Buckow: A Sketch-Map of Misreading in Brecht's Poetry," in Tom Kuhn and Karen Leeder, eds, *Empedocles' Shoe: Essays on Brecht's poetry* (London: Bloomsbury Methuen, 2002), S. 178–205, heißt es: Brecht "is writing poetry as a form of communication closely akin to teaching or instruction" (S. 179), insbesondere in den Jahren des Exils, und: "reader response and the relationship with the reader . . . become most important to Brecht" (S. 183). Hierzu wird S. 274, Anm. 46, ausgerechnet auf das Gedicht "Die Nachtlager" als frühes Beispiel hingewiesen.

[41] Erck/Gräf, "Bertolt Brechts Gedicht *Die Nachtlager*," S. 240.

[42] Ebd.

[43] Scheichl, "Vom Text zum historischen Kontext," S. 131.

[44] Vgl. hierzu den Beitrag des Verfassers: "Es war für mich selbstverständlich, dass ich die Sphäre der politischen Auseinandersetzung vermied." Peter Suhrkamps Auswahl *Bertolt Brechts Gedichte und Lieder* (1956), der in Kürze erscheint.

[45] Es handelt sich um drei typierte Blätter (BBA 791/84–86).

Dieter Goltzsche, *Herr Puntila und sein Knecht Matti*, 1972, Tusche.

Overlooked or Banished? Hanns Eisler's *Bilder aus der Kriegsfibel*

After multiple delays, Brecht's *Kriegsfibel* was finally published in 1955, and Eisler completed his *Bilder aus der Kriegsfibel* a few years later. *Kriegsfibel* is a well-known work by Brecht, but the *Bilder* have had a more modest profile in the overall image of Eisler's work that has formed over time. The main objective of this article is therefore to introduce this composition, despite its proximity to Paul Dessau's *Deutsches Miserere*, as a significant work of its own. Eisler's *Bilder* are small, concentrated works of art, each one a delicate configuration that blends the musical, the poetic, and the photographic in a new aesthetic unity while at the same time expressing different, even contradictory impulses. The work shows Eisler's renewed commitment to testing and demonstrating his artistic freedom through intricately drawn pieces that are at once ambitious fragments and exquisitely rounded, self-enclosed miniatures.

Nach vielen Verzögerungen erschien Brechts *Kriegsfibel* endlich 1955; Eislers *Bilder aus der Kriegsfibel* entstanden wenige Jahre später. Während aber die *Kriegsfibel* bekannt ist, spielen die *Bilder* in der Wirkungsgeschichte Eislers eine sehr untergeordnete Rolle. In dieser Arbeit geht es deshalb vor allem darum, die *Bilder* ungeachtet ihrer Nähe zu Paul Dessaus Werk *Deutsches Miserere* als eine eigenständige, wichtige und interessante Komposition vorzustellen. Eislers *Bilder*—das sind kleine, konzentriert gearbeitete Kunstwerke, delikate musikalische Gebilde, die das Fotografische, das Poetische und das Musikalische zu einer neuen Einheit verschmelzen oder auch Unterschiedliches oder gar Gegensätzliches ausdrücken. Die sorgfältig gearbeitete Komposition der *Bilder* zeigt, dass alles exquisit sein sollte; anspruchsvolle Fragmente sollten es wohl werden, in sich geschlossene, "runde" Miniaturen, kostbare musikalische Perlen, ein Werk, in dem Eisler sein Recht auf künstlerische Freiheit erneut erprobt und demonstriert hat.

Übersehen oder verbannt? Hanns Eislers *Bilder aus der Kriegsfibel*[1]

Arnold Pistiak

"Krieg" war ein Thema, mit dem sich Eisler lebenslang beschäftigt hatte—erinnert sei unter anderem an die frühen Lieder, den zwölftönigen Chor *Gegen den Krieg*, die Svendborger Kantaten, die *Deutsche Sinfonie*, das Chorlied *Der Krieg ist kein Gesetz der Natur* nach einem Text von Ernst Fischer, den Motivkomplex Frieden—Krieg in *Johann Faustus*, an die Bühnenmusik zu Bechers *Winterschlacht*, das *Friedenslied* oder auch an das Chorlied *Regimenter gehn* nach Majakowski. Der späte Eisler fügte diesen Werken eine weitere, höchst individuelle Komposition hinzu—*Bilder aus der Kriegsfibel*:[2] fünfzehn Musikstücke, die jeweils kaum länger dauern als eine Minute. Fünfzehn Musikstücke aber auch, die nicht unabhängig von den Fotografien und Texten der *Kriegsfibel* Brechts verstanden werden können und die darüber hinaus in enger Nachbarschaft zu Paul Dessaus großem Chorwerk *Deutsches Miserere* stehen.[3] Fünfzehn Musikstücke schließlich, die auf eine sehr direkte Weise mit dem *Faustus*-Projekt verknüpft sind—und zwar, genauer, mit jenen Problemen, über die Eisler nach der *Faustus*-Kampagne, aber auch nach dem Brief an das Zentralkomitee der SED Ende 1953 in Wien nachdachte.[4] Denn die tagebuchähnlichen Notizen Eislers sprechen ja nicht nur von Kälte und Verzweiflung; sie sprechen auch über das Vorhaben, die *Faustus*-Oper sehr wohl fortzusetzen, und sie äußern höchst bedenkenswerte Gedanken zu der eigenen kompositorischen Arbeit. Obgleich formuliert mit Blick auf das *Faustus*-Projekt, lassen sie sich in einem weiteren Sinn auch als eine Art Absichtserklärung für sein weiteres Schaffen überhaupt verstehen:

> Mit Zögern und Zagen gehe ich an die Komposition zu meinem Dr. Faustus. Eine enorme Arbeit, ein Berg von Mühsal und Verzweiflung. Misstrauisch blicke ich <an> in die Zukunft. Schmerzhaft sehe ich und voll Sorge, dass ich mit jeder Konvention, auch der modernistischen, zu brechen habe. Voll Sorge <verzichte> sehe ich, dass ich auf Raffinements verzichten muss und mir eine raffinierte Einfachheit erarbeiten muss, wenn ich den Sinn und die Bedeutung auch des Bühnenmäßigen treffen soll. Mutlosigkeit vor all den Schwierigkeiten.[5]

Weisen derartige Überlegungen nicht auf den musikalischen Gestus der (meisten der) folgenden Werke hin—*Nuit et Brouillard* etwa, *Das Schwitzbad, Die Teppichweber von Kujan-Bulak ehren Lenin*, die späten Lieder, die *Ernsten Gesänge*? Auf das eigentliche Spätschaffen Eislers also? Dazu mag man unterschiedliche Auffassungen vertreten. In meinem Verständnis aber lassen sich diese Kompositionen durchaus als Versuche verstehen, diese Ansprüche zu verwirklichen. Im Folgenden aber soll zunächst auf jenes Werk geblickt werden, auf das sich Eislers *Bilder aus der Kriegsfibel* unmittelbar beziehen—Brechts *Kriegsfibel.*

Brecht: *Kriegsfibel*

Gleich Dutzende kürzere oder längere Artikel beschäftigen sich mit jenem Werk, das die Basis, die unverzichtbare Voraussetzung für das Entstehen von Eislers *Bildern aus der Kriegsfibel* bildet: die *Kriegsfibel* von Bertolt Brecht—dem letzten Buch, das Brecht vor seinem Tod herausbrachte, das aber immer noch weitgehend unbekannt ist.[6] Der Widerspruch zwischen der Fülle der Spezialuntersuchungen und dem tatsächlichen Bekanntheitsgrad äußert sich selbst in der wissenschaftlichen Brechtliteratur—so wird die *Kriegsfibel* in Mittenzweis Brecht-Biographie beziehungsweise in Albert Dümlings Arbeit *Brecht und die Musik* nicht oder nur gelegentlich erwähnt. Und noch 2004 stellte Erdmut Wizisla fest: "Brechts Kriegsfibel ist ein Fossil, zusammengestellt in Vorzeiten, heute weitgehend unbekannt."[7]

Angesichts der vorliegenden Literatur kann ich mich im folgenden auf wenige, zunächst resümierende Bemerkungen zur Entstehung der *Kriegsfibel* beschränken: Den Begriff "Fotoepigramm[e]" verwandte Brecht bereits im *Arbeitsjournal*, die ersten drei Fotoepigramme schuf er 1940.[8] Ein interessantes Ereignis fand am 3. April 1943 in New York statt: "Piscator hatte eine Auswahl zusammengestellt und ließ die Texte zu projizierten Dias vortragen."[9] In Los Angeles entstanden dann weitere Fotoepigramme, so dass Brecht bereits 1943-1944 Paul Dessau eine Auswahl übergeben konnte.[10] Ende 1944 oder Anfang 1945[11] sandte Brecht dann eine Zusammenstellung der Blätter an den mit ihm befreundeten marxistischen Philosophen Karl Korsch, der geradezu enthusiastisch erwiderte: "Die Fibel ist das beste, was es über diesen Krieg gibt" (BFA 12, 424).

Nach seiner Rückkehr nach Europa wollte Brecht die *Kriegsfibel* veröffentlichen. Er dachte zunächst an seinen Münchner Verleger Kurt Desch. Desch lehnte jedoch ab, und Brecht forderte am 12. November 1948 die Materialien zurück.[12] Etwa ein Jahr später und trotz des bereits angelaufenen Kampfes gegen den "Formalismus" übergab Brecht dem (Ost-) Berliner Verlag Volk und Welt ein Manuskript zur *Kriegsfibel* mit achtundsechzig Fotoepigrammen.[13] Der Verlag hat das Manuskript dem "Kulturellen Beirat für das Verlagswesen" weitergereicht; einer von dessen Mitarbeitern (Werner Hecht zufolge hieß er Pincus[14]) wandte sich dann am 16. März 1950 an den Ministerpräsidenten der DDR, Otto Grotewohl: Brecht habe "nur allgemein pazifistisch gegen den Krieg Stellung" genommen, und: "Er vergisst hierbei anscheinend ganz den heroischen Partisanenkampf der unterdrückten Völker." Nur drei Tage später antwortete Grotewohl: "Zurück. Ich teile vollkommen Eure Ansicht; völlig ungenügend."[15]

Einen Monat später erhielt Brecht dann einen Brief vom Parteivorstand der SED. Darin meinte Stefan Heymann, er wolle Brecht die "Begutachtung" des Manuskripts mitteilen, die er vorgenommen hatte. Unter anderem schrieb er, unmissverständlich auf Brechts erstes und letztes Fotoepigramm anspielend: "Der neue Faschismus ist nicht ein wiederentstandener Hitler, sondern die Träger des neuen Faschismus sind die amerikanischen Konzernherren und ihre Propagandisten, für uns Deutsche besonders die Verräter in Westdeutschland."[16] In einem Briefentwurf als Antwort auf die Begutachtung und die Kritik an einigen Texten erklärte Brecht dann grundsätzlich: "Jedenfalls wäre es eine Fälschung, wenn ich jetzt, hintennach, da viel hineinänderte; das Buch muss historisch genommen werden." Und er formulierte als Reaktion auf die Kritik die Idee, "am Ende des Buchs Anmerkungen zu bringen, welche das eine oder andere Missverständnis verhindern und die Dokumente erklären könnten."[17]

Aber natürlich: Als Pincus 1950 Brechts *Kriegsfibel* durchsah, muss er sich erschreckt haben. Denn zumindest ein Dutzend der Fotoepigramme thematisierten die individuelle—und damit letztlich auch historische—Schuld derjenigen Deutschen, die sich von den Faschisten hatten einfangen lassen und sich dann, "unwissend," an den deutschen Raubzügen beteiligten. Diese Betrachtungsweise wich erheblich von dem ab, was in der DDR üblich war und reichte hin, in der *Kriegsfibel* eine "pazifistische" Stellungnahme zu sehen. Das war dazumal ein schwerwiegender Vorwurf; als Begriff verwendet, war "Pazifismus" im Grunde eines jener Totschlagwörter, die bis heute aus dem großen Sack von "-ismen" hervorgeholt werden, um Andersdenkende mehr oder weniger denunziatorisch falschen Denkens zu überführen. Denn bis in die 1980er Jahre hinein wurde "Pazifismus" in der DDR nicht im Sinne von Bertha von Suttner oder Käthe Kollwitz ("Nie wieder Krieg!") verwendet. Allgemein ausgedrückt, unterstellte "Pazifismus" damals vielmehr die mangelnde Bereitschaft zu militärischer Selbstverteidigung. Völlig im Geist des gleichsam offiziell vertretenen Verständnisses meinte "Meyers Neues Lexikon" beispielsweise 1963, "Pazifismus" sei eine "bürgerliche Strömung, die unter der Losung des Friedens um jeden Preis den Werktätigen den falschen Gedanken einzugeben versucht, dass ein fortwährender Frieden im Kapitalismus zu erreichen sei;. . . stellt sich damit bewusst oder unbewusst auf die Seite der Imperialisten."[18] Es ist klar, dass Brechts und Eislers Werke der fünfziger Jahre weder in diesem noch in dem ursprünglichen Sinn als "pazifistisch" bezeichnet werden können—weder die *Tage der Commune* noch die *Kinderhymne*, weder das

Faustus-Stück, das Chorlied *Regimenter gehn* nach Majakowski noch der Umstand, dass die *Bilder aus der Kriegsfibel* dem Erich-Weinert-Ensemble der Volksarmee der DDR gewidmet waren, rechtfertigen derart simple Zuschreibungen.[19] Vielmehr sprechen die *Kriegsfibel* wie auch die *Bilder aus der Kriegsfibel* davon, dass Brecht und Eisler bestrebt waren, das scheinbar Unmögliche zu tun: auch in den Jahren des Kalten Krieges ihr antifaschistisches und antikapitalistisches Engagement zu bewahren und gleichzeitig friedliche Impulse zu befördern.

Schloss Grotewohls Notiz ein unmittelbares Erscheinen der *Kriegsfibel* im Verlag Volk und Welt aus, so bedeutet das nicht, dass Brecht nicht weitere Bemühungen unternommen hätte, die auf die Herausgabe der *Kriegsfibel* gerichtet waren. Dass er weiterhin an dem Manuskript gearbeitet hat, belegt eine Notiz des Theaterwissenschaftlers Ernst Schumacher. Nach einem Besuch bei Brecht notierte er am 9. Oktober 1953 in seinem Tagebuch, Brecht sei "mit der Endredaktion der Druckfassung der *Kriegsfibel* befasst, die endlich erscheinen dürfe." Und weiter, sich auf Äußerungen Brechts beziehend: "Aber jetzt, da es mit der Remilitarisierung der Bundesrepublik erneut ernst werde, die noch ganz andere Katastrophen impliziere als die von ihm beschriebenen, sei die Druckerlaubnis gegeben worden."[20]

Eine Druckerlaubnis im Herbst 1953? Dazu kenne ich keine nachprüfbaren Angaben, aber es gibt wohl auch keinen Grund, an Schumachers präzisem Bericht zu zweifeln. Denn immerhin: Stalin war gestorben; die harschen Einsprüche von Brecht, Duncker, Felsenstein, Weigel und Arnold Zweig gegen die Faustuskampagne waren mit Sicherheit noch nicht vergessen; die Erschütterungen, zu denen der 17. Juni geführt hatte, waren noch nicht abgeklungen; die Proteste der Akademie der Künste gegen die Verhaltensweisen Helmut Holtzhauers lagen auf dem Tisch. So ist wohl nicht völlig auszuschließen, dass Brecht ein inoffiziell-vertrauliches positives Signal von "ganz oben" erhalten hätte.

Und dann gab es die überaus wichtige Begegnung zwischen Brecht und Walter Heynowski. Heynowski war seit 1954 Leiter des neu gegründeten Eulenspiegel Verlags. 1953 oder in der ersten Jahreshälfte 1954 besuchte er, vermittelt durch Günter Kunert,[21] Brecht: Denn von Kunert, so schrieb mir Heynowski am 13. Februar 2015, "erfuhr ich von der Existenz der noch nicht veröffentlichten *Kriegsfibel*." Und weiter: "Noch heute rechne ich es mir an, dass ich mit der Unbekümmertheit des Jugend zu Brecht ging und bei ihm die Fotos aus US-Illustrierten mit seinen Texten zu Gesicht bekam. Ich war fasziniert." Heynowskis Faszination, Brechts Interesse an einem Druck der *Kriegsfibel* wie auch die kulturpolitische Situation—jetzt waren wesentliche Voraussetzungen für eine Edition des Brechtschen Werkes vorhanden: Am 1. September 1954 wurde der Vertrag zwischen Brecht und dem Eulenspiegelverlag unterzeichnet (BBA 569/13, Herausgeberin: Ruth Berlau); am 21. Oktober übersandte Brecht dem Verlag weiteres Material (BBA 1774/09); am 13. Dezember wurde festgelegt, dass Peter Palitzsch "die Gestaltung und Ausstattung" der *Kriegsfibel* zu besorgen hätte (BBA Z 44/39).

Aber hinter den Kulissen waren die Auseinandersetzungen darüber, ob die *Kriegsfibel* überhaupt erscheinen dürfe beziehungsweise in welcher Gestalt sie erscheinen solle, noch lange nicht beendet. Am 8. Oktober 1954 hatte der Eulenspiegel-Verlag einen Druckgenehmigungsantrag eingereicht. Zwei Wochen später erhielt er eine zurückhaltende Antwort, verbunden mit dem "Vorschlag," "über Amtsleitung Gutachten von Joh. R. Becher und Johanna Rudolph zu erbitten."[22] Wurde dieser "Vorschlag" akzeptiert? Darüber ist mir derzeit nichts bekannt. Aber wiederum sechs Wochen später, am 29. November 1954, schrieb eine Frau Seipel vom Amt für Literatur und Verlagswesen an Oskar Hoffmann, den Leiter der Abteilung Begutachtung dieses Amtes, einen Brief, der sich auf das *Kriegsfibel*-Projekt von 1950 bezog und dessen Aussagewert wohl kaum überschätzt werden kann:

> Koll. Tschesno war noch Verlagsleiter, als das Manuskript eingereicht wurde. Es ist gegen den Willen von Bruno Petersen beim Kulturellen Beirat eingereicht worden. Koll. Petersen erinnert sich noch sehr genau an den Vorgang. Es ist eine Sammlung von Ausschnitten aus englischen Zeitungen. Dem Inhalt nach reinster Pazifismus, das Ms. war vielleicht 1947 noch tragbar gewesen, aber nicht mehr um 1950.—Es gab eine heftige Auseinandersetzung mit Brecht. Der Kulturelle Beirat hat das Ms. Otto Grotewohl vorgelegt, der entsetzt war. Damit fiel das Projekt ins Wasser.[23]

Dieser Brief und der Kontext, in dem er stand, darf also als ein neuer und wiederum entschiedener Versuch verstanden werden, das Erscheinen der *Kriegsfibel* zu verhindern—mit ungenauen Angaben zum Werk, mit dem Pazifismus-Vorwurf und mit einer denunziatorischen Breitseite gegen den ehemaligen Leiter des Verlags Volk und Welt, Michael Tschesno-Hell. Gleichwohl wurde am 23. Dezember 1954 die Druckgenehmigung von Karl Wloch, dem Leiter des Amtes für Literatur und Verlagswesen, erteilt; sie war versehen mit der Notiz: "Die Angelegenheit wurde vom Koll. Wloch nach Rücksprache mit der Kulturabtlg. d. ZK Gen. Herzog entschieden."[24] Das war fünf Tage nach einer telefonischen Anfrage von Anna Seghers bei Brecht, ob er bereit wäre, den Stalin-Friedenspreis anzunehmen, und genau an dem Tag, da der deutsche Preisträger in Moskau bekanntgegeben wurde!—An diesem 23. Dezember erhielt Brecht das folgende Telegramm der Chefredaktion des Eulenspiegel-Verlags: "lieber berthold brecht wir haben uns ueber ihre ehrenvolle auszeichnung sehr gefreut als geschenk uebermitteln wir ihnen die nachricht dass die druckgenehmigung fuer die kriegsfibel soeben erteil wurde."[25]

Dazu zwei Bemerkungen: Zum einen stellte die Verleihung des Internationalen Stalin-Friedenspreises an Brecht einen Vorgang dar, dessen

Bedeutung schwerlich zu überschätzen ist, da er die Stellung des Ausgezeichneten in der DDR wesentlich stärkte.[26] Dies erlaubte es Brecht, noch vor der Rede Chrustschows auf dem XX. Parteitag der KPdSU die eigene Position zur Sowjetunion in aller Öffentlichkeit anzudeuten. Seine Notizen zur Vorbereitung der kurzen Rede, die er bei der Preisverleihung am 25. Mai 1955 hielt, belegen, wie ernst er selbst die ganze Angelegenheit nahm.[27] Zum andern aber antwortete Brecht auf das Telegramm mit einem Brief vom 4. Januar 1955 und schrieb darin unter anderem, er habe sich die Druckgenehmigung für die *Kriegsfibel* "selbst erteilt. Nachdem ich das Amt für Literatur darauf aufmerksam machte, dass die Arbeiten von Mitgliedern der Akademie der Künste nicht der Kontrolle dieses Amtes unterstehen" (BBA 0745/024). Diese Antwort darf allerdings nicht wörtlich genommen werden. Sie drückte kaum mehr aus als seine Verärgerung über die ständigen Bevormundungen der Künstler. Eine Verärgerung allerdings, der er spätestens am 20. Dezember in einem Telefonat mit dem Amt für Literatur und Verlagswesen Ausdruck gegeben hatte. Einer "Hausmitteilung" des Amtes zufolge hätte Brecht auf die Mitteilung, dass das Manuskript in das ZK geschickt worden sei, etwa geäußert, "er ließe sich nicht in seine Angelegenheiten rein-reden, sondern alles was er schreibt, würde er politisch selbst verantworten und nicht das ZK. Er betrachtet das Amt als Zensurstelle und habe es auch als weltbekannter Dichter nicht nötig, sich auch von hier bevormunden zu lassen. Er weiche zwar von der politischen Linie ab, was Minister Becher in West-Berlin ebenfalls zum Ausdruck gebracht hat, und was auch weiterhin überall bekannt ist."[28] In der Sache selbst aber hätten Verlag und Druckerei niemals die Möglichkeit gehabt, einen derart aufwändigen Druck ohne eine offizielle Genehmigung auch nur zu beginnen. Brechts Status als Akademiemitglied hätte auch nicht ausgereicht, die mehrfache, nachdrückliche Werbung des Verlags für das Buch einzufordern.[29] Vielmehr zeigte es sich, dass es noch nicht sicher war, ob das Buch überhaupt erscheinen könne: Neun Monate später fand im Zentralkomitee der SED eine Besprechung statt, in der man "übereinstimmend" der Meinung war, dass die *Kriegsfibel* "keinen positiven Beitrag zur Entwicklung unserer Literatur darstellt" und sie "eigentlich nicht erscheinen dürfe. Die Erteilung der Druckgenehmigung kann weiter nichts sein als eine eindeutige Konzession an den Namen Brecht." Man wusste nicht, "in welcher Weise das Erscheinen dieses Titels verhindert werden könne" und überlegte, ob nicht die—in späteren Jahren immer wieder praktizierte!—Möglichkeit bestünde, "den Vertrieb des größten Teils der Auflage zu verhindern."[30] Daraufhin hatte sich Seipel am 9. September noch einmal an Hoffmann gewandt und unmittelbar vor dem vorgesehenen Druck im Oktober 1955 vorgeschlagen, "doch noch eine persönliche Aussprache mit B.B. herbeizuführen, um im Hinblick auf die int. Lage den Titel *Kriegsfibel* zu ändern und auf einige Bilder zu verzichten."[31]

Aber was sich auch immer hinter den Kulissen vollzog: Das Jahr 1955 war das Jahr der präzisierenden Arbeit, des Druckes und der Auslieferung der *Kriegsfibel* (BBA 745/36: das Buch zur Begutachtung an Brecht: 10.11.55). Die *Kriegsfibel* wurde eine der ersten großen Buchveröffentlichungen des neuen Verlages, ein geradezu wundervoll gestaltetes anspruchsvolles Buch, das in jeder Hinsicht faszinierend ist. Als sich der Druck unerwartet verzögerte, schlug der Verlag vor, die Druckerei nicht zu wechseln, denn die *Kriegsfibel* sollte "ein Standardwerk werden, und diese Gewähr der Qualität haben wir im Druckhaus Einheit."[32] Über ein halbes Jahrhundert später stellte Grischa Meyer fest: "Der schwarze Grund, auf dem die Zeitungsausschnitte stehen, war (und ist) nicht nur eine Herausforderung für die polygraphische Industrie und eine luxuriöse Verschwendung von Druckfarbe, sie ist auch ein starkes gestalterisches Zeichen." Denn: Nun sind es nicht mehr nur einfache Zeitungsausschnitte, sondern eine "mit Text und schwarzer Deckfarbe aufgetragene 'Übermalung' der Zeitungsseiten."[33] Und der große Regisseur Walter Felsenstein, der Brecht und Eisler während der *Faustus*-Kampagne nachdrücklich unterstützt hatte, schrieb an Brecht:

> In den letzten Tagen ging es mir nicht besonders gut, und so ist es mir erst heute möglich, Ihnen zu sagen, was für eine große Freude Sie mir mit Ihrem wertvollen Geschenk gemacht haben.—Die Kraft dieses Buches in Bild und Kommentar ist von einer so unnachgiebigen Direktheit, dass sich ihr selbst die muntersten Deutschen nicht werden entziehen können.—Die Frage, die sich sehr rasch erhebt, ist: wie bringt man dieses großartige Dokument an diejenigen heran, die es am dringendsten brauchen? Ist diesbezüglich bereits etwas unternommen?[34]

Eisler: *Bilder aus der Kriegsfibel*

Zur Entstehung

Hatte Brecht noch in Los Angeles für Dessaus geplantes abendfüllendes Werk selbst die Texte zusammengestellt und sie Dessau übergeben, so war die Situation bei Eisler völlig anders. Nach dem, was sich belegen lässt, lag der Druck des Eulenspiegelverlags bereits vor, als Eisler begann, sich seinerseits mit der *Kriegsfibel* zu beschäftigen. Haben Brecht und Eisler über Brechts *Kriegsfibel* gesprochen? An Gelegenheiten dazu mangelte es gewiss nicht, aber wir wissen es nicht. Jedoch wissen wir, dass Eisler im Herbst 1955 an der Musik zu dem Film *Nuit et Brouillard* arbeitete und in diesem Zusammenhang seine Reise nach Paris vorbereitete. Auf dem Titelblatt seiner Partitur vermerkte er unter anderem: "Für Georg/ Brechts Kriegsfibl."[35] Er selbst hat also höchstwahrscheinlich die noch druckfrische *Kriegsfibel* mit nach Paris genommen, um sie dort oder wenige Wochen später in Wien seinem Sohn Georg zu geben. Ist die Idee zur Komposition seiner *Bilder* womöglich bereits während der Arbeit an *Nuit et Brouilliard* entstanden? Vielleicht. Jedenfalls stand Eislers Beschäftigung mit der *Kriegsfibel* in engem Zusammenhang mit diesem Film.

Irgendwann im Verlaufe des Jahres 1957 oder Anfang 1958 muss dann die Komposition erfolgt sein. In den Entwürfen zu den *Bildern aus der Kriegsfibel* findet sich die Notiz "Regimenter gehn instrumentieren" (HEA 1802, S. 1). Da *Regimenter gehn* in das Umfeld der Feierlichkeiten zum 40. Jahrestag der Oktoberrevolution beziehungsweise zum 40. Jahrestag der Gründung der Roten Armee gehörte—der vollständige Titel lautet *Regimenter gehn: Zum 40. Jahrestag der Roten Armee*[36]—und da Eisler im Herbst 1957 oder im Januar 1958 an *Regimenter gehn* arbeitete,[37] sind damit die zeitlichen Eckpunkte für seine Arbeit an den *Bildern* annähernd klar. Aber freilich: Eisler mag Brechts Manuskript seit langem gekannt haben und manches, was er nach dem Tode Brechts aufschrieb, mag sich seit langem in seinem Kopf befunden haben.

Es hat gleichwohl den Anschein, als habe Eisler das Buch (oder das dazugehörige Ms.) des Eulenspiegelverlags durchgesehen und sich dabei die Strophen markiert, die er komponieren wollte. Aber wenn für uns Spätere die Gesichtspunkte auch kaum nachvollziehbar sind, die Eisler seiner Auswahl zugrunde gelegt haben mag, eines ist klar: Eisler hat sich sehr genau an den Aufbau der *Kriegsfibel* gehalten; grob gesagt, an die thematischen Komplexe Eroberungen, Waffenproduktion, Kriegsbeginn (*Kriegsfibel* 2–14) / unmittelbare Ergebnisse des Handelns der deutschen Soldaten: Zerstörungen, Leiden der Bevölkerung (15–22) / faschistische Politiker und deren Verbündete (23–32) / Sowjetisches, Außereuropäisches (33–44) / individuelle Schicksale und Verhaltensweisen (45–56) / Reflexionen nach dem Krieg (57–69).[38] Genauer: Eisler hat aus jeder dieser "Gruppen" der *Kriegsfibel* zumindest ein Fotoepigramm ausgewählt und in Musik gesetzt. Schon von der Auswahl her blieb er also dicht an Brechts Vorgehen. Das war durchaus nicht selbstverständlich, denn er hätte sich ja auf eine oder zwei "Gruppen" beschränken und somit eine ganz andere konzeptionelle Grundlinie schaffen können. Zudem hat Eisler die auf der Vorder- wie auf der Rückseite der *Kriegsfibel* abgebildeten großformatigen Fotos sowie die dazugehörigen Texte Brechts verwandt: Er hat Brechts Text zu dem Foto der erschöpften Soldaten, das zum Finale der *Kriegsfibel* gehört, das aber auch gleich einem Motto auf der Vorderseite des Schutzumschlags abgebildet ist, demonstrativ als *Introduktion* seinen *Bildern* vorangestellt, und er hat den Text zur Rückseite des Schutzumschlags *Epilog* genannt und mit ihm die Reihe seiner *Bilder aus der Kriegsfibel* beendet. Andererseits aber hat er die Texte von mehr als fünfzig der Brechtschen Fotoepigramme eben nicht übernommen. Ein drastisches Beispiel: die *Kriegsfibel* beginnt und endet mit jeweils einem Fotoepigramm zu Hitler; Eisler hat weder das eine noch das andere ausgewählt.

Dass Eisler das erste Stück *Introduktion*, das letzte aber *Epilog* nannte und dass er den Schluss der Partitur mit dem energisch geschriebenen Wort "Ende" kennzeichnete, mag deutlich genug belegen, dass er seine *Bilder aus der Kriegsfibel* wahrscheinlich als ein abgeschlossenes Werk betrachtete. Auch die in diesen Jahren mutmaßlich erfolgte Aufführung des Werkes spricht dafür (dazu unten mehr). Nun gibt es jedoch einen Brief von Stephanie Eisler an Ruth Berlau, der einen Monat vor Eislers Tod geschrieben wurde, und in dem Steffi Eisler meint, jetzt, nach Abschluss der Arbeit an den *Ernsten Gesängen*, wollte sich Eisler noch einmal mit der *Kriegsfibel* beschäftigen, sie solle die "nächste größere Arbeit" werden: "Skizzen und auch schon fertige Arbeiten gibt es schon seit 4 Jahren."[39] Hatte Eisler tatsächlich vorgehabt, sich erneut den *Bildern* zuzuwenden? Die Antwort muss wohl offen bleiben. Aber jedenfalls gibt es in den von mir eingesehenen Materialien keinerlei Hinweise, die auf eine beabsichtigte Fortsetzung der Arbeit an den *Bildern aus der Kriegsfibel* schließen ließen. Das bezieht sich übrigens auch auf die Meinung, Eisler hätte beabsichtigt, die einzelnen Teile durch instrumentale Zwischenspiele zu verbinden. Der Wiener Musikwisssenschaftler Rudolf Klein hatte diese Ansicht im Programmheft der Wiener Aufführung von 1971 geäußert (HEA 8452); später wurde sie von Manfred Grabs und Günter Mayer wiederholt.[40]

Hier ein knapper tabellarischer Überblick über den Aufbau der *Bilder* Eislers:

Nr. bei Eisler	**Nr. bei Brecht**	**Beginn des Texts bei Eisler**	**Hinweise auf das Foto**
Introduktion	61 und Schutzumschlag vorn	*Seht unsre Söhne*	deutsche Soldaten im russischen Winter, frierend, hoffnungslos
1	4	*Die Glocken läuten*	ein Platz mit betenden Franco-Soldaten in Barcelona
2	17	*Noch bin ich eine Stadt*	Hafen von Liverpool, noch weitgehend unzerstört
3	19	*Es war die Zeit des Unten und des Oben*	Metro-Bahnhof in London, Menschen suchen vor den Luftangriffen Schutz
4	22	*Such nicht mehr, Frau*	eine Frau, gebückt in den Trümmern suchend
5	30	*Das sind sechs Mörder*	Fotos von sechs deutschen Generälen
6	33	*Ihr Brüder*	Sandkastenübung
7	45	*Wir hörten auf der Schulbank*	Kreuze für getötete amerikanische Soldaten; ein aufgesteckter Handschuh weist nach oben

(continued)

Nr. bei Eisler	Nr. bei Brecht	Beginn des Texts bei Eisler	Hinweise auf das Foto
8	51	*Nicht Städte mehr*	ein erblindeter junger Mann, ergeben sitzend
9	54	*Doch als wir vor das rote Moskau kamen*	zwei sowjetische Partisanen, eine Frau und ein Mann, mit einer Waffe
10	57	*Seht diese Hüte von Besiegten!*	im Wasser treibende deutsche Stahlhelme
11	63	*Ihr in den Tanks und Bombern*	vier Kinder aus verschiedenen Ländern
12	65	*Das sind die Städte*	eine zerstörte deutsche Stadt
13	67	*Ich hör die Herrn in Downingstreet noch schelten*	London, Downingstreet mit Kriegsschäden
14 Epilog (Friedens-fibel)	Schut-zumschlag hinten	*Vergeßt nicht*:	Studierende in einem Auditorium

Annäherung

Brecht nannte seine Verse zu den von ihm ausgewählten Fotos in seinem *Arbeitsjournal* "Fotoepigramme." Dieter Wöhrle beschreibt das Verfahren zu Recht so:

> Die Photographie wird nicht mehr nur dazu bemüht, um etwas auszustellen, sondern in den neuen Kontext des Gedichts gestellt, der das Photo kommentiert. Zugleich wird das Gedicht aus seinem bislang erprobten Zusammenhang reiner Wortgebilde herausgenommen und mit Bildern verbunden. In der Verbindung beider entsteht etwas Neues, das man als Fortsetzung ihrer internen Entwicklung beschreiben kann, indem die jeweilige Grenze des Mediums übersprungen wird.[41]

Analog könnte man, so man denn wollte, Eislers *Bilder* als musikalische Fotoepigramme bezeichnen und hätte damit eine provisorische gattungsmäßige Zuordnung fixiert. Aber was wäre damit gewonnen? Einfacher und vor allem angemessener wäre es meines Erachtens, in diesen kurzen Stücken im Sinne des von Eisler gewählten Titels tatsächlich "Bilder" zu sehen, ein "Gesamtkunstwerk": kleine, konzentriert gearbeitete Kunstwerke, die das Fotografische, das Poetische und das Musikalische zu einer neuen Einheit verschmelzen oder auch Unterschiedliches oder gar Gegensätzliches ausdrücken.[42] Anders gesagt: Eisler seinerseits verhält sich zu den Brechtschen Bild-Text-Kompositionen ebenso, wie sich Brechts Texte zu den von ihm gefundenen und ausgewählten Fotografien verhalten:

souverän. Er verbindet "Einfachheit" und "Subtilität"[43] und versucht weder, die Fotos in irgendeiner Weise nachzuzeichnen noch dem Text genau zu folgen. Vielmehr entwirft er in jedem einzelnen Fall ein durchaus eigenständiges, geradezu delikates musikalisches Gebilde: die Eislerschen "Bilder" gehen weder in den Fotos noch in den Texten der *Kriegsfibel* Brechts auf. Die sorgfältig gearbeitete Komposition der *Bilder* zeigt, dass offensichtlich alles exquisit sein sollte; anspruchsvolle Fragmente, Aphorismen, in sich geschlossene, "runde" Miniaturen sollten es wohl werden, kostbare musikalische Perlen. Eisler setzt nicht nur durch die Auswahl der Fotoepigramme, sondern auch durch deren Komposition *eigene* Akzente—durch die Melodik, die Harmonik, das Lapidare, den Einsatz des Orchesters. Er drückt das Gedankliche spezifisch eisler-musikalisch aus. Gerd Rienäcker vergleicht die *Kriegsfibel*-Kompositionen von Dessau und Eisler und meint: "Darin jedoch, im Versuch radikaler Dialektik, gehen Eislers und Dessaus Kompositionen zusammen—im Aufspüren von Widersprüchen, vor allem in ihrer Emanzipation als Konstituenz und Movens des musikalischen Geschehens zu Wort und Bild."[44]

Wie Brechts Fotoepigramme sind auch alle fünfzehn einzelnen Stücke Eislers kurz, aphoristisch; jeweils haben wir sorgsam gebaute individuelle, originelle Einzelstücke, die gleichsam durch *ein* Prinzip zusammengehalten werden: das der intelligenten Knappheit (oder auch der aphoristischen Originalität). Jedes einzelne Stück ist in sich strukturiert, hat zumindest zwei Teile. Wichtig sind einige Nachspiele, die das Vorhergehende kommentieren/ präzisieren. Locker, abwechslungsreich ist die Folge der einzelnen Stücke angelegt: Wir finden sowohl textliche oder musikalische Anknüpfungen als auch Kontraste. So beginnt und endet das zehnte Stück zwar wie das neunte im *fortissimo*, die Haltungen beider Stücke sind jedoch gegensätzlich. Wenn man nun auf das Ganze der *Bilder* blickt, das von dem jeweils ruhig-nachdenklichen ersten und letzten Stück (*Introduktion*, *Epilog*) umschlossen wird, so zeigt sich eine große Dreiteiligkeit, die an traditionelle Formstrukturen erinnert: im Zentrum befindet sich ein Mittelteil mit den fünf *piano/pianissimo* gehaltenen ruhigen Stücken vier bis acht; demgegenüber sind die beiden "Eckteile" in Tempo und Lautstärke kontrastreich.

Was die Gesamtkonzeption der *Bilder aus der Kriegsfibel* betrifft, so besitzen wir glücklicherweise eine Stellungnahme von Eislers Sohn Georg. Im Jahre 1971 fanden in Österreich zwei Eisler-Konzerte statt, in denen neben den *Ernsten Gesängen* und dem Chorstück *Gegen den Krieg* auch die *Bilder aus der Kriegsfibel* erklangen. Beide Konzertprogramme enthielten einen Text von Georg Eisler, in dem es unter anderem heißt:

> Hanns Eisler wollte bei der Aufführung der "Kriegsfibel" auch das Visuelle einbeziehen. Wie er mir erklärte, war es seine Absicht, die Bildvorlagen, zu denen Brecht die Vierzeiler verfasst hatte, im

> Konzertsaal zu zeigen. Eine Leinwand sollte über dem Podium angebracht und die Bilder darauf projiziert werden. Bei den Brecht-Vorlagen handelt es sich ausnahmslos um Ausschnitte aus Zeitungen und Illustrierten; das heißt, auf gestochen scharfe, präzise Wiedergabe wurde wenig Wert gelegt, denn der Charakter der Drucksache sollte gewahrt bleiben. Dieses Prinzip müsste auch bei den Projektionen gelten. Meinem Vater war es vor allem darum zu tun, bei diesem audiovisuellen Versuch Musik, Text und Bild zu einem Mittel der Information zu verbinden. Der Konzertbesucher sollte nie die Tatsachen, die der Anlass dieser Komposition sind, aus den Augen verlieren.[45]

Leid, Schuld, Widerstand, Ausblick

Wer nicht die Totalität von Brechts Werk im Blick hat (oder danach trachtet, sie im Blick zu haben), sondern sein Brechtbild wesentlich mit dessen Zynismen verbindet, mag sich erstaunt die Augen reiben: Aber es ist unabweisbar, dass in der *Kriegsfibel* nicht nur die Verurteilung der Faschisten und antifaschistischer Widerstand, sondern auch menschliches Leid und die Frage nach der eigenen Schuld zu den zentralen Themen gehören. So auch in Eislers *Bildern*: Nicht nur in der *Introduktion*, sondern auch in nicht weniger als in vier Stücken konzentriert Eisler sich ganz direkt auf die Dimension des vom Krieg verursachten Leidens, zwei Stücke zielen auf die Entlarvung der faschistischen Mörder, drei gelten der eigenen Schuld des deutschen Volkes, vier gelten verschiedenen Facetten des Widerstands, eines nimmt als *Epilog* den Text der letzten Seite des Schutzumschlags der *Friedensfibel* auf. Das alles kann in dem hier gegebenen Rahmen nicht dargestellt werden. Ich gebe jedoch drei Beispiele.

Leid: Im letzten Teil der *Bilder* treten Menschen auf, die im vollen Sinn des Wortes unschuldig sind: Kinder. Anders als in den verschiedenen *Lukullus*-Versionen zeigen Brecht und Eisler nicht, dass und wie die Kinder instrumentalisiert werden, sondern sie zeigen sie als Opfer. Deshalb wohl hat Brecht die vergleichsweise ausführlichen Kommentare zu den Kinderfotos aus vier Ländern (Griechenland, Sowjetunion, Italien, Frankreich) in die *Kriegsfibel* übernommen, deshalb wohl spricht er nicht *über* die Kinder, sondern lässt sie als eine Gruppe gleichberechtigter Sprecher, gleichsam als ein lyrisches Wir, selbst sprechen: Hier formulieren die Opfer selbst ihre Anklagen, indem sie sich mit Verachtung, Hohn und Spott an die "großen Krieger" wenden: "Wir sind's, die ihr besiegt habt, triumphiert!"

Eisler hat für den Gesang der Kinder eine eindrucksvolle Komposition geschaffen: Immer *piano* bleibend und dabei "zart" beziehungsweise "sehr zart" von Hörnern und Posaunen unterstützt, entwickelt sich die e-moll Melodie der Frauenstimme vorsichtig, schrittweise über dem dunklen Untergrund (E bzw. e), der von nicht weniger als fünf Instrumenten geformt wird (Bassklarinette, Fagott, Pauke, zwei Kontrabässe). Und wie nahezu durchgängig in den *Bildern* ist die Struktur der Melodie syllabisch: Alles soll verstanden werden! Drückt schon die leise, präzis artikulierte Frauenstimme Protest und Verachtung aus, so wird diese Haltung noch verstärkt, wenn der Chor die Worte "Triumphiert! Triumphiert!" *pianissimo* vorträgt—und wenn dann dieser Protest, dieser Hohn der Kinder im überraschend beginnenden Nachspiel bestätigt wird—nun aber grell und aggressiv, direkt, offen: eine der nicht seltenen "Explosionen" der *Bilder*.

Mörder: Im vierten *Bild* legt der Sprecher der suchenden Frau nahe, sie möge nicht das "Schicksal" für den Tod ihrer Lieben verantwortlich machen, sondern nach den wirklich Schuldigen suchen—aber bereits zuvor, in dem unmittelbar auf die *Introduktion* folgenden ersten *Bild*, wurde indirekt ein derartiger Hinweis gegeben. Es ist die Komposition von jenem erstaunlichen Fotoepigramm Brechts, das an die Niederlage der Republikaner im Spanischen Bürgerkrieg erinnert: Das Foto zeigt ein Dankgebet der faschistischen Sieger in Barcelona. Brechts Text ist nicht schlechthin lediglich ein Rollengedicht, sondern ein Lied: ein Gesang der spanischen Konterrevolutionäre, die "Gott" preisen, weil *er* ihnen ihren Sieg ermöglicht habe. Brechts bestürzende Idee: Er geht noch weiter und stellt die faschistischen Soldaten und Gott auf eine Ebene: "Gott ist ein Faschist," singen sie. In Übereinstimmung mit seiner Theorie des epischen Theaters verwendet Brecht hier also Formulierungen, die dem Leser/Hörer helfen, eigenes kritisch-distanzierendes scharfes Denken zu entwickeln und in einem produktiven Denkakt die Verlogenheit des Liedtextes zu begreifen und zu entlarven. Dahinter steckt natürlich *auch* die Abrechnung mit allen Konzeptionen, die überirdische Kräfte für die Durchsetzung eigener Ziele und Interessen reklamieren.

Indem Eisler *Die Glocken läuten* unmittelbar der *Introduktion* folgen lässt, beginnt er die Folge seiner *Bilder* sofort mit mehreren scharfen Gegensätzen, die auf die Selbstentlarvung der Sieger zielen. Textlich: Statt der Klage der Mütter nun die brutale Selbstdarstellung der Soldaten in der zynischen Sprache der Schlächter. Musikalisch: Statt dem *pianissimo*-Motiv der Pauke nun ein mehrfach wiederholtes Paukenmotiv in dreifachem *forte*; statt dem *pianissimo* des Chores nun ein Stück, das nahezu durchgängig *ff* bzw. *fff* zu singen ist; statt der stockenden Melodie zu *Seht unsre Söhne* nun eine Melodie, die an einen Choral erinnert: Beginnt das Stück schon choralmäßig in der traditionell "schweren" Tonart b-moll, so wird das Choralmäßige unmittelbar hörbar, wenn in den Takten sieben bis zehn und siebzehn bis zwanzig das Eingangsmotiv des Chorals *Nun danket alle Gott* variiert aufgenommen wird—die faschistischen Soldaten danken mit ihrem Gebet dem "Faschisten" Gott:

Die Bedeutsamkeit dieser Stelle hebt Eisler außerdem dadurch hervor, dass er sie kontrastierend *piano* singen lässt und sie als einen vierstimmig gesetzten *a capella* Einschub behandelt. Das aggressive, "grell" (HEA 507) zu spielende Zwischen- und Nachspiel besteht hingegen aus einer kurzen dissonanten Passage, die das wiederholt gesungene "Gott ist ein Faschist" verstärkt.

Schuld: "Alors, qui est responsable?" fragt der Sprecher in *Nuit et Brouillard* kurz vor Ende des Films, und er schneidet damit ein weiteres der großen Themen an, auf das Eisler im Anschluss an Brecht eingeht, das der *eigenen* Schuld der Deutschen. Gerade dieser Denkansatz war damals von großer Aktualität, da ja die öffentliche Meinung sowohl im Osten wie im Westen Deutschlands weit von der Bereitschaft entfernt war, eigene Schuld anzusprechen oder gar zu akzeptieren. In nicht weniger als drei der fünfzehn *Bilder* wird das durch den Krieg geschaffene Leid mit allem Nachdruck mit dieser Frage verknüpft—und die Schuld wird dabei keinesfalls in der Art der in der DDR offiziell üblichen einseitigen Ansichten allein den Faschisten und ihren Hintermännern zugewiesen. Brecht und Eisler unterstützen auch nicht die Fiktion, dass nach dem Krieg ein ebenso rascher wie gründlicher Umerziehungsprozess stattgefunden hätte, dass derartige Schuldbekenntnisse also unangebracht wären (siehe etwa Brechts *Buckower Elegien* oder Eislers *Ernste Gesänge*). So bezieht sich das zwölfte *Bild* (*Kriegsfibel* 65) auf das Foto einer zerstörten deutschen Stadt.[46] Es sprechen überlebende Soldaten, und zwar solche, die sich angesichts der in Trümmern liegenden Stadt mit Entsetzen über die Untaten äußern, an denen sie doch selbst beteiligt waren. Sie verstehen, dass sie, indem sie den faschistischen Führern ein "Heil" "entgegenröhrten," in Wahrheit Handlanger der "Weltzerstörer" waren und dass die Zerstörung der menschlichen Kultur, an der sie beteiligt waren, sich nicht nur auf ein einzelnes Land bezieht. Sie verstehen, was sie selbst angerichtet haben und welche Konsequenzen ihr eigenes Handeln hatte, und fühlen sich schuldig.

Eislers Musik betont das Entsetzen, die Aufregung, die Selbstanklage dieser Soldaten. "Unruhig (nicht eilen)," fordert er, aber in einer Vorarbeit steht auch "nicht schleppen" (HEA 507). Unruhig ist gewiss die wesentlich aus Achteln bestehende Melodie des einstimmigen Chores, deren erster Teil unverändert wiederholt wird. Unruhig aber ist vor allem der Orchesterpart: die vom ersten bis zum letzten Ton laufenden ostinaten Achtel der Akkordeons, die nichts enthalten als den *fortissimo* zu spielenden Akkord d—es—g und die dadurch eine ganz eigenartige, originelle Klangfarbe hervorbringen; Unruhe erzeugen die *sforzati* Schläge der Bläser und der kleinen Trommel auf "leichten" Taktteilen sowie die synkopierte Dissonanz von Bläsern und Becken, die die Mitte des Stücks beziehungsweise dessen Schluss markiert—einem Entsetzensschrei vergleichbar.

Notendruck, Aufführungen

Die Druckgeschichte der *Bilder* wurde mit einem Faksimiledruck des elften Stücks (*Ihr in den Tanks*) in der Wochenzeitschrift "Sonntag" vom 6. Juli 1958 zum "Thema der Woche: Hanns Eisler zum 60. Geburtstag" eröffnet. Abgebildet ist nicht die Partitur, sondern ein Blatt aus der Entwurfshandschrift HEA 507. Mit Blick auf die *Kriegsfibel*-Vertonung bemerkte der Kommentar: "Er bringt sie dar zum V. Parteitag der Sozialistischen Einheitspartei Deutschlands und widmet sie unserer Nationalen Volksarmee. . . . Wir sehen der Uraufführung des Werkes innerhalb der Berliner Festtage 1958 mit großen Erwartungen entgegen."[47] Im Druck erschienen alle *Bilder aus der Kriegsfibel* dann 1966 im zehnten Band der seit 1955 erschienenen Ausgabe *Lieder und Kantaten*.[48] Für diesen Band war der Herausgeber Nathan Notowicz mithin auf Materialien aus dem Nachlass angewiesen, vor allem natürlich auf die saubere handschriftliche Partitur Eislers (s.o., HEA 508).

Der Briefwechsel zwischen dem Herausgeber und dem Leipziger Verlag Breitkopf und Härtel begann mit einem Brief von Notowicz an Dr. Goetz vom 12. Mai 1965; er bezog sich im Wesentlichen auf den Titel des Werkes, auf die Widmung sowie auf einige Unklarheiten des eigentlichen Notentextes (HEA 7595).[49] In unserem Zusammenhang sind jedoch zwei andere Momente wichtig: Zum einen belegt der Briefwechsel, dass Notowicz wie selbstverständlich davon ausging, dass der Notenband auch die entsprechenden Fotos enthalten müsste. Gleich in diesem ersten Brief schrieb er: "Bitte, prüfen Sie doch, ob man nach den gedruckten Bildern Fotos machen kann, die für den Druck ausreichen" (HEA 7595). Aber am 1.Juli 1966 teilte H. Döhnert vom Verlag Breitkopf und Härtel Notowicz brieflich mit, dass der Verlag vom Sekretariat Helene Weigels folgende Information erhalten hat: "Frau Professor Helene Weigel, die zurzeit nicht in Berlin ist, bat mich, Ihnen mitzuteilen, daß sie nicht einverstanden ist mit dem Abdruck von Bildern aus der Kriegsfibel innerhalb einer Eisler-Gesamtausgabe. Die Bilder mit den Texten, die Bertolt Brecht geschrieben hat, sind eine Sache für sich und können nicht für Kompositionen benutzt werden" (HEA 7595). Die Hoffnung, den ästhetischen Zusammenhang von Bild—Text—Ton sichtbar zu machen, musste damit aufgegeben werden: Soweit mir bekannt ist, existiert bis heute keine Ausgabe, in der Brechts Fotoepigramme und Eislers Kompositionen zusammengeführt werden. Zum anderen gibt der Briefwechsel Aufschluss über die vermutlich erste Aufführung der *Bilder*: Grabs spricht davon, dass Kurt Greiner-Pol "die *Kriegsfibel* seinerzeit in Anwesenheit Eislers mit dem Erich-Weinert-Ensemble einstudiert hatte."[50] Dies wird auch bestätigt durch einen Brief von Goetz an Notowicz (6.5.66, HEA 7595), in dem er von einem "hier noch vorliegenden Lichtpauseexemplar mit dem Stempelaufdruck 'Erich-Weinert-Ensemble Archiv'" sprach. Schließlich verweist auf eine von Eisler begleitete (geplante oder realisierte) Aufführung durch das Erich-Weinert-Ensemble auch eine undatierte Kopie, die in der Mappe HEA 1802/K liegt und den handschriftlichen Vermerk trägt "lag in Mappe: Kriegsfibel." Besonders interessant ist, dass sie Minutenangaben enthält, die mit denen nahezu identisch sind, die Eisler vor der eigentlichen Niederschrift der Komposition fixiert hatte (s.o., HEA 1802). Aber jeder dieser Hinweise gilt lediglich der Einstudierung der *Bilder*—ein Beleg für eine tatsächlich erfolgte Aufführung ist mir nicht bekannt.

Dieser ersten Einstudierung der *Kriegsfibel* folgten bis heute nur wenige andere. Von besonderem Interesse ist zunächst allerdings, dass eine von Eisler angeregte Aufführung nicht zustande kam. Der Leipziger Dirigent Herbert Kegel hatte sich nämlich am 17. Juni 1958 an Eisler mit der Bitte um eine Aufführung der *Deutschen Sinfonie* gewandt. Eisler antwortete in einem Briefentwurf vom 29. Juni abschlägig, da er diese Aufführung bereits der Berliner Staatsoper versprochen hatte. Aber er fragte: "könnten Sie, zu den von Ihnen bestimmten Terminen eine andere Arbeit von mir aufführen? Und zwar in Leipzig u. zu den Festwochen in Berlin?" (HEA 6091 u. 6092). Diese Bitte korrespondierte unmittelbar mit dem Bericht des *Sonntag* vom 6. Juli, der von der "Uraufführung des Werkes innerhalb der Berliner Festtage 1958" mit Bestimmtheit sprach. Allerdings: Obgleich Eisler die Minuten der einzelnen Stücke penibel addiert hatte und also wusste, dass das gesamte Stück etwa fünfzehn Minuten in Anspruch nehmen würde, erklärte er in dem Briefentwurf, "diese meine neueste Arbeit" würde etwa vierzig Minuten dauern. Glaubte er im Ernst, er könnte innerhalb von zwei, drei Monaten über zwanzig neue *Bilder* komponieren? Das ist wohl nicht anzunehmen—und deshalb hat er den Brief womöglich nicht abgesandt. Hinweise auf eine Antwort von Kegel oder auf eine Aufführung der *Bilder* durch ihn scheint es jedenfalls nicht zu geben.

Der Schoß ist fruchtbar noch

"Was immer man ihnen einreden will, die Völker wissen: Der Friede ist das A und O aller menschenfreundlichen Tätigkeiten, aller Produktion, aller Künste, einschließlich der Kunst zu leben," sagte Brecht in seiner hintergründigen Rede, die er in Moskau hielt, als er den Stalin-Friedenspreis erhielt. Niemand anderer als Boris Pasternak hatte sie ins Russische übersetzt. In dieser Rede ist die eigene *Kriegsfibel* aufgehoben—wir dürfen sie aber auch auf Eislers erst später entstandene *Bilder* beziehen. In beiden Kunstwerken treffen wir auf die quantitative Dominanz von Haltungen wie Mitleid, Mitgefühl, Trauer / die nachdrückliche Frage nach der eigenen Schuld / den satirischen Umgang mit der "Geduld" der Völker / die Beschränkung der Frage nach den ökonomisch und politisch Schuldigen auf wenige andeutende Stichworte ("oben"—"unten," die "Herrn") / den Verzicht auf die Verwendung politischer Schlagworte wie "Kriegstreiber" oder

"Kriegsbrandstifter" / die eindringliche Warnung vor dem Verführtwerden: Dies waren und sind Zeichen von politischem Mut und Klarheit von Brecht wie von Eisler; Zeichen einer kritisch-distanzierte Sicht auf militärisches Blockdenken. Vieles von dem entsprach mit Sicherheit nur bedingt dem, was auch noch um 1956-1957 als "volkstümlich" oder "parteilich" verstanden und gefordert wurde. Übereinstimmung im Grundsätzlichen aber bestand im Hinblick auf eine durchaus ernst gemeinte Friedenserziehung. Erst der immer schärfer werdende Kalte Krieg aber brach diese Übereinstimmung zunehmend auf.

Freilich: Angesichts der Erfahrungen mit den Verbrechen Stalins scheint es sich in der Moskauer Rede um blanke Schönfärberei zu handeln. Gleichwohl mögen diese Sätze mehr Verzweiflung enthalten haben, als ihnen äußerlich anzusehen ist. Sie waren aber eben *auch* Ausdruck der inhärent antistalinistischen, demokratischen, friedlichen Programmatik der späten Werke Brechts, die sich mit der Eislers weitestgehend deckte: In ihren Vorstellungen vom Frieden berührte sich gerade das, was Gorbatschow Jahrzehnte später (historisch betrachtet, zu spät) einforderte: die Verbindung des "Klassenmäßigen" mit dem "Allgemeinmenschlichen." Gorbatschow: "Die grundlegende Frage, die sowohl für die Marxisten als auch für deren Opponenten aktuell wurde, ist die Frage der Verbindung des klassenbedingten und des allgemein menschlichen Elements in der realen globalen Entwicklung und folglich in der Politik."[51] So war es mit Sicherheit kein Zufall, dass Ursula Heukenkamp gerade in den "Gorbatschow-Jahren" 1985–1989 schrieb: Brechts in der *Kriegsfibel* entwickeltes Verfahren zielte darauf, "dass weder die Schrecken des Krieges verkleinert werden noch der Humanismus als Maß des Menschen aus dem Blickfeld gerät."[52] Was Gorbatschow 1988 einforderte, hatten Brecht und Eisler schon Jahrzehnte zuvor künstlerisch realisiert. Diesen Gedanken weiter führend, ist es auch angemessen, festzustellen, dass die ästhetische Konzeption der *Kriegsfibel* wie der *Bilder aus der Kriegsfibel* nicht im Widerspruch, sondern umgekehrt in Übereinstimmung mit einigen grundlegenden biblischen Auffassungen sich befinden. Auch dieser Umstand mag den Vorwurf des "Pazifismus" gegenüber diesem "Buch der Propaganda gegen den Krieg"[53] mit veranlasst haben.

Was speziell Eisler angeht, so verhielt er sich, als er nach Brechts Tod zu dessen *Kriegsfibel* griff, in der Komposition der *Bilder* wie auch in den weitaus meisten seiner späten Kompositionen seinem politisch-ästhetischen Selbstverständnis gemäß wohl als Kommunist, jedoch ohne die damaligen offiziell/offiziösen Forderungen an die Künstler und die Künste zu akzeptieren. Wollte man sich jener Terminologie bedienen, so müsste man die *Bilder* wie etwa auch die Kantaten *Das Vorbild* oder *Die Teppichweber von Kujan-Bulak ehren Lenin* als zumindest tendenziell "formalistisch" bezeichnen: Wieder ein Grund für das latente Misstrauen, mit dem Eisler betrachtet wurde. Aber derartige Konstrukte hatten schon damals keinen

Wert. Vielmehr besteht das Wesentliche seiner *Kriegsfibel*-Komposition gerade in ihrer überzeugenden ästhetischen, gedanklichen, ja politischen Konzeption, in ihrem Sein als ästhetisch geronnene Mahnungen, in ihrer nach wie vor niederschmetternden Aktualität.[54] Den *Bildern aus der Kriegsfibel* liegt nicht nur eine überzeugende, ja ich scheue mich nicht zu sagen: eine ergreifende kompositorische Idee zugrunde, sondern alle Details sind auf das sorgsamste ausgearbeitet—ohne jeden Bezug auf dodekaphone oder serielle Techniken, aber auch ohne sich an irgendwelchen quasi-offiziellen Vorgaben zu orientieren. Hinsichtlich der ästhetischen Spezifik des Ganzen kann man wohl auch sagen: Ein Prinzip (das Grundprinzip) der *Bilder* scheint darin zu bestehen, dass Eisler hier versucht hat, sein Recht auf künstlerische Freiheit nicht nur erneut zu erproben, sondern es zu demonstrieren. Wieder einmal gab er "des Eislers, was des Eislers ist."

Freilich: Vermögen die *Bilder aus der Kriegsfibel* (auch) heute, ästhetisches Wohlgefallen zu erzeugen, gibt es Musikerinnen und Musiker, Hörerinnen und Hörer, die sie als interessant, überzeugend, beeindruckend, schön—oder gar als "cool" empfinden? Und vor allem: Vermögen diese "Gesamtkunstwerke," wie erhofft, friedliche Impulse zu befördern? Wer weiß. Aber wie schrieb doch Felsenstein an Brecht: "Die Frage, die sich sehr rasch erhebt, ist: wie bringt man dieses großartige Dokument an diejenigen heran, die es am dringendsten brauchen?"

Anmerkungen

[1] Bertolt Brecht, *Kriegsfibel* (Berlin: Eulenspiegel Verlag, 1956), im Weiteren zitiert als *Kriegsfibel*; Hanns Eisler, *Bilder aus der Kriegsfibel*, in Eisler, *Lieder und Kantaten,* Bd. 10 (Leipzig: Breitkopf und Härtel, 1966), S. 33–60, im Weiteren zitiert als *Bilder*.

Folgende Sigeln werden verwendet:

AJ Bertolt Brecht, *Arbeitsjournal 1938–1955*, Werner Hecht, Hrsg. (Berlin und Weimar: Aufbau Verlag, 1977).

BBA Bertolt Brecht Archiv, Akademie der Künste, Berlin.

BFA Bertolt Brecht, *Werke. Große kommentierte Berliner und Frankfurter Ausgabe*, Werner Hecht u. a., Hrsg. (Berlin und Frankfurt am Main: Aufbau und Suhrkamp, 1988–2000).

HEA Hanns Eisler Archiv, Akademie der Künste, Berlin.

[2] Während es weit über ein Dutzend Arbeiten gibt, die sich mit Brechts *Kriegsfibel* beschäftigen, gibt es bis heute lediglich eine knappe Schallplatten- bzw. cd-Einführung von Günter Mayer sowie den angegebenen Aufsatz von Gerd Rienäcker, der sich sowohl auf Dessau wie auf Eisler bezieht. Eine spezielle Arbeit zu Eislers *Bildern* existiert bislang offensichtlich nicht. Siehe Günter Mayer, ["Einführung"] zu: Hanns Eisler, *Goethe-Rhapsodie* (Berlin: VEB Deutsche Schallplatten, 1980), NOVA 855 183; unwesentlich verändert auch in Hanns Eisler, *Vokalsinfonik* (Berlin: Classics 0092342BC, 1996), S. 14–15; Gerd Rienäcker, "Fibel-Musik?

Anmerkungen zu Hanns Eislers und Paul Dessaus Vertonungen der *Kriegsfibel*," in *Fokus "Deutsches Miserere" von Paul Dessau und Bertolt Brecht*, Festschrift Peter Petersen zum 65. Geburtstag, Nina Ermlich Lehmann, Sophie Fetthauer, Mathias Lehmann, Jörg Rothkamm, Silke Wenzel und Kristina Wille, Hrsg. (Hamburg: von Bockel Verlag, 2005), S. 87–110.

[3] Paul Dessau, *Deutsches Miserere*, Partitur, Nachwort von Peter Petersen (München: Musikproduktion Höflich, 2006); s. a. Paul Dessau, *14 Stücke aus "Internationale Kriegsfibel" (Bertolt Brecht) für Einzelstimmen, gemischten Chor und Orchester* (1945-1970), Partitur (Leipzig: Edition Peters, [1980]). Vgl. *Fokus "Deutsches Miserere" von Paul Dessau und Bertolt Brecht.*

[4] Siehe dazu meine Arbeit *Essays zu Hanns Eislers musikalischem und poetischem Schaffen* (Berlin: Bodoni Verlag, 2013), Bd. 3: *Nie und nimmer! Überlegungen zu Hanns Eislers Projekt einer Faustoper.*

[5] Hanns Eisler, *Musik und Politik: Schriften 1948–1962. Textkritische Ausgabe*, Günter Mayer, Hrsg. (Leipzig: Deutscher Verlag für Musik, 1982), S. 309. Siehe auch HEA 2613.

[6] Siehe Anya Feddersen, "Kriegsfibel," in Jan Knopf, Hrsg., *Brecht Handbuch*, Bd. 2 (Stuttgart und Weimar: J. B. Metzler, 2001), S. 382–397.

[7] Erdmut Wizisla, "Virtuelle Kriegserfahrung mit Brecht-Texten: *Die Kriegsfibel*," in Sabine Kebir und Therese Hörnigk, Hrsg., *Brecht und der Krieg—Widersprüche damals, Einsprüche heute: Brecht-Dialog 2004* (Berlin: Theater der Zeit, 2005), S. 160–161; hier, S. 161; Werner Mittenzwei, *Das Leben des Bertolt Brecht oder Der Umgang mit den Welträtseln*, Bd. 2 (Berlin und Weimar: Aufbau, 1986), S. 714–715; Albrecht Dümling, *Lasst euch nicht verführen: Brecht und die Musik* (München: Kindler, 1985). Eislers Vertonung der *Kriegsfibel* wird auch in Feddersens umfänglichen Artikel im Brecht Handbuch nicht erwähnt.

[8] Die ersten Fotoepigramme, die in die *Kriegsfibel* eingegangen sind: *noch bin ich eine stadt* (2.10.40), *es war zur zeit* (23.11.40) und *such nicht mehr frau* (24.12.40).

[9] Grischa Meyer, "Kann man von Bildern des Krieges etwas für den Frieden lernen?" in *Brecht und der Krieg*, S. 70–85; hier, S. 79.

[10] Paul Dessau 1894–1979. *Dokumente zu Leben und Werk*, Daniela Reinhold, Hrsg. (Berlin: Henschel-Verlag, 1995), S. 43–45 u. S. 75–77.

[11] BFA 29, 345.

[12] Siehe Werner Hecht, *Brecht Chronik 1898–1956*, zweite Auflage (Frankfurt am Main: Suhrkamp, 1998), S. 838. In dem Ergänzungsband zu seiner Brecht-Chronik notiert Hecht, dass Brecht noch von Santa Monica aus Helene Weigel "um Zusendung der Fotoepigramme" bat. Siehe Hecht, *Brecht Chronik 1898—1956: Ergänzungen* (Frankfurt am Main: Suhrkamp, 2007), S. 56.

[13] Hecht, *Brecht Chronik*, S. 915.

[14] Ebd., S. 915.

[15] Anonymus, "Bert Brecht. Mit 'Ungenügend' zu den Akten," *Literatur Revue* (Würzburg) 2.3 (1960), S. 15–17. Hier nach BBA 3422. Erdmut Wizisla, "Virtuelle Kriegserfahrung mit Brecht-Texten," S. 160.

[16] Stefan Heymann, Brief an Brecht, 26.04.50, in Mappe Berlau, BBA 1774/02; vgl. Hecht, *Brecht Chronik*, S. 919.

[17] BBA 1774/04. o. D. Vgl. die späteren "Nachbemerkungen zu den Bildern" am Ende der *Kriegsfibel.*

[18] *Meyers Neues Lexikon in acht Bänden*, Bd. 6 (Leipzig: VEB Bibliographisches Institut, 1963), S. 439. Einschränkend wird hinzugefügt: "Diese negativen Seiten schließen jedoch nicht aus, dass der P., insofern er gegenwärtig gegen den imperialistischen Krieg und vor allem gegen die Vorbereitung eines dritten Weltkrieges auftritt, zugleich eine positive Rolle zu spielen vermag."

[19] Brecht wehrte sich. Siehe seinen Brief an den Eulenspiegel Verlag (4.1.1955, BBA 0745/024); darauf antwortete Heynowski (14.1.1955, BBA 166/33): "Soweit mir bekannt ist, haben einige Mitarbeiter des Amtes für Literatur in Ihre *Kriegsfibel* eine 'pazifistische Tendenz' hineingelesen." Im Auftrag Brechts wandte sich Isot Kilian an den Leiter des Amtes für Literatur, Hoffmann, und erklärte, dass Brecht "eine schriftliche Erklärung haben möchte, warum es nötig war, dass das Manuskript der *Kriegsfibel* im Amt für Literatur längere Zeit zur Druckgenehmigung vorlag" (5.2.1955, BBA 2 0742/019).

[20] Ernst Schumacher, "Reinhart Gasch: Gesichtet und verdichtet. Meine Kalte-Kriegs-Fibel 1964–1970," in *Brecht und der Krieg*, S. 92–97; hier, S. 93.

[21] Kunert seinerseits meinte, er habe um 1948 bei Brecht "diese großen schwarzen Kartonblätter" mit den Fotos zu der *Kriegsfibel* gesehen: "Und ich habe mir das dann geben lassen von ihm, es war ja sehr kühn, dass er es aus der Hand gegeben hat, es war ja ein Unikat. Und ich bin damit dann zum Eulenspiegelverlag gegangen und hab gesagt, also hier, das muss unbedingt veröffentlicht werden, das ist grandios, großartig" (Zitiert nach *Bertolt Brechts Kriegsfibel: Assoziationen zu einem wenig bekannten Buch. Ein Film von Vera Böhm und Markus Böhm*, ZDF/3sat, 1998). Siehe auch Kunert, "Ein Nachwort zur Herausgabe der Kriegsfibel," in Brecht, *Kriegsfibel*, 1. erweiterte Auflage (Berlin: Eulenspiegel, 1994).

[22] 10.10.54, BBA Z44/42 und Z44/43.

[23] BBA Z44/44.

[24] Z 44/42. Die Abkürzung "ZK" ist wahrscheinlich, aber nicht einwandfrei zu entziffern.

[25] Eulenspiegel Verlag an Brecht, 23.12.1954 (BBA 878/50).

[26] Siehe dazu Werner Hecht, "Die andere Seite der Medaille. Thomas Mann fand ihn 'unannehmbar'—wie Bertolt Brecht vor fünfzig Jahren zum Stalin-Preis kam," *Berliner Zeitung* 17.12.2004: S. 26.

[27] Datum nach Hecht, *Brecht Chronik*, 1136.

[28] Hausmitteilung des Amtes für Literatur und Verlagswesen, 20.12.1954 (BBA Z 44/45).

[29] Mehrere *Eulenspiegel*-Nummern vom April bis Juni 1955 brachten Vorabdrucke der Fotoepigramme (BBA 1335/24–36).

[30] BBA Z 44/45: Amt für Literatur und Verlagswesen, Schreiben von Selle an Seipel, 5.9.55. Nach Auskunft von Dr. Matthias Oehme von der Eulenspiegel Verlagsgruppe erschienen in der DDR vier Auflagen der *Kriegsfibel* (1955, 1968, 1977

und 1983). Die erste Auflage betrug 10.000 Exemplare. "Aus den Unterlagen in unserem Verlagsarchiv ist eine Verhinderung des Druckes nicht ersichtlich" (Brief Dr. Matthias Oehme an den Autor, 8.9.15).

31 BBA Z 44/42. Ich fand keinen Hinweis darauf, dass diesen Vorschlägen entsprochen worden wäre.

32 Brief des Eulenspiegel Verlags an Brecht (1.7.1955, BBA 745/29).

33 Grischa Meyer, "Brechts *Kriegsfibel.* Ein Bilderbuch aus der Zeitung," in Christian Hippe, Hrsg., *Bild und Bildkünste bei Brecht* (Berlin: Matthes und Seitz, 2011), S. 29–40; hier, S. 40. Zu der *Kriegsfibel* meint Peter Palitzsch, "Es ist große Kunst und dafür ziemlich vergessen," und Stefan Soldovieri schreibt: "The *Kriegsfibel* is one of Brecht's most fascinating experiments and occupies a unique place in his lyric production." Siehe Palitzsch, "Die Fibel, ein Hilfsbuch zum Lesenlernen für Anfänger," in *Brecht und der Krieg*, S. 177–178; hier, S. 179; und Soldovieri, "War-Poetry, Photo(epi)grammatry: Brecht's *Kriegsfibel*," in Siegfried Mews, Hrsg., *A Bertolt Brecht Reference Companion* (Westport, CT: Greenwood Press, 1997), S. 139–167; hier, S. 139.

34 Felsenstein an Brecht, 9.12.1955 (BBA 2 0750/086).

35 Titelblatt zu *Nuit et Brouillard* (HEA 93/1r).

36 Siehe HEA 146 (Partitur), HEA 147 (Klavierfassung), HEA 766 und HEA 1202.

37 Hanns Eisler an Stephanie Eisler, 6.9.1957 (HEA 6733).

38 Theo Stammen sieht drei Ordnungsstrukturen: eine "weitgehend chronologische Anordnung," "die antithetische Präsentation von Akteuren und Opfern" sowie Brechts "Antifaschismus und seine Antikriegseinstellung, positiv gewendet: sein Pazifismus." Siehe Stammen, "Brechts *Kriegsfibel.* Politische Emblematik und zeitgeschichtliche Aussage," in Stammen, *Brecht und der Nationalsozialismus: Drei Studien* (Würzburg: Ergon Verlag 2006), S. 61–106; hier, S. 80. Siehe auch Dieter Wöhrle, "Bertolt Brechts *Kriegsfibel*—wie man Photos zum Sprechen bringt," *literatur für leser: Zeitschrift für Interpretationspraxis und geschichtliche Texterkenntnis* 5 (1982): S. 1–22.

39 Siehe Eisler an Ruth Berlau, 6.8.62 (HEA 8361).

40 Gründe für die Äußerung Kleins sind mir nicht bekannt. Manfred Grabs meint: "Das Werk gilt als nicht vollendet. Unter anderem sollten die Vokalteile durch Zwischenspiele verbunden werden." Siehe Manfred Grabs, *Hanns Eisler: Kompositionen. Schriften. Literatur* (Leipzig: Deutscher Verlag für Musik, 1984), S. 42. Ähnlich Günter Mayer, ["Einführung"], S. 15: "Es gilt als nicht vollendet. Unter anderem sollten die Vokalteile durch Zwischenspiele verbunden werden."

41 Dieter Wöhrle, "Von der Notwendigkeit einer 'Kunst der Betrachtung': Bertolt Brechts *Kriegsfibel* und die Gestaltung von Text-Bild-Beziehungen," in Hecht, Hrsg., *alles was Brecht ist . . . Fakten—Kommentare—Meinungen—Bilder* (Frankfurt am Main: Suhrkamp, 1997), S. 232–244; hier, S. 240.

42 So Kunert, in *Bertolt Brechts Kriegsfibel: Assoziationen zu einem wenig bekannten Buch.*

43 Rienäcker, "Fibel-Musik?" S. 99ff.

44 Ebd., S. 101; vgl. auch Mayer, ["Einführung"].

[45] In den Programmheften der Aufführungen 19.10.1971 (Studio Steiermark, HEA 8452) und 4.11.1971 (Wien, HEA 8452).

[46] Es handelt sich um die Stadt Bitburg. Das Foto wurde "nach dem Einmarsch der Amerikaner am 28.02.1945" aufgenommen. Siehe Burkhard Kaufmann, "Bitburg 1945—und ein Gedicht von Bertolt Brecht," *Heimatkalender 2005: Landkreis Bitburg-Prüm* (Bitburg-Prüm: Anders GmbH, 2005), S. 155–159.

[47] "Thema der Woche: Hanns Eisler zum 60. Geburtstag," *Sonntag* 6.7.1958.

[48] Siehe Thomas Ahrend, "Materialien zur Editionsgeschichte der *Lieder und Kantaten* von Hanns Eisler," in Matthias Tischer, Hrsg., *Beiträge zu den Musikverhältnissen eines verschwundenen Staates* (Berlin: Kuhn, 2005), S. 238–259.

[49] Der endgültige Titel sollte nicht *Kriegsfibel*, sondern *Bilder aus der Kriegsfibel* heißen (HEA 7595, 6.5. und 10.5.1966).

[50] Notowicz an Dr. Julius Goetz vom Verlag Breitkopf und Härtel, 5.10.1965 (HEA 7595).

[51] Michael Gorbatschow, "Rede auf dem Plenum des ZK der KPdSU," *Neues Deutschland* 19.2.1988: S. 5.

[52] Ursula Heukenkamp, "Den Krieg von unten ansehen: Über das Bild des zweiten Weltkrieges in Bertolt Brechts *Kriegsfibel*," *Weimarer Beiträge* 31.8 (1985): S. 1294–1312; hier, S. 1303.

[53] Kunert, "Ein Nachwort zur Herausgabe der Kriegsfibel."

[54] Siehe dazu Käthe Reichel, "Der entfesselte Welthandel, die Armut, der Krieg," in *Brecht und der Krieg*, S. 162–176.

Dieter Goltzsche, *Die Dreigroschenoper (Eifersuchtsduett)*, 1973, Durchdruckzeichnung.

Framing Two Accompaniments to *Brecht, Music and Culture: Hanns Eisler in Conversation with Hans Bunge*

Sabine Berendse

In 1954, while working as one of Bertolt Brecht's assistants at the Berliner Ensemble, Hans Bunge began recording Brecht in rehearsal. Thanks to these recordings, we have today a unique, firsthand source of information on the way in which Brecht worked. As well as recording rehearsals, Bunge also interviewed many of Brecht's friends and colleagues and asked them about their experiences of their artistic association with Brecht, the nature of their collaboration, and their thoughts about the Brechtian theater. Among those he interviewed was the composer Hanns Eisler, one of Brecht's professional collaborators and his closest friend.

The conversations, although part of the German edition of Eisler's complete works (published in the GDR in 1975 under the title *Hanns Eisler Gespräche mit Hans Bunge: Fragen Sie mehr über Brecht*), have never been fully translated into English. Fifty-three years after Eisler's death and fifty-nine after Brecht's, these fascinating conversations are now available to an English-speaking audience for the first time. Sabine Berendse (Hans Bunge's daughter) and Paul Clements translated and edited the German original. It was published in October 2014 by Bloomsbury under the title: *Brecht, Music and Culture: Hanns Eisler in Conversation with Hans Bunge*.

The two texts that follow connect with that volume but are not found in its pages. The first is one of the introductions for the 1975 edition, by the renowned Marxist musicologist, conductor, and pianist Georg Knepler. For reasons of space, the English translation of Knepler's text was not included in the Bloomsbury volume. I am pleased that it can appear here because it gives a detailed and informative overview of the Eisler-Bunge conversations and establishes the book's rightful place in history.

The second text, written by Manfred Bierwisch, the internationally acclaimed German linguist and Hans Bunge's close friend, was originally a memorial address on the occasion of Bunge's ninetieth birthday and the opening of his personal archive to the public at the Academy of Arts in Berlin. The article provides a sensitive and fascinating view of Bunge's remarkable life, a life, furthermore, that was formed through World War II, by his decision to settle in the socialist GDR and that was immensely influenced by Bertolt Brecht and his work. Like the Knepler introduction, Bierwisch's tribute to Bunge adds a dimension to our understanding of the book, as well as to the lives and work of those at its center.

The GDR has ceased to exist, but that does not mean that the lives and stories of the people who lived there—and how they came to their ideals—are not worth telling. It would be wrong to claim that Eisler's life between 1898 and 1962 and Bunge's between 1919 and 1990 are typical German lives, but they certainly represent important facets and parallels that, combined with all other life stories of this time, form the political, social, cultural, and intellectual kaleidoscope of the twentieth century.

Dieter Goltzsche, *Brecht*, 1979, Kreide.

Accompaniment 1

Introduction to *Hanns Eisler Gespräche mit Hans Bunge: Fragen Sie mehr über Brecht*

Georg Knepler

It goes without saying that Eisler's conversations with Dr. Bunge are an integral part of his collected works.[1] In the field of music, their richness of information puts them on a par with Brecht's writings on the theater, Walter Benjamin's theoretical works, or Christopher Caudwell's essays. In other words, they form part of that not very long list of contributions to Marxist-Leninist aesthetic and cultural theory that have something to say beyond the confines of conventional aesthetic theory.

With printed conversations, one usually has to ask oneself how accurately what is written corresponds to what has been said. Lapses of memory, false recollection, in certain circumstances even deliberate tampering—for whatever reason—can impair the documentary character of the account, perhaps inevitably so. From this point of view, the use of microphones and tape recorders, as was the case here, turns out to be far more than of technical significance. The transfer from tape to typewriter, and from there into print, has preserved everything, apart from intonation, inflection, and speed of delivery. The unavoidable partial losses in the then traditional method of transmission, involving intensive note taking and the subsequent faulty memories of the participants, have been avoided. It should be noted that interested readers can (and should) familiarize themselves with Eisler's way of speaking by listening to any of the several recordings of him available.

The modern method of recording conversations with important composers with such thoroughness and in such detail, for reproduction at full length and unedited was probably used here for the first time. The special, indeed unique nature of this kind of documentation needs to be emphasized. The fact that the conversations were planned to be revised by both speakers, and that this revision never took place, forms part of its special nature. What might normally be considered a regrettable fact has its advantages: Eisler's line of reasoning appears with an immediacy that might not have survived an editorial reworking.

At the center of Eisler's position is the realization that the working class can and will, by revolutionary means, ensure a socialist-communist future for humanity. These conversations confirm that Eisler developed this awareness during the First World War. This book offers an insight into how this belief was strengthened and how it influenced his way of thinking and reflection. It is thus an outstanding demonstration of the old Marxist thesis that human history will only have meaning and resonance for those who have a firm grasp of its future—and vice versa—a notion that, for understandable reasons, bourgeois history and historiography strongly reject. Whether Eisler speaks of ancient history and personalities of the past or talks about the more recent past—his and Brecht's exile plays a significant role here—the relationship to the present and the future is always the important point. The process of learning from history, however important, is but one aspect of historical consciousness. "Wisdom cannot be bought off the shelf," he says, and elsewhere, "If you want to understand the future, you have to come to terms with the past." However, just as important is the awareness of the necessity of maintaining and transmitting to the proletariat the achievements of the bourgeoisie or other ruling classes, despite the flaws and scars they may carry as a result of their contradictory origins. As Dr. Bunge summarizes, the result of such a perspective is that history is never static. Eisler says he has read Goethe "five times" and perceived him differently every time, just as Beethoven and Richard Wagner did.

Eisler's relationship to "contradiction" has to be understood in the same vein. For him it is not just a category that he, as an educated Marxist, has learned to accept as important in nature, society, and thought. He is positively enthusiastic about it. When a problem seems to be easily resolvable, one probably hasn't sufficiently looked into it; only when contradictions appear, can one hope to have come close to understanding it. This is mentioned every so often, but more frequently demonstrated. More than once Eisler can be seen to follow a thought to its extreme, until an objection or merely a doubt leads him to pursue a different aspect of the same problem with the same intensity. Sometimes this leads to a synthesis of two, or even more, aspects; sometimes they remain—unresolved—side by side. Eisler says at one point: "The demands on the intelligence of an artist are enormous."

Also on the intelligence of the reader. One could maybe see it as a disadvantage of this documentary version of the talks—if it is indeed a disadvantage—that it demands an intelligent, critical, and active reader, who knows how to read the protocol character of the documentation. Eisler himself occasionally remarks, having listened to a part of the talk: "Here, my theories become superficial . . . I probably ought to correct myself." But this warning has to be treated with understanding and discrimination too. After all, this is not a "work" in the narrow sense of the word. The simple absence of paper and writing implements during their creation removes these talks from the normal category of a "work." Here spontaneity and finished product lie much closer together than can be reconciled with the concept of a "work." The reader should bear that in mind. Not only should one read conversations differently from theoretical essays, but their origin, conception, and technical realization should be taken into account. For Eisler's responses are spontaneous only with regard to their wording; the questioning and opinions on which they are based are anything but spontaneous. It was not Eisler's aim to formulate final maxims, but to open up problems and to provide food for thought, especially in areas that seemed to him to be missing in current Marxist aesthetic theory; they are largely still missing today.

For this reason Eisler welcomed the suggested conversations. Initially the suggestion was inspired by the desire to preserve what Eisler had to say about Brecht. But right from the start, and especially beginning with the sixth conversation, they ranged wider; Eisler himself became the focus. Repeatedly it becomes apparent that Eisler had carried entire thought processes around for some time—they had already partly cropped up in this essay or that lecture—but either the time or opportunity had not been right to put them down on paper, or he hadn't quite completed them. In this situation, an understanding and insistent interlocutor with a tape recorder must have seemed a better medium than writing paper.

What was said a decade ago is so up-to-date and contains such revolutionary attitudes and wisdom, sparkles with such intellect and wit, and effortlessly unites enjoyment and seriousness—it doesn't require a foreword to point this out.

—Translated by John Knepler

Anmerkung

[1] *Hanns Eisler Gespräche mit Hans Bunge: Fragen Sie mehr über Brecht*, Gesammelte Werke, Bd. 7 (Leipzig: Deutscher Verlag für Musik, 1975).

Dieter Goltzsche, *Mäckie Messer am Donnerstag*, 1979, Tusche.

Accompaniment 2

Memories of Hans Bunge: on the occasion of his ninetieth birthday, 3 December 2009

Manfred Bierwisch

"A man in the century of wolves"—this phrase coined by Heiner Müller during Hans Bunge's funeral on 7 June 1990 at the Dorotheenstädtische Cemetery says it all, but it would be wrong to remember Bunge only for this. Whoever thinks of Bunge should, beside the twists and turns, and the unavoidable failures, also be conscious of his delight in discoveries, experimentation, and accomplishments. In his independent and resolute way Bunge remained true to himself even under difficult and hostile circumstances. The following memories are a kind of kaleidoscope, incomplete and haphazard, but they're in keeping with the vicissitudes of life, the search and the occasional, unexpected resolution. This is not, therefore, a biographical account of his education and career; instead, snapshots, large and small, of the qualities and twists of fate that made an indelible impression on me.

This bright boy from a German nationalist—later strict National Socialist—family is beyond my knowledge. Already in school he had the nickname "Blitz" because he was always top in mental arithmetic; a boy who joined the Nazi Party out of conviction at the age of nineteen and who went into the worst of all wars at twenty; who advanced to the rank of regimental adjutant during the invasion of Russia, who was taken prisoner and who, thus, survived; who, after the collapse of the Third Reich and six years of hard labor in different Russian prison camps returned—unreformed: the century of wolves had a relentless grip on him from the beginning.

Bunge was already thirty when, with an incredible *volte-face*, he began his real life. His studies in Greifswald made him aware—initially from an antagonistic point of view—of what would become the most important point of reference in his life, namely Brecht. Unquestionably, a kaleidoscope that recollects fragments of Bunge's past must start with Brecht. And what comes naturally to mind is the "Legend of the Origin of the Book Tao-Te-Ching on Lao-Tsu's Road into Exile":

> But the honor should not be restricted

to the sage whose name is clearly writ.
For a wise man's wisdom needs to be extracted.
So the customs man deserves his bit.
It was he who called for it.[1]

One doesn't need long to guess what this poem's final verse has to do with Bunge, for what the customs man deserves is a leitmotiv of Bunge's life. Nobody displayed more understanding and instinct, stamina and talent to recognize the wise man's wisdom, to question and to document it than he. Brecht knew and valued the importance of questioning and documentation, of course, and the intellectually interested customs man is anything but an extra. Bunge, however, far outstripping conventional methods, made a science and an art, or actually several arts, out of them. Because the documentation of the *Kaucasische Kreidekreis* rehearsals at the Berliner Ensemble, arising almost from a moment of inspiration, demanded a completely different set of skills from the resolute questioning of Hanns Eisler, or the patient and difficult conversations with Ruth Berlau. And to the art of questioning always belongs the technique of documentation. Bunge wanted to be up-to-date in this field as well.

However, for Bunge it wasn't just a matter of writing things down. At times he literally came up with a new science of documentation. Soon after Brecht's death the idea for a historical-critical edition of his works was proposed and of course that couldn't be a simple, traditional, standard project. The German Academy of Arts and the German Academy of Sciences competed to present the best editorial model in which not only the various versions of texts but also Brecht's unusual production method could be demonstrated. Bunge was the Academy of Art's protagonist, and opposite him, for the Academy of Sciences, as a competitor and friend, stood my friend Klaus Baumgärtner. I met Bunge for the first time during those vehement debates about the presentation of the most suitable way of reading, for example, Brecht's versified *Kommunistische Manifest*. Big displays with graphics about the development of the text weren't enough in those discussions. Cybernetics, which had just had a breakthrough in the GDR, was called as the main witness; and once Bunge documented his special scientific ambition by beginning the presentation of his model with Einstein's famous formula, $E = mc^2$, which didn't belong there at all. No, Bunge did not lack self-confidence.

The ideas around which the debate centered were exciting and really new, but the planned edition did not, in spite of the diplomatic efforts of the mediator Wolfgang Steinitz, come about; it failed because of legal issues before it could begin. And the worst part for Bunge, who had in 1956 set up the Brecht Archive, on which the whole discussion was based, was that it led to harsh words and a split between him and Helene Weigel. On 31 March 1960 Bunge wrote:

> Dear Mrs. Weigel, today is my last working day at the Archive. I don't need to mention that leaving my work, which I understood until a short while ago as my life's work, is very difficult for me. But a productive continuation of Brecht's work seems to me only guaranteed if a team, which plans, advises, and coordinates most—if not all—measures in connection with the maintenance of Brecht's legacy, is constituted under government supervision and government control of its implementation.

Bunge lost this earnest and uninhibited argument in which he believed he represented the public interest, while Weigel wanted to fend off government intervention. And it wasn't just the infamous Eleventh Plenum of the Central Committee of the SED [in 1965] that brought him to accept this as a just defeat. The rift with Weigel and the subsequent abandonment of his own conviction—those are two aspects of the same integrity under difficult circumstances. Because it was proper that the state in which we then lived should not have had the custody of Brecht's work. Bunge was realistic enough to admit: Weigel had possessed the greater wisdom.

In the meantime, the building of the Wall meant that our mutual friend, Klaus Baumgärtner, was lost to the West; from there he commented sardonically in January 1962:

> Dear Hans, that the *Manifest* is now not even to be edited is a cause for despair. We know how good you are at making bread rolls. But I wouldn't like to see you wasting your good looks and talent on that. No one seems to understand any more that you could also be a low-level manager of a mine, a frigate commander, a director of timetables, or an astronaut.

This is a facet, by the way, that no Bunge kaleidoscope can bypass: baking, cooking, and of course carpentry—in each and every craft Bunge was skillful and he enjoyed craftsmanship every bit as much as the fulfilment of friendships and writing. In 1967, while in a quite difficult situation, he writes to Baumgärtner:

> Of course it is an unconfirmed rumor that Klaus has heard: I could be finished with all the bookshelves; with Mao; and with Eisler and with the whole shebang. I will still find things to do. My bookshelves are my lasting works. Should I stop building them? After all, I can always carry on altering them. And if you could see my new, self-built kitchen . . .

Besides the bookshelves and the built-in kitchen there is Eisler, the second main reference point in Bunge's oeuvre. He came back to Eisler again and again: from the fourteen extended conversations to the scandal surrounding the documentation of the *Faustus* libretto, which Bunge finished only shortly before his own death. A *Lehrstück* in its own right, the way he stimulated Eisler's interest in the form of documented conversation, a conversation in which both ingeniously complement each other. Delightful, for example, the last conversation in which they compare their experiences from the two great wars—the socialist Eisler in the Austro-Hungarian army and Captain Bunge in the fascist Wehrmacht. Bunge, turning down all of Eisler's offers for him to criticize the war, is very well aware of his past in which he entertained no doubts about this war's legitimacy: "I'd like to be able to say something more sensible than I can. But I don't want to turn my attitude of those days into something else." Being able to learn means not to deny things that need correcting. And with this attitude Bunge was—with one exception—always true to himself, calm but determined, maybe skeptical, but definitely able to look at things objectively and always to see the other point of view.

Bunge was a master in the art of bringing people together and of promoting understanding and communication. One could easily gain the impression that Berlin was built around his apartment, around the strange courtyard behind the Marstall in Breite Strasse, and then, after the move, around entrance E in Hackesche Höfe. There was no one you wouldn't have met there. To list all the names would be pointless, but to name but a few there were Augstein and Dönhoff, Everding, Neuss and Johnson, Cremer and Hermlin, and, of course, Biermann, Heiner Müller, and Havemann. Berlin was exciting even as a divided city. At Bunge's the city was suddenly reunited. In the terminology of Stasi surveillance reports, it was a place for the "nurturing of uncontrolled contacts with the enemy." (Attempting to control those contacts was impossible, and it could turn out that a car journey that was supposed simply to convey the guest to the border would develop into a wild pursuit in which, almost sportsmanlike, the driving skills of both parties were demonstrated.)

For all his openness to other people and all his natural relish in gatherings that he cultivated and generously arranged, Bunge was no mere socialite. For him life was about something else; he was interested in participation and communication. Bunge's apartment was only a stone's throw away from the Academy of Sciences in Otto-Nuschke-Strasse, where I worked at that time, and I don't know how often I just dropped in for a quick visit but then stayed late into the night. Bunge was a person with whom you could have these wonderful open talks in which you actually really begin to understand yourself, in which opinions can change so fundamentally that what appears at first completely wrong suddenly becomes absolutely right, and in which utopias seem at the same time irrational and suddenly also feasible.

To return to Lao-tzu—and to the odd memory of an image: Bunge and the Chinese. It has little, if anything, to do with Brecht's artfully stylized

China. In 1966 the Maoist illusions of left-wing students came into existence, and at the same time the conflict escalated between China and the Soviet Union. The ultimate vision of socialism could not have been more contradictory. The Chinese Embassy in Karlshorst was guarded like enemy territory; each visit there was jealously recorded by the security service as a provocation. And that was why Bunge wanted to know more. Was there, maybe, a possible alternative? He was soon a regular guest of the Embassy whose culinary delicacies, by the way, he appreciated as much as their high-proof schnapps called Mao Tai. But the insights he got proved deadly. Maoism was a pigheaded idealization of the state; resistance was found only, if at all, in their barely concealed hostility to the deformed Soviet model of communism; doubts about their own doctrine were impossible; and the Mao bible had its derisory nickname for a good reason.

This curiosity about the Cultural Revolution derived from the same sense of conviction as the position with which Bunge—in the face of all hostility—was to stick by Heiner Müller when in 1961 Müller was made a literary and political non-person because of the marvelously contentious world premiere of *Die Umsiedlerin* by students of the Economics Polytechnic in Berlin. Bunge backed him not only intellectually and morally. Financial help was needed too. And a courageous, intelligently argued, written plea by Bunge on behalf of Müller ended with Bunge applying to join the party—a hara-kiri act that fortunately failed.

Another important facet: Bunge and *Sinn und Form*. After the rift with Weigel, there was no longer a place for Bunge at the Brecht Archive, and the Academy of Arts took him into the editorial office of the Academy journal *Sinn und Form*—where things were difficult. After the incorruptible Peter Huchel, whom Bunge knew very well, was scandalously driven out, and his successor, Bodo Uhse, with whom Bunge had a professional relationship, had died, there now presided the justifiably feared cultural official, Wilhelm Girnus. Bunge's responsibility was for special issues and, with those devoted to Thomas Mann and Eisler he had almost made an autonomous institution out of it. This was doomed to fail. Bunge used the journal's status, which it had gained through its quality and through the continuing support of members of the academy, to promote independent interpretations and judgments, which, with the Eisler issue, led immediately to disputes. For example: was Eisler Schönberg's pupil? Dare we mention that he studied under Schönberg?

In connection with the infamous Eleventh Plenum of the party's Central Committee, a special issue was to be planned, concerned with new drama in the GDR. Bunge's suggestion to focus on Volker Braun, Peter Hacks, and Heiner Müller was dismissed by Girnus as outrageous. Bunge's conformist alternative—Helmut Sakowski, KuBa, Alfred Kurella, and Wilhelm Girnus—was interpreted by the latter exactly as it was intended: as savage irony. The reaction came promptly. Bunge was once more finished, but this time not through his own decision. On 7 January 1966, the academy's party secretary together with its director of administration delivered notice to Bunge, in person, effective immediately. Bunge was home on sick leave.

The GDR's definition of a sovereign state included laws intended to withhold, when necessary, reasons for official measures. Bunge did not receive from any institution a reason for his dismissal and he found himself in a situation which, officially, didn't exist: he was unemployed or, more correctly, barred from following his profession, and very strictly, too. All institutions had to abide by this kind of expulsion—publishing houses, editorial offices, radio, theater. No one in the country was allowed even to publish a book review by him, and if anyone risked it, he or she had at least to omit Bunge's name. Needless to say, he was now also forbidden from traveling to "the other side": gone were the visits of the past when he had skillfully and often successfully worked to promote people's understanding of Brecht, especially during the absurd Brecht boycott by most of the West German theaters after the building of the Wall.

Idleness, to which he seemed to be condemned, wasn't Bunge's thing and so a completely different facet suddenly appears: the beautiful farmhouse at the "Sachsenberg" in the Mecklenburg region. In all honesty, it was a functionless relic of the blood-and-soil ideology of the Nazi period, but it didn't look it. It was simply a well-proportioned, spacious house, built in the old style, which fit wonderfully into the hilly landscape, a good hour away from any railway station. The house's big threshing floor was the place for all kinds of Bunge's practical skills. It was not only necessary to build in shelves and a kitchen, but also a shower, a swing, and a garden. And of course soon the visitors gathered again, including the "enemy forces." On top of this, Bunge was also a respected, welcome neighbor of the local collective farm. I spent three wonderful summers there, walking, swimming, and cycling, after the GDR officials (also without giving any reasons and probably on the same grounds) categorically forbade me from leaving the country.

Now follows a rather disturbing facet in the kaleidoscope: Normannenstrasse, the headquarters of the Ministry for State Security. We cannot see the "Sachsenberg" as an idyll in no-man's-land. Acquiring the property was the result of his exclusion from everything else that was important to him, bearing in mind that such an exclusion would clearly not have been possible without the omnipresent security services. It was simply in the nature of things that we, with our interests and unruliness, would come into the Stasi's field of vision. But the nastiness of the actual circumstances was even worse. Already in the autumn of 1963 Bunge had written to Baumgärtner: "For the rest, I had a lot of trouble with Biermann. He is going about claiming that I must be an informer. He would have an instinct about that. That's especially awful, because it's impossible to disprove it." Biermann's instinct was wrong, even if it was born of his painful experience, but his suspicion poisoned relationships. Of course, we were prepared for our telephones being bugged, but we would never get involved with *them*, I was sure about that. However, as is now known from the Stasi files, they started as early as 1959 "to work on the investigation of Dr. Bunge." Dr. Bunge refused to work with them, though. In the Stasi's paranoid worldview our everyday conversations became smear campaigns against the state, our get-togethers subversive cliques, and in 1965 an operational plan was formed. The events in the editorial office of *Sinn und Form* in 1966 were, on the direct orders of the Stasi, the reason for Bunge's immediate and unfounded dismissal from the academy.

What happened next is a perfect example of the despicable way the Stasi operated. Bunge was boycotted by all the institutions with which he had worked. In a degrading way his livelihood was reduced because it now depended on his wife's student loan, on donations from unintimidated friends, and from a source that actually wasn't permitted at all—the West German Radio (WDR). They rebroadcast seventeen of the twenty conversations between Bunge and Eisler that had originally been broadcast on Radio GDR. The existence of this blind spot between the fronts of the Cold War was made possible thanks to Eisler's widow and particularly to the powerful Gerhard Eisler, who wanted to do something on behalf of his late brother. It only fetched a pittance because Bunge couldn't manage his own affairs. But the spite of the Stasi reached further. They planned to remove Bunge from Berlin, to cut him off from his surroundings. And so he was offered, after two years of wearisome isolation, a place at the Volkstheater Rostock under the supervision of Hanns Anselm Perten, manager and artistic director and member of the party's Central Committee. That looked like a buy-off, and Bunge understood it as such, with all the ambivalence attached to such an official pardon, and he acknowledged it by directing a successful, innovative stage version of Brecht's *Flüchtlingsgespräche*. On top of all this, his marriage in Berlin broke down, a blow that hit him very hard because what had happened to him threw him off balance. Through his compulsory exile from Berlin, the Stasi had created a situation whose outcome could now be shamelessly manipulated. In 1970 it says in the files: "because of the previous operational action it can be established that the circumstances in which Dr. Bunge now lives are particularly favorable to the investigation of whether he's now suitable to be recruited." In *Mutter Courage* it says,

> When they finally came to feel that they were through with me
> They'd got me groveling on my face.

In January 1971 Bunge delivers a handwritten, rather devout declaration of commitment as an IM [unofficial informer] and chooses as his alias the name "Hans," and by doing so adds an uneasy connotation to the "Deutsche Hans" [the given name of Faust]. This is the only situation in which he wasn't his own man. It was blackmail, the exploitation of a cruelly calculated, impotent despair. I am still puzzled by it, though. What Bunge didn't do was seek a discussion with his friends, the kind of discussion whose liberating effects we were, unfortunately, not aware of at the time.

In 1970 he came back to Berlin, as part of Perten's entourage, to work at the Deutsche Theater. He fulfilled his commitment as IM Hans solely as and when he saw fit. He didn't harm anyone; he never said what he didn't think was right to say anyway, and the records confirm this. Like Heiner Müller, he stuck to the maxim "I speak to anyone if I think it to be necessary and practical," and that also went for the Stasi officer who was his minder.

Of course, they were all mistaken, those, including Bunge and Müller, who thought their fate was in their own hands. It was also a delusion to believe one could teach the Stasi or the party anything. The apparatus was beyond reform; this was still evident during its disintegration. But his position of wanting to teach officialdom something was at least a piece of self-determination and wholly in keeping with Bunge's fundamental theme: to enter into dialogue. In the end he did start talking more with his friends about the Stasi than with the Stasi about his friends. For him, the contact with the minder was simply an additional experience that was interesting to talk about. And the way in which he then used this experience was rather the opposite of what was expected of him as an IM. When, for example, in 1979 the party instigated proceedings against Frank Hörnigk as "head of a counterrevolutionary platform at the Humboldt University"—once again the context was Heiner Müller, about whom Hörnigk was writing his postdoctoral thesis—it was Bunge who explained to him how to survive such a situation and not to give up. In 1979 the Stasi resigned itself to the fact that the collaboration with IM Hans was fruitless because of "uncontrolled contacts with enemy forces and exposure," as its final report had it—the next best thing to a badge of honor.

Bunge and the theater—this particular facet demands another, much broader view. For theater is involved in nearly everything Bunge did, from his PhD thesis, comparing the character of Antigone in Sophocles, Hölderlin, and Brecht, up to the documentation of Eisler's *Faustus*. Bunge consistently made visible things that others had overlooked or didn't think important. As early as 1951, through Bunge's critical commentary on the volume *Theaterarbeit*,[2] Brecht was convinced by this young man, to whom Ruth Berlau had introduced him, and who very soon became an integral part of the work of the Berliner Ensemble. The things Bunge came up with fifteen years later, while he was directing the *Flüchtlingsgespräche*, to make the characters' obscure logic and their unique situation aesthetically credible, well, that was an intellectual *tour de force* achieved with studied ease. The pleasure of this performance remains in the memory of all those who saw it. But even so, we won't keep Bunge foremost in mind as a theater artist. Naturally, his theater work in Rostock and at the Deutsche Theater was constrained by the circumstances. He made the best of his opportunities, but he also knew where his real strengths lay, and so it wasn't that remarkable, but in fact consistent, when he gave up the Deutsches Theater in 1978, at some cost to himself, in favor of pursuits that aligned more closely with his unique talent. Consequently, in addition to other works, and as the result of long conversations with Ruth Berlau, his wonderful book on Brecht's Lai-tu came into existence; a work where he displayed both persistence and discretion, a work that reflects much of the loyalty and stamina with which Bunge stuck to the principles that determined his life.[3]

Lai-tu—the name and the symbolism are deliberately intended by Brecht to be simultaneously transparent and opaque—belongs to Brecht's very idiosyncratic China myth, a game in which Berlau was not the only player. It brings us back once more to Tao-te-Ching, because it is not just any wisdom that is to be extracted from the legendary Lao-tzu, but a completely Brechtian wisdom, and that in two respects:

> He learned how quite soft water, by attrition
> Over the years will grind strong rocks away.
> In other words, that hardness must lose the day.[4]

The thought here is interesting because it's unexpected. It has to be emphasized because it contradicts everyday experience. In both art and science it is always the unexpected that is interesting, something that changes one's point of view. Receptivity to the unexpected, and the playfulness within it, is unquestionably one of Bunge's fundamental qualities. But there is a second point. It's not only about random surprises. It is the particular, defiant belief that weakness has power and that rigidity, even if it appears to be stronger than anything, can fail. This paradox is at the same time what emancipates us. Wouldn't that be wonderful?

I was able to experience with Bunge the reality of Lao-tzu's Brechtian wisdom, "He learned how quite soft water, by attrition / Over the years will grind strong rocks away": twenty years ago the strong rock, which went right down the middle of Berlin, was ground away, and nobody had predicted it. Meanwhile the views of the "tyrannical GDR state" have become strangely shallow and monotonous. Anyone who isn't given to nostalgia and to glossing over problems now reflects only on the deformities; the constraints; the deprivation of freedom (which were there right from the start); and the increasing symptoms of decline, harassment, and mendacity into which the state collapsed. Of course, the GDR is also an element of the century of wolves—there are many traces of it in the Bunge Archive. But it was the country to which Brecht and Eisler, Steinitz and Bloch, and many others returned after the emigration because they expected it to be the better Germany. Yes, the GDR was gray, its socialism never worked, and at the end it was simply a country in ruins and beyond help. But there was more to it than can be seen only through sullen retrospection. There was rebelliousness and curiosity, there was no less intelligence or acumen than in other areas of the world, and in between the shades of gray other precious hues were visible—and you'll also find plenty of evidence of that in Bunge's archive.

A final look into the kaleidoscope: once again Brecht, the great elegy "An die Nachgeborenen," because here too is a phrase that is easily overlooked and to which Bunge draws attention in the sixth conversation with Eisler when they speak about the setting of this poem. It was part of Brecht's vision of a better society, that man will be a helper to other men. The moving final verses are based on this expectation. Eisler was more skeptical, more realistic—or maybe even more optimistic? His vision, in any case, demands less but it lies closer to us—but perhaps also still farther away. He doesn't ask for help but for an end to brutality and fear. His hope was that the time of the wolves was at an end. So, not without irony about the arrogance that is hidden in Brecht's plea for forbearance, he changed Brecht's final verses. As a result, Brecht's hope, Eisler's realism, Müller's pessimism, and the great care with which Bunge documented it all, come together in a single line. The elegy that Eisler set to music ends:

> But you, when the time comes at last
> And man is no longer a wolf to men
> Think of us
> With forbearance.[5]

—Translated by Sabine Berendse and Paul Clements

Notes

[1] "Legend of the Origin of the Book Tao-te-Ching on Lao-tzu's Road into Exile," English translation in Bertolt Brecht, *Poems 1913–1956*, edited by John Willett and Ralph Manheim (London: Eyre Methuen, 1976), p. 314.

[2] Ruth Berlau, ed., *Theaterarbeit: 6 Aufführungen des Berliner Ensembles* (Dresden: Dresdner Verlag, 1952).

[3] Hans Bunge, ed., *Brecht's Lai-Tu: Erinnerungen und Notate von Ruth Berlau* (Darmstadt and Neuwied: Luchterhand, 1985); English translation: *Living for Brecht: The Memoires of Ruth Berlau*, edited by Hans Bunge, translated by Geoffrey Skelton (New York: Fromm International, 1987).

[4] Brecht, *Poems*, p. 315.

[5] "An die Nachgeborenen" ["To Those Born Later"], in Brecht, *Poems*, p. 318.

Dieter Goltzsche, *Mahagonny*, 1979, Tusche.

The "Reunion": The Chinese Poet and Germanist Feng Zhi and Bertolt Brecht

During his visit to the GDR in 1954, the renowned Chinese poet and German scholar Feng Zhi met Brecht and gave him a volume of Chinese paintings as a present. In the dedication, there are two Chinese characters that look like "Hui Jian" ("See you again"). But they are, in fact, the signature of another Chinese poet (Tian Jian). Feng Zhi and Brecht shared many points of contact in their work. A reunion seemed conceivable. After the meeting with Brecht, Feng Zhi was in charge of an important translation of Brecht into Chinese and became an important person in the early reception of Brecht in China. Shortly after this (1959), Feng Zhi revisited Germany, but a reunion with Brecht was impossible owing to his death in 1956. From a Chinese perspective, Feng Zhi met Brecht "spiritually" during Feng Zhi's coincidental yet moving visit to Brecht's grave.

Während seines Besuchs in der DDR im Jahre 1954 traf der renommierte chinesische Dichter und Germanist Feng Zhi Brecht und schenkte ihm einen Sammelband chinesischer Malerei. In der auf Chinesisch verfassten Widmung gibt es zwei Zeichen, die ähnlich wie "Hui Jian" ("Auf Wiedersehen") aussehen, aber in der Wirklichkeit die Unterschrift vom chinesischen Dichter Tian Jian sind. Feng Zhi und Brecht hatten viele Berührungspunkte in ihrer Arbeit, weshalb ein Wiedersehen aus heutiger Sicht nicht auszuschließen ist. Nach dem Treffen mit Brecht leitete Feng Zhi eine wichtige Brecht-Übersetzungsarbeit und wurde somit eine bedeutende Person in der frühen Brecht-Rezeption in China. Kurz nach dieser Arbeit (1959) besuchte Feng Zhi die DDR abermals. Jedoch konnten sie sich nicht mehr wiedersehen, weil Brecht 1956 verstorben war. Ein zwar nicht reales, doch seelisches Wiedersehen für Feng Zhi mit Brecht—so wurde es aus chinesischer Sicht empfunden, ging in seinem zufälligen aber berührenden Besuch des Brecht-Grabs in Erfüllung.

Das "Wiedersehen": Der chinesische Dichter und Germanist Feng Zhi und Bertolt Brecht

Lin Cheng

Die chinesische Widmung für den Genossen Brecht

Nachdem die deutschen Schriftsteller Bode Uhse und Ludwig Renn ihren China-Besuch beendet hatten, trafen die chinesischen Besucher Feng Zhi[1] (1905–1993) und Tian Jian[2] (1916–1985) am 30. Juni 1954 in Ost-Berlin ein. Sie nahmen u. a. "an der literarischen Diskussion zur Vorbereitung des IV. Deutschen Schriftstellerkongresses" teil.[3] Feng Zhi war ein prominenter Lyriker der neueren chinesischen Literatur und die wichtigste Person der früheren Germanisten-Generationen in China. 1923 begann er mit dem Deutsch-Studium in Peking. Zwischen 1930 und 1935 studierte er Literatur, Philosophie und Kunstgeschichte in Berlin und in Heidelberg. 1935 promovierte er in Heidelberg mit einer Dissertation über das Thema *Die Analogie von Natur und Geist als Stilprinzip in Novalis' Dichtung*. Unter den vielen chinesischen Germanisten, die Brecht übersetzt oder erforscht haben, ist Feng Zhi wohl der Einzige, der den deutschen Dramatiker und Dichter persönlich getroffen hat. Über das Treffen von Brecht und Feng Zhi ist weder direkt bei Brecht noch bei Feng Zhi Genaueres zu finden. In den Notizbüchern von Feng Zhi, die von seiner Frau Yao Kekun (1904–2003) bearbeitet wurden,[4] heißt es, Feng Zhi habe Brecht zweimal während seines Aufenthalts in Berlin im Jahre 1954 getroffen: Einmal besuchte er, in Begleitung von Franz Carl Weiskopf und Tian Jian, Johannes R. Becher. Brecht und Helene Weigel waren bei diesem Treffen anwesend. "Das Gruppenbild von ihnen bewahrt Feng Zhi immer noch sorgfältig auf."[5]

Die Erinnerung, die Feng Zhi während dieses Besuches am stärksten im Gedächtnis blieb, war ein weiteres Treffen mit Brecht: Am 13. August, einen Tag vor seiner Abfahrt, besuchte er Brecht in dessen Haus. Im Gespräch mit ihm hinterließ Brecht einen humorvollen Eindruck.[6] Zur Kenntnis zu nehmen ist noch, dass er Brecht eine Sammlung *Ausgewählte Kunstwerke des Neuen China* (新中国美术作品选集) schenkte, die noch heute in der privaten Bibliothek Brechts erhalten ist.[7] Es handelt sich nicht um traditionelle chinesische Malerei, wie sie Brecht in seinem kurzen Essay "Über die Malerei der Chinesen" (1935) wertschätzte. Diese Sammlung vielfältiger Kunstwerke, z. B. der Abbilder von Statuen und Holzschnitten, der Öl- und Pinselmalerei sowie der Frühlingsfestbilder, hat

Bild 1. Gruppenbild. Besuch Feng Zhis (2. von links) bei Johannes R. Becher, 1954. Used by permission.

eine starke zeitgenössische Prägung und stellt z. B. das neue Leben auf dem Land und die Kriege dar. Das Inhaltsverzeichnis ist auf Chinesisch, Englisch und Russisch verfasst. Demnach war die Sammlung vermutlich ein vorbereitetes Geschenk für ausländische Freunde.

Auf die Hülle schrieb Feng Zhi in chinesischen Schriftzeichen "敬赠—布雷希特同志," d. h., "Respektvoll schenke ich Genossen Brecht (diese Sammlung)." Feng Zhi schrieb diese kurze Widmung an Brecht nicht auf Deutsch, obwohl er als Germanist in der Lage war, eine deutsche Widmung zu verfassen. Dies lässt sich mit den folgenden Vermutungen begründen: (1) Er wusste, dass Brecht Interesse an der chinesischen Kultur hat; (2) er schrieb auf Wunsch von Brecht auf Chinesisch; (3) der Dichter Tian Jian, der der andere Geschenkgeber war und der tatsächlich nur unterschrieben hatte, beherrschte die deutsche Sprache nicht. Jedenfalls sollte es Brecht auch nicht stören, die chinesischen Zeichen zu "lesen": Er hatte sowohl ein chinesisches Rollbild mit einem chinesischen Gedicht als auch das Gedicht *Schnee* von Mao Zedong, eine Kalligraphie, in seiner Wohnung in der Chausseestraße in Berlin.

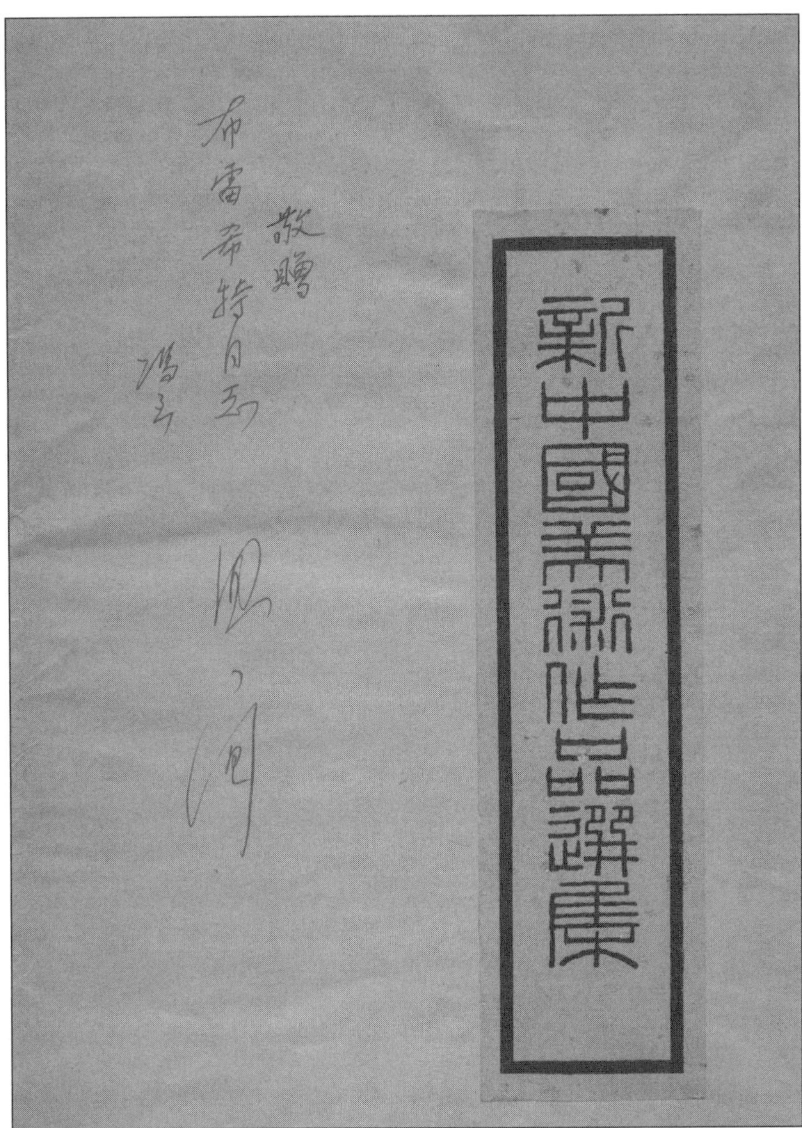

Bild 2. *Ausgewählte Kunstwerke des Neuen China*, mit der chinesischen Widmung von Feng Zhi und der Unterschrift von Tian Jian. Used by permission.

Unter die Widmung von Feng Zhi hat der Dichter Tian Jian (田间) seinen Namen nicht so deutlich auf die Hülle der Sammlung geschrieben, sodass diese zwei Zeichen, die den Namen von Tian Jian bilden, auch für Chinesen schwer zu lesen sind und bei der Entzifferung dieser Zeichen leicht Missverständnisse auftauchen könnten. Eine für deutsche Leser logische Entschlüsselung dieser Zeichen ist "hui jian" (回见).[8] Das aus zwei Zeichen bestehende Wort "hui jian" bedeutet auf Chinesisch "auf Wiedersehen." Als Literaten legten Feng Zhi bzw. Brecht großen Wert darauf, Inspirationen aus der deutschen bzw. chinesischen Kultur und Literatur für ihre eigene Dichtung zu finden. Angesichts des regen Austausches der Schriftsteller Chinas ist ein "Wiedersehen" in der Entzifferung der Widmung zwar ein Missverständnis, jedoch aus heutiger Sicht nicht auszuschließen.

Feng Zhi und seine Brecht-Übersetzung

Vor den 1950er Jahren gab es bereits chinesische Übersetzungen von Brechts Werken, von deren Wirkung allerdings nicht zu sprechen ist. Laut Yao Kekun hatte Feng Zhi sich bereits während seines DDR-Besuchs im Jahr 1951 Brechts *Mutter Courage und ihre Kinder* angesehen, in dem Helene Weigel die Hauptrolle spielte. Das sei die erste Begegnung Feng Zhis mit der Theaterkunst von Brecht gewesen, und die Aufführung berührte ihn sehr.[9] Der Dichter Feng Zhi, der nach seiner Promotion vor allem als Germanist arbeitete, veröffentlichte Mitte 1955 sieben Gedichte von Brecht, z. B. "Lob des Lernens," "Fragen eines lesenden Arbeiters," "Und was bekam des Soldaten Weib?" Das Übersetzen von Brecht-Texten war ein neues Arbeitsfeld für ihn. Über diese Übersetzungen von "Feng Tschih" [Feng Zhi] berichtet die Zeitung *Neues Deutschland* mit dem Titel "Chinesische Zeitschrift veröffentlicht Brecht-Gedicht": "Bertolt Brechts 'Friedenslied' ist neben sechs anderen Gedichten des Stalin-Friedenspreisträgers im Juli-Heft der chinesischen Zeitschrift *I Wen* enthalten, die sich die Verbreitung von Werken der Weltliteratur zur Aufgabe gestellt hat. Die Übersetzung der Brecht'schen Gedichte besorgte der chinesische Dichter Feng Tschih. (ADN)"[10] Bevor Brechts Dramen in China in großem Maß rezipiert wurden, war er zunächst als Dichter hoch angesehen. In der 1958 von Feng Zhi herausgegebenen Literaturgeschichte *Kurze Geschichte der deutschen Literatur* wurden vor allem die politischen Gedichte von Brecht als zeitgenössische Texte vorgestellt.[11]

Im Jahre 1959, dem zehnten Gründungsjahr der Volksrepublik China und der DDR sowie ihrer diplomatischen Beziehung, wurde eine Anthologie von Brecht ins Chinesische übersetzt. Dafür gab es außer diesen Jubiläen mehrere Anlässe. Ende 1955 hörte der Dichter und Literaturkritiker Bian Zhilin (1910–2000) während seines Polenbesuchs viel über Brecht. Er fragte sich, ob er chinesische Literaten und Künstler auf Brechts Theaterstücke aufmerksam machen sollte. Diese Frage wurde in einem späteren Gespräch mit Feng Zhi bestätigt.[12] Ein sehr wichtiger Anlass ist der Vorschlag des deutschen Schriftstellers Günther Weisenborn in seinem Gespräch mit Mao Zedong, das Werk von Brecht ins Chinesische zu übersetzen, wie Feng Zhi im Nachwort der Übersetzung erwähnte.[13] Als Mao vorschlug, man solle *Memorial* von Weisenborn übersetzen, und einen chinesischen Kollegen fragte, ob "wir überhaupt einige westdeutsche Bücher ins Chinesische übersetzen wollen," erwiderte Weisenborn: "Ich schlage vor, als einen der ersten Autoren Brecht zu übersetzen."[14] Feng Zhi befand diesen Vorschlag von Weisenborn als sinnvoll, nicht nur weil Brecht ein hervorragender Dramatiker und Dichter sei, sondern auch weil er ein Freund des chinesischen Volkes sei und viele China-Bezüge habe.[15] In diesem Sinne wäre Brecht "der gute Genosse von Deutschland."

Es überrascht nicht, dass dieses Übersetzungsprojekt von dem erfahrenen Germanisten Feng Zhi geleitet wurde, der als ein kultureller und literarischer Botschafter des neuen Chinas zwischen 1950 und 1959 viermal die DDR besuchte. Nicht nur die äußeren und politischen Gegebenheiten spielten dabei eine Rolle. Es ist zu vermuten, dass sein Theaterbesuch in Berlin sowie seine Treffen mit Brecht, die ihn beeindruckten, seine Kenntnisse über Brecht als Dichter und Dramatiker vertieften, wenn nicht sogar seine Übersetzungsarbeit mit veranlassten. Auf jeden Fall schätzte er Brechts Stil z. B. seinen Sprachstil sehr. "Durch seinen besonderen Stil und seine einfache, unkomplizierte Sprache ist Brechts Werk das Kreativste in der deutschen Literatur der vergangenen 30 Jahre," so Feng Zhi, "seine Gedichte sind zwar sehr kurz, aber sehr inspirierend."[16] Feng Zhi gab zu, es sei bereits sehr spät, so einen Schriftsteller wie Brecht erst drei Jahre nach seinem Tod durch eine so geringe Auswahl an Werken in einer Anthologie der chinesischen Leserschaft vorzustellen.[17] Er definierte diese Übersetzungsarbeit der ausgewählten Werke als einen "Anfang" und wünschte sich weitere Übersetzungen und die Rezeption von Brechts Werken.[18] Die Übersetzungsarbeit der Stücke und Gedichte von Brecht hielt Feng Zhi zwar für eine schwierige Aufgabe, aber "angesichts seiner Loyalität zum Proletariat, der Tiefsinnigkeit seiner Gedanken und seiner künstlerischen Innovation sind wir von der Notwendigkeit überzeugt, seine Werke in China vorzustellen."[19]

Als Professor für deutsche Literatur aber, selbst auch als Dichter, hat Feng Zhi mit seinem Studenten Du Wentang (1935–) vornehmlich Brechts Gedichte übersetzt. In *Ausgewählte Werke von Brecht* sind dutzende Gedichte von Brecht zu finden, vor allem die politischen Gedichte und die Gedichte über Kriege aus *Hundert Gedichte* deren fünfte, ergänzte Auflage 1958 im Aufbau-Verlag in Berlin erschien und als Vorlage für die chinesische Übersetzung diente. Darunter sind z. B. "Fragen eines lesenden Arbeiters," "Lob der Partei" sowie "Kantate zu Lenins Todestag." Im Gesamtwerk von Feng Zhi sind die Übersetzungen von insgesamt achtzehn Gedichten von Brecht zu finden.[20] Neben den Gedichten sind außerdem drei Stücke in dem Band *Ausgewählte Werke von Brecht* enthalten: *Die Gewehre der Frau Carrar* (1936–37), *Mutter Courage und ihre Kinder* (1939) und *Herr Puntila und sein Knecht Matti* (1940). Das Stück *Mutter Courage und ihre Kinder*, das von Sun Fengcheng (1934–), einer Studentin

Bild 3. Brecht, *Ausgewählte Werke*, Peking: Volksliteratur-Verlag, 1959 (BBA A 2038). Used by permission.

von Feng Zhi, übersetzt wurde, diente im selben Jahr als Bühnenvorlage für eine Aufführung in Shanghai und erschien zugleich als Einzelausgabe.

Obwohl diese von Feng Zhi geleitete Brecht-Übersetzungspraxis heutzutage in den Forschungen über die Geschichte der chinesischen Brecht-Rezeption eher wenig erwähnt bleibt, wird ihre Bedeutung anerkannt: Diese Übersetzungen seien die ersten chinesischen Brecht-Übersetzungen "in einem relativ großen Umfang,"[21] und Feng Zhi sei "the pioneer"[22] der

Brecht-Übersetzungen. Der Übersetzer Guo Kailan erwähnte die diplomatische Bedeutung dieser Übersetzungen, die im Rahmen des Kulturaustausches beider Länder stand, in seinem Kommentar über diese neu erschienene Anthologie: "Es ist wirklich eine Freude zu sehen, dass wir zum zehnten Jahrestag der Gründung der Deutschen Demokratischen Republik diese Anthologie des vor drei Jahren verstorbenen deutschen Dichters und Dramatikers lesen können."[23] Auch er schätzte die Klarheit und Einfachheit der Sprache von Brecht sehr: "Manche kurzen Gedichte aus der *Deutschen Kriegsfibel* sind nur drei Zeilen und umfassen nur weniger als 20 Wörter, aber jedes Wort ist wie eine Kugel, die unfehlbar das Herz des Gegners trifft."[24] Für den Literaturwissenschaftler Adrian Hsia ist diese Übersetzung ebenfalls ein wichtiger Schritt der chinesischen Brecht-Rezeption: "In this same year [1959], the tenth anniversary of the People's Republic, the literary and the theatrical reception finally converged and became one."[25] Dies ist vor allem dem Engagement von Feng Zhi und dem berühmten Regisseur und Brecht-Experten Huang Zuolin (1906–1994) zu verdanken: "Feng's translation began the literary reception of Brecht's works in China, just as Huang was the initiator of his theatrical reception."[26] Das Stück *Mutter Courage und ihre Kinder* wurde unter der Leitung von Huang Zuolin in Shanghai als Brecht-Debüt auf der chinesischen Bühne aufgeführt. Hinsichtlich der Reaktion des Publikums war diese Aufführung ein Misserfolg, da die chinesischen Zuschauer der Handlung nicht gut folgen konnten, u. a. weil die Geschichte auf sie fremd wirkte, und weil sie an die Stanislawski-Methode gewöhnt waren.[27] Trotz des Misserfolgs dieser Aufführung erreichte die Brecht-Rezeption in China im Jahr 1959 ihren ersten Höhepunkt. In der Preisverleihungsrede für die "Goethe-Medaille" (1983) an Feng Zhi, die von dem damaligen Botschafter der Bundesrepublik Deutschland in Peking Günther Schödel gehalten wurde, wurden seine Brecht-Übersetzungen neben seinen Goethe- und Heine-Übersetzungen genannt,[28] obwohl die Brecht-Übersetzungen vergleichsweise nicht zu den Kernaufgaben seiner umfangreichen Tätigkeiten als Germanist zählte. Diese Übersetzungen sollen auch nicht in Berlin unbekannt geblieben sein. Diese im September 1959 im Volksliteratur-Verlag erschienene Anthologie wurde im Oktober desselben Jahres von Alexander Abusch aus Peking nach Berlin "als Gruß" für Helene Weigel mitgebracht.[29] Als der spätere Brecht-Forscher Bian Zhilin um 1960 Helene Weigel in Berlin besuchte, nahm er diese Anthologie als Lektüre ebenfalls mit.[30]

Das "Wiedersehen" am Grab von Brecht

Der chinesische Germanist Ye Tingfang (1936–), der zwischen 1956 und 1961 an der Peking-Universität und auch bei Feng Zhi studierte, spricht von der Ähnlichkeit des Sprachstils zwischen Feng Zhi und Brecht:

> [Feng Zhi] beherrscht die Muttersprache ziemlich gut, aber sowohl seine Gedichte als auch seine Übersetzungen sind weder geschwollen noch blumig, sondern wie er selber, bescheiden und nicht hochtrabend . . . Er sieht den Gleichgesinnten als seelischen Freund. Er hat einmal Brecht gelobt, dass dessen Sprache kurz und bündig sei, sodass man kein Wort ergänzen oder streichen könne . . . Ja, der Sprachstil von Brecht, sein Alltagsleben sowie sein Haus in der Nähe eines Friedhofs, könnten kaum bescheidener sein.[31]

Aber nicht nur hinsichtlich des Sprachstils sind sie vergleichbar. In den 1950er Jahren scheinen die deutsche Romantik und die Dichtung von Rilke nicht mehr der Arbeitsschwerpunkt von Feng Zhi zu sein, mit denen er sich seit Beginn seiner akademischen Laufbahn intensiv beschäftigt hatte. Stattdessen erscheinen außer Goethe und Heine auch Namen wie Seghers, Weiskopf und Brecht häufig in seinen Schriften. Nun verfasste er zahlreiche politische Gedichte. Ähnlich wie die von Brecht, haben die politischen Gedichte Feng Zhis einen Erzählcharakter. Durchaus sind ähnliche Themen (Partei, Kommunismus und Arbeiterklasse usw.) bei den beiden zu finden. Es ist nicht zu bezweifeln, dass Feng Zhi Brecht als Gleichgesinnten sah, den er sehr schätzte, nachdem er Brechts Dichtung und Persönlichkeit für sich entdeckt hatte. Im Vergleich zu den Gedichten Brechts, die Feng Zhi zwischen 1955 und 1959 übersetzte, und die Brecht zwischen den 1920er und 1940er Jahren verfasste, haben seine eigenen politischen Gedichte zwischen 1949 und 1957 allerdings mehr optimistische Hingabe für die Partei bzw. das Neue China und weniger dialektisches Nachdenken beispielsweise über die Kriege. Das ist nachvollziehbar, denn der Krieg gegen Japan (1937–1945) war ein Anti-Aggressionskrieg, und das neue Nachkriegs-China hatte sich endlich von dem Status eines halbfeudalen Staates befreit.

Nach der Übersetzungsarbeit der besagten Anthologie von Brecht war Feng Zhi im Herbst 1959 wieder in Deutschland und hat in Berlin das Brecht-Archiv besucht.[32] Ein Wiedersehen von Feng Zhi mit Brecht ist nicht mehr möglich, da dieser bereits 1956 verstorben war. Laut Ye Tingfang erzählte Feng Zhi von seinem Besuch auf dem Dorotheenstädtischen Friedhof in Berlin in Begleitung von deutschen Künstlern und Literaten: Er nahm einen Blumenstrauß auf den Friedhof mit, um ihn am Grab des Dichters Becher niederzulegen, nicht nur weil dieser als der ehemalige Kulturminister der DDR einen hohen Posten hatte, sondern auch weil er kürzlich verstorben war.

> [Feng Zhi] wusste nicht, dass sich das Grab von Brecht ganz in der Nähe des Grabs von Becher befindet, noch weniger hatte er erwartet, dass das Grab von Brecht so schlicht und bescheiden ist, Brecht sehr ähnlich als Mensch und seinem literarischen Stil! Der Respekt aus tiefstem Herzen für Brecht brachte Feng Zhi in einen Konflikt . . . Nach

reichlicher Überlegung änderte er seine Absicht und entschied sich dafür, die Blumen auf das Grab von Brecht zu legen.[33]

Diese kurze, zufällige aber berührende Anekdote am Grab von Brecht war dennoch ein "Wiedersehen" für Feng Zhi mit Brecht, zwar kein reales, doch ein seelisches Treffen unter Genossen—und so wurde es aus chinesischer Sicht empfunden.

Anmerkungen

1 In der deutschen Presse wurde der Name von Feng Zhi unterschiedlich wiedergegeben ("Feng Chih," "Feng Chiu" oder "Feng Tschih"). Im vorliegenden Artikel werden alle chinesischen Namen auf chinesische Weise geschrieben. Ich bedanke mich herzlich bei Frau Helgrid Streidt (Bertolt-Brecht-Archiv) für ihre Unterstützung in meiner Recherche; bei Frau Feng Yaoping, die mir das Foto von Feng Zhi und Brecht (Bild 1) zur Verfügung gestellt hat; und beim Bertolt-Brecht-Archiv, das mir die Abbildungen der Buchumschläge (Bilder 2 und 3) zukommen ließ.

2 Tian Jian, Geburtsname Tong Tianjian, ist ein "chinesische[r] Dichter und Lyriker, der das hier bekannte 'Lied vom Karren' schrieb." Vgl. Eig. Ber., "Chinesische Schriftsteller in Berlin begrüßt," *Neues Deutschland*, 1. Juli 1954: S. 4.

3 Ebd.

4 Yao Kekun ist auch die Übersetzerin des Stücks *Die Gewehre der Frau Carrar*.

5 Über diese zwei Treffen siehe Yao Kekun, "Feng Zhis einige Besuche und Arbeit im Ausland und im Inland," in Yao Kekun, *Ich und Feng Zhi* (Nanning: Guangxi Education Publishing House, 1994), S. 147–158; hier, S. 153. Laut Yao Kekun wurden die Fakten aus ihrem Artikel über Feng Zhis Besuche den Notizbüchern von Feng Zhi entnommen. Siehe ebd. S. 158.

6 Ebd.

7 Mit dem Begriff "Das Neue China" ist hier die im Jahr 1949 in Peking gegründete Volksrepublik China gemeint.

8 Siehe Erdmut Wizisla, *Die Bibliothek Bertolt Brechts* (Frankfurt am Main: Suhrkamp, 2007), S. 264.

9 Siehe Yao, *Ich und Feng Zhi*, S. 149.

10 Anon., "Chinesische Zeitschrift veröffentlicht Brecht-Gedichte," *Neues Deutschland*, 29. Juli 1955: S. 4.

11 Siehe Sun Fengcheng, Zhang Yushu und Du Wentang, "Die wichtigen zeitgenössischen Schriftsteller," in Feng Zhi, Hrsg., *Kurze Geschichte der deutschen Literatur*, Bd. 2 (Peking: Volksliteratur-Verlag, 1958), S. 399–402.

12 Bian Zhilin, "Nachwort," in Zhilin, *Eindrücke von den Theaterstücken Brechts* (Hefei: Anhui Education Press, 2007), S. 106–110; hier, S. 107.

13 Feng Zhi, "Nachwort," in Feng Zhi, Hrsg., *Ausgewählte Werke von Brecht* (Peking: Volksliteratur-Verlag, 1959), S. 323–326; hier, S. 325–326.

14 Günther Weisenborn, "Gespräche mit Mao Tse-tung," *Geist und Zeit: Eine Zweimonatsschrift für Kunst, Literatur und Wissenschaft* 6 (1957): S. 79–84; hier, S. 82.

[15] Feng, "Nachwort," S. 326.

[16] Ebd. S. 323.

[17] Ebd. S. 326.

[18] Ebd. S. 323.

[19] Feng Zhi, "Skizze über die Rezeption der modernen deutschen Literatur in China," *Weltliteratur* 9 (1959): S. 81.

[20] Siehe Han Yaocheng, Hrsg., *Gesamtwerk von Feng Zhi*, Bd. 9 (Shijiazhuang: Hebei Education Publishing House, 1999). Die von ihm übersetzten Brecht Gedichten wurden später wieder in einem bestimmten Kontext veröffentlicht: Zehn Gedichte, darunter z. B. "Im Zeichen der Schildkröte," "1940" und "Deutschland" wurden in die *World Anti-Fascist Literature Series: Band der deutschen und österreichischen Literatur* (Chongqing, 1992) aufgenommen.

[21] Yu Kuangfu, *Versuch über Brecht* (Shanghai: Shanghai Foreign Language Education Press, 2002), S. 3.

[22] Zhang Li, "Brecht in China," in ebd., S. 18–27; hier, S. 19.

[23] Guo Kailan, "Über Ausgewählte Werke von Brecht," *Weltliteratur* 11 (1959), S. 158–159; hier, S. 159. Geburtsjahr und Todesjahr von Guo Kailan bleiben unbekannt. Frau Yin Yu aus Shanghai sind diese Angaben zu verdanken.

[24] Ebd. S. 158.

[25] Hsia Adrian, "The Reception of Bertolt Brecht in China and Its Impact on Chinese Drama," in Antony Tatlow und Tak-Wai Wong, Hrsg., *Brecht and East Asian Theatre* (Hongkong: Hong Kong University Press, 1982), S. 46–64; hier, S. 48–49.

[26] Ebd. S. 48.

[27] Ebd. S. 51–52.

[28] Siehe Günther Schödel, "Die Rede des deutschen Botschafters anlässlich der Preisverleihung des 'Goethe-Ordens' an Prof. Feng Zhi," in Zhang Tian, Hrsg., *Gesamtwerk von Feng Zhi*, Bd. 5 (Shijiazhuang: Hebei Education Publishing House, 1999), S. 189–191; hier, S. 189.

[29] Auf dem vorsatzblatt der ausgewählten Werke dieses Exemplars in der Bibliothek des Bertolt-Brecht-Archivs. Handgeschrieben mit dem Datum 10.10.1954. Dieser Hinweis ist Frau Helgrid Streidt zu verdanken.

[30] Bian, "Nachwort," S. 107.

[31] Ye Tingfang, "Der große Gelehrte der östlichen und westlichen Kultur—Zum Andenken an den 100. Geburtstag von Feng Zhi," *Die Tageszeitung des Volkes* (27.09.2005.): S. 15.

[32] Siehe Yao, *Ich und Feng Zhi*, S. 155.

[33] Siehe Ye Tingfang, "Überall schlicht und bescheiden. Besichtigung des Brecht-Hauses in seinen späten Lebensjahren und des Grabes von Brecht (verfasst im Jahr 1998)," in Tingfang, *Suche nach Muse: Essays* (Peking: The Commercial Press, 2004), S. 59–63; hier, S. 63.

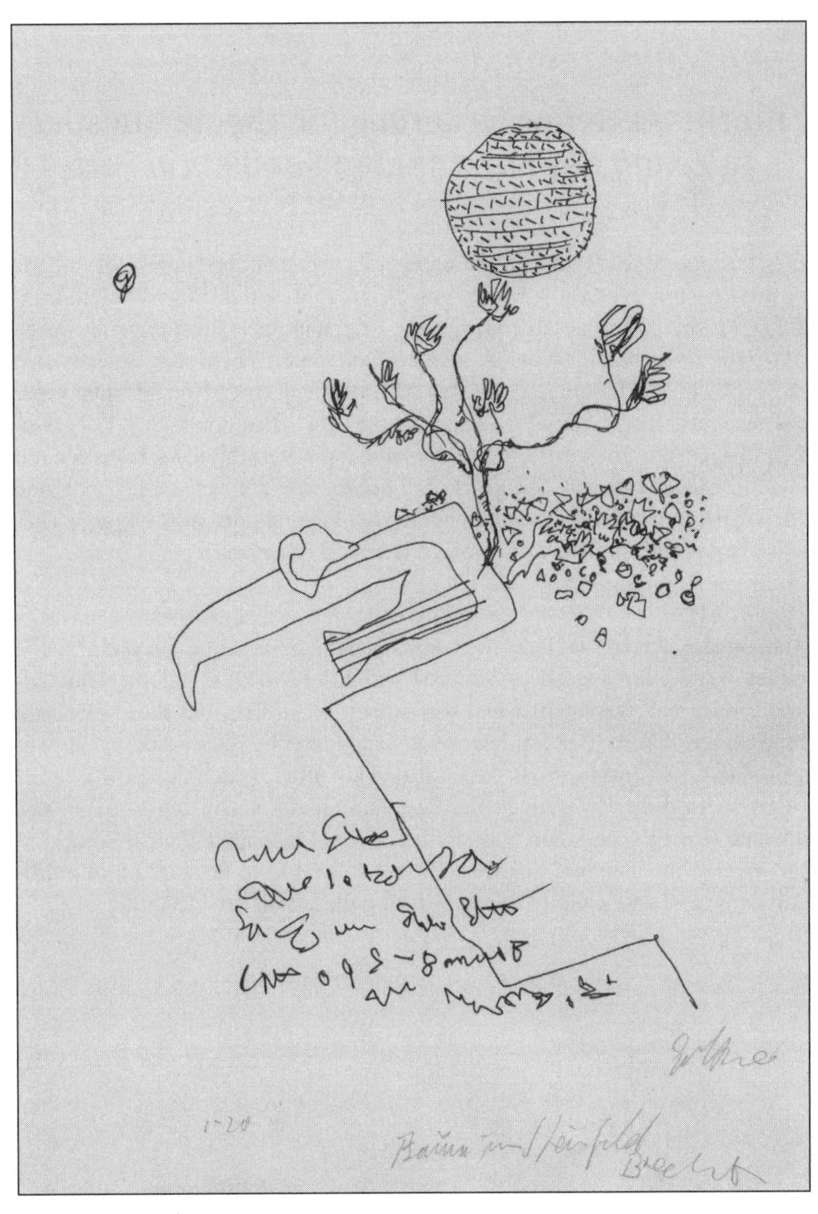

Dieter Goltzsche, *Baum im Steinfeld*, 1984, Lithographie.

Brecht als Herausforderung für Theaterkünstler zu Zeiten des Bewaffneten Konflikts in Peru

Das Theater des peruanischen Mainstreams war nicht im Stande, dringende politische und gesellschaftliche Fragen zu Zeiten des Bewaffneten Konflikts (1980–2000) zu thematisieren. Unabhängige Theaterkreise waren durchaus dazu bereit, aber sie standen vor einem Dilemma: lieferte man theatralische Darbietungen, die den Mächten auf einer Konfliktseite (egal auf welcher) nicht gefielen, dann waren die Theaterkünstler Repressalien ausgesetzt. Dieser Beitrag untersucht, wie verschiedene Künstler mit Brecht während dieser Zeit gearbeitet haben, wie sie sich seine Texte und Ideen aneigneten und diese anwendeten im Versuch, das unabhängige Theaterleben gesellschaftlich und politisch neu zu engagieren.

Mainstream theater in Peru was not capable of tackling pressing social issues during the period of internal war (1980–2000). Independent theater circles had the interest and the capacity to do so, but they were in a bind, given that theater art deemed unacceptable by either side in the war would expose theater artists to reprisal. This article examines how a range of artists in different areas of the Peruvian theater scene appropriated and adapted Brecht's work and ideas in their own independent theater scenes, as the diverse independent theater community sought to become more politically engaged and socially relevant during these two decades.

Brechtian Challenges to Theater Artists during the Internal War in Peru

Carlos Vargas-Salgado

The experience of the internal war in Peru (1980–2000), in which the Shining Path Communist guerrilla and a repressive state faced each other, meant a tremendous challenge to Peruvian theater artists.[1] Located as it was between these two aggressors, the cultural sphere had to find unique ways to tackle issues of conflict and violence without exposing its participants to reprisal. Between two fires, cultural figures had to discover how to face those fires without getting burned. Interestingly, several Peruvian theatrical figures of the era, particularly from the independent theater, focused on the works and ideas of Brecht as a resource for addressing the social injustice of the armed conflict. They did so without being charged or violently attacked by the opposite side.[2] Peruvian theater artists exhibited a persistent concern for discussing the roots of the evil in social violence while rethinking theoretical and aesthetic paradigms taken from Bertolt Brecht's writings.

Before discussing how important Brechtian aesthetics were for politically engaged theater, it is necessary to highlight how the presentation of violence circulated in the Peruvian theater during the internal war. Unlike many other cultural forms, the social nature of performance evinced the intentions of individual producers—often with great risk. Theater exposes civilian participants to greater risks, given the public consumption and transmission of its messages. Unlike the literary field, which did not require a personal confrontation, Peruvian theater during the internal war circulated artistic messages that addressed the violence, intervening in political life and thus exposing the participants (artists and audiences) to the danger of the war.

Such extreme political violence can help us to understand the unique context in which Peruvian theater artists developed their work during these decades. It can also help to comprehend why certain rhetorical devices in plays (such as fables of foreign places, symbolism, and anti-verbal theater forms, and encryption of messages in complex, surrealist speeches), appeared as appropriate strategies to be implemented in scenes that conveyed highly charged political intentions.

All of the works reviewed here were produced by dramatists and writers involved in what is called independent theater production in Peru, and can be seen as expressions of the concerns Peruvian artists experienced regarding their future after the period of violence. Most of these concerns

THE BRECHT YEARBOOK | DAS BRECHT-JAHRBUCH 40
(ROCHESTER, NY: CAMDEN HOUSE, 2016)

were too problematic to expose in the established, *mainstream* circuit of Peruvian theater (namely, theaters and cultural centers). For this reason, most of these works were produced and consumed in the alternative circuits of Lima and other big cities.

Reviewing specific theater practices that arose from a period of acute crisis has implications for a wider inquiry on how any Peruvian theater artists responded aesthetically to the challenge of the historic conflict. In addition, a discussion of Peruvian theater during the internal war is also a discussion about the several coexistent theatrical systems in the country and their heterogeneous ways of understanding the same nation.[3] Given this, what is called independent theater needs to be read as a set of works created by a (still) privileged group of artists who possessed resources to express its voices through theater arts, and being recognized as acceptable discussants of the topic of political violence. At this point, it is convenient to recall Bourdieu's reminder about the role of a *dominated class within the dominating class* that professional artists play in contemporary societies. This is another reason to see their products not as mere illustrations of independent theater agendas, but rather as deeply conceived political statements in their field. Their works and statements should be understood as a dialogue with(in) the ruling class about a set of rules that had led Peru to a social catastrophe. In the case of the works and theater artists reviewed here, the concept of politically engaged art needs to be constantly examined and challenged. This guards against speaking of Peruvian theater as a universal notion, which is deeply problematic.

Bertolt Brecht in a Peruvian War

Brecht has been an influential author for theater artists in Peru for decades. Since the first appearance of his work in the cultural panorama (in the early 1960s), Brecht has been recognized as a politically committed author, serving as a role model for political theater producers in the region.[4] Thus, exploring the uses of Brechtian images in Peruvian theater can be seen as an invitation to look at the recent past, to capture the way in which the author has been read, interpreted, and frequently invoked for Peruvian theater practitioners.[5]

The dissemination of Brecht's works in Latin American theater runs parallel to the initiation of leftist movements, even revolutionary projects. For instance, during the 1960s and 1970s, the influence of the Cuban Revolution took hold of the Peruvian cultural imaginary. Guerrillas and revolutionary movements were formed, some of them even led by young poets, singers, or painters. Also, a long wave of strikes by farmers in rural areas expressed a shifting social momentum in Peru. A revolutionary eruption seemed to be not only imminent but also inexorable.

In the field of Peruvian theater, the influence of Marxist ideology was prevalent. Members of most of the theater collectives founded in the late '60s and early '70s were at the same time Marxist activists, and some framed themselves explicitly as anti-system protesters.[6] At the time when Brecht's influence was first felt, the public image of widely recognized theater collectives such as Yuyachkani or Cuatrotablas, or of authors like Sara Joffré, Juan Rivera Saavedra, or Alonso Alegría, was undoubtedly that of "leftists." It is not surprising that in 1974 Yuyachkani's second production was Brecht's adaptation of *The Mother* by Gorky. That same year, acclaimed playwright and director Sara Joffré created the *Muestra*, the most important Peruvian Theater Festival, expressly encouraged by a phrase attributed to Brecht: "If we don't have a national theater, we will have nothing."[7]

But times changed in May 1980. A group of college students and professors from the Universidad San Cristóbal de Huamanga, in the southern city and region of Ayacucho, started what it called a Popular War, invoking the necessity of revolution in Peru. The students and professors referred to themselves simply as the Communist Party of Peru—the name *Shining Path* was ascribed to them by the Peruvian State Police. They started what at first seemed just another attempted utopia, destined to fail, but their actions and the state's reactions soon escalated into an internal war. As described and analyzed by several scholars over the last decades (Degregori, Stern, McClintock),[8] the violence they perpetrated confirmed that the only revolutionary twist that the Shining Path offered was the transformation from a radical university group into a genocidal and terrorist organization, which allied with drug trafficking cartels from the mid-1980s on.[9] The situation turned even worse when the violent response from the state exponentially increased civilian bloodshed, especially because the state pursued a discriminatory agenda against indigenous populations and their cultures. Thus, the Peruvian armed forces regarded themselves as a democratically sanctioned institution, entitled to suppress the uprising in Ayacucho through massacres of entire indigenous populations. One of the most frequent accusations against indigenous peasants was that they were supporting the Shining Path because they did not speak Spanish and they were poor. The democratic system thus created for itself a way to alienate entire communities of indigenous Peruvians from the entire project of modernity, including democracy itself.[10]

The internal war was the open, violent expression of a set of unresolved historical, racial, cultural, and socioeconomic tensions in Peru, which had worsened steadily over 500 years of colonization and domination by Europe and the subsequent US interventions in Latin America. After twenty years of popular war or war against subversion, depending on the ideological lens through which one observed the facts, the results were horrifying: seventy thousand dead and a national trauma that even now Peruvian society still struggles to manage. It is clear in contemporary Peruvian history that there is a "before and after" when it comes to the internal war. Furthermore, all of the artistic, cultural movements needed and still need to be confronted with this experience. Never before the internal war had Peru faced its deep incapacity to resolve its ethnic and historical divisions.

Several questions regarding Peruvian theater can be posed at this point. First, while this destruction was happening, what were they to do, those theater practitioners who previously had invoked Brecht to support their revolutionary works? Did Brechtian paradigms become part of an open public discussion during the 1980s in Peru, a decade in which being leftist was a synonym for being terrorist? How did theater practitioners respond to the challenge of talking about an unjust society in the face of continuous human rights violations perpetrated in the name of revolution?

As expected, the responses were widely varied; some of them, even surprising. For instance, Víctor Zavala Cataño, the acclaimed playwright and founder of the Teatro Campesino, completely turned in favor of the popular war led by the Shining Path. His commitment to the party compelled him to proselytize through theater, and eventually to join and lead armed attacks against the state and peasant communities. Zavala, arguably one of the most gifted contemporary Peruvian playwrights, suddenly was included in the Central Committee of the Shining Path. Finally, he was caught and condemned to life imprisonment in 1988.

It is reasonable to distinguish two distinct phases of Zavala Cataño's work, one as a leftist and independent producer in rural areas (with *Teatro Campesino*), and one in which he decided to use his theater as a propaganda machine for the Shining Path (the mid-1980s). Zavala's perception of his dramatic work, however, does not divide it. In response to questions on his political writings, many years later (2009), Zavala still perceived his work and political involvement as a whole, integral project. More interestingly, the author insists on describing the many challenges of political writing via Brechtian paradigms:

> It has been debated, discussed (and possibly it will still be), this issue of the relationship between Brecht and the *Teatro Campesino*. Here is my answer: in Peru's reality we cannot, or should not, take Brecht as is, from his plays as well as from his theories and techniques. Problems are not resolved with a literal application, but through a creative application using what is useful and what fits with the social reality of the people. (Zavala Cataño, Personal Blog, 2009; my translation)[11]

The passage illustrates the interpretive horizon of political action in the theater that an author and leader of the Shining Path still gives to the Brechtian ideas. In interpreting his dramaturgical work (*Teatro Campesino*) and linking it to his concrete political action, Zavala seems to underline the need to appropriate the aesthetic legacy of Brecht and to reinterpret it in a Peruvian context. In a sense, Zavala claims for Brechtian theatrical thinking what the Shining Path as a whole claimed for Marxist thought: a Peruvian interpretation. Interestingly, the Peruvian writer never abandons interest in Brechtian aesthetic thinking, conceptualizing its interconnection with revolutionary politics instead. Obviously, between political intentions and political practice are many problematic options (the exercise of violence, in particular) that cannot be strictly attributed to a Brechtian way of thinking but to a particular interpretation made by Zavala.[12]

On the other side of the Peruvian theater spectrum, it is possible to find an opposite trajectory among the so-called "groups of collective creation" (*grupos de creación colectiva*), particularly Yuyachkani and Cuatrotablas. Cuatrotablas (founded in 1971),[13] for instance, has been the most experimental voice to produce and reinterpret Brecht's work. The group did an openly free adaptation of *The Threepenny Opera* called *Los Cómicos* (The Comedians, 1980) using as a framework the shantytowns and the homelessness of Lima. In the production, the group portrayed the miserable situation as a result of a social and economic division that gives rise to violence.

A long silence ensued after this first encounter, but Cuatrotablas returned to Brecht twenty years later, in 1998, with *The Resistible Rise of Arturo Ui*. Toward the end of the nineties, one of the main consequences of the Shining Path's final defeat was the triumph of Alberto Fujimori's fascist/neoliberal dictatorship (1990–2000). Cuatrotablas staged *The Resistible Rise of Arturo Ui*, in which Ui is none other than Fujimori. This staging reproduced with fierce aggressiveness the plot by military forces and capitalist groups in Peru to support Fujimori's regime and its atrocities.

Although Cuatrotablas has always been seen as a politically engaged collective of artists, it is in the work of Yuyachkani where it is possible to find a longer, illuminating conversation between Brechtian ideas and the complex reality of violence in Peru.[14] Although Yuyachkani never has produced plays directly authored by Brecht, Brechtian dialectics are a permanent part of the discussion in almost every Yuyachkani project. That is observable in one of the first plays of the collective, an agit-prop piece titled *Los hijos de Sandino* (Sandino's Sons, 1981), which was strongly inspired by Brecht's political writing. Similarly, Yuyachkani produced *Baladas del Bien Estar* (Ballads of Well-Being, 1985), a show based on songs and poems by Brecht, which was staged during the worst years of Peruvian violence, in many cities around the country. This show, conceived as a one-woman concert for the outstanding actress Teresa Ralli, presented songs (mostly from *The Threepenny Opera*), and some of Brecht's most famous poems, with piano accompaniment. Despite the apparent lack of realistic connection to the internal war, in the context of such ubiquitous violence, every image in the songs and poems was read as a prophecy of a civil and social collapse fulfilled. The aesthetic approach to the internal war did not employ direct depiction. Rather, it discussed the human condition through forms that combined the poetic and the political. The question that this show posed is that of the relative independence of art from politics. Is theater able to find a way to tackle urgent issues (class struggle, the reasons for the insurgency, human rights) without abandoning theater's capacity to entertain? With this production, Yuyachkani found a way to deal with the subject without making direct statements on the political violence of the time. Yuyachkani has continued reflecting on violence over several decades, although the tone of its works has moved increasingly toward proclamation of peace and reconciliation, instead of a confrontational discussion of the war as a social product of historical inequalities in Peru.[15]

By the late 1980s, the violence escalated throughout Peru, particularly affecting the capital city, Lima. As I have shown in my work on the theater of the internal war era,[16] while interest in the conflict could be found in many places around the country, violence was not a focus for the theatrical establishment in Lima. Thus, at the time that violence gripped Lima more and more, the dissociation between the theater produced in establishment venues and the popular theater produced in rural or non-privileged urban areas was increasingly clear. The professional theater establishment began to move away from the subject of violence, taking refuge in classical dramatists of other nations, or in more commercial options: nothing seeming Marxist or Socialist was welcome.

However, not all Peruvian theater practitioners were for a convenient silence. Some voices demanded precisely the opposite, a more dialectical engagement with the war. Among them, the most prominent public interventions came from Alfonso La Torre, critic and playwright, as well as from author and researcher Sara Joffré.[17] La Torre, arguably the most important Peruvian theater critic of the twentieth century, made a direct appeal to the theatrical elites of his time regarding the need to face the theme of violence and destruction. He authored in 1986 a call to Peruvian theater producers, challenging them to address the issue of violence and armed conflict:

> This reality allows us to write in the manner of Bertolt Brecht. Brecht began making an apocalyptic theater, anarchistic, proclaiming the destruction of any system, because there was nothing worth saving. Then Brecht discovered Marxism and came to predict in his mature works a new order, founded dialectically.[18]

For La Torre, it was crucial that theater artists fight against the sort of alienation they were suffering in the context of a tragedy that was killing thousands of people in front of their own eyes. La Torre entitled his diatribe "Is the theater useful for something in Peru?" According to his view, mainstream theater actors, playwrights, and directors had all lost their moral authority to address key issues in Peru because of their silence on war and violence. The only way to recover such authority was to go back to Brecht because such a move would "problematize political treatment of the theater where all the horizons are closing."[19] What La Torre is proposing is the necessity of (re)building an authentic dialectical and revolutionary theater, not a theater opposed to revolution, precisely to face the terrifying course that the Shining Path had charted in the name of social change. La Torre attacked directly the way in which professional companies were avoiding the internal war topic, and he also criticized the ways that the most preeminent experimental collectives (Yuyachkani and Ensayo, among others) opted for symbolism and surrealism instead of a more naturalistic representation of the violence. La Torre calls openly to discuss the war through theater, but always from a progressive, Marxist perspective. He writes, "Those who claimed to fulfill the prediction of Brecht were ominous and alienated from Brecht himself, and they ended by establishing a kind of social doom and gloom."[20]

The Key Figure: Sara Joffré

Sara Joffré (1935–2014), the most important disseminator of Brecht's work in Peru,[21] worked in a vein that was similar to yet distinct from La Torre's. As an author, independent scholar, and promoter of theater festivals (the *Muestra de Teatro Peruano*, for example, inaugurated in 1974), Joffré's work concerning Brecht had two principal trajectories: teaching and creation. As a frequent guest speaker at festivals and events, Joffré was responsible for holding numerous Brechtian workshops (often in grass-roots settings) dedicated to reading and interpreting Brecht's work. As a result of her labor, the workshops have introduced Bertolt Brecht to new generations of artists, researchers, and critics interested in the work of the German writer in Peru. Also, the interest in providing an accessible guide to Brecht brought Joffré to translate the Brazilian scholar Fernando Peixoto's book, *Brecht: Una introducción al teatro dialéctico* (Brecht: An Introduction to Dialectical Theater), which has become a key reference for theater artists in Peru.

Joffré's Brechtian workshops involved thorough, close reading–based discussion of the texts as well as proposed interpretations, appropriations, and participants' experimental writing. A central aim was to promote the use of Brechtian plays among non-privileged circles of theater artists. Since most of her audiences in workshops were youth, the workshops were a compelling opportunity to invigorate the next generation of independent theater through encounters with Brecht's work. Also, Joffré always worked through nonprofit, community-based theaters and festivals in many regions, including remote areas in the Andes. The Brechtian workshops became, in essence, an unofficial educational program for many young theater practitioners in Peru. At a time when Brecht's image (along with that of any socialist icon) was so misunderstood, decried, even prohibited because of its Marxist associations, Sara Joffré spread Brechtian work openly among young audiences. Joffré remained committed and active even in the last years of her life, founding and leading the workshop *Reading Bertolt Brecht* within the Amateur Artists Association (AAA) of Lima from 2010 to 2014.

As a director, Joffré created *La Noche Brecht* (Evening with Brecht, 1984) a yearly event to remember the author among actors and practitioners, reciting or performing passages and poems in cultural centers. Also, during the 1990s, Joffré helped to maintain interest in Brecht among young audiences through her solo performance *Hablando de Bertolt Brecht* (Talking about Bertolt Brecht, published 2000), frequently presented in alternative spaces, bars, schools, and universities. The performance introduced audiences, through a mock conference, to the author's life and work. Joffré used excerpts of Brecht's most acclaimed works with direct challenges to the audiences to appropriate that work and bring it to bear in the public arena. Joffré described the mission that guided her work on Brecht with the underprivileged and youth in her influential book on Brecht and Peruvian theater: "It was not important if what we did was a good production or not, because we knew that the very act of making theater, in itself, can serve the human being. The plays of Brecht convey that."[22]

Joffré was also an acclaimed playwright herself, and she wrote some of the best works to address the historical roots and deep social implications of Peru's chronic violence. Many of these works had an explicitly Brechtian influence. *La Hija de Lope* (The Daughter of Lope, staged 1992, published 1999),[23] based on the historical character of the Spanish Conquistador Lope de Aguirre (1510–60), is an exploration of uncontrolled violence and the many ways in which envisioned utopias can rapidly turn catastrophic for the less fortunate. The failed expedition of Spaniard conquistador Lope de Aguirre in search of El Dorado (1566) serves Joffré as material for a sharp debate about the limits of violence and the value of utopic revolutions. The Aguirre material also fuels an inquiry into the authoritarianism inherent in the very origins of Peruvian history. *La Hija de Lope* (written circa 1990) presents an impossible time, after the death of both Aguirre and his daughter Elvira, a famous episode of the colonial history of America. Historical data about the expedition have confirmed the existence of the Aguirre revolt, an insurgency expressed as stark violence against the original leaders of the El Dorado expedition and ultimately, a rebellion against the power of the king of Spain.

In this regard, the dramaturgical exercise of Joffré distances itself from either a biographical narrative of Aguirre or an account of the events as we find, for instance, in Werner Herzog's film *Aguirre, Wrath of God*, or Ramon Sender's novel *La Aventura Equinoccial de Lope de Aguirre* (The Equinoctial Adventure of Lope de Aguirre). Joffré chooses to *dehistoricize* the history of Aguirre, using distancing effects to place the characters in a time after his death. That way, Aguirre himself narrates his conversion into a violent rebel without consciousness of the eventual implications of the murderous process. Likewise, the discourse alters the time line, creating an assemblage of times and spaces that either overlap or seem to fall into disarray.

The influence of Brechtian drama on the presentation of the plot in *La Hija de Lope* is important to note. The play presents its scenes in an epic fashion, preventing the conventional building of dramatic tension toward a climax. In Joffré's play it is clear that the discourse is non-Aristotelian: beyond time and space and historical vicissitudes, the characters have come to the scene only to tell us the facts of a violent time, dispassionately and, as much as possible, didactically. Characters thus act as agents of memory, selecting and explaining the events. They symbolize the past, explaining the subjects required to better understand the difficult present, a present that seems analogous to the fictive dead time that the play conceives.

It would be legitimate to read this play as an allegorical account of the horrors of the recent Peruvian social violence. There are many links between the utopian adventure of Lope and the bloody Shining Path utopia, and there is more than a little in common between the barbarism and lack of feeling that marked the dawn of Peru's colonization and the internal war-fueled barbarism and lack of feeling that are palpable at the crossroads of Peruvian modernization. Too often, the phenomenon of the Peruvian armed conflict has been defined simply as a time of terror, regardless of its historical or social causes. But both the historical and the social dimensions imbue Joffré's play, mainly due to the author's ability to detach the dramatic language from historical vicissitudes through the rhetorical mechanisms mentioned above. By offering a perspective anchored outside of historical time, *La Hija de Lope* allows the audience to experience it as an allegory of the exercise of memory, not as an illustration of the history itself. And by contrasting a minimal, character-based story with the uncontrollably violent revolt, the text invites the audience to come to terms with such a revolt as a phenomenon that comes into being at multiple junctures of history.

Another play, *Camino de una sola vía* (One-Way Street, 2000),[24] attempts to deal with history in the wake of war. The play presents the last days of Walter Benjamin through the dual lens of his own writings and letters from friends and family. Each depiction in the play is also a meditation on the historical process of violence and the many challenges that the exercise of the memory entails. Even the historical characters are playing the role of discussants, participants in an exchange about the life and works of Benjamin. In this play, for instance, Joffré presents a fictional conversation between Brecht and Benjamin, discussing lessons of historical materialism in order to generate a store of knowledge to be used when the time of violence has passed.

In one of the most interesting moments, Joffré uses Benjamin's texts, extracted from the *Moscow Journals*, to propose the unresolved tension between artists and revolutionary processes. In this section (*Camino de una sola vía*, 26–27), Benjamin asks whether an artist can sidestep an intervention in politics and even try to gain some personal advantage during a revolutionary process. He asks whether it is possible to reconcile an artist's creative work with political activism, even if that activism implies the loss of critical freedom. Joffré does not alter Benjamin's text original. Rather, the play simply draws on the passage's intrinsic dramatic possibilities. This framing and exhibition of Benjamin's idea is at the center of the piece, and it encourages the viewer to shift from an interest in personal-biographical detail to an interest in the conceptual problem that the passage presents.

It is striking, the way that this passage could summarize the dilemmas of the Peruvian Left during the internal war, caught as it was between active participation in, open support of, or conscious distancing from the revolutionary calls that flooded Peru for decades. Joffré succeeds in exposing, through the image of Benjamin, the crucial importance of confronting the artist's perspective with revolutionary practice, especially in a time when Peruvian theater artists saw their work in terms of a commitment to social change.

Given the unresolved dilemmas of artistic creation and political engagement, Joffré uses Brecht again, this time in a poetic way. As a character, Brecht (along with Gerhard [later Gershom] Scholem and Theodor W. Adorno) shows up as a living puppet in an antique store. Before that, Benjamin presents his ideas and discusses his concerns. The Brecht/Benjamin counterposition is the main highlight of the play. Thus, personal images of both writers become images of political commitment in art and intellectual life. They are certainly opposed images, in the different ways that they propose to resolve the dilemma. Addressing the audience directly, Brecht (as puppet) introduces himself and discusses Benjamin's questions extensively, with an intimacy and frankness we only expect from a friend. The scene is presented as a lesson drawn from the historical vicissitudes of Benjamin's life, and by extension, from the lives of a generation of committed thinkers and writers. Facing imminent defeat by fascism, the Brecht character concludes, "In the struggle against them, nothing should be omitted" (*Camino de una sola vía*, 30).

The destruction caused by the Peruvian armed conflict was followed by the consolidation of a neoliberal/conservative ideology, thanks to the political regime of Alberto Fujimori (1990–2000). By 1999, when *Camino de una sola vía* was written, most Peruvians opposed the authoritarian regime that at first promised to defeat the guerrillas and rebuild the economy, only then to destroy incipient Peruvian democracy and to establish market supremacy. Today, Peruvians also begin to wonder whether that regime, as Brecht warned Benjamin, and as Joffré evokes in *Camino de una sola vía* (30), is not planning to stay "for another 30,000 years."

Notes

[1] The internal war was initiated by the Peruvian Communist Party Shining Path but increased significantly due to the response from the government armed forces. Most of those executed and disappeared were civilians, especially in the poorest Andean areas of the country. According to the National Truth and Reconciliation Commission in Peru (2003) most of these victims were peasants, illiterate and Quechua-only speakers (Indians). Thus, Peruvian political violence highlighted an older political and cultural problem: inequality, a weak process of democratization, and the lack of inclusion policies in a Peruvian multiethnic society. However, this tragedy in the recent history of Peru does not appear clarified in the Peruvian official discourse,

particularly in educational programs. A recent study from the Peruvian *Defensoría del Pueblo* states that many of the recommendations of the Report of the Commission of Truth and Reconciliation (2003) have not been implemented yet. See *Informe Final de la Comisión de la Verdad* (Lima: CVR, 2004), available online at http://www.cverdad.org.pe/ifinal.

[2] The topic of violence has been present in many theatrical productions in Peru since the very beginning of the armed conflict (1980). Theater critic Hugo Salazar has shown in his work on theater and violence the presence of the theme in the works of many theater groups in Lima, as well as in other cities of Peru. Salazar demonstrated that structural violence influenced the aesthetic choices of many theater practitioners in Lima. See Hugo Salazar del Alcázar, *Teatro y Violencia: una aproximación al teatro peruano de los 80* (Lima: Centro de Documentación y Video Teatral / Jaime Campodónico, 1990).

[3] The discussion on the parallel theatrical systems in Peru is open. My own dissertation, *Peruvian Theater during Internal Armed Conflict* (2011) suggests the existence of at least three subsystems or fields (Bourdieu) for theater in Peru, which do not intersect and influence one another. One is the privileged theater in formal circuits, the independent and popular theater, and non-artistic systems of theatricality (festivals, dances, and rituals). For more on Bourdieu's concept of *field*, see Bourdieu, *The Field of Cultural Production: Essays on Art and Literature* (New York: Columbia University Press, 1993).

[4] Bertolt Brecht's influence in Latin America has been investigated repeatedly. Among the most known works are Fernando De Toro, *Brecht en el teatro hispanoamericano contemporáneo: acercamiento semiótico al teatro épico en Hispanoamérica* (Ottawa: Girol Books, 1984); Osvaldo Pelletieri, *De Bertolt Brecht a Ricardo Monti: teatro en lengua alemana y teatro argentino (1900–1994)* (Buenos Aires: Editorial Galerna, 1994); Sara Joffré, ed., *Bertolt Brecht en el Perú-Teatro* (Lima: Biblioteca Nacional del Perú, 2001).

[5] My own research retrieved an extensive corpus of dramatic productions connected to the internal war in many regions of Peru. An initial approach, although incomplete and subject to continued investigation will reveal many theater groups of the Independent Theater, particularly incorporating plays and works by Barricada and Expresión, both from Huancayo, and their directors, Maria Teresa Zúñiga and Eduardo Valentín, respectively. Also, the cycle of violence appears very early in the work of dramatists of the shantytowns and marginal urban zones in Lima, the *pueblos jóvenes*; in groups such as Vichama and its director Cesar Escuza at Villa El Salvador, Lima; or La Gran Marcha de los Muñecones, in Comas, northern Lima. See Carlos Vargas-Salgado, "El teatro en las regiones del Perú," *Boletín del Instituto Internacional de Teatro del Perú* (2005); and *Teatro peruano en el conflicto armado interno: estética, derechos humanos y expectativas de descolonización* (PhD diss., University of Minnesota, 2011).

[6] For a detailed description of the beginning of independent theater groups in Peru, see Malgorzata Olezskiewicz, *Teatro popular peruano: del precolombino al siglo XX* (Warsaw: Warsaw University Centro de Estudios Latinamericanos, 1995).

[7] Joffré, *Bertolt Brecht en el Perú-Teatro*, 53.

[8] See Carlos Ivan Degregori, *How Difficult It Is to Be God: Shining Path's Politics of War in Peru, 1980–1999* (Madison: University of Wisconsin Press, 2012); Steve

J. Stern, ed., *Shining and Other Paths: War and Society in Peru 1980–1995* (Durham, NC: Duke University Press, 1998); and Cynthia McClintock, *Revolutionary Movements in Latin America: El Salvador's FMLN & Peru's Shining Path* (Washington, DC: United States Institute of Peace Press, 1998).

[9] On the organization and characteristics of the Shining Path as a revolutionary party, see Degregori, *How Difficult It Is to Be God.*

[10] I echo here the arguments of Jean Franco on the structural causes of contempt for and subsequent elimination of indigenous populations. See Franco, "'Alien to Modernity': The Rationalization of Discrimination," *Journal of Latin American Cultural Studies*: *Travesia* 15, no. 2 (2006): 171–181.

[11] Víctor Zavala Cataño, "Con motivo de los cuarenta años de la publicación del libro Teatro Campesino" *Cuarenta años del Teatro campesino* (teatrocampesino.blogspot.com), 2009.

[12] For further discussion on Víctor Zavala Cataño´s work, see Manuel Valenzuela, "Subalternidad y violencia política en el teatro peruano: El ingreso del campesino como referente de cambio en los discursos teatrales," *Alteridades* 21, no. 41 (2011): 161–174.

[13] For a comprehensive history of Cuatrotablas, see articles and critiques collected in Mario Delgado, *La nave de la memoria: Cuatrotablas, treinta años de teatro peruano* (Lima: Asociación para la Investigación Actoral Cuatrotablas, 2004).

[14] For further information on Yuyachkani´s work, see Miguel Rubio Zapata, *Notas sobre Teatro* (Lima: Grupo Cultural Yuyachkani, 2001).

[15] Yuyachkani is dedicated to staging the social injustice of Peruvian society, as well as to investigate elements of theatricality in Andean and Amazonian regions of Peru. The Yuyachkani "cycle of the violence" includes the works *Contraelviento* (1989), *Adiós, Ayacucho* (1990), *Return* (1996), *Antígona* and *Santiago* (both 2000), *Rosa Cuchillo* (2002) and *Sin título, técnica mixta* (2004).

[16] See Vargas-Salgado, *Teatro peruano durante el conflicto armado interno.*

[17] See the brief tribute in this volume.

[18] Alfonso La Torre, "¿Para qué sirve el teatro en el Perú?" *La República*, 30 March 1986. This manifesto was republished by Joffré in *Muestra, Revista de autores de teatro peruano* 15 (2007): pp. 56–59.

[19] Ibid., p. 59.

[20] Ibid., p. 59.

[21] See the tribute in the opening section of this volume.

[22] Joffré, *Bertolt Brecht en el Perú-Teatro*, 55.

[23] All references are to the version included in José Castro Urioste and Roberto Ángeles, eds, *Dramaturgia peruana* (Lima and Berkeley, CA: Latinoamericana Editores, 1999), pp. 50–66.

[24] All references are to Joffré, *Camino de una sola vía* (Rio de Janeiro: Servicio Social do Comercio, 2013).

Dieter Goltzsche, *Mackie Messer auf der Weidendammbrücke*, 1985, Lithographie.

"*Den guten Menschen* hätte eins von unseren großen Theatern doch vor langer Zeit aufführen sollen." Brecht, die Studenten und das Werden der Neuen Welle des australischen Theaters

Das dramatische Schaffen Bertolt Brechts vor seinem Tode im Jahre 1956 war in Australien fast unbekannt, und die Anfänge der längst überfälligen Rezeption seines Werks sind mit der Arbeit australischer Studentenbühnen eng verbunden. 1960 bis 1963 inszenierten Studierende der Universität Sydney *Der gute Mensch von Sezuan, Die Ausnahme und die Regel*, und *Mutter Courage*, allesamt australische Premieren. Die Mitwirkenden teilten nicht unbedingt die politischen Auffassungen, die den Dramen zugrunde lagen, doch stellten diese Theaterproduktionen ein Protest gegen die herrschenden Formen des damaligen Theaters dar, und die studentische Theaterarbeit änderte im Laufe der Zeit das ganze australische Theaterleben. Unter diesen jungen Künstlern waren viele, die die australische Neue Welle in den 1970er Jahren vorantrieben.

Brecht's work was almost unknown in Australia before his death in 1956, and his long overdue reception is intimately linked to the young people who were the first to stage his work there. From 1960 to 1963 students at the University of Sydney produced *The Good Woman of Setzuan*, *The Exception and the Rule*, and *Mother Courage*—all Australian premieres of his work. While these students were not motivated by the explicitly political underpinnings of Brecht's own theater, their efforts did represent a form of protest against the reigning popular theatrical entertainment of the day, and their work ultimately changed the face of theater in Australia: a decade later, it was these same students who would go on to drive the New Wave of Australian theater in an era characterized by political and social change.

"*Good Woman* should have been done in one of our big theaters long before this":[1] Brecht, the Students, and the Making of the New Wave of Australian Theater

Laura Ginters

In April 1960, nearly two decades after its first production in Europe, *The Good Woman of Setzuan* finally had its Australian premiere. It was produced and performed by undergraduates at the University of Sydney, and it was heralded in the *Bulletin* (an important weekly news journal) as "Sydney's First Brecht." This first encounter between Brecht's socially and politically progressive theater and the impressionable and enthusiastic young people staging it in the 1960s flags not only an important new stage in the reception of Brecht in Australia and these students' explicit efforts to challenge the prevailing theater culture of their time, it also lays the groundwork for a significant shift in the Australian theater landscape—the development of the New Wave of Australian theater and drama in the 1970s, a time also when Brecht's work began to be produced frequently by professional companies.

Some background to the social and political context of the day may help explain why it was left to students to be premiering the work of one of the twentieth century's major playwrights in Australia. In 1960 a conservative government, led by Prime Minister Robert Menzies, had been in power in Australia for eleven years and would continue to rule for another, record-breaking, twelve years. Menzies had also been prime minister from 1939 to 1941.[2] In 1940 he banned the Communist Party for security reasons (a ban that was only lifted in late 1942), and in 1949 he campaigned for election on a platform of again banning the Communist Party. His legislation was ultimately struck down by the High Court of Australia as unconstitutional: Undeterred, Menzies took the question to a national referendum where it was again defeated, albeit by the slimmest of margins (50.6 percent to 49.4 percent).

By the end of the first decade of the Cold War, Australia could be seen as a conservative, somewhat fearful, country, and one that also had not completely relinquished its strong colonial ties (which also extended to all things cultural). Australia had become a Commonwealth in 1901, but the official head of state then (as now) was the Queen of England, and until 1948 even Australian-born citizens were considered to be British subjects. It was an increasingly affluent, "white picket fences" Australia (but also one where its Indigenous inhabitants could not vote in federal elections until 1962). At two million, the population of Sydney was just half its current size, and it was home to the country's oldest and most prestigious university—the University of Sydney.[3] This university was, unsurprisingly, very white, largely middle and upper class, and privileged. Upon graduation, its students would, very often, make the pilgrimage "home" to England for an extended visit.

And while a lively culture of left-wing politics had thrived at the university in the 1940s, in the following decade, the most notable student campaign centered on the famous Pedestrian Crossing Demonstration of 1955 when up to three thousand students swarmed onto the busy road adjoining the university, in protest at the lack of a zebra crossing, which had resulted in a student being knocked over by a car. As Barcan writes, "[t]his was by far the biggest student demonstration for years," but "the cause was local and non-political."[4] Barcan has documented the retreat from leftist student political activity in the "quiet decade" of the 1950s,[5] quoting Martin Davey, an editor of the student newspaper, *Honi Soit*, who noted "the massive indifference of the undergraduates to political questions; the divorce of real politics from student representative bodies"[6] at this time. On campus political engagement was largely restricted to satirical jibes in the annual university revues: These were not the politically radicalized students who re-emerged in the late 1960s. These students were not seeking to create a new social system—but their early productions of Brecht plays *did* represent a deliberate form of protest against the dominant popular stage entertainment of the day.

I will focus here on three early productions of Brecht's plays at the University of Sydney between 1960 and 1963. These were *The Good Woman of Setzuan* (1960), *The Exception and the Rule* (1961), and *Mother Courage* (1963). Perhaps surprisingly, given that Brecht's work had first been produced forty years earlier, these were all the Australian premieres of these works.[7] These productions do not appear in Ulrike Garde's wide-ranging and valuable account of Brecht reception in Australia,[8] nor can they be located in the Australian performing arts database, ausstage. They have, to all intents and purposes, disappeared from the theatrical record. I discovered them while undertaking research into student drama activities at the university in the late 1950s and early 1960s and I found that these students were regularly doing the Australian—and at least on one occasion the world[9]—premiere of contemporary European plays by writers such as Genet, Beckett, Pinter, Borchert, Anouilh, Ionesco . . . and Brecht. These productions were reported, often very favorably, in the mainstream media and attended not just by the friends and family of the students, but also a general theater-going public.

These Brecht productions were part of a flurry of student productions of his plays, beginning in 1958 and continuing through the 1960s, but they can actually be considered as a second "wave" of Brecht reception in Australia.[10] Brecht's theater work was already known in Australia in the 1920s,[11] and the left-leaning New Theatres in New South Wales introduced Brecht to the Australian stage as early as 1938.[12] Garde considers that "Brecht was only genuinely discovered [in Australia] in the late 1950s, after his death," describing a 1939 production as "an exception rather than the start of a series of performances."[13] I believe, however, we might consider the five New Theatre productions in New South Wales from 1938 to 1952 together as a group as being of significance, given the explicitly socially progressive and politically motivated aims of the New Theatre movement, well in line with Brecht's own attitudes to the theater and its purpose. But it was this very political engagement that also, ironically, led to the New Theatre's partial erasure from the Australian theater scene and theater record. Their close association with the Communist Party of Australia meant that the New Theatres in Brisbane, Perth, and Adelaide closed entirely during the wartime ban on the CPA, and the New Theatres in Sydney and Melbourne had to survive underground:[14] The Newcastle New Theatre League disappeared altogether, to be reborn in 1956. The Cold War era threw up its own challenges in relation to the New Theatres' wider visibility and access to audiences, with newspapers sometimes refusing to publicize their shows: The *Sydney Morning Herald*, for example, refused to review or advertise the Sydney New Theatre productions from 1948 to 1961.[15]

This cloak of at least partial invisibility around the New Theatre meant that the path was clear for Brecht to be "discovered" anew in the late 1950s by a crop of decidedly non-political students, heralding a very different kind of Brecht reception in this country. What both groups of this first and second wave of reception had in common, though, was their enthusiastic amateur status, which distinguishes their work, and the attention paid to it, then and subsequently, from the newly professionalizing/professionalized theater from the late 1960s, and the accompanying boom in Brecht productions through the 1970s.[16] I will return to the question of this amateur/professional divide below.

In Sydney in the mid-1950s there was, to all intents and purposes, almost no local professional "serious" theater; the Australian Elizabethan Theatre Trust had begun presenting a small number of plays in Sydney from 1955—but it says much about the local milieu that its first play was Terence Rattigan's *The Sleeping Prince*, starring English actors including Ralph Richardson and Sybil Thorndike, and produced by a commercial producer.[17] For the most part, in Sydney the theatergoer's choices were limited to the (very) occasional professional touring production, imported popular commercial shows from the UK and US, local revues, and the offerings of amateur "Little Theaters." Those plays by leading European writers mentioned above were not being produced by these theaters: but they were by these students.

From around 1957 there was an influx of very enthusiastic and talented undergraduates to the University of Sydney. This concentration of young people interested in drama at the University of Sydney was largely due to two reasons: there was no professional post-school theater training at the time (the National Institute of Dramatic Art [NIDA] took in its first cohort in 1959), and the University of Sydney was one of only two universities in Sydney; the other (the University of New South Wales) had a greater focus on sciences and engineering than arts and humanities. If you were just out of school and keen to be an actor you might well receive the advice—as a number of these young people did—to go to the University of Sydney and do as much drama as you could there. This had been a well-established path into an acting career in the first half of the twentieth century, both in England and in Australia.

The group of undergraduates and recent graduates who produced this work has arguably had a bigger influence on Australian cultural life, right up to the present day, than any single group before or since. Some names will be familiar to an international audience—people like film director Bruce Beresford, the art critic Robert Hughes, the UK-based TV presenter and writer Clive James, the Booker Prize-nominated novelist Madeline St John, and the well-known feminist Germaine Greer. But there are also many others who have made (and indeed in a number of cases continue to make) a major and defining contribution to the arts and professional theater in Australia, like designer and festival director Leo Schofield, playwrights Ron Blair and Bob Ellis, directors Ken Horler and Richard Wherrett, and actor/director John Bell to name just a few.

It is interesting to consider how the students may have come to Brecht at all, given that they were not part, for example, of a New Theatre movement, where suitable left-leaning plays circulated among these like-minded groups and were repeatedly produced, both within Australia, but also internationally. There was, however, from 1957 a burgeoning awareness of Brecht and his work and this developed in several ways.[18] Garde outlines the significance of Edith Anderson's translation of "Vergnügungstheater oder Lehrtheater" published as "Theatre for Learning" in 1958 in a local literary journal for shaping Australian impressions of Brecht's theories,[19] and she also acknowledges the importance of universities for the reception generally of German-speaking playwrights and their work in Australia.[20] I would like to tease this out a little further here, to sketch some of the ways in which knowledge about, and awareness of, Brecht circulated in

Australia—some ten thousand miles (or a six week boat trip) distant from the theatrical centers of London and Berlin.

It is certainly true that some of the intersecting currents of movement and exchange emanated from universities and it was through these that connections were made to the theater, and broader cultural and intellectual life in relation to this interest in, and uptake of, Brecht's plays. University German departments had a natural role to play in introducing their undergraduate students, and others, to significant contemporary German writers—we can see this, for example, at the University of Melbourne where the German Department had staged at least two productions of Brecht's work (in German) with its students by 1958.[21] Academics, including several recently returned from Germany, disseminated their knowledge of Brecht and his theater through public lectures, published articles, and theater productions. Further, they were mobile too, spreading the word as they moved between Sydney, Canberra, and Melbourne for lectures, academic positions, and postgraduate study.[22] But while a relatively small number of students may have been introduced to Brecht in the original language by their German lecturers, it is also clear that there were other sources that sparked more general student interest, and this included firsthand reports from people who had witnessed the impact of Brecht's theater in London and more broadly in Europe. Theater director Wal Cherry, for example, visited the Berliner Ensemble, and wrote about his experience in the *Age* newspaper, just before directing the first professional production of one of Brecht's plays in Australia in 1958 at the Union Theatre at the University of Melbourne.[23] Indeed, in 1958–59 alone there were at least five survey articles published on Brecht, his influence on the contemporary theater, and his role in Australia,[24] in addition to reviews of the three theater productions that took place at the University of Melbourne in that time. This was a good time for newspapers and journals in Australia: The number of quarterly literary journals had been proliferating in recent years, and they were joined in 1958 by two new fortnightly journals, the *Observer* and the *Nation*, both of which reviewed theater productions. This increased general public awareness of theatrical activities across the country, but also played an important role in bringing "new" writers like Brecht to the wider attention of theater practitioners and audiences alike—*Mother Courage*, for instance, was reviewed in both journals.

At the University of Sydney too, a keen interest in what was happening overseas saw students involved in the various drama groups avidly devour theater news from England via theater magazines, records, and/or films, and this must also be considered as a valuable source of information and influence for their own Brecht productions. The Berliner Ensemble's successful tour to London in 1956 was especially significant in bringing Brecht's work to a larger, English-speaking audience—both on the spot and on the other side of the world.[25] As James Lyon has written, this tour "made a marked, lasting impression primarily upon directors and designers who held or were soon to hold key positions at the dominant London companies: George Devine, William Gaskill, Peter Brook, Peter Hall, John Dexter, Tony Richardson, and John Bury, among others."[26] While the same could not exactly be said of Australia, these productions, so far away, did have an impact. These students, raised on a diet of imported theater productions, turned avidly to what was taking place and causing a stir in theater centers like London to inform their own work. Notable, though, is that—despite the reigning cultural cringe that dictated aspiring to all things English, especially in cultural matters—what sparked their interest here was a foreign, "difficult" writer. And armed with this knowledge of Brecht's impact overseas, they put on their own productions, even, perhaps somewhat surprisingly, negotiating with the Brecht estate for rights and royalty payments.

Such productions also led to another form of inter-university exchange across the nation, this time among students, rather than at the level of academics: The Australian Universities Drama Festival was an annual event, where each university was invited to submit a production to the festival, which took place in a different capital city each year. Given Australia's great size (its landmass is only slightly smaller than the United States) and small, dispersed population, this was a valuable opportunity for students to come together and experience productions and playwrights, including Brecht, they may not have previously encountered. These early shared experiences had the potential for long-term repercussions for Australian theater and its practitioners, as I will describe below.

In 1958 Bruce Grant wrote, in an article entitled "Brecht in Australia: The Search for Reality," that

> [o]ne of the advantages of Australia's isolation from the rest of the Western world is that we are not influenced by fashion. By the time whatever is fashionable reaches us, it is also likely to be useful. I am referring to the strength of ideas, not the length of hemlines.[27]

It seemed that Brecht had become "useful" for students by the late 1950s. This, then, was the context in which students at the University of Sydney took up Brecht with such enthusiasm.

The Good Woman of Setzuan (1960)

As noted above, this production was credited as "Sydney's First Brecht." This was not quite true: There had in fact been four productions of plays by Brecht in Sydney between 1939 and 1958. However, the first three of these had been at the New Theatre—hence very little, if any, attention would have been given to them in the local newspapers—and the final production had been produced in German by the Kleines Wiener Theater,[28] so the journalist's mistake is perhaps forgivable.

Leo Schofield, leading light of the Sydney University Players, directed *The Good Woman*. Schofield was better known for his stylish and polished productions of classics like *The Country Wife*, but he had seen photos of Peggy Ashcroft in the play at the Royal Court in London in 1956, and for him Brecht was, as he said, "very modish. Everyone was listening to Brecht and talking Brecht."

The papers of the time welcomed news of *Good Woman*, and an almost concurrent production of *The Caucasian Chalk Circle* at the Independent Theatre.[29] Indeed the commentary and reviews in the major local publications in relation to these Brecht productions continued over a full two months. Brecht's play presented its own particular challenges for Schofield, not least of which were the high expectations of the critics for these plays of a dramatist they recognized as being internationally important, if hitherto mostly ignored in Australia. Fortunately for him, Lindsey Browne, the influential *Sydney Morning Herald* critic, declared that this production "gave Sydney a first exciting taste of the work of much-debated Bertold [sic] Brecht."[30]

Schofield required an experienced and strong actress to play the lead role, the good-hearted prostitute Shen Te, and her male alter ego, Shui Ta—and someone who could sing in a soprano, baritone, and bass voice. He recruited Marlene Horsell, who worked with the downtown Genesian Theatre, to take on this role.[31] While the audiences responded warmly to her, some critics had reservations. While the *Bulletin*'s reviewer praised her as "sensitive in the exhausting central role,"[32] and Browne celebrated "an actress capable of an extraordinarily wide expressive range," another argued that as the Woman, she acted with "so much schmalz [and] was so much the elocuting pretty girl, that the performance was cloying and unconvincing. The Good Woman is a prostitute . . . [S]he is not a . . . girl showing her fellow [Girl] Guides around Daddy's garden!"[33]

He cast the remaining roles from the student body, and the reviewers were generally positive[34] about Schofield's "resourceful"[35] production with its "excellent detail setting and first-class lighting."[36] The shocking acoustics of the lecture theater in which it was performed were not fully overcome by the untrained performers' inability to project their voices well (leading to some critical grumbles), but the production was "cleverly planned and neatly executed"[37]—with one reviewer commenting that "[w]e are very lucky that Mr. Leo Schofield in this production has achieved a good balance between 'doing it with spotlights'" and the "overdressed stage" common to many of the other Sydney theaters of the day.[38] (This last comment, from a student reviewer, was specifically directed at the productions of the Australian Elizabethan Theatre Trust with their sometimes overly fussy, naturalistic sets.)

Even if produced and performed by amateurs, this was a significant production, and was recognized as such by reviewers. One strongly endorsed Players "for their courage in mounting the play," proclaiming "it seems a willful waste not to immediately shift the play downtown and play a season with it. Its merits justify this, and I hope the producer can arrange for it to be done."[39] While its popularity ensured a return season on campus this, alas, did not take place.

Good Woman had been part of an ambitious plan by the Sydney University Players to begin the academic year with a season of three plays: *Good Woman*, *Lysistrata*, and *Twelfth Night*, to be directed by Ken Horler, Schofield's great friend and co-prime mover in the Sydney University Players. *Twelfth Night*, designed by Schofield and starring a very young John Bell (and with Bruce Beresford as the ship's captain), was also a hit and it was invited to the Australian Universities Drama Festival, held in Adelaide that year. It received critical praise—but the "prestige success"[40] of the festival was Michael Boddy's production of Brecht's *The Caucasian Chalk Circle* from the University of Tasmania. Brecht, now newly de rigueur—at least in student circles—had been an obvious student drama choice for the AUDF. Boddy was credited with realizing a production that came close to the core of Brecht's intentions in a production that reached a "powerful climax."[41] It is, I argue, to this moment in 1960, among these undergraduates—and, significantly, located around two Brecht plays—that we can trace the beginnings of the New Wave of Australian theater.

The Exception and the Rule (1961)

In 1961, for the second year in a row, the students opened the year of student drama productions with a Brecht play. *The Exception and the Rule* was directed and designed by Ken Horler. Even as an undergraduate Horler had a clear sense of the importance of theater, often selecting works of large scope, works that he sensed were important, or had historical significance: No other theater director in Sydney could claim to have directed (and designed) two Brecht plays by 1963, much less before turning twenty-five.

In this "short and savage" play,[42] as one critic described this *Lehrstück* at the time, the *Herald* reviewer concluded that Players had offered this pair of plays (it was part of a double bill) "with rather more courage than judgment,"[43] and noted reprovingly that *The Exception and the Rule* "employs normal dramatic technique only in its final court scene" in this "ferociously didactic piece." The reviewer unwittingly continues to betray to us the extent to which Horler *did* in fact grasp and embrace what Brecht was envisaging for this play when he makes comments like "the stage management of Brecht's rather tedious sign-posting of each scene was so meticulous as to be cumbersome" and describes the "brief episodes deliberately clipped of suspense or anything more than rudimentary characterization." Horler, like Schofield before him, was operating in a makeshift venue for this production, in this instance a church hall with very limited stage space and lighting.[44] Turning this to his advantage, he limited the set to a yellow-brown backdrop, accompanied only by signboards to signal the scene changes. This "stark, almost surrealistic" presentation was very effective—and well in keeping, stylistically, with a Brechtian aesthetic.[45]

The Exception and the Rule was coupled in this double bill with a new, award-winning play by a fellow student, Dennis Carroll, *Pluck Your Harps, Cherubs*. Thematically and stylistically the two had nothing at all in common—Carroll's highly realistic play was set in a beach house and was an exploration of the lives of contemporary undergraduates—but the two plays and their production implicitly contributed to larger debates at the time.[46] Carroll's play had been discussed in the media as part of the ongoing, often expressed plaintive appeal that "theatre in Australia will only achieve adulthood when its principal fare consists of new plays of Australian origin."[47] Horler's staging of the play was a deliberate contribution of a local voice to the stage—something that was, in 1961 in Australia, still a rather rare occurrence. The Brecht play, then, functioned as a contrasting/complementing gambit: It not only continued Players' mission to introduce Brecht to Australian audiences, but also in a more complicated move functioned to demonstrate the coming of age of Australian theater more generally, which was, I argue, being at least in part led by these students. Certainly, the dry comment by a student reviewer—"Players must again be commended for staging two plays that have in common only a lack of popular commercial appeal"—indicates the extent to which Horler and company were, quite deliberately, eschewing the conventional path of theater production in Sydney at the time.[48]

A certain theme can be detected across the reviews of these first two productions where the students' "courage" is twice invoked: one in a positive sense, one in a more reproving tone, hinting too at the ambivalence of critics' attitudes toward Brecht as they—and the students staging him—grappled with developing a proper understanding of Brecht's theater, which both parties clearly sensed was significant, but which was so far from the standard theatrical fare of the day. The Players' next exercise in *Courage* provoked a similarly divided critical response: "ambition" is invoked by two reviewers below, again in both positive and negative ways, to address the scope, intention, and impact of Horler's production. "Courage"—apposite or not—and "ambition"—successfully realized or not—are, I think, excellent rubrics through which to interrogate the activities of these students and their engagement with Brecht at this pioneering moment of premiere productions.

Mother Courage (1963)

Two years later Horler directed and designed *Mother Courage*. Unlike *The Exception and the Rule*, *Mother Courage* is not a short play, nor small, and Paul Dessau's demanding score is a stretch for performers who are not trained singers.

Joan Littlewood had premiered *Mother Courage* in English at the Theatre Royal Stratford East in 1955. She both directed and played—somewhat under duress—the title role (Brecht had threatened to withdraw the performance rights if she did not), but it was an under-resourced and under-prepared production which met with a cool critical response and small audiences.[49] The following year Brecht's own company toured its famous production with Brecht's wife, Helene Weigel, in the lead role to London. His director's note in the program indicates that Horler was aware of not only Littlewood's production, but also other recent Mother Courages; Flora Robson, who played the title role in a BBC television production of the play in 1959, and Anne Bancroft who had starred on Broadway in the role earlier that year. The Brecht production film with Helene Weigel was also released in 1961, although it is unclear whether Horler had seen this. That is, even on the far side of the world these students were well aware of developments in other theatrical centers, and were eager to position themselves as *part of* what was new and exciting in contemporary theater.

Horler cast the striking, six-foot-tall Germaine Greer as Mother Courage for her stage presence and strong performance in university revues, and her known singing voice, but even with her background in choirs, this role was demanding for Greer. She recalls that: "[t]he music was hard . . . I didn't really know what it was meant to sound like. All I knew was it didn't sound like any music I was used to singing." This role did not come naturally for her and she never felt suited to it: "I was terribly nervous about Mother Courage . . . You know—too tall, wrong sort of face. Mother Courage needs to be *planted*. Hard to plant someone like me, especially someone as clumsy as I am." Born in the same year as the play itself, she was only twenty-four when she took on this role and her youthful appearance played against her. Ron Blair, who played her son Eilif, pointed to the irony that "Germaine, as Mother Courage, looked years younger than Maree D'Arcy" who played Kattrin, her daughter.

Critical responses to the opening night ranged from openly negative ("an epic drama—an obviously great play—was sacrificed in the cause of ambition . . . We now know that to experience Brecht played poorly is to experience something close to being a monumental bore"[50]) to lukewarm in the *Herald*: "[t]he cast . . . coped gallantly with . . . Paul Dessau's original Berlin song settings . . . [A]ll sang almost as self-reliantly (allowing for first night nerves) as they acted."[51] Of particular interest here though is the fact that the *Herald* reviewer, while deploring this "incorrigibly lagging production," had also, in the ensuing two years, become more reconciled to (or developed a better understanding of?) Brechtian staging techniques: He described the captions—which had so annoyed him in *The Exception and the Rule*—accurately as "intended by Brecht to emphasize the 'epic' and detached nature of his story-telling." They were "excellent." Reviewing a performance later in the season for *The Nation*, "Brek" noted that *Mother Courage*, "the most ambitious undertaking, apparently suffered disastrously from under-rehearsal when first performed before the Festival," but he could now confirm that "[Greer's] performance, and the production as a whole, lucidly outlined the groundplan of Brecht's drama and demonstrated its theatrical vividness."[52] The divergent opinions of this production might well come down to this: that it got rapidly better after a rather poor start. Certainly Greer, long before she became famous outside the Sydney Push and undergrad circles she was then frequenting, was remembered well by people who had seen her in this early role.[53]

Offering me chicken sandwiches for lunch on the day I interviewed her reminded Greer of a less savory aspect of playing Mother Courage:

> You know how Brecht says you have to have real action, no pissing about? You've got to pluck a chicken, so you pluck a chicken. There I was, I started out on the first evening, sitting down plucking a chicken, and of course the poor old chicken wasn't too hot when we got it. They had some trouble getting one with all its head and wings et cetera . . . So there I was, stripping this chicken and by the end of the run the chicken was so wrong that great gobs of it were coming off and oozing . . . I do remember that, my chicken.

This was an experience she shared with Joan Littlewood: Littlewood's chief memory (apart from her one word assessment of the production as "dreadful") was of the nausea she suffered when plucking *her* long-dead chicken.[54] Neither production was a striking critical or popular success—and neither leading lady felt comfortable or confident in her role—but both have entered the history books as the "first" Mother Courage. It was a bold move, in those early days, to produce this epic (and very long) play for audiences who were quite likely to have been suspicious of Brecht's political leanings and who had little experience of his groundbreaking theatrical vision.

I noted earlier that these University of Sydney productions have been, until now, completely absent from the official theatrical record. And this points us to an endemic problem in Australian theater history, and something of a paradox: in Australia, non-professional theater has been a mainstay of the available dramatic offerings since the earliest colonial times—indeed, it formed much of what was on offer in Sydney up to the late 1950s. And yet, amateur theater has been, and continues to be, seriously neglected in academic scholarship.[55] This has meant, then, that little attention has also been paid to the inter-relationship of professional and amateur theater when up until at least the early 1960s there was a much less marked distinction between professional and "non-professional" theater, with participants often moving between both (as for example, with *Good Woman*).

It was only following the introduction of federal arts funding and formal institutional actor (and later director) training in the 1960s,[56] that the "professionalization" of the industry challenged and changed the composition and relationships between professional and non-professional groups. It is as a result of this that Australian theater history has usually been written in retrospect as though it all began with the New Wave of Australian theater from the late 1960s and into the 1970s. The "New Wave" was characterized by explicit efforts to "decolonize" the Australian stage from its conservative Anglocentric origins and influences, embracing a larrikin, irreverent, energetic, humorous, and very Australian theater—both through a focus on new Australian works, and approaches to the classics (Shakespeare with Australian accents for the first time, for example). It was radical in its approach and subject material.

When writers describe the beginnings of the New Wave in Sydney, however, the connection directly back to the University of Sydney is almost completely elided. Geoffrey Milne, for example, dates the "first genuine hit" of the New Wave to the 1970 production of *The Legend of King O'Malley*. This was written, as he says, "by NIDA lecturer Michael Boddy and ABC script-writer Bob Ellis." "John Bell," he continues, "recently returned from overseas, got the job of directing it." A paragraph later he writes:

> John Bell teamed up with a lawyer, Ken Horler, in order to seize the moment. They took over and refurbished a little old stable in Nimrod Street in King's Cross . . . Nimrod [Theatre Company]'s first show was . . . *Biggles*. Like *O'Malley* this was a collaborative creation, written by Boddy with Ron Blair [and Marcus Cooney].[57]

Richard Wherrett, who would later become its co-artistic director, was also instrumental in founding the company and Leo Schofield would design shows for them. It is not at all apparent from this description that, as mentioned above, ten years earlier, Ellis, Bell, Horler, Blair, Schofield (and Wherrett) had all been at university together, all making theater together—and they knew Boddy from his production of *The Caucasian Chalk Circle* at the Adelaide University Drama Festival they'd all attended in 1960. After graduating many of them had then made the trip "home" to England, some working in the theater there, but it was these students of the late 1950s and early 1960s who then returned to Australia and became the professional theater practitioners of the 1970s and changed the face of Australian theater: As undergraduates they were, we might say, the "ripples" before the New Wave.[58]

The important connection between drama activities at universities and the subsequent development of Australian professional theater, particularly in Sydney, has generally been under-recognized.[59] In relation to Brecht more specifically, the three productions discussed above represent a significant contribution to the early reception of Brecht through student premieres and productions in the 1960s, representing not only the Australian premieres of these works, but also a hitherto unrecognized contribution by the University of Sydney to this early reception. There were, in fact, over twenty-five Brecht productions by university groups in the decade to 1970[60]—and this set the scene for what Garde has described as a "boom" in professional productions of Brecht's work in the much more politically engaged, professional theater of the 1970s in Australia.[61] Brecht's reception in Australia, then, is not only intimately tied to young people, but their take up of his work at the University of Sydney was in its own way a form of protest against the status quo of the local theater of the day—and indeed can be linked directly to the subsequent birth of a new kind of theater that was radical, engaged, and above all, Australian.

Notes

[1] "Sydney's First Brecht," *Bulletin*, 13 April 1960. Review of *The Good Woman of Setzuan*.

[2] Menzies was leader of the United Australia Party at that time. The UAP was dissolved in 1945, and Menzies founded and led the subsequent (conservative) Liberal Party. He was prime minister from its election victory in 1949 until his retirement in 1966 and is still Australia's longest-serving prime minister.

[3] The population of Australia has also more than doubled in that time frame: It was 10,392,000 in 1960 and 22,846,000 by 2010 (see http://www.populstat.info/Oceania/australc.htm). The university has grown much more quickly and is now 6.5 times larger than its population of around eight thousand in the late 1950s.

[4] See Alan Barcan, *Radical Students: The Old Left at Sydney University* (Melbourne: Melbourne University Press, 2002), p. 293.

[5] Barcan, *Radical Students*, p. 272.

[6] Barcan, *Radical Students*, p. 274.

[7] *Mother Courage* can only lay claim to being the English language premiere: In 1958 the students from the German Department at the University of Melbourne produced the play in German. For a discussion of this production see Ulrike Garde, *Brecht & Co: German-Speaking Playwrights on the Australian Stage* (Bern: Peter Lang, 2007), pp. 75–77.

[8] See Garde, *Brecht & Co*. Other contributions by Garde on Brecht in Australia include "'Never in Body and Seldom in Spirit': Australian Productions of Brecht's Plays and Their Reviews from 1945 to 1988," *The Brecht Yearbook* 26 (2001): pp.101–125; and "Brecht, der Klassiker 'downunder,'" *Dreigroschenheft* 1 (2009):

pp. 8–12. I consider myself in this article to be in conversation with Garde's groundbreaking work.

[9] Pamela Trethowan, director of the Sydney University Dramatic Society (SUDS), secured Samuel Beckett's permission to adapt his radio play, *All That Fall*, for the stage and produced it in a double bill with *Endgame* (also an Australian premiere) in March 1959.

[10] See Garde, *Brecht & Co*, pp. 377–379. Garde lists a University of Melbourne Marlowe Society production of *The Caucasian Chalk* Circle as taking place in 1959, but contemporary newspaper reviews give a premiere date of 15 July 1958. To her chronology we can also add the following university productions: *Die "Twenties-Show"* staged at the University of Melbourne in the 1940s, which included Brecht (among other authors); *Good Woman* (Adelaide University Dramatic Society, 1960); *The Caucasian Chalk Circle* (Old Nick Company, University of Tasmania, 1960); *The Visions of Simone Machard* (Teachers' College Sydney, 1961); *Good Woman* (Arts Union Festival of Arts, University of Western Australia, Perth, 1962); *Life of Galileo* (Graduate Theatre, Perth 1963).

[11] For example, various newspapers around the country in 1929–30 announced the "eagerly awaited" premiere of *The Lindbergh Flight* ("An Interesting Cantata," *Mercury* [Hobart], 3 July 1929); the stir caused by Brecht's adaptation of John Gay's work in *The Threepenny Opera* ("Books and Writers," *Queenslander*, 31 October 1929); and "a novel musical production which is soon to come to Berlin"—*Mahagonny* ("A Battle of Authors," *Western Mail* [Perth], 22 May 1930).

[12] The New Theatre in Sydney was established in 1932 and is one of the few worldwide that continues today. The Newcastle New Theatre League commenced in 1937 and ceased activities around 1940–41. Garde notes productions of *Señora Carrar's Rifles* (1939), *The Informer* (1941), and *Private Life of the Master Race* (1945), all at the New Theatre in Sydney (the New Theatre's records give a date of 1942 for *The Informer*). We might also note here Brecht's adaptation of *The Germans* by Leon Kruczkowski (New Theatre, Sydney 1952), and, most excitingly, a production of *Señora Carrar's Rifles*, under the title *The Ragged Cap*, produced by the New Theatre League in Newcastle in 1938. This newly discovered production appears to be the premiere of Brecht's work in Australia (and probably the southern hemisphere) and my analysis of this production and company will appear in a later issue of the *Brecht Yearbook*.

[13] Garde, *Brecht & Co.*, p. 69.

[14] See "New Theatre," in Philip Parsons with Victoria Chance, eds., *Concise Companion to Theatre in Australia* (Sydney: Currency Press, 1997), pp. 199–200; here, p. 200.

[15] See Paul Herlinger, "New Theatre—Sydney," in Philip Parsons with Victoria Chance, eds., *Companion to Theatre in Australia* (Sydney: Currency Press in association with Cambridge University Press, 1995), pp. 403–404; here, p. 403.

[16] See Garde, *Brecht & Co.* for a detailed analysis of this era.

[17] The AETT—named to commemorate the recent visit to Australia of Queen Elizabeth II—was established in 1954 to support the performing arts in Australia and to "make the theatre in Australia the same vigorous and significant force in our

national life that it was in the reign of the first Elizabeth." See Helen Musa, "Australian Elizabethan Theatre Trust," in *Companion to Theatre in Australia*, p. 72.

[18] The reception of Brecht was mostly unidirectional, though there are a couple of notable exceptions where Australian artists contributed to Brechtian endeavors in Europe at this time. In addition to visits paid by local directors like Wal Cherry and Brian Barnes to the Berliner Ensemble from the late 1950s, the *Sydney Morning Herald* was pleased to report in 1960, for example, that "[a]nother Australian play has been eagerly taken up in Europe": The Berliner Ensemble had decided to produce Frank Hardy's play about a miner, *Black Diamonds*, which had premiered at the New Theatre in Sydney in 1958. The paper reported that "[o]ther performances are planned in Russia and Rumania" (see: The Herald Music and Theatre Critics, "Moscow Opera Star to Give Recitals," *Sydney Morning Herald*, 2 August 1960). A few years later in 1965 actress Madge Ryan—well known in Australia for her lead role in *The Summer of the Seventeenth Doll*, a play that heralded the "birth" of Australian drama in 1955—was cast as Mother Courage in the National Theatre's production of that play in London.

[19] Edith Anderson, "Theatre for Learning," *Meanjin* 17.3 (Spring 1958): pp. 300–307. See Garde, *Brecht & Co*, pp. 56–63.

[20] See Garde, *Brecht & Co*, pp. 73–75.

[21] *Die "Twenties-Show"* in the 1940s, and *Mutter Courage*—described by the *Age* newspaper as "the first Bertholt [sic] Brecht play to be presented on an Australian stage" (9 July 1958). *Mutter Courage* was the tenth play presented by students of the German Department "in recent years."

[22] For example, Graeme Hughes, a graduate of the University of Melbourne, and whose "special field of research [is] Berthold [sic] Brecht" ("To Lecture at CUC in German," *Canberra Times*, 1 March 1957) was appointed to Canberra University College in 1957 and contributed an essay on "Brecht and Contemporary German Theatre" to the same issue of *Meanjin* (17.3 [Spring 1958]: pp. 292–299) in which Edith Anderson's translation of "Vergnügungstheater oder Lehrtheater" appeared. He completed an MA on "Das Theater Bertolt Brechts" in 1958 at the University of Melbourne, and later directed a production of *The Good Person* at Ormond College at the University of Melbourne in 1961. Dr K. Hommel, a lecturer in German at the University of Sydney and director of the Kleines Wiener Theater, traveled to Canberra to deliver a lecture on "Bertolt Brecht als Dramatiker" to the Canberra branch of the Australian Goethe Society (see: "What People Are Doing," *Canberra Times*, 18 June 1957).

[23] Brian D. Barnes had also worked at the Berliner Ensemble (and other theaters in Europe) before returning to Australia, delivering a lecture on "Theatre in Europe Today" in Canberra (*Canberra Times*, 15 April 1961), and then taking up the artistic directorship of the brand- new Union Repertory Theatre Company at the University of Sydney later that year. His grand plans for the company included staging *Mother Courage* in its first season, but the company was short-lived: the Union Theatre had to wait for another two years for its *Mother Courage*, directed by Ken Horler.

[24] See Graeme Hughes, "Brecht and Contemporary German Theatre"; Wal Cherry, "Brecht's Theatre in East Berlin," *Age*, 5 July 1958; Bruce Grant, "Brecht in Australia: The Search for Reality," *Age*, 19 July 1958; Arthur Phillips, "The Influence

of Brecht on Modern Theatre," *Age*, 31 January 1959; John Moses, "Revolutionary Theories for German Drama," *Sydney Morning Herald*, 3 October 1959. Garde also notes several articles published in the University of Melbourne student newspaper, *Farrago*, in 1958 (see Garde, *Brecht & Co*, p. 74).

[25] In 1956 the Royal Court Theatre had also produced its own *Threepenny Opera* (directed by Sam Wanamaker, designed by Caspar Neher), further exposing Brecht's work to new, English-speaking audiences. The Australian Bruce Grant saw this production, and referred to it in his 1958 article, "Brecht in Australia: The Search for Reality."

[26] James K. Lyon, *Brecht Unbound* (Newark: University of Delaware Press, 1995), p. 189.

[27] Grant, "Brecht in Australia. The Search for Reality."

[28] *The Threepenny Opera* (1958). See Garde, *Brecht & Co.*

[29] The Independent Theatre was one of the city's longest-lived Little Theaters, and had been operating under the direction of Doris Fitton since 1930. Originally begun as an amateur theater, by 1955 Fitton had negotiated a special agreement with Actors' Equity to allow her to employ a sprinkle of professional actors, on salary, in amongst her pro-am casts and thus be designated as "semi-professional."

[30] L. B., "Brecht's Quality Apparent," *Sydney Morning Herald*, 9 April 1960.

[31] The Genesian Theatre, like many of the city's other Little Theaters, used both professional and amateur actors.

[32] "Sydney's First Brecht."

[33] Kevon Kemp, "A Brecht Fable," *Observer*, 30 April 1960.

[34] The most muted praise of the production came from the *Bulletin* whose reviewer felt it "lacked the firmness and clarity essential to the play," but went on to commend the company "for giving at least a passable showing to a piece which many theatergoers must have been waiting to see" ("Sydney's First Brecht").

[35] "Sydney's First Brecht."

[36] Kemp, "A Brecht Fable."

[37] L. B., "Brecht's Quality Apparent."

[38] Chester, "Night Mail to Setzuan," *Honi Soit*, 21 April 1960.

[39] Kemp, "A Brecht Fable."

[40] Max Harris, "Undergraduate Markings," *Nation*, 10 September 1960.

[41] See Harris, "Undergraduate Markings."

[42] The Herald Music and Drama Critics, "Australian Theatre: The Task Ahead," *Sydney Morning Herald*, 14 March 1961.

[43] R. C., "Sydney Uni. Players," *Sydney Morning Herald*, 18 March 1961.

[44] The Student Union's own theater had been demolished in 1959 and the new theater would not re-open until later that year.

[45] John Woodrow, "Players' First Productions," *Honi Soit*, 23 March 1961.

[46] The yellow-brown backdrop was retained for Carroll's play: The addition of a simple wooden frame of three doors created the interior and patio of this beachside home.

[47] The Herald Music and Drama Critics, "Australian Theatre: The Task Ahead."

[48] Woodrow, "Players' First Production."

[49] Peter Thomson, *Brecht: Mother Courage and Her Children*. Plays in Production (Cambridge: Cambridge University Press, 1997), pp. 82–83.

[50] Denis O'Brien, "Great Brecht Play Put on The Chopping Block," *Daily Telegraph*, 7 August 1963. Kevon Kemp noted that "*Mother Courage* . . . seems to have been beyond the resources of both producer and company" ("A Festive Occasion," *Bulletin*, 24 August 1963).

[51] R. C., "Brecht Play at Union Theatre," *Sydney Morning Herald*, 7 August 1963.

[52] Brek [Harry Kippax], "Are We All Met?," *Nation*, 24 August 1963: p. 18.

[53] The Sydney Push was a left-wing Libertarian intellectual group, closely associated with the University of Sydney.

[54] Thomson, *Brecht: Mother Courage and Her Children*, p. 83.

[55] See Katharine Brisbane, *Entertaining Australia: The Performing Arts as Cultural History* (Sydney: Currency Press, 1991), p. 18; Brisbane, "Amateur Theatre," in *Companion to Theatre in Australia*, pp. 38–45; here, 38; Geoffrey Milne, "Theatre in Rural Australia: Theatre of the Region or in the Region?" *Rural Society* 13.3 (2003): pp. 270–286; here, p. 271. A rising recent interest internationally in amateur performance, however, is revealed by the formation of research networks such as RAPPT (Research into Amateur Performance and Private Theatricals), see www.rappt.org. For an important new contribution to this field, see also Janet McGaw, *Country Awakening: Amateur Theatre in New South Wales Regional Communities 1945–1970* (PhD thesis, University of Sydney, 2015).

[56] The Australia Council for the Arts (the federal government's funding and advisory body for the arts) was formed in 1968. The first cohort of students from NIDA completed its training in 1960; a one-year directing course was introduced at NIDA in 1972.

[57] Milne, *Theatre Australia (Un)Limited: Australian Theatre Since the 1950s* (Amsterdam: Rodopi, 2004), p. 130.

[58] The trajectory of the New Wave was rather different in Melbourne: It was centered around the Australian Performing Group (APG), which had largely been formed by a group of radical students coming straight out of universities, primarily Monash University, and into theater-making (initially with the La Mama Company). It was a sign of the changing times and attitudes, especially among young people, that the participants of this group did not make a trip "home" to England first.

[59] Both Garde (*Brecht & Co*, p. 75) and Milne (*Theatre Australia (Un)Limited*, p. 78) also acknowledge this connection in passing, though Garde's point is made in relation to "performances in the German language and at the German departments of Australian universities," and Milne makes no mention in his book of the vibrant and very active dramatic societies at the University of Sydney at this time.

[60] See Garde, *Brecht & Co*, pp. 377–379 and the additional university productions listed above in note 10. The first three university productions listed in Garde's book took place at the University of Melbourne: two by students and one by the professional company resident in the on-campus theatre.

[61] See Garde, *Brecht & Co*, pp. 167–170.

Dieter Goltzsche, *Buckower Elegien*, 2014, Tusche.

Mark Twains "Wohltätigkeits-Literatur" Held und Bertolt Brechts *Der gute Mensch von Sezuan*

Dieser Artikel schlägt vor, dass eine Quelle von Bertolt Brechts *Der gute Mensch von Sezuan* Mark Twains kurzes Stück "About Magnanimous-Incident Literature" sei. Die Autorin diskutiert Parallelen zwischen den zwei Werken und fragt nach der Wahrscheinlichkeit, dass Brecht Twains Skizze kannte. Sie weist auf deutschsprachige Versionen des Textes von Twain in verschiedenen Sammlungen, auf Werke von Twain in Brechts Nachlassbibliothek, und auch daraufhin, dass Brecht Twains Namen in einer Liste von Werken erwähnte, die er für eine Bibliothek für die Nationale Volksarmee empfahl. Twains Skizze, Brechts Parabelstück und ein kurzer Teil von Brechts *Buch der Wendungen* mit dem Titel "Verurteilung der Ethiken" alle handeln von traditionellen ethischen Geboten von Großzügigkeit und Nächstenliebe, die dann verworfen werden, in Hinsicht auf die tragischen Resultate, zu denen sie führen können.

This article proposes that one of the sources for Bertolt Brecht's *Der gute Mensch von Sezuan* is Mark Twain's short essay "About Magnanimous-Incident Literature." After discussing parallels between the two works, the author asks whether Brecht could have known Twain's piece, pointing to its availability in German-language collections of Twain's short sketches, to works by Twain that are in his *Nachlassbibliothek*, and to the fact that he included Twain's name—without proposing specific titles—in a list of works he recommended for a library for the Nationale Volksarmee. Twain's essay, Brecht's play, and a short section in Brecht's *Buch der Wendungen* entitled "Verurteilung der Ethiken" all concern themselves with traditional moral codes that dictate generosity and altruism, which then are rejected in view of the disastrous results to which they can lead.

Mark Twain's "Magnanimous-Incident" Hero and Bertolt Brecht's *Der gute Mensch von Sezuan*

Cora Lee Kluge

Scholars have produced an extensive list of precursors for individual figures, songs, and secondary themes in Bertolt Brecht's *Der gute Mensch von Sezuan*.[1] However, no one has suggested a source for the overarching theme with which the piece both commences and ends—namely the impossibility of following the gods' commandments (in short, "Gut zu sein") while also continuing to survive ("und doch zu leben").[2] This theme, not part of Brecht's original conception of 1930, when his working title was *Die Ware Liebe*, became important in later versions, and was instrumental in introducing both the gods and much of the ensuing critical discussion of the play's content. In this contribution, I argue that the origin of this theme is to be found in a short work by Mark Twain. My purpose is to contribute to an understanding of the play's background, but I would also like to promote interest in investigating further the impact of Twain's work on German literature: on individual writers, the use of dialect in literary works, and more.

In May of 1878 the *Atlantic Monthly* published an essay by Twain, which was entitled "About Magnanimous-Incident Literature."[3] In it the narrator presents a series of four "charming anecdotes" concerning high-minded and noble deeds, sentimental literature written "in the quaint vein of The World's Ingenious Fabulist," which praises virtuous, generous, and benevolent individuals. Though he claims that such stories in the past have taught him a "lesson," given him "pleasure," and brought back his "self-respect" whenever he "thought meanly of [mankind]," the narrator now takes them beyond their "happy climaxes" to focus on their sequels or results. He concludes that magnanimity often leads to disastrous consequences and in the final analysis helps neither the benefactor nor the beneficiary.[4]

The first of Twain's four anecdotes, "The Grateful Poodle," tells of a dog with a broken leg who was healed by a benevolent physician—"who had read the books"—and who then passed his good fortune forward by bringing another broken-legged dog for treatment, each of whom then brought an additional dog, and so forth, until the physician was completely overwhelmed by claims upon his services. The situation is described in detail: "the human spectators . . ., the cries of the wounded, the songs of the healed brutes . . ., the traffic . . . interrupted," and so on. The physician hired assistant surgeons but nevertheless was besieged beyond his capacity and was forced to conclude that he had been "fooled by the books," which "only tell the pretty part of the story, and then stop." He went out with his shotgun (whose purpose is not stated), by chance stepping on the tail of the original poodle, who then bit him. In the end the benevolent physician died of "hydrophobia." The situation had become a catastrophe not only for the benevolent physician, but also for the grateful poodle, both of whom had been attempting to do virtuous work.[5]

The second anecdote, "The Benevolent Author," relates how a generous celebrated author helped a destitute young writer get his first manuscript accepted. "Let this pleasing incident," states Twain, "admonish us to turn a charitable ear to all beginners that need help." But the literary beginner continued to request the author's assistance with additional manuscripts, to the surprise of his benefactor, "because *in the books* the young struggler had needed but one lift, apparently" (my emphasis). Eventually the celebrated author found himself "permanently freighted with the poor young beginner." Fame finally came to the young writer, but it was for a work in which he described the author's private life in "blistering detail," which "broke the celebrated author's heart with mortification." Dying, the author concluded, "The books deceived me; they do not tell the whole story"; and he understood that he had made a mistake in trying to help.[6]

The third anecdote, "The Grateful Husband," tells of William Ferguson, who saved the lives of Mr. McSpadden's wife and son when they were involved in a carriage accident. McSpadden rewarded William and promised him help if ever he should need it. William did need help: a better job, a place for his mother to live in the McSpaddens' home, together with her three younger children, one of whom destroyed a lot of the McSpaddens' valuable furniture and then broke his neck falling down the stairs. Seventeen relatives showed up for the child's funeral, all with requests for assistance. William's mother drank and swore, and the McSpaddens undertook to reform her, out of gratitude for William's good deed. Then William wanted to go to college, and next he needed a vacation in Europe for his health. McSpadden had finally had enough and refused, to the shock of William's entire family. They accused McSpadden of ingratitude, and William's mother complained that her little son had died "in the service of such a reptile!" But McSpadden threw them all out, stating: "I was beguiled by the books, but shall never be beguiled again. . . ." And he saw that his error had been his desire to show gratitude. Incidentally, Twain insists that this incident is based upon a real incident, "within [his] personal knowledge."[7]

The fourth anecdote, which Twain describes as the "text . . . of [his] sermon,"[8] is based on a published report. It is a paragraph directly quoted from an article by Noah Brooks, friend, close associate, and biographer of Abraham Lincoln, which appeared under the title "Personal Reminiscences of Lincoln" in the March 1878 issue of *Scribner's Monthly*.[9] Here one reads of an actor named J. H. Hackett, whose performance as Falstaff Lincoln praised, thanking him in a personal letter. The actor responded by sending him a book and followed up with several notes. Then, to Lincoln's distress, Hackett asked to be sent as consul to London—an unbelievable and upsetting request in Lincoln's view. In these four anecdotes, Twain shows how people abuse the kindness, gratitude, and generosity of others and what the consequences can be. But his point is not merely that good deeds can boomerang, that they are not always a good idea, that we may regret even having done them. Instead, the target of his criticism, as is mentioned in every episode, is "the books," which deceive us into thinking that we should lead lives governed by magnanimity.

Brecht's Shen Te, who wants to keep "the commandments" (*die Gebote*), is like Twain's physician, author, and husband, as well as President Lincoln, whose guiding principles, as they found them in "the books," are gratitude and benevolence. Shen Te refers to recognizable biblical commandments, but also to what could be considered general principles of integrity: "Gebote . . . der Kindesliebe und der Wahrhaftigkeit. Nicht begehren meines Nächsten Haus, . . . und einem Mann anhängen in Treue, . . . aus keinem meinen Nutzen ziehen und den Hilflosen nicht berauben," and the like.[10] But she, like Twain's figures, discovers problems that prevent her from living according to such principles.

There is surprising congruity between the situations presented by Brecht and Twain, particularly between Brecht's second scene and the third of Twain's anecdotes. Like the generous, hospitable, and exploited Mr. McSpadden, who finds himself supporting fully twenty-two members of the Ferguson family, Shen Te finds herself burdened with a number of named guests, in addition to innumerable others, including an "achtköpfige Familie,"[11] until at the beginning of the second scene we read that there are "überall schlafende Leute."[12] She unhesitatingly provides rice for Mrs. Shin and her children, even though hunger is the only basis for their claim to assistance. She offers the elderly couple and their nephew a place to stay, even though they had turned her out in the past when she ran out of money. The unemployed man receives cigarettes, and relatives of the first guests are taken into her house, and then more relatives, though none of them have any legitimate right to her kindness. The recipients of Shen Te's generosity begin to complain that the place is becoming cramped, whereupon she muses: "Der Rettung kleiner Nachen / Wird sofort in die Tiefe gezogen."[13] As with Twain, a person's first act of kindness results in additional demands being made, until the situation gets out of hand, and until one of Shen Te's beneficiaries suggests: "Erkenne nie eine Forderung an, berechtigt oder nicht, denn sofort wirst du überrannt mit Forderungen, berechtigt oder nicht."[14] The figures in Twain's four anecdotes would agree with this recommendation, as their generosity had led to the same result.

Can Brecht have known Twain's essay? It cannot be disputed that Brecht was familiar with Twain's work in general, as he included Twain's name, without specifying particular titles, in a list of authors and works he recommended for a library for the Nationale Volksarmee. Michael Morley, who published this list, surmised that it contains works that Brecht was familiar with and that also reflected his taste.[15] Further indication that Brecht knew Twain comes from the fact that his own personal *Nachlassbibliothek* at the Brecht-Weigel-Gedenkstätte in Berlin contains two volumes of Twain stories—in Danish translation, published in Copenhagen in 1914—, as well as a two-volume Tauchnitz English-language edition of *The Innocents Abroad.*[16] Because the short stories are in Danish, one might postulate that Margarete Steffin is the link between Brecht and Twain, or even a source of Brecht's interest in Twain's work. As his assistant and collaborator in the years between 1932 and her death in 1941, she translated Danish-language texts both for Brecht and for publication, and the significance of her contributions to *Der gute Mensch von Sezuan* is widely known.[17] Admittedly, the essay "About Magnanimous-Incident Literature" is not to be found in either of the volumes.

This particular work by Twain is not well known today. It is, to be sure, one of the 271 short tales, sketches, essays, and speeches included in a two-volume collection published in 1992.[18] Nevertheless, beginning immediately after its original appearance, the approximately 2,300-word piece was often reprinted, both in English and in other languages; and its popularity persisted over a number of decades. In May of 1878, the same month it was first published, it appeared in German in the *New-Yorker Belletristisches Journal*, a major and influential German-American weekly. The journal identifies the piece by the name of its author and its title—"Ein Beitrag zur Wohlthätigkeits- Freundschafts- und Dankbarkeits-Literatur"—and states that this is an "Autorisirte Uebersetzung des 'Belletr. Journals.'"[19] Twain's essay and one additional Twain short story were also included in the second volume of a collection of American humor in August Strindberg's Swedish translation, which was published in 1878.[20] On 11 September 1878, the essay was published in somewhat shortened form for readers of the *Queanbeyan Age* in New South Wales, where it appeared under the heading "Mark Twain on Magnanimous Incident Literature."[21] And it was anthologized in collections of Twain's short stories, such as *The Stolen White Elephant Etc.*[22]

Additional translations of Twain's "About Magnanimous-Incident Literature" into German can be found. It appeared, for example, under the title "Wohlthun trägt Zinsen" in a volume of Twain's sketches translated by Margarethe Jacobi, Henny Koch, and L. Ottmann; under the title "Über Großmuts-Geschichten," as the very first piece in a Reclam collection of Twain pieces translated by H. Oswin; under the title "Geschichten von Groß- und Edelmut" in another volume selected and edited by E. Spiegel;

and under the title "Wohltun trägt Zinsen" in another collection of Twain's works, whose editor or translator was unnamed.[23] Two of these editions appeared after the completion of Brecht's *Der gute Mensch*; but it is nonetheless clear that Twain's story was known to German readers, and it is not difficult to believe that Brecht and his collaborators were familiar with it.

Twain in his essay and Brecht in his play are pointing to the same problem; both authors are questioning whether it is possible to live by the so-called Golden Rule, or whether an attempt to do so is even advisable. They are challenging a seemingly universal moral principle that commands us to lead a life guided by altruism, which can be found in the Old and New Testaments and is basic to the moral codes of many cultures and religions. They confront the principle, reveal its difficulties, point out its problems, and in the last analysis reject it as a viable maxim.

Twain thinks through his three anecdotes to their conclusion, as well as the episode concerning Lincoln, and invites readers to consider the "consequences that flowed" from similar experiences of their own.[24] The consequences in Twain's anecdotes are not trivial: The perpetrators of the good deeds are driven to insanity, death, and the urge to kill; and they learn their lessons about the inadvisability of generosity. As he lies dying, the physician states "Whenever a poor wretch asks you for help . . ., give yourself the benefit of the doubt and kill the applicant"; the benevolent author concludes "Whom God sees fit to starve, let not man presumptuously rescue to his own undoing"; and Mr. McSpadden turns on the young man to whom he had owed a debt of gratitude, shouting "Yes, you did save my wife's life, and the next man that does it shall die in his tracks!"[25] This seems for Twain to be the way of the world, and the tone of his essay remains entertaining and even humorous. Nevertheless, it is clear that by describing inevitable disastrous outcomes, he is protesting against "the books," whose teachings mandate generosity.

Like Twain, Brecht reveals the futility and inadvisability of trying to adhere to time-honored ethical commandments. But he also presents further analysis and suggests revisions for our moral code. In the Me-ti aphorisms that appear under the title "Verurteilung der Ethiken" in his posthumously published *Buch der Wendungen* he is dealing with the same problem. His remarks concerning morality (*Sittlichkeit*), benevolence (*Güte*), justice (*Gerechtigkeit*), abuse (*Missbrauch*), readiness to make sacrifices (*Opferbereitschaft*), and generosity (*Großzügigkeit*), as well as his condemnation (*Verurteilung*) of the traditional moral teachings suggest alternative approaches.[26] Rejecting altruism, Brecht declares that acts of generosity must be judged by their usefulness (*Nutzen*), that people should think of their own well-being, that virtuous deeds, if perpetuated too long, can lead to more problems, and that the disadvantaged people of the world (*die Kleinen*) must not be stingy (*kleinzügig*) but rather generous (*großzügig*)—toward themselves.[27]

Especially the fourth of the Me-ti aphorisms reads like a commentary on Shen Te's story:

> Über den berühmten Satz "Du sollst deinen Nächsten lieben wie dich selbst" sagte Me-ti einmal: Wenn die Arbeiter das tun, werden sie niemals einen Zustand abschaffen, in dem man seinen Nächsten nur lieben kann, wenn man sich selbst nicht liebt.[28]

This is a beautifully contorted assertion: one should *not* love one's neighbor as oneself, because if one does so, the situation will persist where one can love one's neighbor (i.e., be generous) only if one does not love oneself. But it is the lesson Shen Te is forced to learn. Her generosity drives her to ruin, and thus her generosity itself dictates that she must become the selfish, practical Shui Ta, at least from time to time. Frustrated by the situation, she feels trapped and sees no way out. Brecht, however, envisions a better world where love of others can be harmonized with love of self, but to reach this goal, one must refrain from philanthropy. Such a world is not yet the one where Shen Te lives.

This is a central message not only of Brecht's play, but also of Twain's essay; and it seems possible that the German playwright had found his theme in the work of the famous American humorist. The two authors unmask the same problem, and both place the blame in the traditional moral teachings. To be sure, Twain's prose text utilizes irony that allows his readers to smile or laugh at his anecdotes, while still remembering similar difficult situations in their own experience; and Brecht, who meanwhile was also engaged in a more philosophical exploration of the dilemma and in suggesting new maxims to make possible a better future, employs a serious tone and allows his heroine to express her absolute sense of helplessness. But both Twain and Brecht are censuring the teachings of the old moralizers, the idealistic ethicists, the sentimental bourgeois code, "the books," which command us "gut zu sein."

Notes

The author wishes to express her thanks to Heike Schwenecke of the Deutsche Nationalbibliothek in Leipzig, Ingrid Grossmann of the Deutsches Literaturarchiv Marbach, and Helgrid Streidt of the Bertolt-Brecht-Archiv in Berlin, for their assistance.

[1] See, for example, Wolf-Egmar Schneidewind and Bernhard Sowinski, *Bertolt Brecht: Der gute Mensch von Sezuan*, 2nd ed. (Munich: Oldenbourg, 1996), pp. 24–27.

[2] Bertolt Brecht, *Der gute Mensch von Sezuan*, in Brecht, *Werke: Große Berliner und Frankfurter Ausgabe*, Werner Hecht et al., eds, vol. 6 (Berlin and Frankfurt am Main: Aufbau and Suhrkamp, 1988–2000), 275. Hereafter BFA volume, page.

[3] Mark Twain, "About Magnanimous-Incident Literature," *Atlantic Monthly* 41.247 (May 1878): pp. 615–619. I quote the essay from the more easily accessible edition: *Mark Twain: Collected Tales, Sketches, Speeches, & Essays*, vol. 1 (New York: Literary Classics of the United States, 1992), pp. 703–709.

[4] *Twain: Collected Tales*, p. 703.

[5] Ibid., pp. 703–704.

[6] Ibid., pp. 705–706.

[7] Ibid., pp. 708, 709.

[8] Ibid., p. 708.

[9] *Scribner's Monthly* 15.5 (March 1878): pp. 673–681, here p. 675.

[10] BFA 6, 184.

[11] Ibid., 176, 211.

[12] Ibid., 195.

[13] Ibid., 193.

[14] Ibid., 189.

[15] Michael Morley, "Zu zwei Bücherlisten Brechts aus den fünfziger Jahren," *Brecht-Jahrbuch 1974* (1974): pp. 106–113. See especially pp. 109 and 111–113.

[16] Bertolt-Brecht-Archiv, ed, *Die Bibliothek Bertolt Brechts: Ein kommentiertes Verzeichnis* (Frankfurt am Main: Suhrkamp, 2007), p. 158.

[17] She is even listed as one of the collaborators. See BFA 6, 176.

[18] *Twain: Collected Tales*. See note 3. This essay can also be found online at http://www.online-literature.com/twain/3267/ (accessed 31 January 2016).

[19] *New-Yorker Belletristisches Journal* 27.10 (3 May 1878): p. 147. The translator was probably Udo Brachvogel (1835–1913), who is known today as an author, a translator, and a German-American publisher, and who had just become the journal's co-owner and co-editor. Brachvogel's translations introduced several major American writers to readers of German, including Bret Harte, who recognized his assistance by dedicating to him his work "The Story of a Mine" (1877). An early German-language collection of Twain's short sketches translated by Brachvogel, which did not include "About Magnanimous-Incident Literature," appeared in Germany in 1886 under the title *Unterwegs und daheim: Neue Sammlung humoristischer Skizzen* (Stuttgart: Robert Lutz, 1886). See Karl Bleibtreu, ed., *Das Magazin für die Litteratur des In- und Auslandes* 109.38 (September 1886): p. 600.

[20] See Carl L. Anderson, "Strindberg's Translations of American Humor," in Harald S. Næss and Sigmund Skard, eds, *Studies in Scandinavian-American Interrelations* (Oslo–Bergen–Tromsö: Universitetsforlaget, 1971), pp. 153-194, esp. pp. 161, 172. Despite the fact that Strindberg's initials appear on the title pages, indicating that he was the translator, Anderson argues that much of the work was done by others; but he concludes that this was probably not true of the Twain pieces. This volume was published by Seligmann in Stockholm.

[21] Available online at http://trove.nla.gov.au/ndp/del/article/30674114/ (accessed 31 January 2016).

[22] Mark Twain, *The Stolen White Elephant Etc.* (New York: Charles L. Webster and Co., 1894).

[23] These works, which are undoubtedly not a complete list, are as follows: Mark Twain, *Skizzenbuch* (Stuttgart: Lutz, 1914[?]); Mark Twain, *Ausgewählte Skizzen*, vol. 4 (Leipzig: Reclam, 1919 [?]); Mark Twain, *Locht, Brüder, locht!: Humoresken und Satiren*, E. Spiegel, ed. (Wädenswil-Zurich: Villiger, 1945); Mark Twain, *Erzählungen* [Illus. by Ruprecht Haller] (Berlin: Aufbau-Verlag, 1952, repr. 1953).

[24] *Twain: Collected Tales*, p. 709.

[25] Ibid., pp. 704, 706, 708.

[26] BFA 18, 152–154. The aphorisms, a short section consisting of just over six hundred words, were probably written around 1936. See ibid., 486.

[27] Ibid., 154.

[28] Ibid., 152.

Dieter Goltzsche, *Im Dickicht der Städte*, 2015, Tusche.

Navid Kermanis literarische Betrachtungen über Kafka, Brecht und den Koran

In seinem Essayband *Zwischen Koran und Kafka: West-östliche Erkundungen* setzt der deutsch-iranische Intellektuelle und Autor Navid Kermani klassische deutsche Autoren in Beziehung zu östlichen und islamischen literarischen und kulturellen Traditionen. Sein Buch eröffnet eine kosmopolitische, weltoffene Perspektive auf die deutsche Literatur, die im Angesicht der jetzigen Flüchtlingskrise eine neue Bedeutung erhält. Während Kermani offiziell Kafka als sein literarisches Rollenmodell definiert, beweist sein Aufsatz über Brecht ein tiefes Verständnis von Brechts dramatischer Theorie und Praxis. Kermani, der selbst als Dramaturg theatralische Erfahrung hat, kritisiert Brechts Gegenüberstellung von Verfremdung und Einfühlung als sich gegenseitig ausschließende Kategorien. In seiner Analyse des schiitischen Passionsspiels *Taziyeh* zeigt er auf, dass verfremdende Schauspielstrategien mit tief empfundener Einfühlung einhergehen können. Seine ästhetischen Ansichten über die Möglichkeit einer Koexistenz von Distanz und Leidenschaft lassen sich übertragen auf die Forderung nach dem Verständnis für "andere" und Minderheiten im heutigen Deutschland.

In his volume of essays, *Zwischen Koran und Kafka: West-östliche Erkundungen*, the German-Iranian intellectual and author Navid Kermani views classic German authors in relation to Eastern and Islamic literary and cultural traditions. His book creates a cosmopolitan and worldly perspective on German literature that has acquired a new significance in light of the recent refugee crisis in Germany. While Kermani formally defines Kafka as his literary role model, his essay on Brecht displays a deep and critical understanding of Brecht's dramatic theory and practice. Kermani, who himself has theatrical experience as a dramaturge, critiques Brecht's juxtaposition of alienation and empathy as mutually exclusive categories. In his analysis of the Shiite passion play *Taziyeh*, he shows that alienating acting strategies can coexist with deeply felt empathy. His aesthetic views on the possibility of a coexistence of distance and passion may be translated into a call for understanding the "other" and minorities in contemporary Germany.

Navid Kermani's Literary Reflections: On Kafka, Brecht, and the Koran

Vera Stegmann

> *Der Pass ist der edelste Teil von einem Menschen. Er kommt auch nicht auf so einfache Weise zustand wie ein Mensch. Ein Mensch kann überall zustandkommen, auf die leichtsinnigste Art und ohne gescheiten Grund, aber ein Pass niemals. Dafür wird er auch anerkannt, wenn er gut ist, während ein Mensch noch so gut sein kann und doch nicht anerkannt wird.*
>
> —Bertolt Brecht, *Flüchtlingsgespräche*

> *Pässe sind keine Ikonen, sondern Papiere.*
>
> —Navid Kermani, *Wer ist Wir? Deutschland und seine Muslime*

Navid Kermani has emerged as a major public intellectual in Germany, raising the nation's conscience particularly on questions of immigration and religious tolerance. Born in Siegen, Germany, as the son of Iranian parents, Kermani is an author of literary works and of essays, as well as a scholar of religion. He studied "Orientalistik" (Near Eastern Studies), philosophy, and drama in Cologne, Cairo, and then Bonn, where he completed his doctorate in 1998 and his *Habilitation* in 2005. Throughout his studies he worked in theaters, as a directorial assistant ("Regieassistent") and later as dramaturge at the Schauspiel Frankfurt and the Theater an der Ruhr in Mülheim, a theater that played an important role in the development of migrant theater, especially Turkish-German theater, in the 1980s. (Mülheim, incidentally, is also the German city in which Brecht's *Fatzer* is set.) Besides writing journalistically for *Der Spiegel*, *Die Zeit*, *Süddeutsche Zeitung*, and *Frankfurter Allgemeine Zeitung*, among others, he is the author of an astounding variety of books. He authored creative prose works such as the children's book *Ayda, Bär und Hase* (2006) and novels such as *Das Buch der von Neil Young Getöteten* (2002), *Dein Name* (2011), or *Große Liebe* (2014). He wrote travel reports on his many voyages to the Middle East and North Africa that invite comparisons to the work of the Weimar-era "rasende Reporter" Egon Erwin Kisch. Kermani's

THE BRECHT YEARBOOK | DAS BRECHT-JAHRBUCH 40
(ROCHESTER, NY: CAMDEN HOUSE, 2016)

journalistic writings and travel reports from regions in turmoil include the books *Schöner neuer Orient: Berichte von Städten und Kriegen* (2003) and *Ausnahmezustand: Reisen in eine beunruhigte Welt* (2013).[1] In the summer of 2015, he traveled along the route of the thousands of refugees who are fleeing Syria via Turkey, Greece, and the Balkans toward Northern Europe; and he published his experiences and impressions in *Der Spiegel* and in the book *Einbruch der Wirklichkeit: Auf dem Flüchtlingstreck durch Europa* (2016). Kermani's scholarly and essayistic writings range from the book *Der Schrecken Gottes: Attar, Hiob und die metaphysische Revolte* (2005) to *Wer ist Wir? Deutschland und seine Muslime* (2009). Kermani's recent book *Ungläubiges Staunen: Über das Christentum* (2015) is a sympathetic aesthetic treatise on Christianity by a renowned German-language Muslim author who meditates on Christian imagery in religious practices as well as in great art by Botticelli, Caravaggio, and Rembrandt.[2]

For his prolific writings, as well as his attempts to mediate between Christianity, Islam, and Judaism in Germany, he has been awarded numerous prizes, among them the *Buber-Rosenzweig-Medaille* (2011), the *Hannah-Arendt-Preis* (2011), and the *Kleist-Preis* (2012). In 2015, he was chosen for the *Friedenspreis des deutschen Buchhandels* (Peace Prize of the German Book Trade), possibly his greatest honor to date. The jury described Kermani as one of the most important voices in contemporary German society, and Kermani shares this prize with luminaries such as Jaron Lanier, Anselm Kiefer, Orhan Pamuk, Saul Friedländer, Susan Sontag, Jürgen Habermas, and Václav Havel, to mention only a few recipients of past years.

Those who have never read a line by Kermani may have heard his memorable speech in front of the German parliament, on the occasion of the sixty-fifth anniversary of the announcement of the *Grundgesetz*, the German constitution or basic law, on 23 May 2014. His speech, which is also included as an epilog in his book *Zwischen Koran und Kafka*, contains a passionate plea for tolerance and cosmopolitanism in Germany's emerging diverse society. Kermani's "Friedenspreisrede," a speech which he delivered upon receiving the peace prize at the end of the Frankfurt Book Expo in the Paulskirche in Frankfurt on 18 October 2015, raised the German public's consciousness on the suffering of all Syrian people.[3] In this speech Kermani, a Muslim by birth and belief, focused on the plight of Syria's Christian minority, which he illustrated movingly through the example of Pater Jacques Mourad, who was abducted by the Islamic State (ISIS). His speech was broadcast on the ZDF television network and reviewed widely in national newspapers. Reviewers admired his eloquence and his ability to reach out to all faiths. His decision to ask the audience of the Paulskirche, which has been used as a secular place since the end of World War II, not to clap at the end of his speech, but rather pray for captive Christians in Syria in a moment of silence, met with general acceptance, but also a few mixed reviews.

Brechtian References and Connections

Navid Kermani does not mention Brecht among his major literary influences, although he clearly knows and understands Brecht's work well, both in its theory and its theatrical practice. He also frequently appears as an invited guest speaker at the Berliner Ensemble. But Kermani's fascination with mysticism alone might place him on the opposing end of the spectrum compared to Brecht, who professed a more rational and scientific approach to art. Furthermore, Kermani is a religious believer, unlike the atheist Brecht. In his book *Der Schrecken Gottes* Kermani cites Brecht's story "Der Blinde," an early short prose work from 1921 about a man who suddenly turns blind at age thirty, becomes bitter, and eventually commits suicide,[4] as an example of modern atheist adaptations of the theme of Job.[5] Both Brecht and Kermani are profoundly influenced by religious texts in their writings. When asked in 1928 which book had left the strongest impression on him, Brecht famously answered: "Sie werden lachen: die Bibel" (BFA 21, 248). Kermani, for his part, dedicated his dissertation, later published as a seminal book entitled *Gott ist schön: Das ästhetische Erleben des Koran*,[6] one of his few works that have currently been translated into English, to the subject of the aesthetics of religion, in this case the aesthetic experience of the Koran. But while both authors read religious texts as literature and acknowledge them among their important influences, Brecht's statement on the Bible is decidedly more ironic.

Kermani, who dedicated *Gott ist schön* to the idea and concept of the Theater an der Ruhr—"Der Idee des Theaters an der Ruhr" (5)—cites Brecht numerous times in this work. He particularly invokes Brecht in his discussions of the intersections of ethics and aesthetics in religion and literature: "Weder bei Aischylos noch bei Lessing noch bei Brecht lassen ästhetische und inhaltlich-ideologische Rezeption mit dem Seziermesser sich scheiden" (*Gott ist schön* 50–51). Just like the Book of Job or a speech by Martin Luther King, a poem by Brecht can be read as a poetic text, a historical document, an ideological manifesto, or as a reflection on personal or worldly experience (*Gott ist schön* 98). Following the structuralist approaches of Roman Jakobson, Kermani discusses the poetic functions—"die Poetizität" (*Gott ist schön* 98, 132)—that are present both in a poem by Brecht and in the Koran. He focuses on Brecht's poem "Der Radwechsel" and particularly the lines "Ich bin nicht gern, wo ich herkomme. / Ich bin nicht gern, wo ich hinfahre." Their "Poetizität," according to Kermani, consists in the fact that these lines reach beyond the original intentions or associations of the author and can invoke new associations in entirely different and future contexts. This same "Poetizität" exists in the Koran as well (*Gott ist schön* 132–133). Brecht becomes a foil in Kermani's discussions of whether the Koran can be considered as poetry. But Kermani considers a *l'art pour l'art* reading that certain critics have attempted with Brecht's poetry impossible for the Koran: A religious text like the Koran is never exclusively beautiful but intends to portray divine truth, unlike Brecht's plays "die ebenfalls ideologisch sein wollen, aber in vielen Fällen 'nur' als Dichtung wahrgenommen worden sind" (*Gott ist schön* 168).

Despite differences in aesthetic and ideological approaches, Kermani has an acute awareness of Brecht's work. Many of the questions of concern to Kermani, as an important public intellectual in Germany today, were of concern to Brecht in his time: questions of intercultural dialogue and refugee crises, for example. The current refugee crisis in Europe and the Middle East recalls Brecht's own exile experiences, and both can be related to the field of exile studies. A passage from Brecht's poem "An die Nachgeborenen" brings to mind the plight of today's desperate migrants who are fleeing their countries in Africa and the Middle East in an attempt to reach Europe.

> Gingen wir doch, öfter als die Schuhe die Länder wechselnd
> Durch die Kriege der Klassen, verzweifelt
> Wenn da nur Unrecht war und keine Empörung (BFA 12, 87)

Brecht's poem, published in 1939, could easily describe sentiments of the current refugee populations that are at the heart of Kermani's concerns, although Kermani would be less likely to characterize the contemporary wars as class wars exclusively.

Zwischen Koran und Kafka

While Kermani's concerns for the suffering of migrants are most directly reflected in his journalistic travel writings, they are also subtly present in his literary writings and his essays on literary criticism. Western literary traditions or classic authors such as Goethe, Kafka, Kleist, or Lessing are seen in a new light in Germany after the arrival of a million Middle Eastern and North African migrants, or by these migrants themselves. A recent book of creative literary criticism, in which Kermani reflects on German language literature from a Middle Eastern perspective, is *Zwischen Koran und Kafka*.

Published in 2014, *Zwischen Koran und Kafka: West-östliche Erkundungen* is a beautifully written collection of fifteen loosely associated essays that connect Western and Islamic authors, cultures, and traditions.[7] Many of these essays have been published previously in earlier versions, but they are revised, expanded, and newly contextualized for this edition. Kermani covers a wide spectrum of authors and artists ranging from Faridoddin Attar, William Shakespeare, Gotthold Ephraim Lessing, Johann Wolfgang von Goethe, Heinrich von Kleist, Bertolt Brecht, Richard Wagner, Franz Kafka, Sadegh Hedayat, Stefan Zweig, Hermann Hesse, Hannah Arendt, Martin Mosebach, to Huschang Golschiri. A majority of the authors covered in this book wrote in the German language. Kermani offers new and original interpretations that connect Eastern and Western authors, see Western artists in light of Eastern traditions, or relate classical literary works to contemporary political events and debates. A brief overview of a few of his essays provides a sense of his approaches to linking Eastern and Western literatures and thoughts.

Kermani opens with a chapter on the Koran that focuses particularly on the impact that the poetry, the aesthetic beauty, and the language of the Koran has had on the Arab world, not unlike the impact of Luther's Bible on Protestantism and the German language (*Zwischen Koran und Kafka* 26). His article entitled "Lessing und der Terror" interprets Lessing's dramas politically by reading two of his plays—a lesser known one-act tragedy *Philotas* and his most famous play, *Nathan der Weise*—in light of contemporary German debates on multiculturalism. Kermani views Lessing's plays in the context of the right-wing terrorist acts by Uwe Mundlos, Uwe Böhnhardt, and Beate Zschäpe, who were responsible for the murder of ten innocent citizens in Germany, eight of Turkish origin, one of Greek heritage, and a German policewoman. Looking at Lessing's play *Philotas*, Kermani contrasts the protagonist Philotas, who was willing to die for his patriotic beliefs, with his antagonist Aridäus, who gave up political power in favor of human kindness and empathy. Kermani sides with Lessing in favoring Aridäus as a model for a more open-minded Germany.[8]

Kermani's thoughts on Goethe are covered in the chapter "Gott-Atmen: Goethe und die Religion," in which Kermani explores the spiritual dimension of Goethe's work. Through the metaphor of "breathing," a central religious act in Christianity and Islam, Kermani looks at Goethe's representations of *systole* and *diastole*, inhaling and exhaling, in his writings on science, poetry, and religion, as they are reflected in his *West-östlicher Diwan*, especially the poem "Talismane." Kermani's essay on Heinrich von Kleist focuses on the concept of love; and in his analysis of the play *Amphitryon*, Kermani compares the act of love in Kleist's dramas with its representation in Islamic mysticism, particularly by the great Sufi philosopher Ibn Arabi. While Kermani's essay on Kleist was written independently of his receipt of the Kleist Prize, his chapter on Hannah Arendt is based on his acceptance speech in Bremen where he was awarded the *Hannah-Arendt-Preis für politisches Denken*. Kermani wonders how to define political thinking, how political thinking distinguishes itself from non-political thinking, and whether his own writing and thought can indeed be classified as political. The main body of his essay focuses on Arendt's thoughts on the nation-state and its inherent potential for failure; on her theories of empathy, sympathy, and compassion; and on her book *On Revolution*[9] that compares the French and American Revolutions, which Kermani takes as a point of departure for his musings on contemporary revolutions of the Arab Spring and their possible outcomes.

Two essays in Kermani's volume are devoted to Franz Kafka, and as the author's mention in the book's overall title suggests, Kafka plays a pivotal role. Kermani's title, *Zwischen Koran und Kafka*, reminds the reader of another provocative title in an earlier book by a Turkish-German author: Zafer Şenocak's essay "Zwischen Koran und Sexpistols" was first published in 2005 and later, in 2006, integrated in his book *Das Land hinter den Buchstaben: Deutschland und der Islam im Umbruch.*[10] Şenocak's essay discusses the inner conflict of a Muslim immigrant who is torn between a strict Islamic upbringing, symbolized by the Koran, and day-to-day teenage life in Germany's Western society, embodied by the Sex Pistols, a British punk rock band of the 1970s. Şenocak could only overcome this conflict by his immersion in the poetry of Yunus Emre, a thirteenth century Anatolian mystic whose poems he translated. Despite the seeming similarity of these two titles, Kermani's intended meaning and the inner tensions that he describes are quite different. For Kermani, Koran and Kafka embody the opposing intellectual and spiritual poles and principles between which his writing moves, such as revelation and literature, religious and aesthetic experience, Islamic and German intellectual history: "zwischen Offenbarung und Literatur, religiöse und ästhetische Erfahrung, islamisch geprägte und deutschsprachige Geistesgeschichte, Orient und Okzident" (*Zwischen Koran und Kafka* 16). But Kermani allows also for another reading of his title. Beyond seeing Kafka and the Koran as intellectual polar opposites, he emphasizes their resemblances, since both embody the outsider in German culture. Kafka "signalisiert etwas Fremdes, Randständiges, niemals ganz Dazugehöriges" (*Zwischen Koran und Kafka* 16). The Koran later began to signify for him what the Torah and Jewish traditions embodied for German Jewish thinkers: "die selbstbewusste Affirmation des Andersseins, wenn man so will des dauerhaft Exilhaften der eigenen Situation" (*Zwischen Koran und Kafka* 16). In this sense, they are not opposing forces that pull him in different directions, but rather complementary intellectual models that have influenced Kermani in similar ways. Interestingly, Kermani claims to have read Kafka long before studying the Koran, as he immersed himself in Kafka's books at age fifteen, when Kafka was likely taught in the German school system. On the other hand, Kermani did not seriously read the Koran until his college years as a student of religion and "Orientalistik" (*Zwischen Koran und Kafka* 17). Nonetheless, he entitled his book *Zwischen Koran und Kafka*, rather than the biographically more correct "Zwischen Kafka und Koran." He cites musical and aesthetic reasons for his choice, since he prefers to close with the long open vowel "a" in Kafka (*Zwischen Koran und Kafka* 17). Aesthetic reasons also contributed to the choice of his overall title, since Kermani was attracted to the alliteration of the letter K present in both Koran and Kafka (*Zwischen Koran und Kafka* 16).

The first of his two essays on Kafka, entitled "Nachmittag Schwimmschule: Kafka und Deutschland," is based on an earlier essay pointedly entitled "Was ist deutsch an der deutschen Literatur?" Kermani describes Kafka as the exemplary German-language writer. Asked who represents his German literary "Heimat," Kermani responds: "Für mich ist es nicht Goethe oder Schiller, nicht Thomas Mann oder Bertolt Brecht, sondern der Prager Jude Franz Kafka" (*Zwischen Koran und Kafka* 211). Unlike Brecht or Mann, who wrote in German as members of a German nation, Kafka wrote in German from a more distanced perspective, as a Jewish author from Prague; and

Kermani identifies with this more distanced viewpoint. One could argue, however, that Brecht and Thomas Mann developed a similarly distanced perspective to Germany through their long years of exile during World War II.

It is particularly Kafka's conflicted relationship to Germany as a nation and even to the German language that draws Kermani to him. Kermani cites an entry in Kafka's diary on August 2, 1914, shortly after the beginning of World War I, when Kafka laconically wrote only two sentences: "Deutschland hat Russland den Krieg erklärt.—Nachmittag Schwimmschule."[11] Kafka's emotional distance to the onset of the First World War and his complete lack of identification with Germany, as well as his trivialization of the event, could not have been brought out more poignantly than by noting the second event of that day: swimming lessons. Although Kafka's native language was German, he cultivated a similar indifference to the German language as to the German nation. Kermani quotes from a letter by Kafka to his friend Milena Jesenská, whose native language is Czech: "Ich habe niemals unter deutschem Volk gelebt, Deutsch ist meine Muttersprache und deshalb mir natürlich, aber das tschechische ist mir viel herzlicher" (*Zwischen Koran und Kafka* 225). Kermani emphasizes that Kafka was bilingual, speaking both German and Czech. Kafka was actually multilingual, since he was raised in German by his parents and learned Czech from his family's employees and at school, where he also studied French, Latin, and Greek. Later, he taught himself Italian, Yiddish, and Hebrew.[12] But his literary language remained German. Kermani points out that precisely the certain artifice of the German language in Prague, as a linguistic minority, and the lack of a natural or native environment may have contributed to Kafka's obsession with linguistic purity that allowed him to become one of the "penibelsten Wächtern über die deutsche Sprache" (*Zwischen Koran und Kafka* 225). For Kermani, Kafka's alienation and distance from the German language turned him into a role model, an ideal or paradigmatic German writer, and an author with whom Kermani, a German author of Iranian descent, can easily identify. In his book *Wer ist Wir?* Kermani described his own literary writings as "so deutsch wie Kafka."[13]

This distance that Kermani describes from a personal perspective may also be seen as a description of "minor literature," as Gilles Deleuze and Félix Guattari have defined it:

> A minor literature doesn't come from a minor language; it is rather that which a minority constructs within a major language. But the first characteristic of minor literature in any case is that in it language is affected with a high coefficient of deterritorialization.[14]

This deterritorialization of the German language, in Kafka's case the German spoken by the Jews of Prague, a minority within a minority that was far removed from the masses that spoke the language, can be seen as a form of alienation.

Following Deleuze and Guattari's definitions, Yasemin Yildiz describes how Kafka intensified and subverted the German language from within and how German became Kafka's "uncanny mother tongue" (Yildiz 30–34).

While Kermani's first essay on Kafka contextualizes him within German literature, his following essay, entitled "Der Auftrag der Literatur: Hedayat und Kafka," draws connections between Kafka and Iranian literature, especially the twentieth-century modernist author Sadegh Hedayat. Hedayat, who was born in Tehran in 1903 and who died in Paris by committing suicide in 1951, has been called Iran's Kafka (Kermani, *Zwischen Koran und Kafka* 240). Hedayat's creative writings were Kafkaesque in style, and he translated several stories by Kafka from French into Persian and wrote an influential essay, "The Message of Kafka," his last publication, in 1948. Kermani describes Hedayat's short story characters as a kaleidoscope of marginalized figures, a "Kaleidoskop der Randgestalten" (*Zwischen Koran und Kafka* 236), since his protagonists are usually lonely, psychologically debilitated characters who cannot survive in life's mundane day-to-day reality. Hedayat, who is now considered one of Iran's best-known twentieth-century authors, was frequently isolated and censored in his day. He did not fit in any established religious or ideological community. Of aristocratic background, Hedayat was also openly atheist and persecuted by Islamists. Even though he originally sympathized with communism, he later turned away from Iranian dogmatic left-wing ideologues who perceived him as too pessimistic and removed from reality. According to Kermani, Hedayat was a socialist with his heart, more than with his mind. His socialist sympathies resulted less from ideological convictions than from love for the creatures of this earth, humans as well as animals (*Zwischen Koran und Kafka* 238). Hedayat was one of the earliest modernists in Iran; his essay "The Message of Kafka" displays an understanding of Kafka at a time when Kafka's greatness was not yet as universally acknowledged as it is now.

Alienation and Empathy

Although Kermani claims that not Brecht but Kafka represents his German-language literary home, and although Kafka, as a counterpoint to the Koran, is highlighted in the book's title, Kermani's two Kafka essays do not analyze Kafka's specific works in great detail, beyond his references to Kafka's diaries. However, his article on the dramatic theory of Bertolt Brecht, whose writings are clearly not examples of a minor literature in the sense of Deleuze and Guattari, is one of Kermani's longest and most deeply analytical essays in his volume. His article on Brecht and alienation, followed by his essay on Wagner and empathy, is centrally placed in the book, directly preceding the two Kafka essays. Given Kermani's theatrical studies and his long experience as a dramaturge, he is certainly familiar with Brecht's theatrical theory and practice. In the essay entitled "Die Wahrheit des Theaters: Das schiitische Passionsspiel und die Verfremdung," Kermani draws connections between the Persian Shiite passion play and Brecht's epic theater.

Taziyeh, the Shiite passion play, represents a founding myth of Shiite Iran and is the only indigenous Iranian drama engendered by the world of Islam. The word *taziyeh* literally means sympathy, mourning, and consolation in Persian and recalls the suffering and the heroic martyrdom of Imam Hossein, a grandson of the Prophet Muhammad. The Shiite passion play's background is a historical event: after Mohamed's death in 632 the Muslim community needed new leadership and was divided into two factions, those who espoused the ancient Arabic tradition of succession by election and those who desired succession by inheritance, through blood relationship to the Prophet. The former are known as Sunnites (or Sunnis), the latter as Shiites. When Ali, the cousin and son-in-law of Mohamed and Shiite leader, was assassinated and his elder son Hassan was poisoned, his younger son Hossein was asked by a Shiite group near today's Baghdad to join them as their head. Hossein accepted, and in the year 680 set out from Mecca with his family and an entourage of seventy-two followers. But near Kerbela, a city southwest of Baghdad, they were caught in an ambush set by the Sunnite caliph, Yazid. Although defeat was certain, Hossein refused to surrender. Surrounded by a great enemy force, Hossein and his company existed without water for ten days in the burning desert of Kerbela. Finally Hossein and the male members of his group were brutally murdered by Yazid's army; the women and children were taken as captives. Hossein himself was beheaded, and his head was sent to Damascus and shown there as a trophy.[15]

The battlefield and tombs at Kerbela became a place of sacred pilgrimage for Shiites, and the *Taziyeh* of Iran evolved. *Taziyeh* is ritual theater that can become a mass spectacle, since the *tekiyeh*, the tents that were constructed for its performance, often offered space for up to twenty thousand spectators (Kermani, *Zwischen Koran und Kafka* 164). *Taziyeh* derives its form and its content from deep-rooted religious traditions that later received royal encouragement in Iran; so the spectacle became a patriotic as well as a religious act. The critic Peter Chelkowski describes *Taziyeh* as "Indigenous Avant-Garde Theatre of Iran" (Chelkowski 1), and Kermani reminds us that great theatrical directors such as Peter Brook, Jerzy Grotowski, and Tadeusz Kantor were fascinated by the dramatic tradition of *Taziyeh*. Brook especially was profoundly moved by *Taziyeh* during his historic visit to Iran in 1970 and transmitted its aesthetics to Western audiences. In 1979 he transposed Iranian dramatic conventions and cultural themes to the Western stage when he adapted a twelfth-century Persian mystical tract by Attar, *The Conference of the Birds*, into a theatrical play.

Kermani focuses particularly on Brechtian elements of the Shiite passion play, since it makes ample use of the practice of *Verfremdung*. Kermani lists a range of alienating, anti-illusionist and anti-naturalist strategies that have been part of *Taziyeh* for centuries, both in stage design as well as in acting approaches. Theatrical aids such as racks for costumes, stage props, the orchestra, or lights for illumination are not hidden under or behind the stage, but openly displayed. The backstage, if it exists, is visible to the audience, and the fourth wall is broken and has disappeared. The stage design is sparse and multifunctional. A table, for example, can signify a throne in one scene, a hideout in the next, and later a stretcher or a grave (*Zwischen Koran und Kafka* 170). The actor maintains distance and does not identify with his or her role; s/he presents the figure rather than embodying him/her and often has a text in the hand. In Brecht's words, the actor cites his or her character and does not transform fully into her or him (BFA 22, 204). There are futher commonalities: *Taziyeh* performances usually have a prolog and an epilog, and frequently there is a narrator figure, played by the director who holds the script and visibly gives instructions to the actors. As in many plays by Brecht, this authorial narrator can comment on actions on stage, recompose the scenes, and interrupt the course of the plot. This interruption of the action, *ta'liq* in Persian, is a classic epic device in a Brechtian sense (*Zwischen Koran und Kafka* 173). The protagonists and heroes often sing their text, while the antagonists recite their parts, anticipating a Brechtian form of *Gestus*.

Yet, while Brecht's theory of alienation is formulated in direct contrast to Aristotle's concept of catharsis, Kermani posits that "Verfremdung und Katharsis" are not opposing principles but rather coincide harmoniously in the Shiite passion play (*Zwischen Koran und Kafka* 168). He agrees with Brecht that empathy is the basis for catharsis. Catharsis—"die Reinigung durch Furcht und Mitleid, oder von Furcht und Mitleid," as Brecht defined it in *Kleines Organon für das Theater* (BFA 23, 67)—requires empathy: "Diese Reinigung erfolgt auf Grund eines eigentümlichen psychischen Aktes, der *Einfühlung* des Zuschauers in die handelnden Personen, die von den Schauspielern nachgeahmt werden" (BFA 22.1, 171). In *Taziyeh*, however, despite the alienating acting strategies of the performers, the spectators do not remain rational and reflect critically on the stage action, but they empathize with the characters and are encouraged to let their emotions flow. They are moved to tears at seeing Hossein's suffering and to emotional outbursts of lamentation that can border on hysteria. The spectacle, which in the nineteenth century could stretch over several days, resembles a mythological ritual. Shedding tears over Hossein's death is an established part of this ritual for the entire audience. It is the task of the theater director to animate the audience with gestures of mourning to participate in outbursts of lamentation. Beyond crying, spectators are encouraged to beat themselves rhythmically on their chests. Audience members have in the past torn off their clothes in pain and despair, and even flagellated and hit themselves to the point of bleeding. In this context Kermani cites Elias Canetti, who was also fascinated by *Taziyeh*: "Die Raserei, von der die klagenden Massen bei diesen Festen ergriffen werden, ist beinahe unvorstellbar" (*Zwischen Koran und Kafka* 168). In his book *Masse und Macht* Canetti distinguishes between religions of war and religions of lament.[16] While he sees Islam as a "Kriegsreligion," he describes the beliefs of Shiite Muslims, like those of Christianity, as a "Klagereligion" (Canetti 162). Canetti analyzes in great detail the emotional effect that the Shiite reenactment of Hossein's martyrdom has on large human masses.

How then is it possible that the alienating strategies on the part of the actors still produce deep empathy in the spectators, against Brecht's prescriptions? In the specific case of *Taziyeh*, the answer may lie in the fact that *Taziyeh* is not a secular theater performance, but an identity-forming religious ritual in which all spectators are expected to participate. Since audience members know the story before they enter the performance, there is no dramatic tension in the traditional sense; and actors can present their characters in a distanced, alienating fashion. The religious nature of the spectacle also explains the actors' alienating presentation of their characters. The tragedy of Kerbela is considered a unique and holy event for Shiites, and many of the characters in the play are either prophets, angels, holy figures like Hossein or brutal, satanic figures such as Yazid. Therefore, an empathetic form of acting in which a human actor identifies with superhuman or demonic characters is impossible or prohibited by religious conventions. Kermani explains that the empathy felt by the spectators is therefore not an empathy or identification with the performer or his/her role, but with the action on stage (*Zwischen Koran und Kafka* 178). A similar dynamic occurs in the medieval Christian passion play in which *Verfremdung* is also used for a very different purpose than the one envisioned by Brecht. Andrzej Wirth explains in his semiological analysis of *Taziyeh* the differences between Brecht's epic theater and the "confessional folk opera of Iran," as he calls *Taziyeh*:

> Comparisons with the Brecht theatre are superficial and misleading, and are provoked mostly through the manner of acting which presents in the eye of the uninitiated Western observer analogies with the *Verfremdungseffekt*. The Western observer is tempted to confuse style with technique. Brechtian V-Effect expresses a revisionistic and polemical attitude toward reality. This attitude is totally foreign to Ta'ziyeh. Ta'ziyeh is interested in the emotional status quo, namely in the reinforcement of the religious feelings of the spectators and the performers with the redemption effect in mind (the therapeutic element). This is philosophically and artistically not a theatre of alternatives but of confirmation and determination.[17]

Because of the essentially religious nature of *Taziyeh*, in which a "performer-believer" communicates a familiar story to the "spectator-believer" in order to achieve a spiritual and mystical union, Wirth asserts that despite its alienating acting approaches, a *Taziyeh* performance is "neither epic nor dramatic, but confessional" (Wirth 34). For this same reason, Wirth also believes that acting in *Taziyeh* stems from the great Asiatic tradition and in Western terms "is neither Stanislawski nor Brecht" (38).

The fact that *Verfremdung* fulfills such a different purpose in *Taziyeh* and in Brecht's dramas can be explained by their different nature, as Andrzej Wirth shows convincingly: modern principles for secular theater may not apply smoothly to ancient religious rituals. Kermani's more general question, whether it is possible that alienation and catharsis, two principles that are diametrically opposed in Brecht's theatrical theory, can coexist harmoniously in modern theater, nonetheless remains an interesting and provocative one. Kermani states:

> Es ist ein bis heute bestehendes Klischee, an dessen Entstehung Brecht ungewollt beteiligt war, dass Illusionsdurchbrechung durch Verfremdung zu einem politisch aufklärenden, eher den Intellekt ansprechenden Theater gehört, während Rührung, Anteilnahme und Identifikation durch eine möglichst natürlich wirkende Spielweise entsteht, die die Echtheit der Gefühle behauptet. (*Zwischen Koran und Kafka* 192)

Kermani believes that an epic theater that breaks illusions with alienation techniques does not always lead to an enlightened, intellectual, progressive attitude in the spectator. Similarly, an emotional, more conservative, status-quo affirming response in the audience does not necessarily require acting strategies that rely on empathy and performer-character-spectator identification. For Kermani, it is possible to be emotionally deeply moved by a theater that breaks illusions and doesn't rely on empathetic acting. Ancient Greek dramas, or the Persian passion play that Kermani analyzes, used alienating epic and narrative techniques that produced catharsis, outbursts of emotion, and empathy in the viewer.

Kermani distinguishes between two levels of empathy: empathy on the part of the actors and empathy on the part of the spectators. In his view Brecht assumed that these needed to coincide, although this hasn't been the case throughout much of theatrical history and may be a rather recent idea, beginning with the "Illusionstheater" of the nineteenth and early twentieth centuries and later with Stanislawski (*Zwischen Koran und Kafka* 189). Indeed, an excerpt from Brecht's essay "Verfremdungseffekte in der chinesischen Schauspielkunst" shows that Brecht believed that alienation on the part of the actor will produce an alienated, critical, reflective posture in the viewer:

> Der Artist wünscht, dem Zuschauer fremd, ja befremdlich zu erscheinen. Er erreicht das dadurch, dass er sich selbst und seine Darbietungen mit Fremdheit betrachtet. So bekommen die Dinge, die er vorführt,

> etwas Erstaunliches . . . Das Sich-selber-Zusehen des Artisten, ein künstlicher und kunstvoller Akt der Selbstentfremdung, verhindert die vollständige, d. h. bis zur Selbstaufgabe gehende Einfühlung des Zuschauers und schafft eine großartige Distanz zu den Vorgängen. Auf die Einfühlung des Zuschauers wird trotzdem nicht verzichtet. Der Zuschauer fühlt sich in den Schauspieler als in einen Betrachtenden ein: so wird seine betrachtende, zuschauende Haltung kultiviert. (BFA 22, 202)

In Brecht's dramatic theory, *Verfremdung* occurs on both levels, that of the actor and the spectator. *Einfühlung* or empathy may also exist exclusively between the spectator and the performer as a person who inspires the audience member to assume a similarly observing, distanced attitude. Here Kermani differs from Brecht, since Kermani believes that *Verfremdung* can be present on one level only, the level of the performing artist, and need not transfer to the spectator who can be profoundly and empathetically moved emotionally by the stage characters and action, despite alienating acting approaches on the part of the performers. Kermani demonstrates this convincingly in his analysis of the Iranian *Taziyeh*, and he also proposes that Western dramatists and directors can learn from the ancient Persian stage and adapt these principles to contemporary Western performances, as Peter Brook has done.

In the volume's following essay on Richard Wagner, entitled "Befreit Bayreuth! Wagner und die Einfühlung," Kermani continues his discussions on alienation and empathy. He critiques the "abgestandene[s] Einfühlungstheater" that frequently rules Bayreuth (*Zwischen Koran und Kafka* 197). In order to revitalize Bayreuth and create a new balance in the "Beziehungslosigkeit von Bild und Musik," between the beauty of the music and the often unimaginative acting and stage design, Kermani proposes a Brechtian approach to salvage Wagner: Contradicting Wagner's prescriptions, the orchestra should not be invisible and below the stage, but brought back to the top of the stage (*Zwischen Koran und Kafka* 195, 205). However sacrilegious this might sound to committed Wagnerians, a visible orchestra might modernize Wagner for a contemporary audience, and in Kermani's view it would produce a staging that combines the principles of alienation and empathy. Ultimately Kermani considers Shakespeare's dramas as a model of a theater that unites "radikale Verfremdung und ergreifende Einfühlung" (*Zwischen Koran und Kafka* 206).

The Artist and the Refugees

"You can only truly love the *other*," Kermani states in his acceptance speech upon receiving the Peace Prize of the German Book Trade. He explains that self-love always needs to involve self-criticism, while a love of the other may be more effusive, enthusiastic, and emotional:

> Die Liebe zum Eigenen—zur eigenen Kultur wie zum eigenen Land und genauso zur eigenen Person—erweist sich in der Selbstkritik. Die Liebe zum anderen—zu einer anderen Person, einer anderen Kultur und selbst zu einer anderen Religion—kann viel schwärmerischer, sie kann vorbehaltlos sein. Richtig, die Liebe zum anderen setzt die Liebe zu sich selbst voraus. Aber verliebt, wie es Pater Paolo und Pater Jacques in den Islam sind, verliebt kann man nur in den anderen sein. Die Selbstliebe hingegen muss, damit sie nicht der Gefahr des Narzissmus, des Selbstlobs, der Selbstgefälligkeit unterliegt, eine hadernde, zweifelnde, stets fragende sein. ("2015 Friedenspreisrede")

He delivered this statement in the context of describing two Christian priests in Syria who greatly respected Islamic religion and culture; and in light of the recent killings by ISIS Kermani called on all Muslims who love their religion to do so in a spirit that admits doubt and self-criticism: "Wer als Muslim nicht mit ihm hadert, nicht an ihm zweifelt, nicht ihn kritisch befragt, der liebt den Islam nicht" ("2015 Friedenspreisrede").

These ideas also guide his perception of literature and art. In his essay on the Persian poet Faridoddin Attar, Kermani concludes that literature and intellectual pursuits in general are essentially self-critical acts: "Kritik an anderen Kulturen ist immer affirmativ gegenüber der eigenen Kultur und damit das Gegenteil dessen, was Literatur zum Antrieb und zur Aufgabe hat. Literatur—Kunst und Intellektualität insgesamt—ist im Kern ein selbstkritischer Akt" (*Zwischen Koran und Kafka* 69). Brecht's poem "Deutschland" opens with a similar emphasis on the importance of self-critique: "Mögen andere von ihrer Schande sprechen, ich spreche von der meinen" (BFA 11, 253).

Kermani's distinction of different forms of love, a passionate love for the other and a more critical love of oneself, may also be seen in view of his thoughts on the coexistence of alienation and empathy in drama, as he expressed them in his essay on Brecht and the *Taziyeh*: A focus on the other, and on distance, does not impose strict rationality. On the contrary, it may be highly emotional. Kermani's aesthetic views on the coexistence of passion and distance, or empathy and alienation, may also be applied to ethical values and contemporary political developments. He stresses the importance of respect for and love of the other, for example in the current refugee crisis or in the relationship between Islam and the West. As an artist, he has a heightened sensitivity toward the outsider in society. It is a belief that he not only preaches but practices: His recent book *Ungläubiges Staunen*, which contains his reflections on Christian art, was also designed to help Islamic populations understand Christianity. Kermani visited countless mosques in Germany, where he discussed his book and explained Christian iconography to a resident Muslim minority that knows little about Christian beliefs.

Similarly, *Zwischen Koran und Kafka* is a creative and educational work of literary criticism that bridges aesthetic boundaries and addresses Western audiences not only to teach them the wisdom of Eastern art and thought, but also to help them see Western artistic works in light of Eastern traditions' literary perceptions and productions. When Kermani reads Hannah Arendt's theories on revolution in light of the recent Arab Spring, or when he compares Kleist's theories of love with those of the Sufi philosopher Ibn Arabi, or when he interprets Goethe's poetry in relation to the aesthetic beauty of the Koran, to mention a few examples, he not only widens the creative scope of the possibilities of literary criticism, he also politicizes them. *Zwischen Koran und Kafka* is not a directly political work, unlike his travel reports from war-torn regions, such as *Ausnahmezustand*, in which Kermani shows how much the suffering of refugees is at the core of his writings, or his essay collection *Wer ist Wir?*, which was reissued in its sixth edition in 2015 and which addresses questions of migration on a more personal and political level. But the recent dramatic increase in a flow of refugees to Germany, amounting to almost a million in one year, will shed new light on Kermani's book, which may have started as a literary project, but acquired a political dimension as well in the process of this mass migration. *Zwischen Koran und Kafka* appeared in 2014, as the movement of refugees from the Middle East was just beginning. This influx of new immigrants will change German literary and political identity, as Kermani's book admirably reflects in its rereading of classical Western authors.

Zwischen Koran und Kafka is a timely and essential book. Beyond its political significance in light of the current refugee crisis, it is an important poetic work that transgresses formal and thematic boundaries. Formally, it can be seen as a hybrid, as a collection of critical essays by an author who is primarily a creative writer—a writer who is steeped in mysticism. Kermani is strongly influenced by Islamic mysticism, by Sufi poets like Attar, Rumi, and Ibn Arabi who infuse his literary writings. Thematically, this book elegantly eliminates boundaries between Eastern and Western literary traditions and explores possibilities of a cosmopolitan literature in German language today.

While Kermani's stated role model remains Kafka, he actually engages with Brecht's writings at a deeper level and in greater detail in *Zwischen Koran und Kafka*. As his discussion of Brecht and *Taziyeh* shows, Kermani understands Brecht well and respects him profoundly, but also critiques him and proposes to adapt his theories to experiences of Eastern theatrical traditions. In Kermani's book, his fellow exile Brecht assumes a central, albeit critically reflected space.

Notes

[1] Navid Kermani, *Schöner neuer Orient: Berichte von Städten und Kriegen* (Munich: Beck, 2003) and *Ausnahmezustand: Reisen in eine beunruhigte Welt* (Munich: Beck, 2013).

[2] Kermani, *Ungläubiges Staunen: Über das Christentum* (Munich: Beck, 2015).

[3] Kermani, "Über die Grenzen: Jacques Mourad und die Liebe in Syrien. 2015 Friedenspreisrede," accessed 18 October 2015, http://www.friedenspreis-des-deutschen-buchhandels.de/819312/. Hereafter "2015 Friedenspreiserede."

[4] Bertolt Brecht, *Werke. Große kommentierte Berliner und Frankfurter Ausgabe*, Werner Hecht et al., eds., vol. 19 (Berlin and Frankfurt am Main: Aufbau and Suhrkamp, 1988–2000), 147–41. Hereafter BFA volume, page.

[5] Kermani, *Der Schrecken Gottes: Attar, Hiob und die metaphysische Revolte* (Munich: Beck, 2005), p. 259. Hereafter *Der Schrecken Gottes* page.

[6] Kermani, *Gott ist schön: Das ästhetische Erleben des Koran* (Munich: Beck, 2003). Hereafter *Gott ist schön* page.

[7] Kermani, *Zwischen Koran und Kafka: West-östliche Erkundungen* (Munich: Beck, 2014). Hereafter *Zwischen Koran und Kafka* page.

[8] For more on Kermani's advocacy for tolerance, see Karolin Machtans, "Navid Kermani: Advocate for an Antipatriotic Patriotism and a Multireligious, Multicultural Europe," in Jill E. Twark and Axel Hildebrandt, eds., *Envisioning Social Justice in Contemporary German Culture* (Rochester, NY: Camden House, 2015), pp. 290–311.

[9] Hannah Arendt, *On Revolution* (New York: Penguin Books, 1985).

[10] Zafer Şenocak, "Zwischen Koran und Sexpistols," *Das Land hinter den Buchstaben: Deutschland und der Islam im Umbruch* (Munich: Babel Verlag, 2006), pp. 29–33.

[11] Franz Kafka, *Gesammelte Werke: 8 Bände*, vol. 7 (Frankfurt am Main: Fischer, 1983), p. 305. Hereafter Kafka, *Werke* volume: page.

[12] Yasemin Yildiz, *Beyond the Mother Tongue: The Postmonolingual Condition* (New York: Fordham University Press, 2012), p. 223. Hereafter Yildiz page.

[13] Kermani, *Wer ist Wir? Deutschland und seine Muslime* (Munich: Beck, 2014), p. 133. Hereafter *Wer ist Wir* page.

[14] Gilles Deleuze and Felix Guattari, *Kafka: Toward a Minor Literature*, trans. Dana Polan (Minneapolis: University of Minnesota Press, 1994), p. 16. Hereafter Deleuze and Guattari page.

[15] Peter J. Chelkowski, ed., *Ta'ziyeh: Ritual and Drama in Iran* (New York: NYU Press, 1979), pp. 1–2. Hereafter Chelkowski page.

[16] Elias Canetti, *Masse und Macht* (Frankfurt am Main: Fischer, 1981). Hereafter Canetti page.

[17] Andrzej Wirth, "Semeiological Aspects of the Ta'ziyeh," in Chelkowski, ed., *Ta'ziyeh: Ritual and Drama in Iran*, pp. 32–39, here p. 34. Hereafter Wirth page.

Dieter Goltzsche, *Der gute Mensch von Sezuan*, 2015, Tusche.

Karl Kraus and Bertolt Brecht: On the Comparability of the Incomparable

If Karl Kraus is mentioned in the secondary literature on Brecht at all, he comes up only in regard to those two poems in which Brecht in 1933–34 expressed his disappointment about the long silence of Kraus regarding Hitler's seizure of power in Germany as well as Kraus's support of the Dollfuß regime in Austria. But this is only one facet of a much deeper and more complex connection between these two authors. A closer analysis reveals that they had a very intensive, even friendly relationship during the last years of the Weimar Republic in Berlin, where Kraus performed a number of Offenbach's operettas as a solo actor and singer and even participated actively in the rehearsals of the *Dreigroschenoper*, thereby having an important influence on Brecht's concept of the epic theater. In spite of Brecht's disappointment at Kraus's political stance in the years 1933–34, he never lost his admiration for Kraus's highly critical attitude towards bourgeois society and even still tried hard in the GDR to prevent any and all critiques of Kraus.

"Falls Karl Kraus überhaupt in der Brechtforschung erwähnt wird, so ist es meist nur im Hinblick auf jene zwei Gedichte, in denen er 1933–34 seine Enttäuschung über Kraus' Schweigen angesichts der nationalsozialistischen Machtergreifung und dessen Unterstützung des Dollfuß-Regimes ausdrückte. Dies ist aber nur ein Aspekt einer tiefreichenden, vielschichtigen Verbindung zwischen diesen zwei Autoren. Eine genauere Analyse ergibt eine wesentlich intensivere, ja freundschaftliche Beziehung zwischen beiden am Ende der Weimarer Republik in Berlin, wo Kraus mit seinen Offenbachiaden beachtliche Erfolge feierte und sogar an den frühen Proben der *Dreigroschenoper* aktiv teilnahm. Kraus beeinflusste dadurch die Entwicklung des epischen Theaters, und trotz der Enttäuschung in den Jahren 1933–34 hörte Brecht nicht auf, Kraus' kritische Haltung der Bourgeoisie gegenüber zu schätzen und ihn auch noch zu DDR-Zeiten zu verteidigen.

Karl Kraus und Bertolt Brecht: Über die Vergleichbarkeit des Unvergleichlichen

Jost Hermand

I

Auf den ersten Blick kann man sich kaum einen größeren Unterschied als den zwischen Karl Kraus und Bertolt Brecht vorstellen. War nicht der Eine—einmal etwas vereinfacht gesehen—ein bürgerlicher Einzelgänger, der in seiner Umwelt nur Untergangssymptome wahrnahm, auf die er mit beißendem Spott reagierte, und war nicht der Andere—ebenfalls etwas vereinfacht gesehen—ein unermüdlicher Optimist, der sich unter marxistischem Vorzeichen bis zum Ende seines Lebens für eine "Bewohnbarmachung" der Welt eingesetzt hat? Was soll daher bei einem Vergleich dieser beiden Autoren herauskommen? Nur Unterschiede oder eventuell auch Vergleichbares? Das wäre die Frage, die es in dieser Hinsicht zu stellen gilt.

In der relativ spärlichen Sekundärliteratur zum Verhältnis dieser beiden so verschiedenartigen, ja unvergleichlichen Autoren zueinander gibt es darum auf diese Frage bisher kaum befriedigende Antworten. Zugegeben, dass Brecht nach 1933 von Kraus eine scharfe Ablehnung des Nazifaschismus erwartet hatte und über ihr Ausbleiben lange Zeit verstimmt war, davon ist in vielen Brecht-Studien mehr oder minder ausführlich die Rede.[1] Aber all das, was dieser Erwartungshaltung in den zwanziger Jahren vorangegangen war, bleibt meist unerwähnt oder wird eher beiläufig behandelt.[2] Ja, wenn in den bekannteren Brecht-Darstellungen Kraus überhaupt auftaucht, dann lediglich als eine unbedeutende Randerscheinung oder gar als Antipode, auf den man nicht näher einzugehen braucht.

Schuld an dieser Nichtbeachtung ist weitgehend jene zum Teil ins Hagiographische tendierende Kraus-Darstellung, wie sie sich unter seinen engsten Anhänger ausbildete und dann auf weite Kreise der bürgerlich-liberalen Literaturkritik übergriff.[3] In ihren Schriften wird Kraus fast ausschließlich als ein "einsamer Kämpfer" gegen das herrschende Presseunwesen charakterisiert, der kein Blatt vor den Mund genommen habe, um mit triumphierender Gehässigkeit gegen eine Welt von Feinden zu Felde zu ziehen, in denen er—aufgrund seiner intellektuellen Überlegenheit—lediglich ein Sammelsurium tölpelhafter Spießer oder nichtswürdiger Duckmäuser gesehen habe.[4] Diese Kritiker stellten daher Kraus zumeist als einen ihnen zutiefst verwandten Spötter, Nörgler oder

Querulanten hin, der stets darauf aus gewesen sei, sich auf gut- oder bestbürgerliche Weise über all jene lustig zu machen, die er als geistig minderbemittelt empfunden habe.

Nun, es gibt zum Glück auch andere Kraus-Verehrer, die in ihm nicht nur einen arroganten Zyniker gesehen haben, dem es in seinen in der *Fackel* abgedruckten Dramen, Gedichten, Glossen und Aphorismen allein darum gegangen sei, seine intellektuelle Überlegenheit zu demonstrieren, sondern der dabei selten oder nie die gesellschaftskritische Absicht seiner Invektiven gegen die grundsätzliche "Verkehrtheit" der politischen Entwicklung von der späten Habsburger Doppelmonarchie über den Ersten Weltkrieg bis zur ersten Österreichischen Republik der zwanziger Jahre vergessen habe. Und in ihren Schriften taucht auch der Name Brecht hin und wieder auf.

Ja, es gibt sogar schon einige Studien, die—wenn auch in unterschiedlicher ideologischer Perspektive—etwas näher auf die persönlichen Beziehungen zwischen Kraus und Brecht, ja sogar auf gewisse Ähnlichkeiten oder Übereinstimmungen in den Anschauungen und literarischen Darstellungsmitteln dieser beiden Autoren eingegangen sind. Eher positivistisch, das heißt sich auf die Wiedergabe faktisch nachweisbarer Bezüge beschränkend, verfuhren hierbei Kurt Krolop[5] und Caroline Cohn.[6] Friedrich Rothe akzentuierte vor allem den linksliberalen Aspekt dieser Beziehung,[7] während sich James K. Lyon—unter Bezugnahme auf die sich angeblich widersprechenden Aphorismen "Gleich zu gleich gesellt sich gern" sowie "die Gegensätze ziehen sich an"—eher um eine "dialektisierende" Sicht im Hinblick auf diese beiden Autoren bemühte.[8] Dagegen versuchte ein Marxist wie Georg Knepler auch die "linke" Komponente in den Werken von Kraus und ihre Bedeutsamkeit für Brecht herauszustellen.[9] Um etwas mehr Klarheit in die komplizierten und zugleich folgenreichen Bezüge zwischen diesen beiden Autoren zu bringen, soll daher im zweiten Abschnitt dieses Essays erst einmal all das in chronologischer Reihenfolge dargestellt werden, was mir in dieser Hinsicht bedeutsam erscheint, um dann gegen Schluss die notwendigen Folgerungen daraus zu ziehen.

II

Der erste nachweisbare Beleg, dass Brecht eine der Schriften von Kraus gelesen hat, findet sich in seinen frühen *Tagebüchern*. Dort heißt es am 15. September 1921 im Rahmen einer Lektüreübersicht: "Außerdem lese ich Kraus."[10] Damit könnte entweder ein Heft der *Fackel* oder das Drama *Die letzten Tage der Menschheit* gemeint sein, das 1919 erschienen war und viel Aufsehen erregt hatte. Kraus scheint spätestens 1924 auf Brecht aufmerksam geworden zu sein. Das geht aus einer seiner Polemiken gegen Herbert Jhering hervor, in der Kraus zugleich Arnolt Bronnen und Bertolt Brecht, diesen "beiden Fasolte des deutschen Expressionismus," wie so vielen Dramatikern ihrer Generation, eine "mangelnde Ausdrucksfähigkeit" vorgeworfen hatte.[11] Auch in den folgenden drei bis vier Jahren holte Kraus gelegentlich gegen Brecht aus. So warnte er etwa 1926 in seinem Essay "Winke für Schwangerschaft" eine junge Frau, keineswegs Brecht zu lesen, da sie bei der Lektüre seiner Werke sicher "brechten" würde.[12] Doch das wird Brecht sicher nicht "geritzt" haben, wie man damals sagte. Er war zwar in seinen Urteilen nicht so scharfzüngig oder bildungsbetont wie Kraus, gab sich aber manchmal ebenfalls recht abschätzig, wenn es galt, einen seiner Widersacher niederzumachen. Und auch kalauernde Wortspiele gefielen ihm durchaus. So warf er etwa dem fünfzigjährigen Kraus vor, den siebzigjährigen George Bernard Shaw nicht genug zu schätzen, sich "über die Welt nur in Zeitungen zu informieren" oder sich wie ein "moralischer Narziss" aufzuspielen, der lediglich seine "eigne Reinheit" beweisen wolle.[13]

Doch derlei Gerangel war in literarischen Kreisen damals allgemein üblich, wenn man an die scharfen Polemiken Alfred Kerrs und Kurt Tucholskys denkt. Als sich daher Kraus im Herbst 1928 längere Zeit in Berlin aufhielt, entwickelte sich zwischen beiden—trotz des großen Altersunterschieds, des verschiedenartigen Herkommens und ihrer politisch abweichenden Meinungen—dennoch relativ schnell ein gutes Einvernehmen, ja fast eine offen demonstrierte Waffenbrüderschaft. Wie es dazu kam, hatte folgende Ursachen. Wohl die wichtigste war, dass Kraus im Jahr zuvor aktiv in die österreichische Politik eingegriffen hatte und darauf als Kritiker der herrschenden Reaktion von großen Teilen der Wiener Bourgeoisie abgelehnt, ja gehasst wurde. Während er zuvor vornehmlich gegen das "schmierige" Presseunwesen vorgegangen war, hatte er nach einer am 15. Juli 1927 vor dem Wiener Justizpalast stattgefundenen Arbeiterdemonstration, bei der von der Polizei fast hundert Protestierende ermordet worden waren, in aller Schärfe gegen den regierenden Polizeipräsidenten Johann Schober vom Leder gezogen, ja sogar eine Plakataktion gestartet, welche die Aufforderung an Schober enthielt, sofort zurückzutreten. Und das hatte sich auch in Berlin herumgesprochen und ihm unter den dortigen Linken eine Reihe neuer Freunde verschafft, während sich in Wien die herrschenden Schichten, ja selbst führende Sozialdemokraten weiterhin mit Schober gegen den "Pöbel" solidarisierten.[14] Darauf richtete Kraus sein Augenmerk zusehens auf Berlin, wo er sich ein verständnisvolleres Publikum für seine antibürgerlichen Ansichten erhoffte.[15] Und das traf auch ein. Seine ersten Erfolge erzielte er dort in der letzten Märzwoche des Jahres 1928 mit seinen zeitkritisch bearbeiteten Offenbachiaden, und zwar der *Großherzogin von Gerolstein*, dem *Blaubart*, der *Madame L'Archiduc* und dem *Pariser Leben*,[16] deren Texte er nicht nur vortrug beziehungsweise sang, sondern die er zugleich gestisch verdeutlichte, um damit eine neue Art von Theater zu initiieren, das in seiner parodistischen Darbietung nicht nur vergnüglich, sondern auch aufreizend, ja gesellschaftkritisch "eingreifend" sein sollte.[17]

Man fragt sich unwillkürlich: warum bevorzugte Kraus bei diesen Darbietungen ausgerechnet die Opéras bouffes jenes Jacques Offenbach, der inzwischen längst durch Operettenkomponisten wie Johann Strauß, Franz von Suppé, Emmerich Kalman und Franz Lehar in den Hintergrund gedrängt worden war? Doch deren Werke erschienen ihm zu albern, zu sentimental, auf bloßen Ohrenschmaus bedacht, kurzum: als Konsumgüter einer irregeleiteten Welt—und damit menschlich und ästhetisch "unwürdig." In Offenbach, der weder die französische Grand Opéra noch das Wagnersche Musikdarama geschätzt hatte, sah er dagegen einen ihm kongenialen Satiriker, der sich über die erbärmliche Großmannssucht und zugleich kapitalistische Veräußerlichung des französischen Zweiten Kaiserreichs unter Napoleon III. ebenso unbarmherzig lustig gemacht habe wie er über die inzwischen untergegangene habsburgsche k. und k. Monarchie sowie die auf sie folgende, von vielen Widersprüchen durchzogene österreichische 1. Republik der zwanziger Jahre. In Offenbach glaubte daher Kraus einen ihm zutiefst verwandten Künstler gefunden zu haben, der als jüdischer Außenseiter, gnadenloser Satiriker und Feind aller nationalen Überheblichkeit der bürgerlichen Welt seiner Zeit einen nicht minder entlarvenden Spiegel vorgehalten habe, wie er es mit seiner *Fackel* und seinen Dramen versuchte.

Als Kraus darauf hörte, dass Kurt Weill und Bertolt Brecht im August 1928 im Theater am Schiffbauerdamm mit den Proben zu ihrer *Dreigroschenoper* begonnen hatten, der eine ähnliche vergnügliche und zugleich parodistische Absicht wie seinen Offenbachiaden zugrunde lag, nahm er zunächst "heimlich" an den Proben teil und gab sich schließich als der zu erkennen, der er tatsächlich war.[18] Darauf entwickelte sich zwischen Kraus und Brecht, dem Vierundfünfzigjährigen und dem Dreißigjährigen, ein geradezu kameradschaftliches Verhältnis, ja Kraus behandelte Brecht, dieses "junge Genie," wie Elias Canetti berichtet, geradezu wie seinen "erwählten Sohn."[19] Und auch andere bestätigten die menschliche Vertrautheit, die sich in diesen Wochen zwischen beiden entwickelte. So schrieb Heinrich Fischer, der damals am Theater am Schiffbauerdamm als Dramaturg tätig war, in seinen Erinnerungen an Kraus, dass beide während dieser Zeit "fast jeden Abend mit einigen Freunden in einem Bierkeller in der Friedrichstraße" zusammen gesessen hätten.[20] Auch im Künstlerlokal Max Schlichters in der Lutherstraße trafen sich Kraus und Brecht oft, wie Friedrich Rothe herausgefunden hat.[21] Bei den dort stattfindenden Diskussionen, an denen sich auch John Heartfield und Hanns Eisler beteiligten,[22] muss es zu vielen anregenden Gesprächen über jene theatralische Praxis gekommen sein, die sowohl Kraus als auch Brecht damals beschäftigte, nämlich den Verlauf der Handlung mit Songs und Sprechdialogen aufzubrechen, um so jene naturalistische Psychologisierung zu vermeiden, die damals im Gefolge Ibsens und Hauptmanns trotz gewisser expressionistischer Experimente noch immer das gängige Theaterwesen bestimmte. Ja, Brecht—großzügig in Fragen geistigen Eigentums—erlaubte Kraus sogar, in dem kurz darauf schnell berühmt werdenden Eifersuchtsduett der *Dreigroschenoper* noch eine weitere Strophe hinzuzudichten.[23] Selbstverständlich nahm Kraus—mit Georg Knepler, dem Klavierbegleiter seiner Offenbachiaden—auch an der am 31. August 1928 stattfindenden Uraufführung der *Dreigroschenoper* teil. Als kurz darauf Alfred Kerr, der bürgerlich Überkorrekte, Brecht bezichtigte, sich ohne genaue Kennzeichnung an der Ammerschen Übersetzung der Gedichte François Villons "vergriffen" zu haben, setzte sich Kraus unverzüglich für Brecht ein, ja ließ sich sogar dazu hinreißen, den "Trottel" Kerr, mit dem er sich wegen dessen kriegsverherrlichender Gedichte schon seit Längerem in den Haaren lag,[24] als den "größten Schuft im ganzen Land" zu bezeichnen. Aus Dankbarkeit für diese Art von Rückendeckung empfahl daher Brecht kurz darauf dem Berliner Regisseur Leo Reuß für dessen *Macbeth*-Inszenierung, sich bei der Hexenszene auf die Nachdichtung von Karl Kraus zu stützten, die von "unerhörter sprachlicher Schönheit" sei.[25]

Und bei diesem guten Einvernehmen zwischen Kraus und Brecht blieb es auch in den darauffolgenden Monaten und Jahren. Schließlich war Kraus von der Theaterbesessenheit des jungen Brecht geradezu fasziniert. Zugleich hoffte er, dass Brecht nach dem Erfolg der *Dreigroschenoper* nun auch einige seiner Stücke aufführen würde. Aufgrund der in dieser Hinsicht kursierenden Gerüchte meldete daher das *Neue Wiener Journal* am 25. Januar 1929, dass es sicher bald zur Einstudierung des ein Jahr zuvor von Kraus verfassten Dramas *Die Unüberwindlichen* durch Bertolt Brecht und Erich Engel kommen würde. Doch erwies sich das als eine Ente. In diesem Stück hatte sich Kraus sowohl den Wiener Polizeipräsidenten Johann Schober als auch den korrupten Zeitungsverleger Imre Békessy vorgenommen, die bei ihm unter den Namen Wacker und Barkassy auftreten. In der Einsicht, dass dieser Angriff letztlich im Leeren verpuffen würde, hatte er dem Ganzen allerdings das Kierkegaard-Motto vorangestellt: "Ein einzelner Mensch kann einer Zeit nicht helfen oder sie retten, er kann nur ausdrücken, dass sie untergeht." Schließlich war der von ihm angegriffene Schober nicht nur im Amt geblieben, sondern wurde 1929 sogar österreichischer Bundeskanzler. Und so blieben *Die Unüberwindlichen* in Wien unaufgeführt. Lediglich im Dresdner Residenztheater wagte Paul Verhoeven im Mai 1929 eine Inszenierung dieses Stücks. In Berlin kam dieses bewusst als Farce angelegte Drama am 20. Oktober des gleichen Jahres an der Berliner Volksbühne am Bülowplatz mit Peter Lorre, der vorher den Galy Gay in Brechts *Mann ist Mann* gespielt hatte, in der Rolle des Barkassy heraus und wurde von Herbert Jhering im *Berliner Börsen-Courier* als eins der besten Zeitstücke dieser Ära begrüßt.[26] Doch schon einen Tag später musste es aufgrund einer Intervention der Österreichischen Botschaft in Berlin wieder vom Spielplan abgesetzt werden.

Auch Anfang 1930 verbrachte Kraus wiederum einige Zeit in Berlin, wo am 15. Januar sein Stück *Die letzte Nacht*, bei dem es sich um den

Epilog seines Dramas *Die letzten Tage der Menschheit* handelte, in der Regie von Heinrich Fischer und der Begleitmusik von Hanns Eisler auf der Versuchsbühne des Theaters am Schiffbauerdamm aufgeführt wurde. Sechs Wochen danach hielt Kraus mehrere "Vorlesungen" einer Bühnenfassung der *Letzten Tage der Menschheit*, die trotz ihrer Dialektintonationen beim Publikum gut ankamen. Ja, am 9. März begann er in der von Hans Flesch-Brunnigen geleiteten Berliner "Funkstunde"—unter der Mitwirkung von Ernst Busch, Trude Hesterberg, Peter Lorre und Helene Weigel—zwölf seiner Offenbachiaden in eigener Wortregie einzustudieren, worauf sich die allem Neuartigen durchaus zugängliche Krolloper entschloss, seine Fassung der Offenbachschen *Périchole* im April 1931 in Szene zu setzen.

Und das beglückte Kraus selbstverständlich. Nicht nur Teile der gebildeten und zugleich liberal eingestellten Oberschicht jubelten ihm in dieser Stadt zu, sondern auch viele der dortigen Linken, darunter neben Bertolt Brecht vor allem Walter Benjamin, Hanns Eisler, Heinrich Fischer und Herbert Jhering, die nicht nur seine Vortragskunst, sondern auch die satirische Schärfe seiner Angriffe gegen das bürgerliche *juste Milieu* geradezu hinreißend fanden. Trotz seiner unverhohlenen Abneigung gegen den Kommunismus, mit dem viele seiner Berliner Freunde seit dem Ausbruch der Weltwirtschaftskrise im Oktober 1929 und dem sensationellen Wahlerfolg der Nationalsozialisten im September 1930 zu sympathisieren begannen, fühlte sich Kraus in seiner radikalen Kritik der abgelebten Bürgerwelt von diesen Kreisen durchaus verstanden. Und er erwiderte die ihm entgegengebachte Sympathie durchaus. So erklärte er Anfang März 1932 in der *Fackel*, dass er Brecht für "den einzigen deutschen Autor" halte, "der heute in Betracht zu kommen hat," weil er der "einzige" sei, der ein "Zeitbewusstsein" besitze, statt jener "Flachheit und Ödigkeit" der "beliebteren Reimer der Lebenprosa" zu huldigen, die sich unter den Autoren der Neuen Sachlichkeit verbreitet habe.[27] Am besten gefiel ihm zeitweilig Brechts *Aufstieg und Fall der Stadt Mahagonny*, von dem er Teile, darunter das Lied von den zwei Kranichen und die Gerichtsszene, sogar in seine "Vorlesungen" aufnahm und sich dabei von Kurt Weill am Klavier begleiten ließ. Ja, im gleichen *Fackel*-Heft schrieb Kraus sogar: "Für die Verse 'Kranich und Wolke' gebe ich die Literatur sämtlicher Literaten hin, die sich irrtümlich für seine Zeitgenossen halten."

Seine letzte "Vorlesung" in Deutschland hielt Kraus im Dezember 1932. Anschließend kehrte er nach Österreich zurück, allerdings nicht ohne vorher noch mit Brecht den Plan einer Wiener Aufführung der *Mutter* an einem der dortigen Theater zu besprechen. Auch von einem möglichen Vortrag, den Brecht in Wien halten würde, war bei diesen Gesprächen die Rede. Doch aus beiden wurde nichts. Schließlich waren nach dem 30. Januar 1933, an dem Hindenburg auf Drängen der deutschen Großindustriellen und Großagrarier Hitler das Kanzleramt übertrug, um die Weimarer Republik vor einer drohenden "Bolschewisierung" zu retten, weder in Österreich noch in Deutschland irgendwelche linken Aktivitäten möglich. Ja, für alle, die sich diesem Trend entgegenzusetzen versuchten, wurde die Lage von Tag zu Tag immer prekärer. Helene Weigel trug zwar Anfang Februar 1933 auf einer Arbeiterversammlung in Begleitung Georg Kneplers noch Brechts "Wiegenlieder einer proletarischen Mutter" vor, doch danach waren selbst solche Auftritte nicht mehr möglich. Den Schlusspunkt dieser Entwicklung bildete schießlich der Reichstagsbrand vom 27. Februar, der von den Nazifaschisten der KPD angelastet wurde. Danach mussten alle exponierten Linken versuchen, dem braunen Terror zu entkommen, um nicht sofort verhaftet, eingekerkert oder gar umgebracht zu werden. Brecht und Weigel verließen angesichts dieser Situation bereits am folgenden Tag Berlin. Ihr erster Zufluchtsort war Wien, wo Weigels Vater in der Berggasse 30 wohnte und Brecht zugleich Kraus wiedertreffen wollte, der ihn als "weiser Freund," wie Brecht später schrieb, mit den Worten begrüßte: "Die Ratten besteigen das sinkende Schiff."[28] Kraus war zwar hocherfreut, beide in Sicherheit zu wissen, riet aber Brecht ab, in Österreich zu bleiben, da sich auch dort die "Barbarei" ausbreite. Daher reiste Brecht, nachdem ihm der hilfsbereite Kraus finanziell unter die Arme gegriffen hatte,[29] schon Anfang März in die Schweiz, um dort—weiterhin auf die Chance eines "eingreifenden Denkens" vertrauend—mit seinem Freund Lion Feuchtwanger mögliche antifaschistische Aktivitäten zu besprechen.

Aufgrund seiner die Schaffung einer proletarischen Einheitsfront gegen das Hitler-Regime ins Auge fassenden Einstellung, wofür sowohl Brechts in dieser Zeit entstandenen Gedichte gegen den "Anstreicher" Hitler als auch das Drama *Die Rundköpfe und die Spitzköpfe* sprechen, war er zutiefst enttäuscht, dass in den folgenden acht Monaten kein einziges *Fackel*-Heft erschien, in dem sich Kraus gegen die auch von ihm gehassten "Hakenkreuzler" ausgesprochen hätte. Und als dann im Oktober 1933 doch ein, wenn auch nur acht Seiten umfassendes Heft dieser bisher so engagierten Zeitschrift herauskam, war er noch enttäuschter, da sich in ihm—nach einer kurzen Gedenkrede auf Adolf Loos—lediglich jenes kurze, auf einen resignierenden Ton gestimmte Gedicht befand, das mit den Zeilen begann: "Man frage nicht, was all die Zeit ich machte. / Ich bleibe stumm, / und sage nicht warum," und dann mit dem Statement schloss: "Das Wort entschlief, als jene Zeit erwachte."[30] Ähnlich wie Kurt Tucholsky empfand er zu diesem Zeitpunkt, "dass Gewalt kein Objekt der Polemik, Irrsinn kein Gegenstand der Satire" sei.[31]

Fast alle aus Deutschland vertriebenen Linken fanden dieses Gedicht empörend. Gerade von Kraus, dem unerbittlichen Gegner der "verkehrten Welt," hatten sie einen besonders scharfen Angriff gegen die "braune Barbarei" im Nazireich und nicht einen so resignativ gestimmten Abgesang erwartet. Musste das nicht auch Brecht zutiefst verstören? Dass er nicht ebenfalls empört reagierte, wie manche seiner Gesinnungsfreunde von ihm erwarteten, beweist, dass er in Kraus weiterhin einen alle literarischen

Kleingeister überragenden Autor sah, dessen gesellschaftskritische Haltung er durchaus zu schätzen wusste und der ihm durch sein persönliches Entgegenkommen auch menschlich beeindruckt hatte. Ja, Brecht lud Kraus Anfang Juli 1933 sogar zweimal brieflich ein, ihn doch in Thüro bei Svendborg, wo er sich inzwischen niedergelassen hatte, zu besuchen.[32]

Doch danach verstimmte auch ihn das monatelange "Schweigen" von Karl Kraus über die inzwischen verübten Untaten der Nazifaschisten so sehr, dass er sich Ende 1933, also nach dem Erscheinen des besagten *Fackel*-Hefts, entschloss, sich wenigstens in einem Gedicht unter dem Titel "Über die Bedeutung des zehnzeiligen Gedichtes in der 888. Nummer der Fackel" (Oktober 1933) damit auseinzusetzen.[33] Es begann mit den Zeilen:

> Als das Dritte Reich gegründet war
> Kam von dem Beredten nur eine kleine Botschaft.
> In einem zehnzeiligen Gedicht
> Erhob er seine Stimme, einzig um zu klagen
> Dass sie nicht ausreiche

Brecht schloss mit den halbwegs verständnisvollen Zeilen:

> Als der Beredte sich entschuldigte
> Dass seine Stimme versage
> Trat das Schweigen vor den Richterstuhl
> Nahm das Tuch vom Antlitz und
> Gab sich zu erkennen als Zeuge.[34]

Darauf schickte er dieses Gedicht an einige Wiener Kraus-Freunde, um es in dem Band *Stimmen über Karl Kraus zum 60. Geburtstag* zu veröffentlichen, in dem es dann 1934, allerdings erst im Herbst, auch erschien.[35]

Ja, Brecht verfasste Anfang 1934 sogar noch mehrere kurze Prosatexte über Karl Kraus, die offenbar ebenfalls für die geplante Kraus-Festschrift gedacht waren.[36] In ihnen betonte er zwar wiederum, dass man gerade in einer "Zeit blutiger Verwirrung" als Autor Leistungen erbringen müsse, die "für unseren Kampf verwendbar sind," also etwas, was er auch von Kraus erwartete. Dennoch pries er in diesen Notaten Kraus weiterhin als einen bedeutenden gesellschaftskritischen Methodiker, ja verglich ihn in dieser Hinsicht sogar mit Marx und Engels, indem er erklärte:

> Die großen Marxisten haben untersucht, warum die Menschheit bei dem Aufbau der modernen Produktion in einen Zustand geraten musste, wo jeder neue Fortschritt, beinahe jede einzige Erfindung, die Menschen in immer tiefere Entmenschung hineintreiben muss. In einem riesigen Werk stellt Kraus, der erste Schriftsteller unserer Zeit, die Entartung und Verworfenheit der zivilisierten Menschheit dar. Als Prüfstein dient ihm die Sprache, das Mittel der Verständigung zwischen

> Mensch und Mensch. Seine Entdeckungen auf diesem Gebiet und die Methoden, die sie ermöglichen, sind Legion.[37]

Um so mehr war Brecht schockiert, als er Ende Juli 1934 jene *Fackel*-Hefte zu Gesicht bekam, in denen sich Kraus zum klerikalen Austrofaschismus des Dollfuß-Regimes bekannte und zugleich die Niederschlagung des Wiener Februaraufstandes rechtfertigte,[38] da Kraus darin die einzige Chance sah, den "Anschluss" Österreichs an Hitler-Deutschland zu verhindern, den zu diesem Zeitpunkt sogar viele Wiener Sozialdemokraten befürworteten.[39] Brecht reagierte auf diesen Gesinnungswandel mit dem Gedicht "Über den schnellen Fall des guten Unwissenden," in dem er seine bisherigen Verteidigung des langanhaltenden Schweigens von Karl Kraus zurücknahm und unter Bezugnahme auf sein Gedicht "Über die Bedeutung des zehnzeiligen Gedichtes in der 888. Nummer des Fackel" vom Oktober 1933 unmissverständlich erklärte:

> Als wir den Beredten seines Schweigens wegen entschuldigt hatten
> Verging zwischen der Niederschrift des Lobs und seiner Ankunft
> Eine kleine Zeit. In der sprach er.
>
> Er zeugte aber gegen die, deren Mund verbunden war
> Und brach den Stab über die, welche getötet waren.
>
> So bewies er
> Wie wenig die Güte hilft, die sich nicht auskennt
> und wie wenig der Wunsch vermag, die Wahrheit zu sagen
> Bei dem, der sie nicht weiß.
>
> Der da auszog gegen die Unterdrückung, selber satt
> Wenn es zur Schlacht kommt, steht er
> Auf der Seite der Unterdrücker.[40]

Das war hart formuliert, beweist aber weniger "Spott und Hohn als Zorn und Trauer," wie es bei Kurt Krolop heißt.[41] Um nicht als grundsätzlicher Kraus-Gegner missverstanden zu werden, ließ Brecht dieses Gedicht nicht drucken und es Kraus lieber in Wien von Helene Weigel persönlich übergeben.[42] Ja, er schrieb sogar im November 1934, dass sie bei ihren Wien-Besuchen weiterhin "nett" zu ihm sein solle, obwohl er zutiefst "bekümmert" sei, dass Kraus gegen die Floridsdorfer Arbeiter Stellung genommen habe, die sich gegen "die Beauftragten von Unternehmern, Bankiers und Grundbesitzern" zur Wehr gesetzt hätten.[43] Doch in seinen Veröffentlichungen der Folgezeit schwieg sich Brecht über Kraus stets aus. Nur in einem Kurzgedicht aus dem Jahr 1938 unter dem Titel "Tafel" heißt es einmal im Hinblick auf "Die uns geholfen haben": "In Österreich Karl Kraus."[44] Ein weiterer Hinweis auf Kraus findet sich lediglich in einem Notat seines *Arbeitsjournal* vom 15. Juli 1942, wo es heißt: "Möchte Schweyk machen, mit Szenen aus *Die letzten Tage der Menschheit* dazwischen geschnitten, so dass man oben die herrschenden Mächte sehen kann und unten den Soldaten, der ihre großen Pläne überlebt."[45]

Dass Brecht auch in seinen späteren DDR-Jahren—trotz aller Enttäuschung über den politischem "Umfall" von Kraus in den Jahren 1934-35—weiterhin an seiner Hochschätzung des "linken" Kraus der späten zwanziger Jahre festgehalten hat, haben aus eigener Erfahrung sowohl Caroline Cohn als auch Hans Mayer bestätigt.[46] Ja, dafür sprechen sogar noch drei andere Belege. So schlug Brecht in einem Brief vom 3. Januar 1952 an die Sektion Dichtkunst und Sprachpflege der Deutschen Akademie der Künste in Ostberlin vor, in die Lektürelisten der Grundschulen der DDR unbedingt den Text "Ein sterbender Soldat" aus dem Epilog der *Letzten Tage der Menschheit* von Kraus aufzunehmen.[47] Anfang Juli 1954 erklärte er in einem Gespräch mit Lotte Sternbach-Gärtner (d. i. Caroline Cohn), die ihn in Paris anlässlich eines vielbeachteten Gastspiels des Berliner Ensembles im Théâtre Sarah Bernhardt interviewte, im Hinblick auf Kraus:

> Ein echter Theatermensch! Jedesmal, wenn er in Berlin war, kam er an den Vormittagen zu uns ins Theater. Er wusste mehr über Theaterdinge als alle Kritiker, alle Fachleute zusammengenommen! Ich habe von ihm unendlich viel gelernt und wir hatten leidenschaftliche Diskussionen. Wie gerne würde ich einen Nestroy oder einen Shakespeare in seiner klugen und künstlerisch durchdachten Fassung spielen! Einmal werde ich es sicher tun![48]

Als darauf Franz Leschnitzer im Herbst 1954 einen marxistisch gemeinten Angriff auf Karl Kraus in *Sinn und Form* veröffentlichen wollte, teilte ihm Peter Huchel, der Herausgeber dieser Zeitschrift, in einem Brief vom 16. November dieses Jahres mit, dass

> das Redaktionskollegium (Brecht, Jhering, Renn) die Ansicht vertrete, dass man in der gegenwärtigen Situation unmöglich eine so scharfe Karl-Kraus-Abrechnung publizieren könne, zumal es in Westdeutschland weite Kreise gebe, die Kraus verehren und mit uns Schulter an Schulter gegen das Adenauer-Regime und für eine friedliche Lösung der deutschen Frage kämpfen . . . Brecht meinte, man könne Ihre Arbeit erst veröffentlichen, wenn man vorher eine positive Analyse über Karl Kraus gebracht habe.[49]

Dieser Aufatz erschien darum unter dem Titel "Der Fall Karl Kraus" erst nach Brechts Tod im November 1956 in der *Neuen Deutschen Literatur*.[50]

III

Welches Fazit soll man aus der Fülle dieser nachweisbaren Fakten, ob nun den persönlichen Begegnungen, den gedruckten oder den privaten Äußerungen oder den literarischen Bezugspunkten zwischen Kraus und Brecht ziehen? Schließlich gibt es hier sowohl Positives als auch Negatives, sowohl Gleichbleibendes als auch Sichwandelndes, sowohl Bedeutsames als auch Beiläufiges, so dass jeder Versuch, darin einen vergleichbaren Grundzug aufzuspüren, von vornherein unmöglich erscheint. Und doch spürt man bei näherer Betrachtung immer wieder, dass es zwischen diesen beiden Autoren nicht nur menschlich und literaturgeschichtlich, sondern auch ideologisch viele Berührungspunkte gibt.

Beginnen wir bei dem Versuch, vor allem die Gemeinsamkeiten zwischen Kraus und Brecht zu betonen, mit einem Hinweis auf ihr soziales Herkommen. Beide waren fehlgeleitete "Bürger," die zeit ihres Lebens das ihnen angeborene Oberklassenbewusstsein gewaltsam zu unterdrücken versuchten: der eine mit hasserfüllten, wenn auch hochgestochenen Invektiven gegen das ihn umgebende *juste Milieu*, der andere mit einer sich im Laufe der späten zwanziger Jahre angeeigneten marxistischen Grundorientierung, die sich an den revolutionären Zielen der Arbeiterklasse ausrichtete. Beim ersten Zusehen lassen sich diese beiden Haltungen kaum auf einen sie verbindenden ideologischen Nenner bringen. Und doch haben sie in ihrer Frontstellung gegen die "verkehrte Welt" durchaus manches Gemeinsame. Schließlich wollten beide in letzter Konsequenz das ganz Andere, ob nun eine Rückkehr zum "Ursprünglichen" wie bei Kraus,[51] oder ein Fortschreiten zu einer "besseren, bewohnbaren Welt" wie bei Brecht, in der es keine Kriege und keine Ausbeutung mehr geben würde. Sowohl Kraus als auch Brecht verfuhren dabei so radikal wie nur möglich: der Eine als Einzelgänger, der jedoch in den späten zwanziger Jahren auch nach möglichen Bundesgenossen Ausschau hielt, der Andere als selbsternannter Parteigänger der Arbeiterklasse, der er bis zu seinem Tode die Treue hielt. Beide waren daher unerbittliche Gegner des Nazifaschismus, wenn auch Kraus seine 1933-34 geschriebene *Dritte Walpurgisnacht*, in der er dem Dritten Reich in aller Schärfe die Leviten las, nicht zu veröffentlichen wagte, während Brecht nach 1933 in seinen Angriffen gegen den "Anstreicher" Hitler auch in der Öffentlichkeit, wie auf dem Pariser Kongress "Zur Verteidigung der Kultur" von 1935, kein Blatt vor den Mund nahm.

Obwohl also Brecht in den Jahren 1933-34 erst über das Schweigen von Kraus und dann über dessen Bekenntnis zum Dollfuß-Regime zutiefst enttäuscht war, ließ er sich auch in der Folgezeit nicht davon abbringen, in Kraus weiterhin einen seiner bedeutendsten Mentoren zu sehen. Schließlich hatte ihn in den schwierigen Jahren vor und nach der Machtübergabe an Hitler nicht nur dessen persönliche Zuneigung, sondern auch die satirische Schärfe der Krausschen Schriften nachhaltig beeindruckt. Dafür ließen sich viele der Brechtschen kritisch gemeinten Wortspiele und Zitatverdrehungen, und zwar nicht nur in seinen *Geschichten von Herrn Keuner*, den *Flüchtlingsgesprächen* sowie dem *Me-ti*, sondern auch in zahlreichen seiner Dramen, Essays und Gedichte aus dieser Zeit, heranziehen. Ebenso beeindruckend müssen die vielen öffentlichen "Vorlesungen" von Kraus auf den jungen Brecht gewirkt haben. Schließlich waren die Krausschen Offenbachiaden, mit denen er 1926 in Wien begann und darauf 1928 in Berlin fortsetzte, alles andere als bloße "Vorlesungen," mit denen er lediglich die französischen Grand Opéras und die Wagnerschen Musikdramen parodieren wollte. Indem Kraus dabei sowohl sprach, sang und gestikulierte, erwies er sich damit zugleich als ein wichtiger Anreger jener Form des Epischen Theaters, das auch Brecht in den gleichen Jahren mit seiner *Dreigroschenoper*, dem *Aufstieg und Fall der Stadt Mahagonny* sowie den darauffolgenden Lehrstücken anstrebte. In dieser Hinsicht gibt es daher für die an theatergeschichtlichen Aspekten Interessierten zweifellos noch viel zu entdecken.

Worauf man bei solchen Vergleichen in der älteren Sekundärliteratur zu Brecht bisher eingegangen ist, beschränkt sich meist auf rein Stoffliches. Eine der ersten, die auf derartige Bezüge aufmerksam machte, war Lotte Sternbach-Gärtner, die bereits 1958 darauf hinwies, wie sehr gerade *Die letzten Tage der Menschheit* auf Brechts Dramatik eingewirkt hätten.[52] Darauf war es Jens Malte Fischer, der 1974 im Hinblick auf *Die Unüberwindlichen* von Kraus erklärte:

> Wie hier Elemente des Dokumentartheaters, der Revue, des Zeitstücks, des surrealistischen Theaters, des Shakespearschen Monologs, des Kabaretts vereint werden, das steht weltliterarisch einzigartig da und hat nicht nur auf Brecht und das Theater der zwanziger Jahre Eindruck gemacht, sondern auch vieles vorweggenommen, was später als Neuerung bestaunt wurde.[53]

Georg Knepler stellte darauf 1984 vor allem den durchaus ähnlichen Antinaturalismus in den dramatischen Bemühungen von Kraus und Brecht heraus, mit dem beide versucht hätten, den Eindruck der "Scheinwirklichkeit" zu vermeiden.[54] Ja, Günter Hartung charakterisierte 1987 *Die letzten Tage der Menschheit* von Kraus im Sinne Brechts als durchaus "antiaristotelisch."[55] Nadežda Dakova betonte dagegen im gleichen Jahr, welche Bedeutung der Aphorismus und vor allem der sokratische Dialog für Kraus und Brecht gehabt hätten, wobei sie unter anderem auf die strukturelle Ähnlichkeit der Gespräche zwischen dem Nörgler und dem Optimisten in den *Letzten Tagen der Menschheit* mit den Dialogen zwischen Kalle und Ziffel in Brechts *Flüchtlingsgesprächen* hinwies.[56] Wohl die ausführlichste Analyse dieser Art legte 1991 Dieter Reinhold Krantz vor, der darauf hinwies, dass bereits Kraus, wie später Brecht, in seiner Abneigung gegen das "Schauspielertheater" die Opernbühne in einen "Hörsaal" zu verwandeln suchte, um den Zuschauern "keine Identifikation" mit den auftretenden Akteuren zu erlauben.[57] Beide hätten sich gleichermaßen um "Lehrstücke" bemüht, bei denen man den Schauspielern die Rolle von "Zeigenden" zugewiesen habe, was er anhand eines detaillierten Vergleichs der Stücke *Die letzten Tage der Menschheit* und *Furcht und Elend des Dritten Reichs* zu belegen versuchte. Eine solche Untersuchung wäre sicher noch überzeugender ausgefallen, wenn er dafür auch Stücke wie *Der aufhaltsame Aufstieg des Arturo Ui* sowie *Schweyk im zweiten Weltkrieg* herangezogen hätte.

Kurzum: in dieser Hinsicht ließe sich sicher noch vieles anführen. Dazu konnte jedoch in Form eines kürzeren Essays nur ein erster Ansatz geboten werden, in dem sowohl auf das Gemeinsame als auch auf das Trennende hingewiesen werden sollte, statt lediglich—wie meist zuvor—den grundsätzlichen Unterschied zwischen diesen beiden Autoren herauszustellen. Schließlich handelt es sich bei Kraus und Brecht um die zwei bedeutendsten Satiriker der deutschen Literatur des zwanzigsten Jahrhunderts, die beide zeit ihres Lebens gegen die reaktionäre Übermacht der bürgerlichen Gesellschaft anzuschreiben versuchten. Mag auch der Eine dabei von einer grundsätzlich negativistischen Sicht der herrschenden Verhältnisse ausgegangen sein, das heißt sich nie mit "der Möglichkeit einer Ablösung durch ein anderes Gesellschaftssystem befasst" haben,[58] während sich der Andere seit seiner Wendung zur Marxismus in den späten zwanziger Jahren—entgegen allen Zweifeln an der Realisierung einer andersgearteten, auf den Maximen des Sozialismus beruhenden Gesellschaft—immer wieder zu der Hoffnung auf eine "Veränderbarkeit" der bestehenden Verhältnisse durchgerungen hat. Dieser Unterschied sollte keineswegs übersehen werden. Aber in der Schärfe ihrer Kritik sowie ihrer Vorliebe für den lehrstückhaften Charakter des epischen Theaters waren sich beide durchaus einig. Und das bleibt letztlich das Vergleichbare im Unvergleichlichen ihrer literarischen Bemühungen.

Anmerkungen

[1] Kurt Krolop, "Bertolt Brecht und Karl Kraus," *Philologica Pragensia* 4 (1961): S. 95–112, 203–230; Werner Mittenzwei, *Das Leben des Bertolt Brecht oder Der Umgang mit den Welträtseln*, 2 Bde. (Berlin: Aufbau, 1986), I: S. 464–469; John Pizer: "Why Silence Becomes Golden: Brecht's Poetry on Karl Kraus," in *Brecht Yearbook* 28 (2003), S. 155–172; und Jan Knopf, *Bertolt Brecht: Lebenskunst in finsteren Zeiten* (München: Hanser, 2012), S. 262–277.

[2] Friedrich Rothe, *Karl Kraus: Die Biographie* (München: Piper, 2003).

[3] Leopold Liegler, *Karl Kraus und sein Werk* (Wien: Lányi, 1920) und Paul Schick, *Karl Kraus* (Reinbek: Rowohlt, 1965).

[4] Hans Hennecke, "Einer gegen alle. Ein kritischer Versuch über Karl Kraus," *Neue Deutsche Hefte* 5 (1959): S. 974–988, 1081–1096.

[5] Krolop, "Bertolt Brecht und Karl Kraus."

[6] Caroline Cohn, *Karl Kraus* (Stuttgart: Metzler, 1966).

[7] Rothe, *Karl Kraus*.

[8] James K. Lyon, "'Gleich zu gleich gesellt sich gern' und 'Gegensätze ziehen sich an.' Das dialektische Verhältnis Karl Kraus—Bertolt Brecht," in Joseph Strelka, Hrsg., *Karl Kraus: Diener der Sprache. Meister der Ethik* (Tübingen: Francke, 1992), S. 267–285.

[9] Georg Knepler, "Karl Kraus und die Bürgerwelt," *Sinn und Form* 27 (1975): S. 332–370.

[10] Bertolt Brecht, *Tagebücher 1920–1923: Autobiographische Aufzeichnungen 1920–1954*, in Herta Ramthun, Hrsg. (Frankfurt am Main: Suhrkamp, 1975), S. 146.

[11] *Fackel* 649–656 (1924): S. 45.

[12] *Fackel* 743–750 (1926): S. 86.

[13] Lyon, "'Gleich zu gleich gesellt sich gern,'" S. 268, und Werner Hecht, *Brecht Chronik* (Frankfurt am Main: Suhrkamp, 1997), S. 185.

[14] Alfred Pfabigan, *Karl Kraus und der Sozialismus: Eine politische Biographie* (Wien: Europaverlag, 1976), S. 222 ff.

[15] Cohn, *Karl Kraus*, S. 42.

[16] Georg Knepler, *Karl Kraus liest Offenbach: Erinnerungen. Kommentare. Dokumentationen* (Wien: Löcker, 1984), S. 213.

[17] Vgl. dazu demnächst meinen Aufsatz "Karl Kraus und Georg Knepler," in Johann Dvořák, Hrsg., *Karl Kraus und die Musik* (Wien, 2016).

[18] Ernst Josef Aufricht, *Erzähle, damit du dein Recht erweist* (Berlin: Propyläen, 1966), S. 73.

[19] Elias Canetti, "Die *Fackel* im Ohr," in Erdmut Wizisla, Hrsg., *Begegnungen mit Bertolt Brecht* (Leipzig: Lehmstedt, 2009), S. 83.

[20] Krolop, "Bertolt Brecht und Karl Kraus," S. 104, und Heinrich Fischer, "Erinnerung an Karl Kraus," *Forum* 8 (1961).

[21] Rothe, *Karl Kraus*, S. 24.

[22] Ebd.

[23] Ebd., S. 35.

[24] Krolop, "Bertolt Brecht und Karl Kraus," S. 99, und Cohn, *Karl Kraus*, S. 280.

[25] Hecht, *Brecht Chronik*, S. 257.

[26] Günther Rühle, *Theater für die Republik 1917–1933: Im Spiegel der Kritik* (Frankfurt am Main: Fischer, 1967), S. 949.

[27] *Fackel* 868–872 (1932): S. 1f. und 36f.

[28] Hecht, *Brecht Chronik*, S. 349.

[29] Mittenzwei, *Das Leben des Bertolt Brecht*, I: S. 468.

[30] *Fackel* 888 (1933): S. 4.

[31] *Fackel* 890–905 (1934): S. 26. Vgl. dazu auch Mittenzwei, *Das Leben des Bertolt Brecht*, I: S. 468, und Lyon, "'Gleich zu gleich gesellt sich gern,'" S. 284.

[32] Bertolt Brecht, *Werke. Große kommentierte Berliner und Frankfurter Ausgabe*, Werner Hecht u. a., Hrsg., Bd. 28 (Berlin und Frankfurt am Main: Aufbau und Suhrkamp, 1988–2000), 368–369 (Brief 490 und 491). Im Folgenden BFA Band, Seite.

[33] Vgl. zum Folgenden vor allem Krolop, "Bertolt Brecht und Karl Kraus," S. 203–230.

[34] BFA 14, 195–197.

[35] *Stimmen über Karl Kraus zum 60: Geburtstag*, hrsg. von einem Kreis dankbarer Freunde (Wien: Lányi, 1934), S. 11.

[36] BFA 22.2: 33–36.

[37] Ebd. 35.

[38] *Fackel* 890–905 (1934): S. 21ff.

[39] Rothe, *Karl Kraus*, S. 171.

[40] BFA 14, 216–217.

[41] Krolop, "Bertolt Brecht und Karl Kraus," S. 226.

[42] Werner Kraft, *Das Ja des Neinsagers: Karl Kraus und seine geistige Welt* (München: Boorberg, 1974), S. 219.

[43] BFA 28, 460 (Brief 613).

[44] BFA 15, 22.

[45] BFA 27, 114.

[46] Caroline Cohn, "Bert Brecht, Karl Kraus et le Kraus-Archiv," *Études Germanique* 4 (1956): S. 342–348, und Hans Mayer, "Karl Kraus und die Nachwelt," *Sinn und Form* 5 (1957): S. 945.

[47] BFA 30, 102 (Brief 1635).

[48] Lotte Sternbach-Gärtner (d. i. Caroline Cohn), "*Die letzten Tage der Menschheit* und das Theater von Bert Brecht," *Deutsche Rundschau* 84 (1958): S. 836.

[49] Zit. in Krolop, "Bertolt Brecht und Karl Kraus," S. 230.

[50] Franz Leschnitzer, "Der Fall Karl Kraus," *Neue Deutsche Literatur* 4 (1956): S. 59–82.

[51] Mayer, "Karl Kraus und die Nachwelt," S. 939 ff.

[52] Sternbach-Gärtner, "*Die letzten Tage der Menschheit* und das Theater von Bert Brecht," S. 836–842.

[53] Jens Malte Fischer, *Karl Kraus* (Stuttgart: Metzler, 1974), S. 30.

[54] Knepler, *Karl Kraus liest Offenbach*, S. 94.

[55] Günter Hartung, "Bertolt Brecht, Karl Kraus und die antifaschistische Satire," in *Brücken: Germanistisches Jahrbuch DDR-CSSR* (1987-1988), S. 27.

[56] Nadežda Dakowa, "Karl Kraus und Bertolt Brecht. Vergleichende Betrachtung einiger poetologischer Grundsätze," *Philologia* 19/20 (1987): S. 49.

[57] Dieter Reinhold Krantz, *Karl Kraus und Bertolt Brecht: Dramentheorie und Realisierung. Ein Vergleich* (PhD diss., Waterloo, Ontario, 1991), S. 43.

[58] Ebd. S. 63ff.

Book Reviews

Hermann Haarmann und Christoph Hesse, Hrsg. *Briefe an Bertolt Brecht im Exil* (1933–1949). Bd. 1, 1933–1936. Bd. 2, 1937–1945. Bd. 3, 1945–1949. Berlin und Boston: Walter de Gruyter, 2014. 2028 Seiten.

Was man von einer guten Briefedition erwartet, sind vor allem eine möglichst vollständige Wiedergabe aller vorhandenen Texte, eine sorgfältige Kommentierung, ein exaktes Namenregister, ein Verzeichnis aller Abkürzungen und Siglen, eine Chronologie der abgedruckten Briefe, die nötigen Copyrighthinweise sowie eine wohldurchdachte Einführung. Allen diesen Anforderungen werden die hier zu besprechenden Bände auf eine kaum zu überbietende Weise gerecht.

Während bisher fast nur jene Briefe in gedruckter Form vorlagen, die Johannes R. Becher, Walter Benjamin, Hanns Eisler, Lion Feuchtwanger, George Grosz, Karl Korsch, Erwin Piscator, Margarete Steffin und Sergej Tretjakow während der Exilzeit an Brecht geschrieben haben, wurden in diese Edition auch alle Briefe aufgenommen, die bisher—mehr oder weniger unbekannt—im Berliner Brecht-Archiv oder, oft über viele Länder verstreut, in anderen staatlichen Archiven oder privaten Nachlässen lagen und daher selbst manchen Brecht-Experten oder -Expertinnen unvertraut waren. Und so wuchs das Ganze, das höchst umständliche und zeitraubende Recherchen erforderte, von den ursprünglich ins Auge gefaßten fünfhundert Briefen auf fünfzehnhundert Briefe an, was zwangsläufig eine dreibändige Ausgabe erforderte.

Da sich die damit verbundene Sammeltätigkeit als höchst geld und zeitaufwendig erwies, war Hermann Haarmann, der Herausgeber, nicht nur auf die Unterstützung des Instituts für Kommunikationswissenschaft an der Freien Universität zu Berlin, sondern auch auf die Förderung der Fritz-Thyssen-Stiftung, der von Jan Philipp Reemtsma geleiteten Hamburger Stiftung zur Förderung von Wissenschaft und Kultur sowie der Preußischen Seehandlung und der Wall AG angewiesen. Außerdem halfen ihm bei der Herausgebertätigkeit anfänglich Toralf Teuber und dann vor allem Christoph Hesse, der die oft mühsame Kommentierung aller in diese Bände aufgenommenen Briefe übernahm, wodurch das Ganze nach jahrelanger Such und Aufbereitungsarbeit endlich dem Walter de Gruyter Verlag übergeben werden konnte.

Und so liegt diese Edition jetzt in drei gewaltigen Bänden vor, die zwar immens teuer sind, aber von jeder wissenschaftlich orientierten Bibliothek sofort angeschafft werden sollten. Nicht nur Brecht-Kenner und -Kennerinnen, sondern auch alle, die sich weiterhin mit den Exiljahren nach 1933 befassen, werden hier eine Fülle brauchbarer Materialien finden und zugleich neue Einsichten gewinnen, die für ihre weitere Arbeit nützlich sein könnten. Dabei wird ihnen auch die fünfzig Seiten umfassende Einleitung "Dear Bertie!" von Hermann Haarmann helfen, der im Spiegel der zwischen 1933 und 1949 an Brecht gerichteten Briefe sowohl dessen prekäre materielle Situation als auch seine im Exil weiterhin vertretenen politischen Grundpositionen so detailliert wie nur möglich darzustellen versuchte. Allerdings bediente sich Haarmann dabei stellenweise weiterhin jener Rhetorik des Kalten Kriegs, auf die selbst manche der eher konservativen Literaturkritiker inzwischen verzichtet haben. Natürlich soll die stalinistische Perversion des Marxismus in dem hier behandelten Zeitraum nicht verschwiegen werden, aber Brecht eine "gewollte Blindheit" ihr gegenüber vorzuwerfen, wie Haarmann das tut, ja ihn als einen sensiblen Ästheten hinzustellen, der gegen Ende seines Lebens einer weitgehenden Desillusionierung in politischer Hinsicht verfiel, hätte man als ideologisches Fazit von einem genauen Kenner der brechtschen Werke wie Hermann Haarmann an sich nicht erwartet.

Doch nicht nur die an politischen und historischen Themen und Fragestellungen, auch die an lebensgeschichtlichen Aspekten Interessierten werden beim Lesen oder zumindest Durchblättern dieser drei Bände auf ihre Kosten kommen. Schließlich findet sich in ihnen vieles, was menschlich bewegender ist als das, was der eher karge und brieffaule Brecht in diesen Jahren entweder selbst verfaßte oder zum Teil an andere delegierte. Und zu diesen Dokumenten gehören nicht nur die von einer grenzenlosen Liebe zeugenden, stellenweise ins Poetische überhöhten Briefe von Margarete Steffin, sondern auch die episch langen Lebensberichte der in den USA vereinsamten Elisabeth Hauptmann, welche direkt oder indirekt jene Ausstrahlungskraft unter Beweis stellen, die von Brecht nicht nur als Autor, sondern auch als Mensch ausging.

Jost Hermand, University of Wisconsin–Madison

Stephen Brockmann. *The Writers' State: Constructing East German Literature, 1945–1959.* Rochester, New York: Camden House, 2015. 368 pages.

The Writers' State is both conceptually and methodologically a kind of sequel to Stephen Brockmann's *German Literary Culture at the Zero Hour* of 2004. In this earlier book, rejecting the conventional notion of a bleak *Nullpunkt*, Brockmann explored the rich body of writing and wide range of literary activity that in fact characterized postwar German culture in all four occupation zones. The present study, its thematic focus East German literature from 1945 to 1959, makes a no less convincing plea for the reassessment of a crucial but largely neglected literary era within GDR studies. While scholarship especially on this side of the Atlantic—and it is this readership to which the book primarily appeals—has tended to focus on GDR literature of the 1960s, 1970s, and 1980s, it has, so Brockmann argues, mostly dismissed or ignored entirely the import and influence of literary discourse in the late 1940s' and 1950s' era of East German political and cultural reconstruction. As in his 2004 book, Brockmann attributes the cultural energy of the era he describes not to the authority of its institutions, but to the individual and interpersonal engagement of its writers and intellectuals. And once again he develops his arguments on the basis of extensive primary, secondary, and archival sources, and grounds these arguments within the larger framework of political-historical development.

Written in a style that can engage a wide audience, Brockmann's book provides a trove of information and critical assessment by which those interested in GDR studies (e.g., historians, political scientists, Germanists alike) are called upon to engage with the wide range of important issues and debates that were crucial to the development of literature and culture in the postwar period. In contrast to the conventional fare in GDR studies that gauges literature, especially in the *Aufbau* years, according to the degree of its reflection of or opposition to socialist reality at a given time, Brockmann argues on behalf of literature's autonomous qualities, as its own *assertion* of social and political reality—hence: "The Writers' State." For this purpose he relies above all on examples of narrative prose. Citing Katarina Clark's *Moscow, The Fourth Rome* (2011), he reminds us that the course of East German literature in many respects paralleled that of the Soviet Union in the 1930s, where the "novel of development or 'fictionalized biography' became . . . a synecdoche 'for the national biography, for the movement of man and nation over time'" (p. 17). Thus writers and intellectuals who, as the book's subtitle suggests, were "constructing East German literature" in its early years, created what we might call a "national literature" upon which succeeding generations would build. The resulting national consciousness inherent in GDR literature also allowed it to become—unlike the nation's newspapers—a crucial source of information for readers as to the actual, or possible, state of the society and the nation. During the 1950s this national consciousness was represented by the public engagement and literary works of notably Johannes R. Becher, Anna Seghers, and Bertolt Brecht, and in subsequent years by such writers as Christa Wolf, Heiner Müller, Volker Braun, and Christoph Hein.

Brockmann's book opens with a twenty-three-page introduction that presents his main arguments as to why we should renew our attention to early East German culture. We ignore it "at our peril" (p. 9), he writes: Early on, unlike its counterpart in the West, it raised questions of German identity as they pertained to the events of the Holocaust and the experiences of soldiers and civilians; its discussions and debates were still open, and relations with West German writers and intellectuals porous; finally, even if the GDR "was an experiment that failed," its literary culture did not as it "constituted an ambitious attempt to mobilize literature for the creation of a new and better state" (p. 13). This "ambitious attempt" is then examined in the ensuing chapters. *The Writers' State* is not a chronological survey in the traditional sense. Its four main sections are organized around what Brockmann calls "key nodal points" of East German literary and cultural history. As indicated by the section headings, these are: The Absence of State (1945); Constructing the State (1949); Contesting the State (1953); The State Cracks Down (1956). Each of the main sections is then subdivided into cultural-political concerns that circle around specific issues from a variety of discursive constellations and perspectives.

The central question governing this book is this: How is literature constituted in a society in which its role is equally important to its writers and intellectuals and to its political leaders? For the latter, Brockmann focuses almost exclusively on the positions taken by the acerbic SED leader Walter Ulbricht and his cohorts. For the former, Brockmann draws on myriad public statements and writings by such luminaries as Johannes R. Becher, Bertolt Brecht, Anna Seghers, and Georg Lukács, also the philosopher Wolfgang Harich and the publisher of Aufbau-Verlag Walter Janka, and writers less familiar to non-aficionados such as Eduard Claudius, Willi Bredel, and Erich Loest. These are only a fraction of the writers and intellectuals, also among them journalists and critics, whose activities are considered. More might have been said about the prolific Friedrich Wolf whose critical presence and contributions to culture in various venues were significant; and about the GDR president Wilhelm Pieck, respected and trusted unlike Ulbricht, and whose mitigating role often had conciliatory results, as in the *Lukullus* affair involving Brecht and Paul Dessau.

The discussions and debates included in this book are far too numerous, the range of their subtly interlocking topics much too intricate to be enumerated here. The controversies leading up to and following the Hungarian Revolution of 1956 in themselves, in some cases resulting in political trials and incarcerations, comprise numerous pages that, based on archival souces, reveal significant new insights into this crucial period. Brockmann's book is neither a history of literary texts and intellectual thought, nor a survey of *Kulturpolitik*. Rather, it intertwines these expressions of culture in such a way as to show us their always shifting critical interdependence. Accordingly, literary texts are not assessed solely on the basis of their aesthetic value, but primarily in terms of their specific cultural-political relevance, while *Kulturpolitik* involves not only SED policies but also its existence as created and defined by a wide range of writers and intellectuals. Reading this book is a must for anyone who wants to dig deeper into the complexity of early East German culture and to gain a better understanding of how intellectual and literary endeavor—that in other cultures would merely have been yet another passing trend or movement—became the vital cornerstone of a "writers' state."

Helen Fehervary, The Ohio State University

Pamela Katz. *The Partnership: Brecht, Weill, Three Women and Germany on the Brink*. New York: Anchor Books, 2015. 496 pages.

This new biography of the collaboratory group that includes Bertolt Brecht, Kurt Weill, Helene Weigel, Lotte Lenya, and Elisabeth Hauptmann is an interesting addition to the non-academic works about Brecht in English. Pamela Katz has woven the stories of her main characters around their relationships and their productions. As a playwright herself, she writes about writers and composers, actors and actresses in a tone of immediacy, and in a less judgmental and strident way than used in other biographies. Brecht biographers tend to cast Kurt Weill as a talented musician who needed Brecht's ideas and scripts to create their box office successes, and Weill biographers tend to cast Brecht as a heartless cad surrounded by intellectual women partners to do his work for him.

Brecht, Weill, Lenya, Weigel, and Hauptmann were radically dissonant personalities but in accord with aesthetic and political goals, and their working habits, as flawed as they may have been, were somehow compatible. Brecht procrastinated, Hauptmann would stay up nights finishing the manuscripts they had edited the day before, Weill spent days alone composing until his projects were almost finished. The *Mahagonny Songspiel* in 1927 was their training ground, and they were able to move on and produce *The Threepenny Opera*; *The Yes-Sayer, The No-Sayer*; *Happy End*; *Rise and Fall of the City of Mahagonny*; and a ballet, *The Seven Deadly Sins*.

Katz writes the story of writing the stories. Hauptmann's translation of John Gay's *Beggar's Opera* started a stream of coincidences that resulted in writing one of the most popular musicals worldwide, *The Threepenny Opera*, and the song they composed for the star, "Mack the Knife" has been recorded by everyone from Brecht to Bobby Darin to Sting. Before that box office hit, they had arranged texts first collected in a parody of a home "book of prayer" into the "Mahagonny Songspiel," and then into their musical, *The Rise and Fall of the City of Mahagonny*.

The Partnership has fifteen chapters with generous notes to help readers understand the context of these intellectuals and their times. They only worked together from 1927 until they left Berlin to escape National Socialism in 1933. Both Brecht and Weill spent some time in Paris hoping that the Nazis would be short-lived, and worked on a ballet, *Seven Deadly Sins*, finally leaving for different countries, Weill to New York and Brecht to Scandanavia with his family. The chapters tell the story of their work together in those few, but extremely productive years, and include a biography for each of her characters, woven into the chronology of their collaboration. Photos illustrate their differences and document early productions of the *Mahagonny Songspiel* and the *Threepenny Opera.*

Other reviewers have criticized assumptions Ms. Katz made about the characters' actions and motivations, reminding readers that she is a scriptwriter and novelist. The reliability of the information about the artistic and intellectual context in Weimar Germany has also been questioned (by Alexis Soloski in the *TLS* of 5 January 2016), but with all of the criticism, *The Partnership*: *Brecht, Weill, Three Women and Germany on the Brink* is helpful as an English language text that describes the constellation of influences on Brecht's and Weill's works in Weimar Germany. As the *Times Literary Supplement* so accurately describes Brecht's presence in England and America in the review of Stephen Parker's biography *Bertolt Brecht: A Literary Life*, both England and the United States "are, if not quite Brecht-free zones, nevertheless territories where he has persistently been misunderstood, unappreciated, unloved and under suspicion . . .; and the man and his ideas are routinely and casually butchered" (13 August 2014).

Katz looks at her protagonists' backgrounds, at their approach to work ethic, and their personal lives, and provides a layman's context for the political situation, as well as sources for their theories about the theater. The descriptions may lack a historian's exactitude, and there is little about the actual political gridlock resulting in government by decree. Metaphors like the "darkening clouds" of National Socialism describe their context, and some geography has not been carefully researched, as pointed out by Modris Eksteins in the *Wall Street Journal* about their whereabouts while writing the *Threepenny Opera* in St-Cyr-sur-Mer, not Le Lavandou—but Katz's goal is to tell the story of their work together. The unsung heroine of Brecht's pre-war Berlin years, Elisabeth Hauptmann, she describes as an introvert, highlighting Hauptmann's preference for working behind the scenes: "She was powerfully drawn to anonymity." An example of her working habits is her uncredited inclusion of her own English song texts in their musical, *The Rise and Fall of the City of Mahagonny*: "The Alabama Song," and the "Benares Song," both of which have the handwritten note "Elisabeth Hauptmann" on the archived originals. These songs were so popular that Otto Klemperer sang them to friends, high praise indeed for the texts and the writer who created them. Hauptmann's talent is described as dependent on Brecht: "The poem could never have been written without her profoundly symbiotic relationship with Brecht," though Hauptmann had been writing poetry and short texts in German and English long before she met Brecht, and first wrote the songs at the very beginning of what became that close relationship, when she was helping edit his first book of poetry, *Hauspostille*, back in 1925.

This book provides a captivating look at a group of artists and how these artists managed to produce some of the twentieth century's most intellectual and entertaining art. More about their political and historical context, the Weimar Republic, would have supported the story. Elisabeth Hauptmann's role in most of Brecht's early works is sometimes lacking, but the "remarkable Hauptmann" is credited with important texts and ideas, especially her support of Brecht's "teaching plays," which included using a Japanese "Noh"-play she had translated for their "Lehrstück," or teaching play project *The Yes-Sayer / The No-Sayer*. Many Brecht/Weill productions would not have been as successful nor been written without Hauptmann's constant support.

Paula Hanssen, Webster University

Christian Hippe (im Auftrag des Literaturforums im Brecht-Haus), Hrsg. *Über Brechts Romane*. Berlin: Verbrecher Verlag, 2015. 224 Seiten.

Weder beim breiten Publikum noch in der Literaturwissenschaft hat Brechts Romanwerk auch nur im Entferntesten jenes Maß an Aufmerksamkeit gefunden, das seinem Theaterschaffen und seiner Lyrik zuteil wurde. Das liegt sicherlich nicht zuletzt an der außerordentlich uneinheitlichen und zudem vielfach fragmentarischen Gestalt dieses Textkorpus. Vollendet und zu Lebzeiten des Autors als Ganzes veröffentlicht wurde lediglich der umfangreiche *Dreigroschenroman*, der stofflich an die berühmte *Dreigroschenoper* anknüpft und in die frühe Phase des Exils gehört. Von dem Projekt eines historischen Romans *Die Geschäfte des Herrn Julius Caesar* führte Brecht während der Exilzeit immerhin große Partien im Zusammenhang aus, die die Konzeption des Werkes deutlich erkennen lassen, bevor er die Arbeit abbrach, während ein als Intellektuellen-Satire angelegter Tui-Roman schon im Stadium der Planungen und Vorbereitungen stecken blieb: Es liegen zahlreiche Bruchstücke und Notizen vor, doch kam Brecht offenbar nicht einmal dazu, ein definitives Handlungsgerüst zu entwickeln. Im Übrigen besteht das Material zu seiner Beschäftigung mit der Gattung Roman aus verschiedenen kleineren Fragmenten und Ideen sowie aus einer Anzahl theoretischer Reflexionen.

Der vorliegende Band vereint die Beiträge zu den Brecht-Tagen 2014, die speziell dem Romancier Brecht gewidmet waren. Neben acht wissenschaftlichen Vorträgen, die ganz unterschiedliche Aspekte ins Auge fassen und naturgemäß ein äußerst heterogenes Gesamtbild ergeben, stehen drei Podiumsgespräche mit Gegenwartsschriftstellern und Publizisten. Die Ergebnisse dieser Diskussionen mit Jörg-Uwe Albig, Georg M. Oswald, Gerhard Henschel und anderen fallen leider ziemlich enttäuschend aus, weil erstaunlicherweise kein einziger der Beteiligten so recht etwas mit Brechts unkonventionellen Romanen anfangen kann oder sich auch nur näher auf deren experimentelle Techniken einlassen will. Angesichts der Erwartungen und der literaturtheoretischen Idealvorstellungen, die dabei bisweilen zur Sprache kommen, kann das freilich auch nicht verwundern: Wer von einem Roman beispielsweise "episches Behagen" in breiten, plastischen Schilderungen verlangt—so Stephan Speicher im Gespräch mit Lorenz Jäger (S. 14)—wird bei Brecht in der Tat nicht fündig werden!

Von den Aufsätzen behandeln die meisten sehr spezielle Gesichtspunkte, die hier nur kurz benannt seien. Martin Brady stellt in knapper Form den Film *Geschichtsunterricht* von Jean-Marie Straub und Danièle Huillet, eine Adaption des *Caesar*-Fragments, aus dem Jahre 1972 vor; Ernest Schonfield diskutiert die manipulative, verschleiernde Rhetorik der Figuren im *Dreigroschenroman*, die von Brecht ideologie- und sprachkritisch vorgeführt wird; und Marja-Leena Hakkarainen rückt Brechts Erzählprosa in die Tradition der menippischen Satire und der karnevalesken Literatur, wobei es allerdings überwiegend bei der Aufzählung recht oberflächlicher Motiv- und Strukturparallelen bleibt. Frank D. Wagner rekonstruiert anhand der Tui-Fragmente und der *Flüchtlingsgespräche* das Hegel-Bild Brechts und zeigt seine Auseinandersetzung mit der vielberufenen Unverständlichkeit und dem harmonisierenden metaphysischen Systemdenken des Philosophen, aber auch das Porträt Hegels als eines "Humoristen," das geeignet ist, die Distanz abzubauen und das Schwerverständliche näher zu bringen; Helen Fehervary gibt einen kursorischen Überblick über die Parallelen zwischen Brecht und Anna Seghers, die sich indes auf die Vielschichtigkeit und ästhetische Komplexität sowie auf die generelle politische Funktionalisierung des epischen Schreibens beschränken und damit auf einer sehr allgemeinen Ebene bleiben, während die literarischen Techniken der beiden Schriftsteller im Einzelnen doch höchst unterschiedlich aussehen.

Die gewichtigsten Beiträge des Bandes erörtern dagegen grundsätzliche Probleme, die Brechts Poetik des Romans und ihre praktische Umsetzung betreffen, und versuchen auf diesem Wege, auch die besondere Stellung des Autors in der Geschichte der modernen Romanliteratur genauer zu bestimmen. Sophia Ebert bringt die für Brecht zentrale Frage auf den Punkt: Er sucht nach "schriftstellerischen Verfahrensweisen, mit Hilfe derer politische und ökonomische Zusammenhänge anschaulich gemacht werden können, ohne sie einfach nur abzubilden, die das Interesse des Publikums wecken und es in einer aktiven, nicht-konsumierenden Rezeptionshaltung schulen" (S. 193). Es geht also um den entscheidenden Schritt weg vom traditionellen Individualroman, der auf plastische Gestaltung, Psychologie und Einfühlung setzt, um neuartige Möglichkeiten, die strukturellen Bedingungen der modernen Lebenswelt mit Hilfe narrativer Formen zu erfassen und zu durchdringen—und zugleich notwendigerweise um den Anspruch, der Leserschaft (ähnlich wie dem Publikum des epischen Theaters) eine nüchterne, kritisch-distanzierte Einstellung nahe zu legen. Konkret widmet sich Ebert einem bislang kaum beachteten fragmentarischen Kriminalroman-Projekt, an dem Brecht 1933 gemeinsam mit Walter Benjamin arbeitete und in dem es nicht nur um einen Mord, sondern auch um ausgedehnte Erpressungsmanöver vor dem Hintergrund des zeitgenössischen Aktienrechts gehen sollte. Sie arbeitet einleuchtend den Experimentalcharakter des Vorhabens heraus, dessen Schöpfer sowohl die Chancen einer kollektiven Produktion als auch die politische bzw. gesellschaftskritische Umfunktionierung populärer künstlerischer Formen und Genres erproben wollten—zwei Themen, denen Brecht bekanntlich auch sonst große Bedeutung beimaß. So ergeben sich aufschlussreiche Einblicke in Brechts (und Benjamins) epische Strategien und Zielsetzungen, was umso beachtlicher ist, als Ebert sich nur auf eine äußerst schmale Materialbasis stützen kann, die überwiegend bloß aus spärlichen Notizen besteht.

Dem *Dreigroschenroman* wendet sich Stefan Willer zu, der das Thema Wirtschaft in den Vordergrund rückt. Er erörtert zunächst Brechts finanzielle Lage zu Beginn des Exils und geht dann auf die "Ökonomie der Selbstbearbeitung" (S. 93) ein, die sich in der produktiven "zitierenden" Aufnahme des bereits in der Oper gestalteten Dreigroschenstoffs und seiner Figuren zeigt. Zuletzt werden die einzelnen Handlungsstränge und die verschiedenen Gestalten des Romans in ihrer Determiniertheit durch ökonomische Zwänge betrachtet. Für die Frage nach Brechts allgemeiner Romanpoetik ist diese Partie des Aufsatzes gewiss die interessanteste, weil sich hier erhellende Beobachtungen zu der Kernfrage finden, wie übergreifende sozio-ökonomische Strukturen und Mechanismen überhaupt *erzählt* und in der Interaktion individueller Protagonisten abgebildet werden können.

Der am stärksten systematisch und gattungspoetologisch geprägte Zugriff kennzeichnet schließlich den Aufsatz von Klaus-Detlef Müller zum *Caesar*-Fragment. Wie sich das epische Theater programmatisch von einem idealtypisch erfassten aristotelischen Theaterkonzept abgrenzt, so entwirft Brecht in seinen theoretischen Überlegungen—mit einer gewagten Begriffsprägung!—auch einen "aristotelischen Roman," um vor diesem Hintergrund sein eigenes Modell profilieren zu können: Der "antiaristotelische Roman" soll, um der modernen Wirklichkeitserfahrung gerecht zu werden, mit dem Primat des autonom handelnden, psychologisch komplexen Individuums brechen und damit zugleich das Einfühlungsangebot an den Leser durch distanzierende Verfremdungsstrategien ersetzen. Anhand der *Geschäfte des Herrn Julius Caesar* erläutert Müller, wie Brecht seine Vorstellungen umsetzt: durch die satirische Entlarvung vermeintlich "großer" historischer Gestalten, wie sie die traditionelle bürgerliche Historiographie so gerne verherrlichte, durch ein materialistisches Geschichtsbild, das die altbekannten antiken Quellen in völlig neue Zusammenhänge stellt, aber beispielsweise auch durch eine virtuos gehandhabte Vielfalt der Figuren- und Erzählperspektiven.

Brechts Bemühungen um den Roman sind ein essenzieller Bestandteil seines Schaffens, und seine Romanpoetik bleibt in ihrem Anspruch und ihrem Reflexionsniveau keineswegs hinter den entsprechenden Überlegungen zum Theater und zur Lyrik zurück. Überdies demonstrieren zumindest der *Dreigroschenroman* und *Die Geschäfte des Herrn Julius Caesar*, dass Brechts Experimente mit neuen Formen, Techniken und Sujets des epischen Erzählens durchaus zu spannenden, intellektuell und ästhetisch anregenden Resultaten führen konnten, dass sich also realistische Belehrung und vergnüglicher Genuss auch hier—wie beim epischen Theater—keineswegs ausschließen. Diesen Themenkomplex systematisch zu erörtern, bleibt nach wie vor eine wichtige Aufgabe der Brecht-Forschung. Der vorliegende Sammelband gibt dazu einige nützliche Impulse. Wünschenswert wäre aber vor allem eine aktuelle monographische Untersuchung von umfassendem Zuschnitt, die insbesondere auch die Einbettung der Brecht'schen Erzählkunst in das (literar-)historische Umfeld der zeitgenössischen Avantgarde zu berücksichtigen hätte.

Ulrich Kittstein, Universität Mannheim

David Barnett. *Brecht in Practice: Theatre, Theory and Performance*. London: Bloomsbury, 2014. 257 pages.

In a period when questions of Brechtian theater have been revitalized with publications of books such as *Brecht on Performance* (Marc Silberman, 2015) and *Bertolt Brecht: A Literary Life* (Stephen Parker, 2014), a new book on Brechtian theater by David Barnett further confirms and defines this trend. An overview of this revivalist trend immediately brings to light one of its unique characteristics in the context of Brecht. This characteristic, evident in almost all recent publications on Brecht, articulates a shift from biographical life to literary life in general and theory to praxis in particular. On the first page, Barnett confirms this shift when he writes that the book "aims to introduce students, practitioners and those interested in theatre in general to the principles and nuances of Brecht's thought and its implications for the practice of making theatre." In other words, the book "reintroduces" Brecht by presenting him not only as an important theoretician of theater but also as a practitioner of theater.

Broadly, the book debunks "the myths" (8) surrounding Brechtian theater, in two stages. First, Barnett re-examines a selection of Brecht's important concepts and their usage in literary history, beginning with the meaning of the term "Brechtian" to demonstrate how it is misunderstood across the length and breadth of literary history. He cites examples to show how the term is misinterpreted either to acknowledge "the reality of the theater" (1) or to underline productions that are "slow, ponderous, didactic" (1).

Once Barnett has underlined the problems associated with the secondary literature on Brecht, he turns to actual productions. Here again, he demonstrates how the problems related to Brechtian concepts remain unresolved: "Brecht's plays neither implicitly nor explicitly provoke a Brechtian production: directors can take and have taken a great many approaches to staging them that have followed, resisted or ignored Brecht's ideas for a dialectical theatre" (181). Barnett believes that the reason behind failed attempts to understand Brecht's idea of theater is the "de-politicization" (4) of Brecht. To emphasize this point, Barnett tracks down the genesis of de-politicization by reminding us of the epic moment when Martin Esslin separated Brecht's art from his politics. For Barnett, this separation of art from politics has remained a crucial reason behind our erroneous notions of Brechtian theater. Thus, the book offers Brecht's "politicized positions on theatre making" (6).

Barnett proceeds from Brecht's political principles throughout the book and does not separate Brecht's art from his politics, as has been done by numerous critics in the past. As a part of his methodological approach, Barnett clearly states that the theme running across the eight chapters of the book "is method over means" (5). That is to say that Brecht's stage innovations and radical stagecraft (his "means") are all products of the way he thought about the world (his "method"). Over the course of 245 pages, readers learn how Brecht's theoretical concepts can be applied to practice (and thus the title of the book *Brecht in Practice*). Barnett with his own examples and coinage (such as "micro-*Fabel*") demonstrates how one might apply Brecht's method in practice.

The first six chapters of the book engage with Brecht's much discussed concepts and practices and enlighten the readers in how to make "theatre politically" (160). The seventh chapter, "Brecht, Documentation and the Art of Copying," embarks on a journey often avoided or always discussed in hushed tones. Brecht, in the course of his career, courted many controversies for not acknowledging his literary sources. As if to clarify Brecht's stand on copying, in this chapter Barnett reflects on the "constructive role" Brecht ascribed to copying (161). Barnett further throws light on the condition of theater documentation in the 1940s by focusing on the transformation process of Brecht's *Notate* (records of rehearsals) to the "model book."

One of the most insightful chapters is the eighth, called "Using Brecht's Method," which shows the practical application of the much debated and discussed concept of the dialectical method. Barnett chooses two examples—*The Resistible Rise of Arturo Ui* (1941) and Patrick Marber's *Closer* (1997)—and demonstrates through them the application of the dialectical method.

Barnett is to be commended for how he engages not only with the plays but also the short stories and parables in order to throw light on Brecht's idea of dialectical theater. One such engagement is in chapter 3 where Barnett uses the parable "Meeting Again" featuring the fictional Mr. Keuner, to elucidate the working of dialectics. The example of this parable, which is only two lines in its entirety, works well in explaining the dialectical method of Brecht. This example further shows how Barnett brings to light the invisible political thread of dialectics that runs across the oeuvre of Brecht. Furthermore, with this example, Barnett states that one essential feature of a Brechtian performance is the use of dialectical method. For Barnett, "the Brechtian method, then, is the dialectical investigation of dramatic material" (84).

An important quality of the book is its lucidity. Barnett's style of writing is not only crystal clear but also jargon free. Barnett simplifies even the most complicated concepts such as *Haltung* and *Arrangement* in the course of a couple of pages. To make the narrative even more concise, Barnett has organized each chapter into many subparts using subheadings. These subheadings are programmed to keep the readers focused, and in a way they work like Brecht's text panels (an instance of the *Verfremdungseffekt*), as they inform the readers what is about to come and thus keep them active.

Although subheadings and bulleted points help the readers, sometimes an excess of them turns the book into an undergraduate reader. Despite this, the book is an important and timely contribution to Brechtian scholarship, and probably a starting point for all the practitioners and students of Brecht.

Prateek Prateek, The University of Queensland

Matthias Neumann und Mayte Zimmermann, Hrsg. *In Gemeinschaft und als Einzelne_r*. Mülheimer Fatzerbücher 3. Berlin: Neofelis, 2014. 202 Seiten.

Aller guten Dinge sind drei! Nach den *Mülheimer Fatzerbüchern 1* und *2* von 2012 und 2013 über *Kommando Fatzer* bzw. *Räume, Orte Kollektive* geht es nun um den Aspekt der Gemeinschaft aus historischer, soziologischer, politischer und vor allem literatur- und theaterwissenschaftlicher Sicht, ein Begriff der mit der *community*-Bewegung wieder an Aktualität gewonnen hat.

Am aktuellsten sind sicherlich die Abschnitte über *Fatzer* und das politische Theater in Athen. Wegen der geopolitischen Situation in Europa sowie angesichts der politischen Lage in Griechenland und dem Elend der dortigen Flüchtlinge (siehe deren Texte) ist die Darstellung der Workshops und der (Theater)arbeit "zwischen Verweigerung und Organisation" (S. 145) von "FATSA / KOINA" in Athen besonders spannend, hier erhält das "Verhältnis des_der Einzelnen zur Gemeinschaft" eine ganz besondere "Dringlichkeit" (S. 146). *Fatzer* dient dabei "als Versuchsanordnung" für "kollektive Alternativen des Zusammenarbeitens und -lebens 'zur

Selbstverständigung'" (S. 146), wie Brecht es nennt. Mit Derridas Begriff der "'Politik(en) der Freundschaft'" sollen "Assoziationen" "freier, selbstbewusster Individuen" (S. 170) entstehen, denn, wie Marx und Engels betonen: "die freie Entwicklung eines jeden [ist] die Bedingung für die freie Entwicklung aller"—und nicht umgekehrt! Durch "den Rundgang des Fatzer durch die Stadt Athen" wird Griechenland "als ein Ort der 'Krise' gegenwärtig" (S. 17): "*Athen* ist heute das Arschloch Europas—ein Labor des Kapitalismus" und d. h. "ein technokratisch verwaltetes Experimentierfeld des ins Stocken geratenen Triumphzuges des Neoliberalismus" (S. 154). Das "selbstverwaltete EMBOS-Theater in Athen, welches im November nach jahrelangem Leerstand von Künstler_innen und Anarchist_innen besetzt und reanimiert wurde," steht dem als "'Inseln der Unordnung' oder ein() 'positive(s) Loch()'" (S. 159) entgegen. Im "Athener Lehrstück" (S. 146) mit seiner "existentielle(n) Krise des Sozialen" geht es jedoch nicht allein um Fatzers "Exodus und Desertion" (S. 161) im Kontext von Individuum und Gemeinschaft, also um inhaltliche Fragen, sondern gleichermaßen um neue ästhetische Formen und veränderte Arbeitsweisen. Das Nachdenken über das Theater in der Krise verbunden mit Überlegungen, wie man "*politisch* politisches Theater Machen" (S. 181) kann, führt zu einem "Theater der Sorge" (S. 181): "unter Berücksichtigung eines erweiterten Sorge-Begriffs (als Interesse, Anteilnahme und Solidarität)" soll "ein Theater der Aufmerksamkeit und Sensibilisierung" (S. 199–200) entstehen.

Der vorliegende Band bezieht sich wieder auf die Mülheimer Fatzer-Tage, er enthält neben den Abschnitten zum politischen Theater in Athen vier theoretische Texte vom Symposium. Juliane Spitta zeigt Fatzer vor der Folie der "gemeinschaftliche(n) und gemeinschaftsstiftende(n) Erfahrung" (S. 24) des Ersten Weltkriegs und diskutiert am Beispiel von Ferdinand Tönnies die nur in der deutschen Sprache existierende Trennung von Gemeinschaft und Gesellschaft; Claas Morgenroth verlängert diese Diskussion um Ansätze von Jean-Luc Nancy, Giorgio Agamben und Maurice Blanchot. Martin Kaluza konzentriert sich auf Fragen der Moral und Interessenkonflikte und Mayte Zimmermann thematisiert das Paradox, dass mit der Auseinandersetzung um das Asoziale in Brechts Theatertext diese Haltung schon "verpasst und verspielt" (S. 13) werde.

Es folgen zwei Praxisberichte über Fatzer-Gastspiele in Mülheim: Stefan Suschkes Inszenierung von *Fatzer* in Marburg und die theatrale Veranstaltung *Scheiß auf die Ordnung der Welt* des Jugendtheaters P 14 der Volksbühne Berlin stehen für zwei theatrale Möglichkeiten, sich mit Brechts *Fatzer* in der Bühnenfassung von Heiner Müller auseinanderzusetzen. Sehr unterschiedlich sind die Installation *You can wash all that shit away* von Karin Hylla und der "Versuch, auf dem Podium sich einzurichten" von Scholtysik und Schauf, in dem es um die Potentialität des *Fatzer* für ein Laientheater mit Blick auf "Reden ohne Bedeutung, Handeln ohne Konsistenz" (S. 136) geht und sich "die Frage nach dem Verhältnis des

Einzelnen zu einem Ganzen auf inhaltlicher" und im Spielprozess zugleich "als formale Frage" stellt (S. 139). Die zentralen Fragestellungen sind dabei die "Konflikte von Gemeinschaft und Einzelnem_Einzelner" (S. 7), das "soziale(. . .) oder politische(. . .) Gemeinsam-Sein" (S. 9) und die "Anerkennung der Daseinsberechtigung von Differenz" (S. 11).

Diese wieder mit vielen Farbfotos versehene und dadurch sehr anschaulich und lebendig wirkende Publikation liefert am Beispiel von Brechts *Fatzer* sehr unterschiedliche Zugänge zu dem Aspekt Gemeinschaft, deren Möglichkeiten und Begrenzungen, auch und gerade mit Blick auf die politische Theater-Arbeit von Gruppen oder Kollektiven.

Florian Vaßen, Leibniz Universität Hannover

Contributors

Sabine Berendse, the daughter of Hans Bunge, is a Librarian and Information Specialist in Cardiff, Wales, and a freelance translator.

Lin Cheng hat in Qingdao (Ocean University of China), Beijing (Renmin University of China) und Tübingen (Universität Tübingen) Germanistik und Deutsche Literatur studiert. Zur Zeit promoviert er an der Freien Universität Berlin und seit 2013 erforscht er im Rahmen seiner Dissertation *Das Unheimliche der Puppe in der deutschen Literatur um 1800 und 1900*. Forschungsschwerpunkte von Lin Cheng sind vor allem literarische Phantastik und die wechselhafte Beeinflussung der deutschen und chinesischen Literatur und Kultur.

Kattrin Deufert und Thomas Plischke (gemeinsam der Künstlerzwilling deufert&plischke) leben und arbeiten in Berlin. In den letzten fünfzehn Jahren realisierten sie zahlreiche Theaterprojekte, die sich mit Situationen künstlerischer Produktion und der komplexen sozialen Dynamik und Logistik künstlerischer Prozesse befassen. Ihre Arbeiten reichen über den Rahmen von Tanz und Theater hinaus und fokussieren die individuelle Teilhabe und den sozialen Alltag im künstlerischen Geschehen. In ihren Arbeiten entstehen immer unterschiedliche künstlerische Umgebungen, die den Alltag aufheben, indem sie ihn umfassend in die Kunst integrieren und aufarbeiten.

Laura Ginters is Chair of the Department of Theatre and Performance Studies at the University of Sydney. Her current research is focused on historical and contemporary rehearsal processes and production histories, including German theater of the 18th and 19th centuries, and early productions of Brecht in Australia. Her translations of German and Austrian plays have been performed, published and adapted, and she also works as a script assessor and dramaturg. She serves on the editorial board for the journals *About Performance*, *Australasian Drama Studies Journal* and *Philament*, and is a member of the Seymour Theatre Centre's Artistic Advisory Group.

Jost Hermand, Vilas Research Professor Emeritus of German Culture at the University of Wisconsin-Madison and Honorary Professor at the Humboldt University, Berlin; co-founder of the International Brecht Society and co-editor of the first ten volumes of the *Brecht Yearbook*; publications on

Brecht: *Brecht und die bildenden Künste* (1983), *"Das ewig Bürgerliche widert mich an." Brecht-Aufsätze* (2001), and *Die Toten schweigen nicht. Brecht-Aufsätze* (2010).

Jürgen Hillesheim, Leiter der Brecht-Forschungsstätte Augsburg, Professor h.c. der Staatl. Iwan Franko Universität, Zhytomyr, Ukraine, PD an der Universität Augsburg. Promotion mit einer Arbeit über Thomas Mann, Habilitation mit einer Arbeit zu Brechts Epischem Theater. Seit 2002 Mitherausgeber des Brecht Yearbooks, von 2006 bis 2015 Mitherausgeber der Buchreihe "Der neue Brecht," seit 2016 Herausgeber der Buchreihe "Brecht – Werk und Kontext." Hillesheim ist Autor bzw. Herausgeber von über 30 Büchern und über 100 Beiträgen zu Themen der Neueren Deutschen Literaturgeschichte, vor allem zu Wilhelm Müller, Georg Büchner, Thomas Mann, NS-Literatur, Musikrezeption in der Literatur und Bertolt Brecht.

Cora Lee Kluge, Department of German at the University of Wisconsin–Madison, specializes in German-American studies, especially the history of immigration from German-speaking lands and America's German-language literature. In addition to articles on various aspects of modern German literature and culture, she is known for her *Other Witnesses: An Anthology of Literature of the German Americans, 1850–1914* (2007). She has served as the editor of *Monatshefte* and is Co-Director of the UW–Madison's Max Kade Institute for German-American Studies, where her current larger project concerns Milwaukee's German-language theater.

Klaus-Dieter Krabiel, Studium der Germanistik, Anglistik und Philosophie in Frankfurt am Main und Manchester; 1970 Promotion. 1973 bis 1980 Dozent am Deutschen Seminar der Goethe-Universität Frankfurt am Main. 1988 bis 2015 Redakteur und Editor an der Kritischen Hofmannsthal-Ausgabe. Wissenschaftlicher Beirat und Mitarbeiter am neuen *Brecht-Handbuch*. Publikationen zur deutschen Romantik und zur Literatur des 20. Jahrhunderts, insbesondere über Brecht (Schwerpunkte: Lehrstücke und Lehrstücktheorie, Lyrik, Theaterpraxis und Theatertheorie, Radiotheorie), über Hofmannsthal und Thomas Mann, über Editionsprobleme und zur Rezeption deutscher Literatur in Frankreich.

Hans-Thies Lehmann, University Professor Emeritus of Theatre, Film, and Media Studies at the Johann Wolfgang Goethe-Universität Frankfurt am Main, is a former president of the International Brecht Society and a pioneering theorist of postdramatic theater. His extensive body of scholarship encompasses Brecht, Heiner Müller, performance, aesthetic theory, and the intersection of theater and politics. As a theater practitioner he has been involved in productions throughout the world, and his seminal 1999 study *Postdramatisches Theater* (1999) has been translated into multiple languages.

Thomas Pekar wurde nach dem Studium der Germanistik, Philosophie und Politologie in Freiburg im Breisgau und Berlin mit einer literaturwissenschaftlichen Arbeit über Robert Musil promoviert; dann Habilitation in Neuerer Deutscher Literaturwissenschaft in München mit einer Untersuchung über die europäische Japan-Rezeption. Verschiedene Stipendien und Forschungsprojekte in Deutschland, Japan und den USA. Unterricht an Universitäten in Oldenburg, Bayreuth, Heidelberg und München; Arbeit als Assistant-Professor an der Keimyung Universität in Daegu, Süd-Korea und als DAAD-Lektor am Germanistischen Seminar der Universität Tokio. Seit 2001 ist er Professor für deutsche Literatur- und Kulturwissenschaften an der Gakushuin Universität in Tokio. Zu seinen Forschungsinteressen gehören besonders die Exil- und Kulturkontaktforschung sowie die deutschsprachige Literatur der Klassischen Moderne.

Arnold Pistiak, Studium Humboldt-Universität; Promotion in Potsdam; Universität Bagdad (Irak), Universität Antananarivo (Madagaskar), Fachhochschule Frankfurt (Oder), Universität Potsdam (bis 2006). Wissenschaftliche Schwerpunkte Heine und Feuchtwanger, Kompositionen Hanns Eislers, Wechselbeziehungen zwischen Literatur und Musik. Veröffentlichungen (Auswahl): "Heimkehr als Aufbruch. Feststellungen und Lesarten zu Schuberts Heineliedern," *Heine-Jahrbuch* (2009); "Skovbostrand 1937: Nein und Ja. Erinnerung an Hanns Eislers Kantaten auf Texte von Ignazio Silone und Bertolt Brecht," in *Feuchtwanger und Exil. Glaube und Kultur 1933 – 1945* (2011), *Essays zu Hanns Eislers musikalischem und poetischem Schaffen* (4 Bände, 2013).

Matthias Rothe, Associate Professor of German at the University of Minnesota, works on Critical Theory and theater. His most recent publication is *The Frankfurt School: Philosophy and (political) Economy,* a special issue of *History of the Human Sciences* (29.2, April 2016), co-edited with Bastian Ronge.

Vera Stegmann is Associate Professor of German at Lehigh University in Bethlehem, Pennsylvania. She specializes in modern German literature, film, and theater, as well as in comparative arts, particularly the relationship between literature and music. Her publications include the book *Das epische Musiktheater bei Strawinsky und Brecht*, as well as articles on Pina Bausch, Thomas Bernhard, Ferruccio Busoni, Hanns Eisler, Pablo Neruda, Anna Seghers, and Kurt Weill. Her new research project focuses on contemporary transnational German-language literature.

Carlos Vargas-Salgado is Assistant Professor of Spanish at Whitman College in Washington. He has published on performance studies applied to Latin American culture, Andean literatures, and human rights and memory studies in the Spanish-speaking world. His work has been published in *Latin American Theatre Review*, *Hispanic Issues Online*, *Revista de Crítica Literaria Latinoamericana*, and various other scholarly journals in Peru, Chile, Brazil, and Spain.

Helene Varopoulou holds degrees in law from the University of Athens and in theater from the University of Paris III. She has taught in theater studies departments at the University of Athens and the University of Patras. She has also been active as a theater theorist, critic, and practitioner, including work as the artistic director of the Argos Festival and as president of the Greek Centre of the International Theatre Institute. She writes essays and theoretical articles on theater, art, and culture, and she has translated from German into Greek a series of works by Heiner Müller.